British Foreign Secretaries in an Uncertain World, 1919–1939

The nature of international diplomacy and Britain's world role changed immeasurably after the end of the First World War, and this book shows how the various men who headed the Foreign Office during the inter-war years sought to operate in the shifting political and bureaucratic environments that confronted them.

British Foreign Secretaries in an Uncertain World examines the careers of each of the inter-war foreign secretaries, including Lord Curzon, John Simon and Anthony Eden. Using an extensive range of primary sources both published and unpublished, official and private, Michael Hughes offers a detailed assessment of how the foreign secretaries approached their role and how influential they were in international diplomacy. The book also looks at the foreign secretaries' successes and failures within the British political system, analysing how influential the Foreign Office was under each foreign secretary in determining British foreign policy.

Michael Hughes is Reader in Modern History at Liverpool University, UK.

British foreign and colonial policy
Series Editor: Peter Catterall
ISSN: 1467–5013

This series provides insights into both the background influences on and the course of policy making towards Britain's extensive overseas interests during the past 200 years.

Whitehall and the Suez Crisis
Edited by Saul Kelly and Anthony Gorst

Liberals, International Relations and Appeasement
The Liberal Party, 1919–1939
Richard S. Grayson

British Government Policy and Decolonisation, 1945–1963
Scrutinising the official mind
Frank Heinlein

Harold Wilson and European Integration
Britain's second application to join the EEC
Edited by Oliver Daddow

Britain, Israel and the United States, 1955–1958
Beyond Suez
Orna Almog

The British Political Elite and the Soviet Union, 1937–1939
Louise Grace Shaw

Britain, Nasser and the Balance of Power in the Middle East, 1952–1967
From the Egyptian Revolution to the Six Day War
Robert McNamara

British Foreign Secretaries Since 1974
Edited by Kevin Theakston

The Labour Party, Nationalism and Internationalism, 1939–1951
R.M. Douglas

India's Partition
The story of imperialism in retreat
D.N. Panigrahi

Empire as the Triumph of Theory
Imperialism, information and the Colonial Society of 1868
Edward Beasley

The British Intervention in Jordan, 1958
Stephen Blackwell

The Office of the Permanent Under-Secretary of the Foreign Office, 1854–1945
Thomas Otte

Mid-Victorian Imperialists
British gentlemen and the empire of the mind
Edward Beasley

Britain's Policy Towards the European Community
Harold Wilson and Britain's world role 1964–1967
Helen Parr

British Policy in Aden and the Protectorates 1955–67
Forwards and backwards
Spencer Mawby

British Foreign Secretaries in an Uncertain World, 1919–1939
Michael Hughes

British Foreign Secretaries in an Uncertain World, 1919–1939

Michael Hughes

Routledge
Taylor & Francis Group

LONDON AND NEW YORK

First published 2006
by Routledge
2 Park Square, Milton Park, Abingdon, Oxon OX14 4RN

Simultaneously published in the USA and Canada
by Routledge
270 Madison Ave, New York, NY 10016

Routledge is an imprint of the Taylor & Francis Group

© 2006 Michael Hughes

Typeset in Garamond by Wearset Ltd, Boldon, Tyne and Wear
Printed and bound in Great Britain by MPG Books Ltd, Bodmin

The publisher makes no representation, express or implied, with
regard to the accuracy of the information contained in this book and
cannot accept any legal responsibility or liability for any errors or
omissions that may be made.

British Library Cataloguing in Publication Data
A catalogue record for this book is available from the British Library

Library of Congress Cataloging in Publication Data
A catalog record for this book has been requested

ISBN 0–714–65715–8

Contents

General editor's preface

For no period of British history has foreign policymaking been subjected to as much critical scrutiny as for the inter-war years. Much of this literature, however, looks primarily at how policymakers responded to the externalities and threats that presented themselves in these years, and particularly in the 1930s. Less attention has been paid to the subjects of this book, the Foreign Secretaries themselves who had responsibility for protecting Britain's international interests in the period, or to how they discharged their duties.

They faced an era which, even leaving aside the rise of aggressive dictators, was complicated by a number of factors which had been comparatively absent before 1914. Ideology had previously animated actors with international pretensions, such as the Second International, but the Great War had made manifest its limitations. In its aftermath, however, it was to be used as an arm of foreign policy as never before by states which to differing degrees portrayed themselves as the principal proponents of particular ideologies.

Meanwhile, multilateral diplomacy had hitherto been an occasional and subject-specific exercise. The Victorian and Edwardian eras saw nothing similar to the series of international naval conferences launched at Washington in 1921, the results of which were to constrain the British ability to project power, not least in the Far East. Such exercises proved deeply problematic, witness not least the failings of the various international economic conferences of the 1920s and early 1930s. But they, not to mention the League of Nations, provided in many ways the main arena in which international relations were articulated for much of the inter-war years.

In such circumstances the approach of a Salisbury to foreign affairs, seeing it as the occasional fending off of crises whilst using parliamentary privilege as an excuse to avoid international entanglements, was no longer possible. Nor could British Foreign Secretaries, unlike their long-serving Edwardian predecessor Sir Edward Grey, avoid the necessity of travel. Diplomacy was not necessarily a more open activity, as those reformers who blamed its failings for the outbreak of war in 1914 would have wished, but it was a more public one. In consequence Prime Ministers were increasingly drawn into the diplomatic arena. Lloyd George may have been the only one to have, in the unique circumstances of post-war peacemaking, set up his own foreign policy machinery within the Cabinet Secretariat. Others, such as Baldwin in 1924–29, were less inclined to involve themselves in foreign affairs. However, as becomes clear from this book, the predominance of the Prime Minister in foreign policymaking, so marked in Kevin Theakston's recent book in this series on *British Foreign Secretaries since 1974*, was already an established trend during the inter-war years.

This remained true even as the 1930s wore on and the tentative moves towards multilateral diplomacy of the previous decade broke down in the face of economic crisis, the impossibility of resolving Franco-German differences at the 1932–34 World Disarmament Conference and the advent of governments determined to revise the international map in their favour in Germany and Japan. Although the 1930s in consequence were to see a revival in the importance of more traditional forms of bilateral diplomacy, Foreign Secretaries could still struggle to pursue their own line in the face of a determined Prime Minister, as the case of Eden's resignation in 1938 makes clear.

Despite the constraints, however, of Prime Ministerial interference, differences with officials or external challenges – all of which Michael Hughes here examines in detail – in the end responsibility for British diplomacy remained with the Foreign Secretary. Contemporaries clearly felt that this responsibility was discharged with very varying success. One later Foreign Secretary, Harold Macmillan, was apt to describe Sir John Simon as the worst Foreign Secretary Britain had ever had. However, as Michael Hughes shows, many of the failings attributed to Simon then by hostile Tory backbenchers like Macmillan were shared by the Cabinet as a whole. A Foreign Secretary's performance needs to be assessed not just by the diplomatic fruits of their period in office, which in Simon's case were undoubtedly meagre, but by how they approached their task. How imaginative were they in addressing the problems confronted? How good were they at persuading colleagues to pursue a particular course (Simon may have had the disadvantage of being the leader of a minor party in a coalition government, but that never seemed to hold back Joseph Chamberlain in 1895–1903)? Were they primarily reactive or did they attempt to shape the political weather? Did they, like Halifax, adjust their policies to fit the circumstances? And how much influence did they have, if not in choosing the issues they had to deal with, then at least in determining how they were handled?

One of the guiding principles of the Foreign Secretaries of the modern era considered in Theakston's book is the desirability of ensuring that Britain 'punches above its weight' in the international arena. The task of the diplomat in such circumstances is to search for leverage which compensates for the lack of military hardware. For the inter-war Foreign Secretaries considered here, however, their role was a rather different one, as a principal actor seeking to maintain international order in a difficult era. The objective was not so much to punch above weight, but to avoid punching below it.

This, as least as much as the eventual inability to prevent the drift to war, should be the criterion by which the Foreign Secretaries discussed in this book should be judged. By offering for the first time a detailed assessment of how the various Foreign Secretaries of the inter-war years approached their role, and of the effect of their personalities on their management of policy, Michael Hughes here provides a means to do just that.

Peter Catterall
21 September 2004

Acknowledgements

A vast amount has of course been written on the subject of inter-war diplomacy over the past sixty years or so. The main purpose of this book is not therefore to focus in any detail on the complex diplomatic manoeuvres of the period that have been dealt with at great length elsewhere. It instead seeks to concentrate on the decision-making process itself, focusing in particular on the role that was played by British foreign secretaries between 1919 and 1939. This is not of course to denigrate the excellent work that has appeared in recent years emphasising how foreign policy decisions between the wars were shaped by a vast number of factors, ranging from financial considerations through to military preparations. It is, however, always salutary to remember that the critical decisions were in the last resort taken by individuals trying to master an almost unbearably complex domestic and international environment.

The author of any study of this kind naturally has a huge debt to the authors of the voluminous secondary literature. Although I have tried in the bibliography and references to give some sense of the extent of my debts, it has not of course been possible to list every book and article that I have consulted over the past few years. I have also made a point of making extensive use of the primary sources – published and unpublished, official and private – in order to gauge how successive foreign secretaries went about their business. I therefore owe a great debt to the staff of the various archives and libraries in which I have worked on this project: the Special Collections Reading Room at Birmingham University Library; the Reading Room at the Borthwick Institute of Historical Research (York); the British Library (Department of Manuscripts and Oriental and India Office collections); the Department of Manuscripts Reading Room at Cambridge University Library; Churchill College Archives Centre; the Department of Special Collections at the London School of Economics and Political Science; the Special Collections Reading Room at the Robbins Library, University of Newcastle-upon-Tyne; the Modern Papers Reading Room of the Bodleian Library (Oxford); the Public Record Office (Kew); and last but not least the Sidney Jones Library at the University of Liverpool. I am particularly grateful to all those who have given me permission to quote from material in their care or

of which they are the copyright holders. Material in the Baldwin, Templewood and Crewe Papers is reproduced by permission of the Syndics of Cambridge University Library; Crown copyright material in the Public Record
Office is reproduced by permission of Her Majesty's Stationery Office. A
British Academy Small Research Grant helped to fund my visits to the
various archives listed above, whilst the University of Liverpool provided me
with sabbatical leave that was used in part to complete the final draft of the
book.

I have also incurred other debts too numerous to list during the time I
have been preparing this manuscript. I must therefore confine myself to
thanking Dr Peter Catterall of the University of London for his detailed and
helpful comments on the whole manuscript, and to my fellow historians at
Liverpool for putting up with an increasingly weary and bad-tempered colleague. The greatest debt is, as ever, a personal one. This book is dedicated
with love to Katie, who knows no Russian, but understands full well the
spirit of the Russian proverb that proclaims '*zhizn' prozhit'* – *ne pole pereiti*'.

1 Introduction

The changing Foreign Office

This book examines the careers of the men who served as British foreign secretary between 1919 and 1939, focusing in particular on the ways in which they sought to mould foreign policy during their time in office. A vast amount has of course been written on international relations during the inter-war years, including a number of valuable biographies about the various individuals who headed the Foreign Office, but there has been less interest in analysing the complex array of factors that helped to determine the *modus operandi* of a particular foreign secretary.[1] The chapters that follow are designed to help fill this gap in the literature.

The nineteenth-century Foreign Office was one of the defining institutions of Victorian Britain, an institutional expression of the country's enormous international wealth and power.[2] The names of the most prominent foreign secretaries, such as Lord Palmerston and Lord Salisbury, resounded across the globe. At a time when Britain's international prestige and power rested on a tantalisingly elusive mix of economic and military strength, the Foreign Office appeared to symbolise the effortless hegemony of a country that had created the greatest empire yet seen in human history. The reality was, however, a good deal more complicated than this simple sketch conveys. The nineteenth-century Foreign Office was a remarkably small organisation, seldom employing more than fifty diplomatic clerks, many of whom spent their day engaged in the routine work of copying dispatches and making up the diplomatic bag.[3] Most other departments of central government dwarfed the Foreign Office in size. The Foreign Secretary himself was widely perceived as the second most important member of the Cabinet, behind the Prime Minister, but in a fluid system of collective government such notional rank did not automatically translate into real power. The formulation of Britain's overseas policy was in any case never conducted through the Foreign Office alone. The Colonial Office and the India Office naturally took the lead in questions of imperial administration, whilst both institutions also played a vital role in ensuring the security of the territories for which they were responsible. The War Office and the

Admiralty offered advice about strategic problems that inevitably both constrained and moulded broader deliberations about foreign policy. The Cabinet provided a formal setting in which the perspectives and concerns of the major departments could be discussed by all its members, and the background 'hum' of discussions in *ad hoc* committees and informal meetings gave further opportunities for ministers and senior officials to discuss international questions. The role and status of both the Foreign Office and the Foreign Secretary therefore fluctuated throughout the nineteenth century according to the personalities involved and the issue under review.

The organisation and operation of the Foreign Office changed sharply in the early years of the twentieth century,[4] following a series of reforms in 1903–06 designed to create a more efficient administrative system, capable of responding to the increasing flow of dispatches and telegrams. These changes were partly a reflection of a broader pattern of administrative modernisation that had been taking place in other Whitehall departments for many years.[5] They were also, though, related to a broader shift in the organisational culture of the Foreign Office, characterised by the attempts of a younger group of officials to establish greater influence over the policy-making process.[6] When Lord Salisbury served as Foreign Secretary and Prime Minister, from 1895 to 1900, he seldom paid very much attention to the views of Foreign Office staff about policy.[7] His successor at the Foreign Office, Lord Lansdowne, was more willing to consult his officials, but he instinctively believed that the Cabinet was the most appropriate body for making important decisions about foreign policy.[8] However, when Sir Edward Grey became Foreign Secretary, at the end of 1905, a sharp change took place in the role of the Foreign Office. Sir Charles Hardinge, who became Permanent Secretary a few weeks after Grey's arrival, was determined to assert his influence on Britain's foreign policy.[9] Grey himself established good working relations with his senior officials, and consulted them extensively, with the result that discussions about important issues of policy within the Foreign Office became a more genuinely collaborative effort than before. There were of course occasions when pressure from other ministers placed real constraints on Grey's freedom to pursue his chosen policies unquestioned, but the Foreign Secretary was generally adept at insulating foreign policy from outside scrutiny. In the eight years or so leading up to the First World War, the Foreign Office was more often than not the primary location for initiating important proposals about foreign policy.

The outbreak of war in 1914 naturally had huge consequences for the role both of the Foreign Office and the Foreign Secretary. Grey himself recognised that diplomats had to take second place to soldiers at times of war, and became less inclined to assert the right of his department to act as the principal location for decisions about foreign policy. Foreign Office staff themselves became increasingly preoccupied with such specific war-time tasks as fostering new patterns of alliance diplomacy and promoting the blockade against Germany. The Grey Foreign Office had in any case already become a focus for considerable unease in the years before 1914, particularly among radical critics such as the journalist E.D. Morel, who repeatedly claimed throughout the early years of the twentieth century that the organisation was 'closed to men of brains, intelligence and education'.[10] Morel also vigorously attacked the secrecy that surrounded the conduct of diplomatic relations between governments, arguing that greater efforts should be made to assert parliamentary control over the supposed machinations of the diplomats.[11] Such assaults on the old diplomacy were magnified when hostilities finally erupted in 1914, since the conflict seemed to symbolise the dangers inherent in giving too much freedom to the foreign policy 'experts', and organisations such as the Union of Democratic Control were set up to campaign for greater public control over foreign policy.[12] In Britain, as in most of the other belligerent countries,[13] traditional patterns of diplomacy were subjected to a searing critique designed to demystify their authority. At the same time, considerable energy was devoted across the political spectrum to devising new and imaginative ways of ensuring that the present war would be the 'war to end all wars', most obviously via the establishment of a new international organisation intended to foster closer co-operation between governments. All these changes made it increasingly unlikely that the British public would willingly accept a return to the diplomatic *status quo ante* once war was over.

The outbreak of war in 1914 also helped to change the way in which at least a section of the political elite viewed the institutions and procedures associated with the old diplomacy. When Lloyd George replaced Asquith as Prime Minister, at the end of 1916, he quickly showed himself to be a strong critic of the Foreign Office.[14] He remained enough of a radical to believe that the typical diplomat or Foreign Office clerk was, like Sir Edward Grey himself, a well-born 'conventional' master of a 'serene flow of unexceptionable diction' that counted for little at a time when the international system was in turmoil. In his memoirs, Lloyd George condemned the erstwhile Foreign Secretary for lacking 'vision, imagination [and] breadth of mind' – qualities that he believed were also missing in the institution over which Grey had presided for so many years.[15] It was partly for this reason that the Prime Minister was determined to involve himself personally in the diplomatic process, taking part in numerous international conferences and bilateral meetings with foreign leaders. Lloyd George's visceral dislike of professional diplomats also helps to explain why he paid so little attention to the views of Balfour, who took over from Grey as Foreign Secretary in 1916, as well as accounting for the Prime Minister's efforts to place greater responsibility for the conduct of foreign affairs in the hands of a small group of officials based at Number 10.[16] Growing dissatisfaction among politicians with the traditional conduct of diplomacy after 1914 was not, though, confined to those of a more radical political disposition. It even extended to sections of the Conservative Party, most notably Robert Cecil, who played a great part in promoting the cause of the League of Nations.[17]

Whilst some of those who served in Lloyd George's war-time coalition government laboured under the illusion that the conduct of British foreign policy would return to normal after the end of hostilities, the more prescient understood that changes set in motion by the war made such an outcome unlikely.

The distinctive texture of inter-governmental relations that developed between the allied powers during the war exercised a powerful effect on the pattern of international diplomacy that evolved after 1918. In the years before 1917, close co-operation took place between the British, French and Russian governments over a whole range of strategic, diplomatic and financial questions – a phenomenon that was extended when the United States entered the war as an 'associate power' in 1917. By the time of the armistice, the relationships between the victorious powers had gone far beyond the conventional military agreements that marked most traditional alliances. The Paris Peace Conference was dominated by the major victor powers, whose representatives met in a complex web of committees set up to discuss questions ranging from reparations payments through to the future of Eastern Europe.[18] The creation of the League of Nations, which eventually developed its own elaborate institutional structure in Geneva, also helped to re-enforce a growing international recognition of the value of conference diplomacy for dealing with such matters as rearmament and trade.[19] Although traditional patterns of bilateral diplomacy continued to flourish in the post-war world, the emergence of new forums for discussion between national governments had profound ramifications for the role of diplomatic establishments across the globe.

The post-war role of the British Foreign Office was inevitably affected by changes in the way in which foreign policy was made within the core executive, understood here as 'all those organisations and procedures which co-ordinate central government policies, and act as final arbiters between different parts of the government machine'.[20] The nature of the international agenda changed considerably after the end of the war. Financial and economic questions became more important than had been the case in the years before 1914. The vexed question of war debts and reparations loomed large in international discourse throughout the 1920s, in large part because their resolution had such important consequences for the financial health of most major countries. The economic crisis of the early 1930s encouraged governments around the world to think systematically about the way in which their existing trading patterns served to promote or damage their domestic welfare. In the words of one acute scholar of the post-war Foreign Office, 'the blurring of the distinctions between foreign and domestic policies not only meant that decisions taken in one field had significant repercussions in others, but also made it difficult to keep a sharp division of functions between the Foreign Office and neighbouring departments'.[21] The Treasury became an increasingly important actor in determining the pattern of Britain's external relations, most notably over the reparations question in the 1920s and the configuration of defence priorities in the 1930s, whilst the War Office and the Admiralty emphasised the military dimension of the various international crises that erupted periodically between 1919 and 1939. The Colonial Office, Dominions Office and India Office also continued to take an interest in the development of British foreign policy towards regions where they had particular responsibilities, as well as articulating in London the views of the various imperial governments on such questions as British policy towards Europe. Throughout the post-war years, then, the Foreign Office had to adjust to a constantly evolving international and domestic environment, responding to a whole host of changes that placed constraints on its ability to act as a gatekeeper determining the course of British foreign policy.

Individuals and the policy-making process

The decision to concentrate on individual foreign secretaries throughout the following chapters may need to be justified to some readers. It could, after all, be argued that such an approach is rooted in an unwarranted assumption that individual men and women represent the motive force of history. And, given the emphasis in previous paragraphs on the complex bureaucratic setting within which British foreign policy was made between 1919 and 1939, a focus on individuals might seem to run the risk of ignoring the importance of formal institutions and administrative structures on policy outcomes. A good deal of recent literature on international history and political science has, however, shown that individuals can exert great influence on the way in which complex political processes develop.[22] It is a view that has been widely supported by those who have actually held positions of power. In the words of Henry Kissinger, 'as a professor, I tended to think of history as run by impersonal forces. But when you see it in practice, you see the difference individual personalities make'.[23]

The days have of course long since gone when historians believed that great men shaped the evolution of human history. The ideas of nineteenth-century writers such as Thomas Carlyle come across to a modern reader as almost impossibly quaint. The dawn of psychoanalysis in the early twentieth century has done irreparable harm to the assumption that the statesmen and politicians who populate the pages of the past always acted out of a conscious and coherent set of rational motives. The development of the social sciences has in any case challenged traditional and unproblematic notions of human agency, focusing instead on the importance of complex social processes that seemed to leave little place for ideas about personal autonomy and freedom. The evolution during the past few decades of 'diplomatic history' into 'international history' – characterised by a focus on a wide range of economic, ideological and cultural factors[24] – has reflected broader changes in historical scholarship in the second half of the twentieth century. There is no doubt that all these approaches have enriched the research of historians and political scientists, helping to break down earlier paradigms that emphasised high politics at the cost of a more sophisticated understanding of the way in which politics formed part of a complex structural whole. It remains possible, though, to mount a robust defence of the study both of high politics in general and the role of the individual in shaping developments in particular.

The following pages rest on the assumption that the Foreign Secretary at least had the potential to be a pivotal actor in influencing British foreign policy between the wars. This in turn raises the question of what is meant by such vexed terms as 'power' and 'influence'. The formal constitutional power of the Foreign Secretary was almost non-existent, given the fluid administrative and political character of the British governmental system.[25] Since the convention of collective responsibility meant that all Cabinet members were bound by collective decisions, ministers were always likely to entertain more than a passing interest in the policies pursued by their colleagues. In addition, as has already been seen, the changing pattern of international relations after 1919 challenged the Foreign Office's gate-keeping role and allowed other departments and individuals to assert themselves in the conduct of international relations. When Lord Curzon served as Foreign Secretary from 1919 to 1924, he repeatedly complained that the activities of Lloyd George and his 'garden suburb' of advisers undermined the status of the Foreign Office. However, even so formidable figure as the erstwhile Viceroy of India could not really argue that such a development was actually *unconstitutional*, given the uncertainties and complexities of the British constitution in distributing functions and responsibilities among ministers and departments. A foreign secretary who wanted to assert his control over the foreign policy-making process could not rely on his formal position alone when seeking to achieve his objectives.

Most of the foreign secretaries featured in the following chapters came to office with at least some ideas about the direction in which they hoped to direct British foreign policy, whilst all of them developed their own views on the various international problems that confronted them once in post. In order to ensure that they prevailed within the clamour and confusion of the policy-making process, successive foreign secretaries therefore had to identify ways of mobilising support and limiting opposition. The decision-making process within the core executive was in practice both complex and fluid. Although the Cabinet served as the formal constitutional focus for authoritative rulings about all aspects of public policy, decision-making was in practice incremental and multi-locational: discussion about foreign policy took place at many levels, in many different settings, and with a shifting cast of actors. Nor was the decision-making process insulated from the wider political environment. Ministers and senior officials were all, to a greater or lesser extent, sensitive to the way in which decisions about foreign policy were likely to be received in parliament and the press as well as among the wider public. Since the foreign policy-making process was so fluid and complex, foreign secretaries (like all other ministers) had to engage in an almost constant struggle to assert themselves. They could not, to put it crudely, sit on their laurels.

The impact of an individual head of the Foreign Office on policy-making depended to a great extent on their personal qualities and political *nous*. The very fact that they rejoiced in such a title as 'Foreign Secretary' created certain expectations both within and beyond government about their central role in guiding Britain's relations with other countries. Some of the men who became foreign secretary in the inter-war years had developed a considerable public reputation prior to their appointment, with the result that they already commanded a certain political *gravitas* on taking office. Lord Curzon, for example, had served as Viceroy of India in the opening years of the twentieth century, whilst Austen Chamberlain filled a number of important ministerial posts before going to the Foreign Office in Baldwin's second government. Once in post, though, prior reputation counted for little unless it was skilfully used to enhance an individual's authority. It will be seen in the next chapter that Curzon failed to establish his authority while at the Foreign Office in large part because he could not understand that the personal and political attributes required to be a successful Foreign Secretary were very different from those needed to be an effective Viceroy. A successful foreign secretary needed to mobilise support for his policies among a wide range of politicians and senior civil servants in order to see them accepted as general policy. If he lacked the skills to achieve this, then he was likely to find himself marginalised and condemned to comparative impotence, whatever his status upon taking office.

The whole question of personality as it relates to performance in government is naturally a very vexed one. Although a good deal has been written about the nature of charismatic leadership, there has been little agreement among scholars about how to categorise something so inherently intangible and elusive.[26] It has in any case been a rarity in the ordered world of twentieth-century British politics, where patterns of institutional continuity have not provided the kind of vacuum of authority that allows charismatic leadership to thrive. Some politicians such as Lloyd George and Churchill were certainly astute at using their public profile to advance their authority within the dense texture of political and administrative relationships that defined the core executive. By contrast, few of the men who served as foreign secretary in the inter-war years developed the sort of profile capable of providing them with great leverage in their dealings with other ministers and senior officials. The personal qualities that are explored in the following chapters are therefore for the most part more prosaic. A foreign secretary who got on well with his ministerial colleagues was generally in a stronger position to promote his views in Cabinet than one who was more isolated. The same was true of a foreign secretary who established effective working relations with his senior officials. Such ties could be based on friendship or could instead reflect a common outlook on major political problems. They could be confined to the official world of Cabinet committees and depart-mental meetings, or they could spill over into the more private world of per-sonal correspondence and attendance at the same house parties (the place of Cliveden in the mythology of appeasement immediately comes to mind).[27] It is easy in some cases to trace the importance of patterns of personal anti-pathy and sympathy in moulding discussions about foreign policy, whilst in other cases the situation was subtler and more intricate – a matter of 'mood' that escapes precise characterisation, but which nevertheless helped to shape the pattern of policy-making at the heart of government. Although the chapters that follow cannot provide a substitute for the whole series of detailed political histories and biographies necessary to explore this phe-nomenon properly, they can at least offer a series of examples that together cast some light on the process.

The structure of the book

Each of the following chapters focuses on one of the men who served as Foreign Secretary between 1919 and 1939: Lord Curzon, Ramsay MacDon-ald, Austen Chamberlain, Arthur Henderson, John Simon, Samuel Hoare, Anthony Eden and Lord Halifax. There is no room for a detailed discussion of Lord Reading's short-lived tenure at the Foreign Office during 1931. The structure of the various chapters varies from case to case, but they are all explicitly or implicitly built around a series of questions designed to facili-tate a comparative perspective on the factors governing the role and effec-tiveness of inter-war foreign secretaries. The first of these questions concerns the coherence of the views about international politics expressed by the various foreign secretaries during their time in office. In order to judge how successful a particular individual was at promoting their chosen foreign policy objectives, it is necessary to have some idea of what they sought to achieve. Such a task is a good deal harder than it may at first appear. The formulation of foreign policy is by its very nature a reactive process, driven in large part by the actions and decisions of other governments, whilst the dominant political tradition in inter-war Britain was in any case sceptical about locating particular policy decisions within any kind of grand frame-work. The Foreign Office produced annual reports in which it usually paid lip-service to the assumptions that guided its activities, but these seldom went beyond a bland assertion that the British government was committed to peace and the international *status quo*. Such concepts as 'collective secur-ity' and the 'balance of power' also prove on close examination to be less clear-cut and more problematic than sometimes realised.[28] Some individuals nevertheless came to office with marked views about how best to define and promote British interests. Lord Curzon, for example, stood in the grand tra-dition of British imperialism, and although shrewd enough to understand that Britain could not neglect developments in western Europe, he was inclined to devote much of his time at the Foreign Office to defending

British influence in the Near East and Persia. Austen Chamberlain soon became convinced after his arrival in office that the promotion of British security and prosperity across the globe required the establishment of greater stability on the European continent, which explains why he devoted so much of his energy in 1925 to securing the Locarno accords. As the 1920s gave way to the 1930s, the rise of the dictators encouraged foreign secretaries such as Samuel Hoare and Anthony Eden to extend this focus on Europe as the principal arena of British foreign policy. Even so, deciding how to balance Britain's European and imperial responsibilities provided one of the major challenges faced by every British foreign secretary in the inter-war years. Each of them developed their own views about the most effective way of achieving such an elusive goal.

The second major question addressed in the following chapters concerns the relationship between foreign secretaries and the officials in the department over which they presided, not least because the authority of successive foreign secretaries was bound up with the status of the Foreign Office itself. Some, such as Curzon, were extremely vocal in defending the principle that the Foreign Office should serve as the primary location for key decisions about foreign policy. Others, like Sir John Simon, were less concerned by the whole question. During the inter-war years, some foreign secretaries such as Chamberlain and Eden developed a close working relationship with their officials. Others, most notably Curzon and Simon, were viewed with frank dislike by many of those who served under them. The impact of the relationship between a particular foreign secretary and his officials on the operation and status of the Foreign Office was not always clear-cut. A foreign secretary who worked well with his senior officials was on the whole better placed to benefit from their expertise, which could in turn help him to defend his department's views in Cabinet. He could, however, still discover that his fellow ministers ignored his recommendations, a fate that confronted Eden in the months leading up to his resignation from Neville Chamberlain's Cabinet in February 1938, which came about in part because the Prime Minister had already developed a deep suspicion of the whole diplomatic establishment. The precise role of the Foreign Office in the policy-making process was in practice indelibly shaped by the texture of the relationship between the Foreign Secretary and his fellow ministers – and most notably prime ministers – and it is for this reason that the following pages devote a good deal of space to a third question: namely, the way in which foreign secretaries interacted with their Cabinet colleagues.

The fluid nature of the British constitution and the changing pattern of international relations in the years after 1919 made it extremely difficult for the Foreign Office to define a specific sphere of operation. Other ministers could claim that they had a right to help mould decisions about foreign policy *both* because they were bound by the convention of collective responsibility *and* (in some cases) because such decisions were likely to impinge on the activities of their own departments. The Foreign Office was clearly responsible for managing the flow of dispatches and instructions between London and the missions abroad, but this did not mean that ministers automatically accepted that the Foreign Secretary and his officials were entitled to take authoritative decisions about major policy issues. The Cabinet and its elaborate edifice of committees, such as the Committee for Imperial Defence, provided the most obvious location for reconciling competing perspectives on how best to manage all aspects of Britain's relations with the rest of the world: military, colonial, diplomatic, and so forth. This process was, however, extremely *ad hoc* and uncertain in character, with the result that ministers who were determined to advance their own ideas about overseas policy had numerous opportunities to influence decision-making. Winston Churchill, for example, proved to be very adept throughout the 1920s at using his various ministerial portfolios to justify his attempts to influence decisions about a whole range of international issues. In the following decade, Neville Chamberlain used his position as Chancellor of the Exchequer to assert himself on numerous defence and foreign policy questions. When he subsequently became Prime Minister he insisted that his role as head of government gave him a right to intervene on any question concerning Britain's relationship with the wider world. It will indeed be seen in the following chapters that the relationship between the Foreign Office and Number 10 was often the most important factor in shaping the formulation of British foreign policy between the wars.

The fourth major question examined in the following chapters concerns the impact of actors beyond the heart of government on the role of successive foreign secretaries: MPs, journalists, pressure groups and the like. The previous paragraphs have focused almost exclusively on the way in which foreign policy was made within the core executive, but the decision-making process was not of course insulated from the wider political environment, even though the impact of 'public opinion' on foreign policy between the wars remains a vexed issue. The extension of the electoral franchise in 1918 symbolised a major shift in both political practice and political culture. Ministers and senior officials involved in making decisions about foreign policy became increasingly aware of the potential importance of public opinion on questions ranging from disarmament through to the operation of the League of Nations. Some ministers such as Churchill and Birkenhead were astute at using the media to advance both their political careers and their policy preferences. Others, by contrast, found it difficult to adjust to the more open political system that emerged in the wake of the First World War. No foreign secretary could afford to ignore the constraints placed on British policy by popular opinion. Even Lord Curzon was forced to acknowledge that it was impossible for a government to pursue a foreign policy that did not have widespread public support. It therefore made sense for foreign secretaries to play a central role in seeking to 'educate' public opinion, not least because a high public profile also held out the possible added advantage of increasing their influence within the core executive. Some foreign secretaries, most notably Eden, developed a strong and positive public image; others, such as John Simon, did not. Eden's resignation at the start of 1938 nevertheless showed that a public reputation for glamour and effectiveness did not automatically translate into power to determine policy within the confines of government. Although most of the men examined in the following chapters paid at least lip-service to the importance of mobilising public support behind British foreign policy, none of them proved particularly adept at identifying ways of securing such an objective.

There is inevitably some tension in a book such as this between the need for detail and the search for more general comparisons and conclusions. The following chapters are designed to illustrate the complexity of the inter-war foreign policy-making process, but they cannot provide anything approaching a comprehensive review of all the important decisions taken by a particular foreign secretary when in office. They instead concentrate on showing how the various men who headed the Foreign Office during the inter-war years sought to operate in the changing political and bureaucratic environment that confronted them, with the result that the focus of the book is firmly on the domestic decision-making process. Some chapters begin with a general review of the key political and administrative relationships that developed between a particular foreign secretary and other key actors across Whitehall, before using a small number of selected case-studies to show how these operated in practice. Others seek to combine the material into a single narrative. All the biographical chapters are, though, focused on the broad questions set down in the previous paragraphs. The final chapter then seeks to draw some tentative conclusions about the factors that determined the influence of inter-war foreign secretaries on shaping Britain's relationship with the wider world.

It is perhaps worth concluding this introductory chapter with a few words about the sources used in this study. Any book of this kind necessarily relies on the vast secondary literature that has appeared in recent decades on international politics between the wars. It also has to rely on the many excellent biographies that have been written on the eight men who feature in the following pages. The footnotes and bibliography give some sense of the depth of my obligations, but the demands of space make it impossible to list all the works that have informed my thinking over the past few years. During the course of my research, I have sought when possible to return to the original sources, both published and unpublished, in order to interrogate them afresh in the light of the concerns of this book. It has also proved helpful to review a range of private and semi-official correspondence, in addition to the formal Cabinet and Foreign Office records, since such material often provides better insight into the 'atmosphere' in which decisions were taken. The selection of case-studies has inevitably been somewhat arbitrary, but the choice has in each case been designed to facilitate a greater understanding of the way in which individual foreign secretaries sought to navigate the vicissitudes of their job. The role of inter-war foreign secretaries proves, on close inspection, to have depended to a great extent on the strategies pursued by the various incumbents when seeking to stamp their authority on the policy-making process.

2 Lord Curzon at the Foreign Office (1919–24)

Introduction

The agreements reached at the Paris Peace Conference in 1919 had important repercussions for the development of international politics throughout the following twenty years. The raft of measures imposed on Germany by the victor powers, which effectively condemned the country to second-class status, were as the more prescient observers noted at the time bound to create tensions in the future. The same was true of the decision to create a series of multi-ethnic states throughout central and south-eastern Europe, a move that took place in stark contradiction of the principle of national self-determination about which so much was said at the Peace Conference. Nor could the victor powers devise an effective policy for dealing with Soviet Russia, half-heartedly trying to broker an end to the Civil War there, whilst simultaneously promoting outside military intervention that was at least in part directed against the Bolshevik government in Moscow. There was not even much consensus at Paris about the future role of the new League of Nations, seen by some as an entirely new forum for conducting international relations, and by others as little more than a temporary irrelevance. The First World War had ripped apart the social and political fabric of Europe, making it almost impossible for the peacemakers to establish a new international order resilient enough to withstand the tensions and suspicions that were the inevitable legacy of years of bitter fighting and destruction.

Britain appeared at first glance to emerge from the war with its status enhanced – one of the main architects of victory over the central powers – and a beneficiary of political and territorial changes that took place in the Near East and elsewhere across the globe. In reality, though, four years of war had exacerbated many of the problems that were already facing the country before 1914. The huge debts incurred during the years of fighting threatened to place real constraints on the country's international power and prestige. The rise of the independence movement in India symbolised the growing pressure for a shift in the relationship between Britain and its colonies, whilst the white dominions were becoming ever more jealous of their own autonomy. Parity in sea power was effectively ceded to the United

States at the Washington Naval Conference of 1921–2, whilst the Japanese gained local naval supremacy in the Far East. Closer to home, Franco-German tension over subjects ranging from the payment of reparations through to rearmament constantly threatened to undermine European stability. British foreign policy in the 1920s (and indeed the 1930s as well) was based on a desire to sustain as far as possible the international status quo, whilst at the same time accepting that some concessions to change were unavoidable. The logic of this position meant that there could never be any return to the (partly mythical) days of 'splendid isolation'.[1] Britain's weak economic and military position required successive governments to pursue an active diplomacy designed to manage threats in such a way that they did not become serious enough to challenge the country's vital interests. In the 1920s, this led to the Locarno accords. In the 1930s, it led to appeasement.

The man who headed the Foreign Office during the critical years between 1919 and 1924 managed, in the words of one of his biographers, to become a caricature in the course of his own lifetime.[2] Viscount Curzon of Kedleston certainly comes across to the modern sensibility as a potent symbol of British imperialism, a minor aristocrat with an exaggerated sense of *amour propre*, who by dint of hard work and determination managed to become Viceroy of India at the tender age of thirty-eight. After his controversial resignation in 1905, following a struggle with Kitchener over reforms to the administration of the Indian Army,[3] the career of the erstwhile Viceroy stuttered badly for a time, but his reputation as one of the natural *doyens* of the British political establishment remained curiously intact, a striking testimony to his undaunted self-belief and sense of self-importance. The outbreak of war in 1914 provided Curzon with fresh opportunities to display his undoubted talents, particularly when he entered Asquith's Cabinet the following year, having previously dropped a none-too-subtle hint in a letter to the *The Times* that his country could ill-afford to ignore his considerable talents.[4] Despite obtaining a Cabinet post, however, the new Lord Privy Seal fretted almost continuously about his lack of influence on overseas policy. By the end of 1917 he was actively lobbying to take over as Foreign Secretary in place of Arthur Balfour, whose relaxed approach to his duties at the Foreign Office infuriated the workaholic Curzon. His opportunity finally came at the start of 1919, when Balfour accompanied Lloyd George to Paris to take part in the Peace Conference. The Prime Minister asked Curzon to take over as acting Foreign Secretary, an appointment that was made permanent nine months later when Balfour became Lord President of the Council. Curzon hoped that his promotion would allow him to become the principal architect of British foreign policy, whilst simultaneously advancing his progress towards his ultimate ambition of becoming Prime Minister.[5] He was to be disappointed. Over the next few years he was unable to achieve either of his major ambitions, losing out to Stanley Baldwin in the race for Number 10, and repeatedly failing to persuade his ministerial colleagues to accept his lead in discussions about the future of Britain's relations with the wider world.

Curzon may have embodied many of the values that characterised the political establishment of early twentieth-century Britain, but he lacked many of the personal qualities generally deemed to be essential for a successful political career. Whilst he earned a reputation for intellectual brilliance during his time at Oxford, he made little effort to cultivate the kind of friendships that could be so useful in later life, and it was during his time at university that he first attracted derision as a 'Very Superior Person', a tag that stuck to him until his death in 1925. Despite his rather pathetic denial that he was 'a pompous person ... devoid of any sense of humour',[6] he came across to his contemporaries as almost comically self-centred. When he served as Under-Secretary of State for Foreign Affairs, in the 1890s, Curzon's demeanour had grated on many of his listeners in the House of Commons. Nor were things much better when he subsequently moved to the House of Lords, although the more sober atmosphere there did provide a better setting for his speeches. Curzon had no clear following among his ministerial colleagues when he became Foreign Secretary in September 1919, whilst his limited skill as an orator meant that he had found it difficult to make a positive impression on a wider public. During his time in India he had expertly manipulated the symbols of imperial rule in order to enhance his personal authority, but he was much less adept at operating in the more humdrum world of British politics, struggling to adapt to the collegiality of the Cabinet and the pseudo-democratic rhetoric that increasingly characterised public life after 1918. The qualities that made Curzon an imposing Viceroy in the Edwardian era were not on the whole those required to achieve political success in inter-war Britain. His energy and undoubted talent as an administrator nevertheless meant that he remained a force to be reckoned with by all those around him. By the time Curzon became Foreign Secretary, he had been an imposing figure within the British Establishment for so long that he remained a potent presence even at a time when his qualities increasingly seemed to belong to a bygone era.

Curzon arrived at the Foreign Office in 1919 with a greater knowledge of the outside world than most of his predecessors. Sir Edward Grey had taken a veritable pride in refusing to venture abroad during the ten years he served as Foreign Secretary. Curzon had by contrast travelled extensively in the Middle East early in life, acquiring a profound knowledge of the region that he displayed in such magisterial tomes as *Persia and the Persian Question*,[7] whilst his time as Viceroy subsequently helped him to develop an understanding of international politics across Asia. His knowledge of European affairs was more limited, although still by no means negligible. It is tempting to identify Curzon's outlook as one of thoroughgoing and instinctive imperialism, but such a nebulous term does not altogether capture the bundle of instincts and ideas that informed the new Foreign Secretary's perception of Britain's place in the world when he took charge at the Foreign Office in 1919.[8] Curzon was certainly passionately committed to the cause of Empire, but he was shrewd enough to recognise that European questions were likely to play a critical role in British foreign policy during the years ahead, and was ready to make the effort to master the complexities of the whole subject. His general approach towards the conduct of foreign policy was spelled out in his presentations to the two Imperial Conferences of 1921 and 1923. During his time as Viceroy, Curzon had favoured a strong 'forward' policy designed to contain Russian influence in central Asia, manifested most dramatically in his tacit support for the Younghusband Expedition to Tibet, but as Foreign Secretary he took a more measured view of Britain's ability to play an assertive role around the world. He told delegates to the 1921 Imperial Conference that British policy over the previous two years had been marked 'by great caution and reserve. We have, as I read the lessons of the time, to keep what we have obtained [and not] seize anything else'. He subsequently told the 1923 Conference that 'war weariness' and 'profound moral repugnance to the very idea of war among our people' made the pursuit of an ambitious foreign policy quite impossible.[9] On both occasions, Curzon strongly argued that the maintenance of peace was indispensable for Britain's European and global interests, a *credo* that could have been articulated by almost any British Foreign Secretary or senior Foreign Office official in the years that followed. The Foreign Secretary's caution was largely inspired by his recognition that Britain was a *status quo* power, but it also showed that he was quite capable of taking a realistic view of the political and material constraints that governed foreign policy in a new and more democratic age. Although he had little liking for the new League of Nations, he reluctantly accepted that no British government could ignore an institution that was fast becoming a potent symbol in the popular consciousness of the struggle to prevent a 'repetition of the horrors' of 1914–18.[10] When serving as Viceroy, Curzon was impatient with those who counselled the need for caution. As Foreign Secretary, however, he showed himself capable of recognising the virtues of a pragmatic approach to international relations.

Curzon and the Foreign Office

The news of Curzon's appointment as Foreign Secretary provoked a nervous reaction among his new staff. One senior official later recalled that 'It was ... considered an evil day for the Foreign Office when it became known that this potentate, this ex-Viceroy, this "Superior Person", was in fact to rule over it ... I trembled for my peace of mind and I trembled for my daily liberty'.[11] A number of officials did, though, hope that their new political master might prove effective in restoring the battered reputation of the Department. Curzon's relations with Charles Hardinge, who served as Permanent Secretary until the end of 1920, were particularly difficult,[12] although the two men were united in their anger at the decline in the influence of the Foreign Office on policy during the war and post-war years.[13] Hardinge had also previously served as Viceroy of India, and he steadfastly refused to be awed by his new master. He vigorously defended his colleagues when Curzon complained about their laziness and inefficiency, warning that such bullying served only to 'undermine the confidence which does, and should, exist between the Secretary of State and this Office'.[14] Hardinge's successor as Permanent Secretary, the indefatigably diligent Eyre Crowe, was perhaps temperamentally less well-equipped to adopt such a direct tone with his master, leading to (unfounded) rumours that he was driven to a breakdown by the demands placed upon him by the Foreign Secretary. Curzon in fact had a high opinion of Crowe, and fought hard for his appointment in the face of some opposition from Lloyd George, who seems to have given serious consideration to the possibility of bringing in an outsider to head the Foreign Office.[15] Junior officials were often perturbed at the prospect of coming into direct contact with the 'Very Superior Person', and the more nervous among them went to great lengths to avoid even a chance meeting in the corridor. Exaggerated accounts of these tensions inevitably leaked out into the wider world of Westminster and Whitehall, and by 1922 it was widely presumed that Foreign Office staff heartily detested Curzon's 'brutality', and felt a profound 'relief' when he was absent abroad or on his sick-bed.[16] A few officials such as Harold Nicolson did express some affection and admiration for Curzon,[17] but most of his colleagues disliked working for a man whose manner suggested that he viewed them as little more than functionaries, whose main role was to carry out instructions rather than offer detailed advice on important questions of policy.

The Foreign Office experienced a number of organisational changes while Curzon was in charge, including the partial implementation of a pre-war proposal to end the traditional distinction between diplomats posted abroad and Foreign Office clerks stationed in London.[18] The return to peace-time conditions also led to changes in the role of the Political Intelligence Department and the Press Bureau. Since Hardinge and Crowe were both able administrators, Curzon was not required to involve himself closely in the purely administrative work of the Foreign Office, but he was much less willing to delegate important decisions about policy. As a result he felt impelled to review thoroughly all the documentation relating to important issues. Such a *modus operandi* inevitably placed him under great strain, particularly given his indifferent health. He listened with care to the views of Hardinge and Crowe,[19] along with a number of other senior officials,[20] but he seldom discussed foreign affairs with more junior staff (although he did carefully read their minutes on documents passed up the bureaucratic hierarchy). Face-to-face meetings between Curzon and his staff were usually formal affairs rather than opportunities for relaxed and wide-ranging discussion. The pressure of work on the Foreign Secretary and senior officials did, though, mean that staff in the geographical departments sometimes had a considerable degree of autonomy when dealing with issues deemed by their chief to be of secondary importance. The Foreign Office was, like most bureaucracies, a complex hierarchy in which the pattern of decision-making fluctuated according to the dictates of circumstance. Even such a zealous workaholic as Curzon could not involve himself with every issue that came within the formal remit of his department.

There were times when Curzon's views about international questions came into conflict with those of his senior advisers, particularly when European matters were under consideration. Many senior Foreign Office officials including Crowe and Tyrrell were deeply committed to the *entente* with France, believing that a close relationship with Paris was vital to preserve the future peace of Europe. Whilst Curzon was quite willing to recognise the importance of the Anglo-French axis in the post-war world, he made little secret of his contempt for French politicians, whom he condemned derisively as not 'the sort of people one would go tiger shooting with'.[21] He was also acutely aware that France remained Britain's most important imperial rival. Curzon was therefore generally ready to follow Lloyd George's lead in seeking to reintegrate Germany back into the mainstream of European economic and political life, whilst making soothing noises designed to reassure Paris that Britain remained committed in some definite if ill-defined sense to ensuring France's security. Members of the Foreign Office who disagreed with the Foreign Secretary about questions of policy were seldom in a position to change his mind. Tyrrell became involved in a curious plot, apparently masterminded by Lord Derby and H.A. Gwynne of the *Morning Post*, to ease the Foreign Secretary from office in favour of a more francophile successor.[22] Such behaviour was, however, quite exceptional. Foreign Office officials were perfectly well aware of the constitutional conventions governing the relationship between a minister and his staff. Whatever their disagreements with Curzon's 'line' on any particular issue of policy, they tried dutifully to follow his instructions once he had made his views clear to them.

Curzon's relationships with British diplomatic representatives abroad proved difficult on occasion, reflecting the complex array of social and constitutional considerations that governed the status of ambassadors and other heads of mission. Many heads of embassies regarded themselves as *the* expert on the bilateral relationship between the British government and the government to which they were accredited, and were therefore determined to use their position to exercise a real influence on policy. The character of the Foreign Secretary's relations with senior British diplomatic representatives abroad once again varied according to the particular constellation of personalities and circumstances, a pattern that can be illustrated by reference to the two most important embassies: Berlin and Paris. Lord D'Abernon's appointment as ambassador to Berlin in 1920 – on the grounds that he possessed the financial expertise needed to deal with the complex problems of reparations payments and reconstruction – attracted bitter resentment from Foreign Office staff who resented the intrusion of an 'outsider' who did not belong to the diplomatic establishment.[23] Since Lloyd George was largely responsible for securing D'Abernon's appointment, Curzon may have shared the anger of his officials, resenting an appointment over which he had little control. The Foreign Secretary certainly seems to have tried to engineer D'Abernon's removal from Berlin on a number of occasions in the early 1920s, but was stymied by the problem of finding a replacement with the requisite financial expertise. The ambassador in any case had his own extensive contacts with political and financial circles in London, and kept up a lengthy correspondence with individuals ranging from Lloyd George and King George V through to senior bankers and industrialists. He also unashamedly ignored instructions from the Foreign Office from time to time in order to pursue a policy that he considered more appropriate. Although the ambassador usually kept Curzon abreast of the most important developments in Germany, the Foreign Secretary remained wary of an ambassador whose extensive network of contacts back home gave him an opportunity to evade the control of the Foreign Office.

Three men headed the Paris Embassy during Curzon's time in charge at the Foreign Office: Lord Derby, Lord Hardinge and Lord Crewe. Derby, like D'Abernon, was appointed to his post even though he had never been a member of the Diplomatic Service. The erstwhile Cabinet minister enjoyed a formidable array of social and political contacts that allowed him to pursue his duties in an independent spirit, and he corresponded at length with ministers and senior officials outside the Foreign Office throughout his time in Paris.[24] He also entertained on a lavish scale, which gave him a chance to build close links with foreign diplomats and politicians, as well as members of the British social and political elite passing through the French capital. Derby instinctively disliked Curzon's supposed 'conceit',[25] and a veritable feud broke out between the two men when the ambassador eventually returned to the Cabinet in 1922. Nevertheless, whilst he was at the Paris Embassy he maintained an extensive and generally good-natured correspondence with Curzon, providing the Foreign Secretary with the material he needed to remain abreast of 'the rather kaleidoscopic position of affairs in France'.[26] Derby himself was sensitive to attempts by other ministers to marginalise the role of his embassy by relying on their own representatives in Paris for information,[27] which may account for the fact that he was more ready than D'Abernon to keep the Foreign Secretary informed about his activities. The same was true of Charles Hardinge when he took over as British ambassador in France at the end of 1920, and the voluminous private correspondence between the two men was surprisingly friendly and informative.[28] Even so, Hardinge was still, like Derby, able to claim a considerable degree of independence, despite his protestations that he believed it was the duty of an ambassador to 'obey orders' whether he agreed with them or not.[29] The Foreign Secretary was without doubt far more comfortable when Lord Crewe was appointed to the Embassy at the start of 1923, since the two men had been friends for many years, whilst their extensive correspondence reflected a considerable symmetry in their views on most important international questions.[30]

Curzon and the Cabinet

Curzon's relationship with Foreign Office officials and Embassy staff was of course seldom the critical factor determining his influence over the foreign policy-making process. His relationship with his ministerial colleagues was far more important. The cabinets of Lloyd George, Bonar Law and Baldwin contained some of the most familiar heavyweights of twentieth-century British political life, including Churchill, Balfour, Milner and Austen Chamberlain. Such ministers not only possessed enormous experience, but also had their own strong views on international affairs, which they took every opportunity to advance in Cabinet. The elaborate edifice of Cabinet committees that made recommendations to the full Cabinet also set limits on the autonomy of the Foreign Secretary and the Foreign Office, since they provided a setting for other departmental representatives to articulate and defend their own positions on matters of detail. Curzon chaired the Eastern Committee of the Cabinet, a post that allowed him to strengthen his influence over British policy in the Middle East during the early part of his tenure at the Foreign Office, much to the chagrin of other ministers such as Churchill.[31] He seldom attended the Committee of Imperial Defence, however, even though Lloyd George hoped that the post-war CID would play an important role in co-ordinating the activities of the service departments and the Foreign Office.[32] Whilst senior Foreign Office officials attended meetings in his place, the absence of their political master weakened the voice of their department in discussions there. The inter-departmental committees that were set up on an *ad hoc* basis also provided ministers and officials from beyond the Foreign Office with an opportunity to influence decisions about foreign policy.[33] Many discussions naturally took place outside the confines of the formal committee system altogether, allowing senior representatives from different departments to resolve outstanding differences in off-the-record conversations or via private correspondence. However, since Curzon was not adept at establishing an easy *rapport* with his Cabinet colleagues, he found it hard to establish the kind of informal understandings that might have helped him to promote his position within the bureaucratic and political labyrinth of Whitehall and Westminster.

Curzon's relationship with the three Prime Ministers he served under at the Foreign Office played a critical part in determining the scope of his authority and power. The Lloyd George Cabinet that lasted until the autumn of 1922 was an unstable coalition, plagued throughout its life by personal and political tensions.[34] A Liberal Prime Minister, who had made his name in domestic politics as a radical, presided over a Cabinet mainly comprised of traditionally-minded Tories inclined to look askance at their *parvenu* leader. When the coalition finally disintegrated, Curzon was convinced that it was Lloyd George's 'ill-judged and calamitous interference in Foreign Affairs that brought about this doom'.[35] In reality, however, the experience of coalition had placed such strain on both the Liberal and

Conservative parties that the government was always vulnerable to disintegration. Curzon always acknowledged that Lloyd George was a 'wonderful speaker' who excelled in 'invective, persuasion and audacity'.[36] There was also a fair measure of agreement between the two men over the major challenges facing Britain in the post-war world. Both were pledged to maintain the Empire as the foundation of Britain's international power and prestige, as well as committing their country to an active role in European politics, a view predicated on the assumption that a retreat to isolation would simply create a degree of international instability that would threaten British interests across the globe. Beneath this broad level of agreement, though, there was almost constant tension between the Prime Minister and the Foreign Secretary. Both men were convinced that they had the right to set the fundamental direction of Britain's foreign policy, with the result that their relationship was marked by a great deal of friction.[37]

Lloyd George and Curzon co-operated most effectively when policy towards Western Europe was under review. Both men believed that treating Germany as a permanent political and economic pariah would undermine international stability, and were therefore wary of the harsh demands put forward by successive French governments on matters such as reparations and German rearmament. They nevertheless worked hard to maintain reasonable ties with Paris, so as to be in a position to encourage ministers there to take a softer line towards their eastern neighbour. The two men also recognised that international stability could only be achieved once the French government was satisfied that it had gained reasonable security against any possible future German attack. The Prime Minister and the Foreign Secretary were, however, united in their reluctance to offer too binding a security guarantee to the French government (something which became apparent during the abortive negotiations for an Anglo-French defensive alliance that took place before the Cannes Conference of 1922).[38] The comparative harmony between the two men over West European affairs was strengthened by the fact that Curzon was primarily interested in areas beyond the continent. Whilst there is a danger of exaggerating the extent to which the Foreign Secretary ignored developments in Europe during 1920–22, he showed little sustained interest in the kind of complex financial questions that increasingly formed the warp and woof of discussions between European governments after 1919.[39] He was, by contrast, determined to assert himself when policy towards the Middle East and Russia was under review.

Curzon broadly endorsed Lloyd George's handling of the half-hearted British intervention in Russia that took place in the wake of the 1917 Revolution. Although the Foreign Secretary was convinced that Bolshevik Russia posed a major threat to British imperial possessions in Asia, he accepted the Cabinet's decision in 1919 to withdraw British troops from the south of the country in favour of a policy of providing material assistance to the white armies there. He was, however, bitterly opposed to Lloyd George's attempts the following year to build closer relations with the new Bolshevik regime, a move which the Prime Minister hoped would encourage greater moderation in Moscow whilst simultaneously creating new markets for British companies, and was more inclined to favour a policy designed to isolate Russia behind a kind of *cordon sanitaire*.[40] Against the wishes of Curzon and many other ministers, Lloyd George invited a delegation of leading members of the Soviet regime to London to take part in negotiations for an Anglo-Russian Trade Agreement.[41] The Foreign Secretary wrote a series of angry memoranda in the spring of 1920 demanding that no agreement should be signed until the Soviet government guaranteed to stop its campaign of propaganda 'against British interests [and] the British Empire in the East'.[42] The outbreak of war between Poland and Russia in the summer of 1920 added to his anxiety. The Foreign Secretary was particularly incensed by the refusal of British dock workers to load ships bound for Poland with munitions for use against Bolshevik troops, complaining that such militancy was inspired by members of the Soviet delegation, whom he feared were using their presence in Britain 'to stab us in the heart'.[43] Curzon's opposition to establishing *de facto* relations with the Soviet government was supported by a number of his ministerial colleagues, as well as by senior army officers and counter-intelligence officials, but the Foreign Office was not in practice closely involved in the detailed talks that took place with the Soviet delegation in the summer of 1920 (which were largely conducted through the Board of Trade). Although the Foreign Office was regularly consulted, Curzon had few opportunities to intervene directly in the negotiations, largely confining himself to angry memoranda complaining that 'the presence of these unscrupulous agitators is too high a price to pay even for the chances of a peaceful settlement'.[44] Lloyd George was in any case so determined to secure the Trade Agreement with Russia that he was willing to take a tough line with dissenting ministers,[45] and at a Cabinet meeting on 18 November the Prime Minister used his position to push through the Agreement despite strong opposition from Curzon and a number of other senior ministers.[46] The situation was somewhat different two years later, though, in the build-up to the Genoa Economic Conference that met in April 1922. Lloyd George was by now less confident of his political position, and he was forced to promise Churchill and other 'diehards' that he would not extend *de jure* recognition to the Soviet government except under certain strict conditions. Curzon himself remained hostile even to the Prime Minister's wish to improve trade links with Russia, believing that the government in Moscow would never refrain from propaganda whatever commitments it made, and after Lloyd George's departure from office he wasted little time in urging a more forceful line. He was the main architect of the decision to send a strong Official Note to Moscow in 1923 protesting against Soviet violations of the Trade Agreement, and even seriously considered recalling the British representatives from the Commercial Mission that had been sent to Russia in 1921.[47]

The starkest disagreement between Lloyd George and Curzon developed when policy in the Near East was under review. The Prime Minister's support for Greek intervention in Turkey in 1919 perturbed Curzon, since the Foreign Secretary was concerned that the disintegration of the old Ottoman Empire would create further instability in the Near East, whilst a conflict between Britain and Turkey might foster resentment among the millions of Moslems in the Empire.[48] Other ministers such as Montagu at the India Office supported the Foreign Secretary's position. Over the following two years, continual bickering between the British and the French governments helped to create an ill-tempered deadlock in the region. By the autumn of 1922, the Greek position in western Turkey was in the process of disintegrating entirely, along with dreams of building a greater Greece, starkly posing the question of possible British intervention to prevent the nationalist Kemalist regime from gaining control of the Straits. Curzon believed that it was necessary to provide a clear signal to the Turkish government that any further advances would be resisted, but he was reluctant to see Britain commit itself to unilateral military action, and threw himself energetically into the search for a new understanding with the French.[49] The talks that took place in Paris on 20–21 September were however marked by an extraordinarily bad-tempered confrontation between the Foreign Secretary and the French Prime Minister Raymond Poincaré (although a compromise was eventually cobbled together setting down joint terms for the Kemalist regime that would have recognised its claim to eastern Thrace). Curzon himself upon returning to London was more perturbed than ever by the activities of the 'philhellenes' within the Cabinet, above all Lloyd George, and was appalled when ministers took the decision on the morning of 29 September to approve an effective ultimatum demanding the withdrawal of Turkish forces around the town of Chanak. He worked hard to change the views of his colleagues, noting at a second meeting later in the day that a war with Turkey 'would be a most deplorable occurrence',[50] but without much effect. The Foreign Secretary found himself, for once, taking a less hawkish position on a key question of foreign policy than many of his Cabinet colleagues. His views were, though, shared by many prominent Conservatives outside the Cabinet,[51] as well as by senior members of the diplomatic establishment including Charles Hardinge in Paris. Resentment over Lloyd George's handling of the Chanak crisis, fostered above all by Bonar Law, played a significant part in the machinations that led up the celebrated decision at the Carlton Club on 19 October to withdraw Conservative support from the coalition government.[52] Lloyd George made a determined effort to 'lobby' Curzon in the days leading up to the Carlton Club meeting, but the Foreign Secretary seems to have determinedly sat on the fence, keeping his distance both from his fellow ministers and from the plotters. There can be little doubt, though, that he shed few tears at the prospect of Lloyd George's departure from Downing Street.

Curzon had become more irritated than ever by Lloyd George's incursions into foreign affairs in the weeks leading up to the Prime Minister's resignation. At the start of October 1922, when the crisis in the Near East was at its height, he complained yet again that the Prime Minister's failure to keep the Foreign Office abreast of his talks with foreign envoys was placing the department 'in a very invidious position'.[53] A few days later he drafted another and more damning letter – the dispatch of which was in the event forestalled by Lloyd George's own resignation – arguing that:

> There has grown up a system under which there are in reality two Foreign Offices: the one for which I am for the time being responsible, and the other at Number 10 – with the essential difference between them that, whereas I report not only to you but to all my colleagues everything that I say or do, every telegram that I receive or send, every communication of importance that reaches me, it is often only by accident that I hear what is being done at the other Foreign Office; and even when I am informed officially of what has passed there, it has nevertheless been done, in many cases, without the Foreign Office, for which I am responsible, knowing that the communication was going to be made or the interview take place.[54]

The immediate cause of Curzon's anger was of course Lloyd George's 'hellenophile policy', but the Foreign Secretary's words reflected the anger he felt about the way in which the Foreign Office had supposedly been marginalised in the policy-making process throughout the previous few years. The Prime Minister himself had attended twenty-three international conferences during the period 1920–22, a pattern of attendance that symbolised his abiding involvement in foreign affairs.[55]

Curzon's letter also revealed his deep concern about the development of a powerful *institutional* apparatus at Number 10. The Foreign Secretary was not alone in expressing apprehension that the Prime Minister was encroaching on the traditional autonomy of departments, and the survival of a powerful Cabinet Secretariat into the post-war years raised concern in the minds of many ministers. There was even greater perturbation about the Prime Minister's penchant for relying on a so-called 'garden suburb' of nondepartmental advisers, whose activities threatened both to create administrative confusion and to challenge the traditional role and status of departments. It is difficult to evaluate the influence of the Cabinet Secretariat and the garden suburb on the operation of government, particularly given the suggestion that the changes made by the Prime Minister to the operation of the core executive were evolutionary rather than radical in character.[56] Nevertheless, whilst some of the administrative innovations were doubtless little more than an *ad hoc* response to the demands of war, and the fragile peace that followed, other changes certainly represented a deliberate attempt by the Prime Minister to assert himself as the main force in domestic and foreign policy-making.[57] During his time at Number 10,

Lloyd George relied heavily for advice about international affairs on such advisers as Philip Kerr, the future Lord Lothian, who had been one of the leading members of Lord Milner's South African *kindergarten* in the early years of the century. Kerr, who served as Lloyd George's private secretary, was 'perhaps the Prime Minister's most intimate private confidant in the period 1919–20',[58] helping to influence policy towards Germany and Russia, as well as playing a key role during the Versailles negotiations. He also acted on numerous occasions as an intermediary between Downing Street and the Foreign Office, conveying to officials the Prime Minister's views on important questions of foreign policy. When Kerr took up a job in Fleet Street in the summer of 1921, other advisers such as Edward Grigg continued to provide Lloyd George with advice about a whole range of international questions. Curzon roundly condemned the activities of such advisers, condemning Kerr in particular as 'the chosen agent of his master's intrigues',[59] a resentment fuelled by the Foreign Secretary's fear that their activities undermined both his own position and the position of the department over which he presided.

Curzon's attitude towards the Cabinet Secretariat, headed throughout this period by the indefatigable Maurice Hankey, was rather more positive.[60] Hankey was himself a sharp critic of Lloyd George's chaotic style of government, complaining bitterly on more than one occasion that the Prime Minister 'centralises too much ... and then cannot get through the work'.[61] He certainly did not share his political master's dislike of the Foreign Office or of the Foreign Secretary himself. When Curzon complained in the autumn of 1919 that he did not receive enough notice about the discussion of foreign affairs in Cabinet, Hankey helpfully assured the Foreign Secretary that 'I will do my best to give you warning when Foreign Office subjects are coming up'. He added cautiously, though, that 'The fact is that I can very rarely extract from the Prime Minister a decision as to whether he will have a Cabinet meeting until late on the afternoon or evening of the previous day'.[62] Curzon's reasonable personal relationship with Hankey was perhaps surprising given that the Cabinet Secretary himself insisted on playing a very active role in international affairs. He often accompanied Lloyd George to major international conferences, including the Washington Conference on Naval Disarmament of 1921–22, a practice that he justified by claiming that 'the interdepartmental questions dealt with at these Conferences are essentially of the order of Cabinet questions and it is convenient that they should be handled in their secretarial aspects by the same office'.[63] Hankey also helped to ensure that the Cabinet Office took a leading role in dealing with League of Nations business, warning Curzon at the start of 1920 that the Foreign Office could not effectively manage such a task since 'There will be lots of new bodies associated with the League ... and they will need to interact directly with a range of British departments'.[64] Although the Cabinet Office faced considerable hostility from many Conservative ministers throughout the early 1920s, Curzon seems to have appreciated the talents and diligence of the Cabinet Secretary. When the two men did briefly fall out in the autumn of 1922, after Curzon launched an attack on the 'too powerful and too numerous' Secretariat, the Foreign Secretary quickly followed up his harsh words with a private letter of apology.[65] Hankey's predictions about the potential for confusion in the handling of League business did, however, prove prescient. In the summer of 1923 Curzon was forced to fight a bitter battle with Robert Cecil, the newly appointed Lord Privy Seal with particular responsibility for League Affairs, in an effort to prevent him from becoming a kind of 'subordinate Foreign Secretary'.[66]

The Foreign Secretary hoped that the break-up of the coalition government would allow him to increase his influence over foreign policy in the new administration, which was derisively condemned by its critics as 'the Government of the Second Eleven', given the departure of so many senior ministers from office. At first it appeared that his hopes might be fulfilled. The Cabinet Secretariat was cut drastically in size shortly after Lloyd George's departure, although Hankey prevailed on the new Prime Minister, Andrew Bonar Law, to resist pressure from ministers and senior civil servants to eliminate it altogether.[67] The most prominent members of the garden suburb also faded from the scene once a new face appeared in Number 10. At the same time, Curzon's deft handling of negotiations at the Lausanne Conference, which met at the start of 1923 to discuss the situation in the eastern Mediterranean, won him many plaudits and provided a rare taste of popularity.[68] Although the British position prior to the Conference was very weak, following the *débacle* of recent developments in south-eastern Europe, the Foreign Secretary used his presence and negotiating skill to secure a compromise peace that broadly satisfied both Turkey and Britain. Despite these promising developments, though, his reputation quickly began to plummet again. Even the briefest glance at Curzon's final months in office shows that his sensitivity about challenges to his authority survived the departure of Lloyd George and the dismantling of the 'other' Foreign Office at Number 10.

Both Bonar Law and Baldwin were less interested than Lloyd George in international affairs.[69] Bonar Law was a sick man throughout his brief tenure as Prime Minister, with the result that he often lacked the energy to stamp his mark on policy. Baldwin for his part was less ignorant of foreign affairs than his critics claimed, but he was temperamentally inclined to pursue a more consensual style of decision-making than Lloyd George, as well as showing marked reluctance to become involved in departmental minutiae. Curzon nevertheless continued to complain bitterly throughout 1923 about Prime Ministerial interference in areas that he regarded as his own special responsibility. Within weeks of Bonar Law replacing Lloyd George, Curzon was already chiding the new Prime Minister for failing to inform the Foreign Office about a recent conversation with the French ambassador,[70] whilst criticising him in private for his ignorance of 'diplomacy in general'.[71] The Foreign Secretary was even more angry about Baldwin's forays into foreign affairs, most notably his private talks with Poincaré during the Ruhr crisis of 1923, which first erupted in January when French and Belgian troops were deployed in the region following repeated German defaults on reparations.[72] Curzon was appalled at a move which he saw both as a source of confusion in the foreign policy-making process, as well as a direct challenge to his authority, a position that may have been heightened by his suspicion that Baldwin's talks with Poincaré were part of a manoeuvre by the Prime Minister to push policy in a more Francophile direction than his Foreign Secretary was ready to endorse.[73] The differences between the two men over policy towards France were in any case made worse by the personal and political tension that existed between them. The Foreign Secretary had desperately hoped to replace Bonar Law as Prime Minister following the latter's resignation on the grounds of ill-health in May 1923, and his defeat at the hands of Baldwin in the political manoeuvrings that followed left a bitter taste in his mouth.[74]

Curzon in fact commanded very little support in his quest to become Prime Minister. A number of ministers such as Derby made little secret that they would refuse to serve under him, whilst King George V was only too willing to accept Balfour's advice that it would be imprudent to appoint a Prime Minister who sat in the House of Lords.[75] Although Baldwin did provide Curzon with some latitude in his handling of foreign affairs during the second half of 1923, he never gave the Foreign Secretary the freedom he craved. The Prime Minister had a poor opinion of Curzon, whom he believed 'had been more harmful to this country than any previous Foreign Secretary', and was inclined to back other ministers when they came into conflict with him.[76] By October, just a few months after Baldwin came to power, Curzon was already complaining 'about the way in which foreign policy is carried on in this cabinet, which is quite unlike anything in my experience. I receive no support. Any member may make any suggestion he pleases and the discussion wanders into irrelevancies. The Prime Minister *must* give the Foreign Secretary his support'.[77] Despite Curzon's lament that his problems were 'unlike anything in my experience', though, his complaints closely resembled those he had made when Lloyd George was still at Number 10. He had once again failed to grasp that the system of Cabinet government placed inevitable limits on the ability of a Foreign Secretary to define and pursue his own foreign policy without the close co-operation of his fellow ministers.

Curzon's troubled relationship with successive prime ministers undoubtedly weakened his position when dealing with other ministers, while his unpopularity with many of his Cabinet colleagues made it difficult for him to mobilise support for his preferred policies. Leo Amery, who served at the Admiralty during this period, was convinced that the Foreign Secretary was 'arrogant' and 'not really reliable'.[78] J.C.C. Davidson, who was Parliamentary Private Secretary to both Baldwin and Bonar Law, before becoming Chancellor of the Duchy of Lancaster in 1923, condemned Curzon for an 'arrogance which was unbelievable'.[79] Austen Chamberlain, who had long doubted Curzon's judgement, was equally scathing. Lord Derby, who returned to the

Cabinet as Secretary of State for War in 1922, was perhaps Curzon's most vitriolic critic, in part because he believed that the Foreign Secretary placed too little emphasis on the Anglo-French entente to which Derby himself had devoted so much of his recent political career. In the spring of 1922 Derby declined an offer from Lloyd George to become Secretary of State for India, telling the Prime Minister that 'I fear Curzon's and my ideas of foreign policy are so very different that it will make co-operation with him very difficult'.[80] When he did finally return to the Cabinet, he repeatedly complained that Curzon treated his fellow ministers in a high-handed fashion, and refused to keep them informed about policy.[81] Edwin Montagu at the India Office was another powerful critic of Curzon's performance at the Foreign Office. In a letter to Churchill written at the end of 1921, Montagu sarcastically condemned the Foreign Secretary's performance during his first years in office:

> And during the time he has been at the Foreign Office, we have seen the stately array of his diplomatic successes. How he has strengthened the entente and confounded our enemies; how he has seized each opportunity as God presented it to his Vice-Regent; how he has written his great name across the annals of Persia, of Mesopotamia, of Azerbaijan, of Armenia, of Silesia, of France and America, with the result that the word 'Curzon' carries to the inhabitants of all these far-flung countries the same imperishable message.[82]

The tension was aggravated by growing division between the two men over the responsibility for policy towards the Near East. In March 1922 Montagu authorised the Indian Government to deny rumours that the British government intended to provide Greece with munitions and other war material. Curzon was appalled by this decision, which was not approved by the Cabinet, whilst Lloyd George subsequently demanded the resignation of the Secretary of State for India. Montagu responded in a speech at Cambridge by attacking the Prime Minister as a 'dictator', before going on to launch a diatribe against Curzon's foreign policy, attacking its 'disastrous effects' in India, a charge that was calculated to wound the vanity of a former Viceroy who still prided himself on his expertise in Indian affairs.[83] Most of the charges made by Montagu were in fact unfair, and Curzon had few problems defending himself in a powerful speech to the House of Lords, but the whole incident once again illustrated the Foreign Secretary's unrivalled genius for aggravating his colleagues.

Curzon faced a number of battles with the Treasury during his time as Foreign Secretary, a development that reflected the growing importance of financial and economic issues in the foreign policy-making process after the First World War. He was sometimes successful, as in 1919–20, when he fought hard for extra resources to facilitate the successful restructuring of the Foreign Office, and resisted proposals to integrate it more fully into the mainstream civil service.[84] There was nevertheless considerable concern within the Foreign Office about the Treasury's growing involvement in foreign policy, and Curzon himself complained to Austen Chamberlain on more than one occasion about the failure of his staff to keep the diplomats informed of their activities,[85] as well as lamenting more generally to his Cabinet colleagues about 'the casual way in which economic questions were dealt with between Departments'.[86] Sir Warren Fisher, who served as Permanent Secretary at the Treasury throughout the inter-war years, took a sustained interest in foreign affairs, and unashamedly used the Ruhr crisis of 1923 to push his own views on the potential dangers of an Anglo-French policy based on a punitive line towards Germany. Curzon himself had little real understanding of the complex financial questions at stake in the bitter disagreements about reparations that marred international relations during the early 1920s,[87] with the result that he was perhaps less sensitive to incursions on Foreign Office authority over this issue than he was on subjects that were of more immediate interest to him. The five years in which he headed the Foreign Office witnessed the emergence of the Treasury as a major actor in domestic debates on Britain's relations with the rest of the world, as well as a significant player in the international conferences and commissions that provided an increasingly important setting for interactions between governments in the years after Versailles.

Curzon's most protracted battles took place with Winston Churchill, who served at the War Office and the Colonial Office during the years between 1919 and 1924. Although both men were instinctive imperialists, committed to maintaining Britain's position in Asia, they often disagreed about the best way of achieving such an objective. Some of their sharpest disputes took place in 1919, when the civil war in Russia was still raging. Curzon strongly defended the independence of the new states that emerged in the Caucasus in the wake of the 1917 Revolution, believing they could provide a buffer against any future Russian expansion towards Persia, and favoured the maintenance of a British military presence in the region.[88] Churchill was by contrast more willing to see the White forces headed by General Denikin establish themselves in the Caucasus as part of their broader war with the Bolsheviks, despite the danger that they would effectively snuff out the independence of the new states there.[89] Since Curzon for once found himself supported by most of the Cabinet, he was able to defeat Churchill's attempts to determine British policy towards south Russia and the Caucasus during 1919, although the Foreign Secretary faced a constant battle to persuade his ministerial colleagues to maintain British forces in the region.[90] Whilst he was at first successful in persuading them not to evacuate troops from the area around Batum, on the shores of the Black Sea,[91] he had to admit defeat by the summer of 1920 as it became clear that the British position there was untenable.[92]

The battle between Churchill and Curzon had in any case by now largely passed to the whole question of Persia and other parts of the Middle East. The Minister of War dragged his feet when asked in May 1920 to provide troops to support Curzon's policy of supporting a stable pro-British regime in Persia, accusing the Foreign Office of taking important decisions without consulting the General Staff,[93] whilst the Foreign Secretary in turn attacked Churchill for failing to pay attention to the opinions of the Cabinet.[94] Churchill also wrote a memorandum complaining bitterly about the situation that had developed in Mesopotamia since 1918, accusing the Foreign Office of adopting a policy that ignored the financial implications for the War Office, which was expected to provide troops to protect British officials based in the country. He therefore proposed that questions relating to Mesopotamia should be handed over to the Colonial Office.[95] Ironically, as Curzon wasted little time in observing, Churchill was confused about the division of responsibilities in the region since the India Office was in fact responsible for Mesopotamia.[96] Nevertheless, Churchill's complaints about the confusion surrounding British policy in the Middle East struck some chord with other ministers, and extensive debate followed about the desirability of creating a new department charged with managing Britain's interests in the whole region.[97] Curzon argued that such a move would be too costly and proposed the establishment of a new Middle Eastern Department under the control of the Foreign Office. In the event, though, he lost the battle to establish the Foreign Office as the undisputed architect of Middle Eastern policy.[98] Whilst Lloyd George largely supported his Foreign Secretary throughout much of 1920, the Prime Minister eventually asked Churchill to take over at the Colonial Office at the beginning of 1921, charged among other tasks with establishing a new semi-autonomous Middle Eastern Department. In the event, though, the lines of responsibility remained blurred. Egypt, for example, remained the formal responsibility of the Foreign Office, and quickly became the focus for yet more bad-tempered disagreements between Curzon and Churchill, whilst Churchill himself continued to argue that the tensions plaguing British policy could never be resolved unless he was given sole responsibility for the 'whole problem' of the Middle East.[99] The Foreign Secretary for his part bitterly opposed such a development, writing angrily to his wife that Churchill 'wants to grab everything into his new Dept., & to be a sort of Asiatic Foreign Secretary'.[100] Curzon was as ever convinced that he had the right to be something more than *primus inter pares* when dealing with international affairs. Churchill was by contrast determined to assert himself in the foreign policy-making process on the grounds that his departmental responsibilities gave him both the right and the duty to play such a role.

Beyond Whitehall

The previous pages have focused on Curzon's failure to assert himself as the principal architect of British foreign policy within government. The Foreign Secretary himself recognised, however, that 'moral repugnance to the very idea of war' placed great constraints on the freedom of policy-makers.[101] The avalanche of criticism directed against the old diplomacy during the war years reflected growing public scepticism about the behaviour of professional diplomats, whilst the extension of the franchise in 1918 represented an important moment in the development of the British democratic system, symbolising the right of a broader public to pass judgement on the success of government ministers in carrying out their duties. In this new political environment, newspapers, pressure groups and political parties all provided a forum for articulating public sentiment about the conduct of foreign policy. An effective foreign secretary could not afford to ignore such institutions, since they formed an integral part of the political environment that moulded the texture of political and administrative relationships within the core executive. Although Curzon recognised that popular sentiment was increasingly posing a constraint on the freedom of foreign policy makers, he made few sustained efforts to mould public opinion during his time at the Foreign Office. Newspaper proprietors such as Beaverbrook and Northcliffe played a critical role in the British political system after the end of the First World War,[102] seeking to use their publications to promote their chosen opinions and agendas, and most leading politicians were shrewd enough to recognise the importance of the press in swaying the views of newly enfranchised voters. Ministers such as Birkenhead and Churchill understood that the development of their own political careers was likely to be profoundly influenced by the treatment they received in the major newspapers, and eagerly cultivated contacts with leading editors, as well as contributing their own articles to the major newspapers. Curzon, by contrast, was never effective at dealing with the press. Neither his experience as Viceroy, nor his instinctive disdain for the compromises of democratic politics, fostered the skills needed to thrive in the changing political landscape of inter-war Britain.

The Foreign Secretary commented bitterly on the attacks he endured in the press, particularly at the hands of *The Times* and *Daily Mail* (both of which were owned by Northcliffe until 1922). Although *The Times* was traditionally perceived as the voice of the British establishment, particularly abroad, the paper was bitterly critical of Lloyd George's coalition government in the post-war years. Henry Wickham Steed, who edited the paper from 1919 to 1922, was an especially fierce critic of Curzon. The leading articles in the paper seldom proposed a clear direction for British foreign policy, beyond a staunch defence of the Anglo-French entente, but their authors did make numerous attacks on the coalition government's actions. The Government's policy in Mesopotamia was subjected to stinging criticism in the spring of 1920.[103] A few months later, Curzon's policy towards Persia was denounced even more savagely, and the Foreign Secretary was personally blamed for creating a situation that 'is, in all senses, ridiculous'.[104] The most vitriolic criticism came in an extraordinary editorial on 13 July 1921, when a leading article cautioned against including Curzon in a delegation due to depart for Washington to negotiate the naval treaty with the American and Japanese governments, on the grounds that the Foreign Secretary was 'pompous and pretentious' and showed an 'incapacity' for business.[105] Nor did *The Times* usually give Curzon much support even when it agreed with his policies. The paper gave him little credit for opposing the *rapprochement* with Russia in 1921, even though it was itself bitterly critical of such a development, and only grudgingly acknowledged the Foreign Secretary's attempts to promote a moderate policy during the Chanak crisis that helped to destroy the Lloyd George coalition in the autumn of 1922.

Curzon was angered at the attacks in *The Times*, although his reaction was magnified by his habitual penchant for melodrama and self-pity. When he was recovering from a serious bout of phlebitis, in the summer of 1922, he complained angrily to his wife that 'the Northcliffe people will not spare me even in my illness and seem intent on getting me alive or dead'.[106] He never really found a way of dealing with the problem, at least until the death of Northcliffe and the departure of Steed at the end of 1922 led to some changes in the newspaper's coverage of international affairs. After the attack made on him in the build-up to the Washington Conference, Curzon instructed both the Foreign Office and the Embassy in Washington to withdraw news facilities from *The Times*,[107] a decision that was subsequently defended by Lloyd George in the House of Commons. Such a confrontational approach predictably failed to have any discernible effect on the paper's editorials. Nor did the Foreign Secretary make any sustained effort to pursue a more positive approach, for example by engaging in a campaign to cultivate newspaper editors and proprietors in an effort to win them over to his position. The Foreign Office News Department itself failed to develop an effective relationship with most of the British press, whilst it was in any case headed for much of this period by William Tyrrell, himself often a critic of Curzon. The Beaverbrook *Daily Express* was in general less critical of Curzon than *The Times*, even though its proprietor was subsequently responsible for an astonishingly bitter attack on the Foreign Secretary's reputation,[108] but it too periodically called for Curzon's resignation. Curzon's aloofness from the world of journalism, like his isolation within the Cabinet, had the effect of weakening his authority within government.[109]

Although newspapers represented one possible mechanism for mobilising public sentiment on international affairs, Parliament represented the correct constitutional forum for public scrutiny of foreign policy. Since Curzon was a member of the House of Lords, where the procedures and culture were very different from the House of Commons, he was seldom forced to confront shrill partisan questions of the kind routinely encountered by ministers in the lower house. Although the Upper House contained numerous members with extensive knowledge of international affairs, most peers instinctively sought to avoid sharp divisions over foreign policy. Curzon's speeches seldom went beyond broad questions of principle and general reviews of particular problems. The Foreign Secretary was also careful to mask his own private feelings. When Lord Sydenham expressed anxiety in November 1920 about the government's readiness to negotiate over trade with Moscow, Curzon largely concealed his doubts about the wisdom of Lloyd George's policy, noting firmly (and loyally) that foreign policy was never the work of 'an individual minister. The responsibility for that policy is that of the Government as a whole'.[110] The Foreign Secretary would have found such equivocations much harder to sustain in the more robust atmosphere of the House of Commons. Curzon was not able to ignore altogether the sentiments expressed by MPs, not least because his Cabinet colleagues who sat in the lower chamber had to worry far more than the Foreign Secretary about parliamentary opinion. Labour MPs in particular addressed numerous critical questions to ministers about such subjects as policy towards Soviet Russia, a topic that also aroused powerful if contrary emotions among diehard conservatives. MPs also adopted other strategies designed to influence the government's foreign policy. Letters to newspapers such as *The Times* were a popular (if rather futile) option.[111] Delegations from the House of Commons also visited the Foreign Office from time to time, whilst Curzon occasionally agreed to meet with individual MPs who had concerns about a particular issue. The Foreign Secretary was, however, instinctively impatient of attempts by parliamentarians to assert their influence. He was never even a popular figure with Conservative backbenchers. Although Curzon's absence from the Commons allowed him to ignore many of the opinions expressed there, it also tended to increase his political isolation and reduce his influence.

The years after the First World War witnessed the development of a whole constellation of organisations devoted to various aspects of foreign affairs, perhaps most notably the League of Nations Union (LNU), which was created in 1918 to mobilise public support for the principles of collective security.[112] However, the only minister who maintained close links with the LNU during the early 1920s was Robert Cecil. Curzon, like most senior Conservatives, paid lip-service to the League, but privately doubted whether it could ever transform traditional patterns of diplomacy between national governments, a view that was shared by many of his officials in the Foreign Office.[113] He therefore had very little to do with the LNU, an organisation widely regarded by Conservative ministers as the home of cranks and enthusiasts. The Foreign Secretary was much happier to associate himself with organisations such as the imperialist-minded Primrose League, addressing its members on such subjects as 'the evils of bolshevism'[114] (although the Primrose League too was never able to exert real influence on the deliberations of the Foreign Office or the Cabinet).[115] 'Outsider' groups devoted to such diffuse principles as the promotion of collective security or imperial welfare found it difficult to find effective ways of exerting influence on the foreign policy-making process. The same was even truer of the inchoate and transitory groups that sprung up from time to time to protest over such issues as the future of Constantinople and the Turkish Empire.[116]

British policy towards Soviet Russia probably attracted the most wide-spread public interest during Curzon's time as Foreign Secretary. Organisations such as the Association of British Creditors of Russia held numerous meetings with ministers and senior officials in the hope of forcing the government to put pressure on the Bolshevik regime to pay compensation for property nationalised following the October Revolution. Policy towards Russia also attracted strong interest within the British labour movement, leading to the establishment of the 'Hands off Russia' campaign in early 1919, which was designed to oppose British intervention in the country. Although few Labour leaders had much real sympathy for the Bolsheviks, the Russian Revolution continued to command a certain sentimental appeal amongst many on the left in the years following the collapse of the tsarist regime. Despite holding a series of public meetings, however, the leaders of the 'Hands off Russia' campaign found it very difficult to bring pressure to bear on the government, and the Cabinet's decision to scale back British involvement in Russia in the summer of 1919 owed little to its activities. Twelve months later, though, British policy was challenged by a more determined extra-parliamentary campaign, which began when a group of London dockers refused to load a ship with munitions destined for Polish forces involved in a war with Soviet troops. Their union agreed to support the action, triggering the start of a major conflict between the government and the labour movement, and by August 1920 a number of Labour MPs, including Stephen Walsh and George Lansbury, were launching scathing attacks on the 'war party in this country'.[117] Members of the Parliamentary Labour Party and the Parliamentary Committee of the TUC met regularly to discuss how to co-ordinate opposition to the government's policy towards Russia. In reality, of course, Lloyd George was desperate to continue negotiations with the Soviet government over a possible trade agreement, whilst even bitter ministerial critics of the bolsheviks such as Curzon had no desire for war, but it was impossible for the political establishment to ignore a movement that appeared to challenge the basic principles of parliamentary government. On 10 August Lloyd George made a speech warning the Labour Party against challenging 'the institutions upon which the liberties of Europe depend'.[118] *The Times* attacked the behaviour of the Council of Action as alien to the constitution.[119] The crisis eventually blew over when it became clear that Polish troops had succeeded in repelling an attack on Warsaw without direct assistance from the British. Radical extra-parliamentary agitation over foreign policy in any case proved to be the exception rather than the rule during the early 1920s. Curzon predictably showed contempt for those who sought to challenge the traditional character of the domestic foreign policy-making process. Although the Foreign Secretary was intelligent enough to realise that the architects of British foreign policy could not ignore public sentiment altogether, he found it hard to adapt to a world in which ministers had to take parliamentary and public opinion into account before making decisions.

Conclusion

A good deal of debate has taken place among historians in recent years about the extent of Curzon's success as Foreign Secretary. The problems he faced at the Foreign Office were immense. The First World War had destroyed established patterns of international order and created numerous problems and uncertainties, ranging from the economic collapse of Germany through to the future of the Middle East. Despite the comprehensive settlement reached at the Paris Peace Conference, the most intractable problems only became fully visible once efforts were made to put into effect the decisions that were taken there. British foreign policy from 1919 to 1924 certainly lacked an over-arching rationale, but Curzon himself was decidedly sceptical about the wisdom of grounding practical policy decisions in the abstract rhetoric of grand designs. Despite his much-vaunted imperialism and characteristic love of spectacle, the Foreign Secretary was perfectly capable of taking a pragmatic approach to policy-making. It is certainly possible to mount a convincing defence of British foreign policy during the years immediately following the Paris Peace Conference, on the grounds that Britain contributed to the maintenance of peace in Europe, whilst simultaneously managing to defend its imperial interests across the globe. Although there was almost constant disagreement with other governments over subjects ranging from reparations to rearmament, the tensions were never allowed to explode into war. Foreign policy in the Curzon era was, in short, pragmatic, reactive and cautious – three attributes that seldom win great plaudits. Nevertheless, at a time when financial resources were limited, and public opinion was loathe to endorse any action that might lead to conflict, a policy which successfully defended 'what we have obtained' whilst maintaining peace cannot be dismissed as an unmitigated failure.[120]

It is, however, harder to determine the extent to which Curzon really was the architect of British policy during this period – and therefore to decide whether he should receive the praise or blame for its successes and failures. His expectations of the influence he would be able to exercise on policy when he first became Foreign Secretary in 1919 were always profoundly unrealistic. Even such imposing nineteenth-century foreign secretaries as Palmerston and Salisbury were never able to dictate policy without taking into account the views and opinions of their ministerial colleagues. Curzon nonetheless believed that he was repeatedly thwarted in his attempts to set the course of Britain's relations with the rest of the world. There were certainly occasions when he was unable to pursue the policies that he believed were most appropriate for his country – perhaps most notably towards Russia in 1920–21, and then in the Near East during 1921–22 – but Curzon's almost mordant sensitivity led him to focus too much of his attention on those occasions when he was not able to get his own way. His 'sensitive and egocentric' temperament was not one that found it easy to accept the need for compromise.[121] Although he normally couched his frustrations in a quasi-constitutional language, his real anger was aroused by his pervasive sense that ministerial colleagues were failing to treat him with sufficient deference. Curzon's position as head of the Foreign Office meant that he could legitimately (if not wisely) take a hierarchical view of his department, treating all but his most senior staff as glorified clerks, who were not expected to offer much in the way of recommendations about policy. His ministerial colleagues, by contrast, were equals rather than subordinates, who were collectively responsible for all aspects of foreign policy. Ministers like Churchill and Montagu were seldom ready to give Curzon the deference he seemed to expect from them. Nor were they willing to accept uncritically his policy prescriptions. And, to make matters worse, a number of them could not resist the temptation to poke fun at the undoubted pomposity of the Very Superior Person. Lloyd George once frankly admitted that Curzon was the only member of his Cabinet whom he enjoyed bullying. It was quite impossible under these circumstances for the Foreign Secretary to acquire the level of prestige and influence that he believed were his due.

Curzon's frustrations were not, though, simply rooted in personal conflicts with other ministers. There was taking place beneath the sound of clashing egos a more fundamental shift in the bureaucratic and political framework in which decisions about foreign policy were made. The changes in the international and domestic environment, discussed in the previous chapter, made it increasingly difficult for the Foreign Office to assert itself as the only proper channel for relations with foreign governments in the years after 1918. The rise of economic and financial questions up the international agenda gave the Treasury and the Board of Trade an important international role of their own. Ministers and senior officials at departments such as the War Office and the Colonial Office were also in a position to assert their right to influence British foreign policy, whilst the growth in popularity of summit diplomacy broadened the range of actors involved in negotiations between governments. The same was true of the League of Nations. Some historians have found it hard to explain why Curzon was so poor at protecting his authority against incursions from other ministers, particularly Lloyd George, and have questioned why he never followed through on his periodic threats to resign. One of Curzon's early biographers suggested that the Foreign Secretary was always haunted by the memory of 1905, when his resignation as Viceroy led to a prolonged period in the political wilderness,[122] but the real situation was more complex. Curzon was perfectly willing to fight to establish himself as the principal architect of British foreign policy. He simply did not know how to fight effectively in the changing political landscape in which he had to operate. The Foreign Secretary lacked the charisma to establish a strong Cabinet following. Nor did he have the skills required to engage in the kind of informal coalition building that might have helped him to win support from other ministers. The Viceroy in Curzon was never willing to adapt fully to the demands of the modern world, whilst the modern world was certainly never going to adapt to the demands of the Viceroy.

The question still remains as to why Curzon was able to remain for so long as a central fixture in the British political landscape, given his repeated failure to attract the loyalty or sympathy of those with whom he worked. The answer can probably be found at least in part in his sheer energy and 'presence'. Curzon's belief that his talents and aptitudes made him a natural *habitué* of the political world seems to have communicated itself to all those around him throughout his long career. Nor was this self-belief based on purely imaginary foundations. Curzon had real talents. He was intelligent and hard-working. He had wide experience of the world. He was a competent if high-handed administrator. And he could also be a shrewd and effective negotiator. His ministerial colleagues may have found their colleague infuriating and autocratic when he served as Foreign Secretary, but most of them also instinctively recognised that he was one of their 'great contemporaries', whose departure would weaken rather than strengthen the quality of the government. Curzon doubtless expected too much from his time at the Foreign Office, failing to understand that the conventions and practices of Cabinet government would inevitably stymie his independence, but the fact that he found his sojourn as Foreign Secretary profoundly frustrating does not mean that he was a 'failure' at the job. He played an important part in the thankless task of reorienting British foreign policy in a world that had been transformed by war and revolution.

3 Ramsay MacDonald at the Foreign Office (1924)

Introduction

The prospect of a minority Labour Government created a great deal of anxiety in the pages of newspapers and the periodical press during the first few weeks of 1924. The *English Review* warned its readers that 'For the first time in history the party of revolution approach their hands to the helm of the state ... with the design of destroying the very bases of civilised life'.[1] A letter writer to *The Times* solemnly informed readers that the Labour Party 'was supported in Parliament by the votes of Communists, the wild men, the illiterate, and the thousand and one of the submerged or semi-submerged, who, for one cause or another, are thoroughly disgruntled, and who are prepared to denounce every Government in turn which neglects, regardless of merit and cost, to supply homes, food and pensions in abundance for all'.[2] Philip Snowden, who served as Chancellor of the Exchequer in the 1924 government, later recalled that he was asked in all seriousness whether 'it was true that the first thing the Labour Party would do would be to cut the throats of every aristocrat and steal all their property'.[3] There was doubtless something artificial about the hysteria whipped up by sections of the press over the prospect of a Labour Government. The phlegmatic reaction of King George V, who noted ruefully that he had to 'march with the times',[4] was echoed by many denizens of the political establishment who hoped that experience of government might encourage the Labour leadership to abandon altogether its residual commitment to radical socialism. The appointment of the first Labour Government nevertheless had the potential to serve as a significant watershed in the development of British political life.

Most of those who wrote so apprehensively about the prospect of a Labour Government were concerned above all with domestic policy, but the appointment of a Labour administration also held out the intriguing prospect of important changes in the way that British foreign policy was formulated and implemented. Ramsay MacDonald, who served as both Foreign Secretary and Prime Minister in the 1924 Government, had during his earlier career been heavily involved in the activities of the Second International that sought among other things to mobilize the international labour movement against a future war. He subsequently became one of the leading critics of Britain's involvement in the First World War, co-founding the Union of Democratic Control, and contributing countless articles to radical publications such as *The Nation* and *Labour Leader*. His war-time writings were bitterly critical of the methods and practices associated with the old diplomacy,[5] condemning the conflict as 'a diplomatists' war, made by 'about half-a-dozen men'.[6] Whilst his language became more restrained in the post-war years, he was still convinced that diplomacy 'as we have known it has been out of touch with modern political ways', and remained 'a bar to the co-operation of democracies for peaceful and human ends'.[7] These sentiments were firmly endorsed by Arthur Ponsonby, who served as Under-Secretary of State at the Foreign Office in the 1924 Labour Government.[8] Ponsonby had become one of the most strident critics of the old diplomacy after leaving the Diplomatic Service and becoming a Liberal MP, in 1908, and he was the most radical member of the 1914 Royal Commission set up to recommend changes to the pattern of Britain's overseas representation.[9] He was a prolific author of UDC pamphlets during the First World War, making repeated attacks on a diplomatic system that allowed 'a small number of men in each country' to determine whether a country should go to war or remain at peace.[10] Whilst some of the reforms proposed by the Royal Commission were introduced in 1919,[11] Ponsonby made no secret that he believed more radical changes were still required, including the creation of a special Parliamentary Foreign Affairs Committee designed to ensure effective scrutiny of the Foreign Office. He was not alone in hoping that the new Labour Government would continue the process of reform.

The criticisms made by MacDonald and Ponsonby of traditional diplomacy were widely shared across the Labour party, which was in 1924 still the 'residuary legatee of the dissenting tradition in foreign policy which went back to Gladstone, and before that to Cobden and Charles James Fox'.[12] Whilst many of its leading figures such as Arthur Henderson and J.H. Thomas had played an important role in rallying organised labour behind the Government during the war years, they were sharply critical of the direction taken by British foreign policy in the period since 1918, vigorously condemning the Versailles Treaty for its failure to lay the foundations of a lasting peace. The leading figures in the Labour movement were not, though, agreed on how to tackle the formidable range of problems facing Europe in the years after the Peace Conference. There were, for example, substantial differences over the value of the League of Nations, viewed by some as the main hope for establishing international politics on a new foundation, but by others as the unforgiving policeman of a harsh and unsustainable peace settlement. MacDonald's 1923 pamphlet on *The Foreign Policy of the Labour Party* committed a future Labour Government to the rapid *de jure* recognition of the Soviet Government,[13] but his other pronouncements were usually more striking for their rhetoric than their substance. MacDonald himself was determined that a Labour Government should use its influence to transform the texture of European politics by challenging traditional notions of security based upon crude calculations of military force, but at the time he came to office neither the Labour leader nor his colleagues had developed a coherent strategy to advance such a vision. They were still imbued with an oppositional mentality that was too inclined to focus on abstract principles rather than the complex practicalities of day-to-day diplomacy.

The following pages examine the extent to which MacDonald and other Labour ministers in the 1924 Government sought to promote the shibboleths of the new diplomacy during their months in office, focusing in particular on the way in which decisions about foreign policy were made and executed. MacDonald told Parliament in February 1924 that he had decided to become the first British Prime Minister since Salisbury to serve simultaneously as Foreign Secretary, in order to use the 'weight of office' to resolve the country's 'unsatisfactory' relationships with other European governments.[14] In reality, the Prime Minister was generally 'appalled' at the quality of the possible candidates for ministerial office,[15] whilst several obvious contenders for the Foreign Secretaryship, such as J.H. Thomas and Arthur Henderson, were effectively ruled out either by opposition from other Labour leaders or because they could not work harmoniously with MacDonald himself.[16] MacDonald's decision to hold two major posts at the same time inevitably had a profound influence on the pattern of political and administrative relationships within the core executive, which in turn had significant ramifications for the way in which British foreign policy was made under the first Labour Government.

MacDonald, the Cabinet and the control of foreign policy

It was seen in the last chapter that there was almost constant disagreement within Cabinet about the allocation of responsibility for directing Britain's international relations during Curzon's time at the Foreign Office. It was also noted that whilst the tensions were in part due to the personalities involved, they were also a consequence of changes that had taken place during the previous few years, which together served to constrain the Foreign Office's role in the policy-making process. The Labour Cabinet of 1924 was not of course immune to the kind of personal tensions and divisions that had characterised its immediate predecessors. It included individuals such as Arthur Henderson and J.R. Clynes, whose roots were firmly in the trade union movement, as well as erudite Fabians like Sydney Webb, whose writings had played a major role in forging the intellectual consciousness of the Labour movement since the start of the century. Other ministers, including MacDonald himself, were from an Independent Labour Party background. The tensions that were always latent in this ideological and organisational mosaic were given added spice by the kind of personal animosities that invariably play a part in shaping the fortunes of governments. The relationship between Henderson and MacDonald had been a difficult one for many years, reflecting both real political differences and imagined personal slights, and the 'elements of jealousy' between the two men coloured the way in which they dealt with one another.[17] At the same time, the almost legendary acerbity of Philip Snowden won the new Chancellor few personal friends among his ministerial colleagues, and certainly did nothing to smooth his relations with a Prime Minister whose 'brooding Celtic emotions' could on occasion make him over-sensitive to criticism.[18] Even MacDonald's critics such as Fenner Brockway and Emanuel Shinwell acknowledged the Prime Minister to be a 'commanding personality', who was blessed with a great personal 'magnetism' and 'oratorical power', but his undoubted charisma did not always translate into the kind of personal qualities that were required to win support from his colleagues. Clement Attlee subsequently recalled that MacDonald seldom bothered to conceal his low opinion of many other leading figures in the Labour movement, which did little to improve the smooth working of the 1924 government, not least because it aroused suspicion among some ministers that their contributions to debates about policy were unwelcome. The complex political differences and personal animosities that characterised the first Labour Government undoubtedly shaped the way in which Ramsay MacDonald dealt with foreign affairs during his nine months in charge of the Foreign Office. The following pages suggest that he proved adept at using his political authority to carve out a degree of autonomy in setting the broad contours of foreign policy, but that personal conflicts and disagreements meant that MacDonald was never able to ride rough-shod over the opinions of his colleagues.

When Arthur Ponsonby was first appointed Under-Secretary at the Foreign Office, he entertained high hopes that the new administration would be 'in control of foreign policy', noting optimistically that its members might be able 'to carry out some of the things we have been urging and preaching for years'.[19] MacDonald, though, always took a cautious view of what his Government could achieve across the whole range of public policy. In a speech that he made in the House of Commons just a few weeks after becoming Prime Minister, he acknowledged that his Government could not stay in power for long, given its minority status, adding modestly that his main ambition was to carry out 'good work' that could be built on by future governments. The same attitude informed his views about international politics. MacDonald declared that his main ambition on taking office was to promote a 'healthier atmosphere' in Europe,[20] in order to make it easier for governments to reach agreement over the complex problems that continued to plague the continent, most obviously the crisis that had erupted the previous year following the Franco-Belgian occupation of the Ruhr. He did not, however, have very firm views on how this might be achieved. Although MacDonald did not share the francophobia that characterised many of his colleagues in the Labour Party, he was quite unwilling to extend the kind of guarantees to France that would alone have persuaded Paris to be more amenable over security questions. Nor was he by instinct a strong supporter of the League of Nations as an institution, although he was strongly committed to the shibboleth of collective security, even if he had few clear ideas about how such a fine principle could be enshrined in concrete reality. Whilst the Prime Minister was resolutely opposed to any attempt to achieve greater security for Britain through such conventional methods as the establishment of military alliances to maintain the balance of power, he was always less convincing when trying to spell out exactly what it was that he wanted to achieve when dealing with Britain's relations with the wider world.

MacDonald certainly placed emphasis on diluting the 'stiff correctness' and formality that he had long believed were the hallmarks of professional diplomacy.[21] Shortly after coming to office, he drafted a note to the Soviet Commissar for Foreign Affairs, Georgi Chicherin, observing that he had chosen to write a personal letter since 'official communications are apt to appear cold and lifeless'.[22] A few days earlier, he had written a personal letter to the French President, Raymond Poincaré, expressing in an unusually frank manner his hope that 'the strenuous action of goodwill' would make it possible to overcome the suspicion between France and Britain.[23] Such an approach generally met with approval in foreign capitals. Poincaré responded warmly to the tone of MacDonald's initial overtures, whilst the German Foreign Minister, Gustav Stresemann, subsequently noted that the Prime Minister's striking 'absence of formality' during the London Conference on reparations that took place in August was a key factor in smoothing tensions between the various delegations.[24] Lord Parmoor, who dealt with League of Nations affairs in the 1924 Labour Government, agreed that the Prime Minister 'had a genius for creating a sympathetic atmosphere' which was of crucial importance when 'initiating a new international policy'.[25] MacDonald was adept at keeping the more acerbic and dismissive part of his personality at bay when dealing with foreign negotiations (far more so, in fact, than when dealing with his own Cabinet colleagues). His emphasis on establishing close face-to-face relations with foreign leaders did not, though, represent a real shift in diplomatic practice. The advocates of traditional diplomacy had long since maintained that informal receptions and private dinners provided a critical arena when seeking to come to terms with the representatives of other countries.[26] The rise of summit diplomacy in the final years of the war had in any case established the principle that political leaders rather than diplomatic representatives should handle major international negotiations whenever possible. MacDonald ironically possessed in abundance many of the 'soft' diplomatic skills that were frequently viewed with scepticism by critics of traditional diplomacy, who feared they were expressions of a system of class privilege that fostered a diplomatic dialogue impervious to outside scrutiny and review.

MacDonald's decision to hold the two posts of Prime Minister and

Foreign Secretary was a controversial one for many Whitehall insiders. The Cabinet Secretary Maurice Hankey, who established a close working relationship with the Prime Minister, doubted whether any 'man or super-man' could perform the duties associated with the two offices.[27] Most other informed commentators agreed that the vast increase in government business since the age of Salisbury meant that a Foreign Secretary could not work effectively if he had other major calls on his time (although Hankey's deputy, Thomas Jones, believed that such a view was 'twaddle').[28] MacDonald's unusual position did mean, though, that he was spared some of the problems that plagued his predecessor at the Foreign Office. Curzon had been forced to engage in an endless series of pitched battles with other ministers in order to determine the exact scope of his authority. MacDonald's position as Prime Minister, by contrast, meant that he enjoyed much greater latitude when directing British foreign policy.

One of the main criticisms traditionally directed against the old diplomacy by its critics was of course that decisions were not subject to effective scrutiny and control. Even ministers in Asquith's pre-war Cabinet bitterly complained that Sir Edward Grey seldom kept them informed about his activities.[29] Although many on the left insisted that Parliament should be given a greater say in foreign policy, the convention of collective responsibility meant that the Cabinet was bound to remain the most important constitutional setting for authoritative decisions on the subject. MacDonald was not, though, particularly scrupulous at keeping ministers informed about foreign affairs, a trait that doubtless reflected his (decidedly arrogant) conviction that he alone possessed the talents required to master such a complex subject. Beatrice Webb noted in her diary just a few weeks after he took office that 'So far as I can gather from Sidney and other members of the Cabinet, they are not consulted about what the attitude shall be towards France: certainly no documents are circulated prior to dispatch. So far as Henderson, Clynes and Sidney are concerned, the P.M. alone determines what line he takes towards other countries'.[30] She went on to suggest that MacDonald's style became even more autocratic in the weeks following his success at the London Conference on reparations that took place in the summer. Whilst such anecdotal reports of developments in Cabinet are not always reliable, the relevant documents do seem to bear out Beatrice Webb's impressions.

The Cabinet papers for 1924 suggest that the Cabinet was consulted in an inconsistent manner about foreign affairs.[31] MacDonald sought his colleagues' approval before taking action on such questions as the British Government's response to the report of the Dawes Committee, that was established shortly before the Labour Government came to power in order to make recommendations on the best way of responding to the crisis surrounding German reparation payments.[32] The Prime Minister also consulted his Cabinet colleagues before writing to Geneva to confirm that his Government was definitely opposed to the Draft Treaty of Mutual

Assistance, first put forward by Robert Cecil the previous year, in an effort to increase the League's effectiveness by providing its Council with greater powers to respond quickly in case of international aggression.[33] On other occasions, though, he took action on important questions of policy without clearing it in advance with the Cabinet. MacDonald frequently confined himself in Cabinet to making a general statement 'on various questions of foreign policy', an approach that did not give his ministerial colleagues much opportunity to engage in collective debate on detailed points of substance.[34] During the London Conference on reparations, ministers were persuaded to allow 'the Prime Minister to make the best arrangements he thought possible without further reference to Cabinet',[35] with the result that at least some of them had to rely on the press to keep abreast of developments.[36] Most of the Cabinet was also kept in the dark about the detailed progress of the Anglo-Soviet negotiations that took place during the spring and summer of 1924, at least until the middle of July, when it seemed as though an agreement was imminent. Nor did the Committee of Imperial Defence (CID) serve as a particularly important institutional focus for discussion about questions of foreign policy. MacDonald himself did not always attend full meetings of the CID, a practice that caused some tension with Hankey, who was as determined as ever to defend the bureaucratic machinery that he had spent so long developing.[37] The relationship between the Prime Minister and the Cabinet Secretary was nevertheless generally harmonious.[38] Hankey noted in his diary in October 1924 that he had become the Prime Minister's 'principal adviser and counsellor' during the London Conference on reparations, with the result that the 'more delicate diplomatic negotiations on points of high policy ... passed more and more into my hands'.[39] He also maintained, not entirely correctly, that senior Foreign Office officials had no fears that he might be usurping their position.

Although MacDonald enjoyed considerable autonomy when dealing with foreign affairs, his freedom was nevertheless still constrained both by the need to take into account the views of his Cabinet colleagues, and by the intricacies of the inter-departmental policy-making process. The Prime Minister's cautiously sympathetic approach towards the French government aroused strong resentment amongst some other figures in the Labour leadership, a number of whom were convinced that the determination of Paris to maintain a harsh policy towards Germany posed the main threat to European security.[40] Arthur Henderson told an audience at a by-election rally in Burnley at the end of February that revision of the Versailles Treaty 'was very much overdue', even though he knew that such a statement would cause considerable diplomatic embarrassment to the Prime Minister, who was working hard at the time to improve relations with the French government.[41] MacDonald was subsequently forced to make a stumbling defence in Parliament, arguing unconvincingly that the Home Secretary was talking as a private person and that there was 'no change to published policy'.[42] There were also sharp differences between the two men over the Geneva Protocol.[43]

MacDonald was himself the unwitting initiator of the process that led up to the drafting of the Protocol, a document he subsequently came to look upon with considerable concern. When the Prime Minister addressed the League Assembly in early September he suggested, apparently without much fore-thought, the establishment of a new system of international arbitration designed to make a resort to force less likely at times of tension. MacDonald told his audience that the British government placed little store on conventional military alliances, since they often led to mutual suspicion and tension, but wanted instead to see the creation of new machinery that would resolve disputes before they led to war. The Prime Minister's speech was in fact spectacularly short on specifics and made few real suggestions about how to turn somewhat pious platitudes into practical policy. MacDonald himself returned to London shortly after his oratorical triumph, leaving Henderson and Parmoor to carry out the detailed negotiations to set up a system of international arbitration that would be detailed enough to ease the French government's perennial security fears over Germany, whilst remaining vague enough to be acceptable in London. Henderson and Parmoor were, however, far more inclined than most of their Cabinet colleagues to argue that the League of Nations should be at the heart of British foreign policy. Both men believed that the constraints on Britain's freedom of manoeuvre implied by an effective collective security system would be out-weighed by the benefits of greater international stability. Such enthusiasm was looked at askance back in London, where many ministers remained suspicious that the League might become a mechanism by which the French would be able to entangle Britain once again in the problems of the conti-nent. Following discussion at a Cabinet meeting in late September, minis-ters agreed to send an urgent instruction to Parmoor in Geneva, noting that he should make it clear that any agreement he signed was subject to definite approval from ministers in London.[44] Henderson nevertheless persisted in speaking warmly in favour of the Protocol on his return to Britain,[45] raising the prospect of a serious division within the Cabinet, although in the event the collapse of the MacDonald Government took place before the issue became critical and exposed divisions within the Labour movement over the whole vexed question of collective security and the League.

MacDonald came into even sharper conflict over foreign affairs with Philip Snowden, his acerbic Chancellor of the Exchequer, who persistently pushed the Prime Minister to take a tough line with the French government during the London Conference on reparations that took place in July and August. The Chancellor was convinced that the Treasury should play a central role in determining British policy on the whole issue of reparations, which had dominated the European agenda since the Ruhr crisis the previ-ous year, a position in which he was generally backed by his Permanent Secretary Sir Warren Fisher. Snowden favoured a rapid withdrawal of French forces from the Ruhr, on the grounds that international bankers would not advance a loan to Germany until there was greater international political stability, which the Chancellor believed was a prerequisite for German economic recovery. MacDonald was by contrast more willing to accept a slower retreat as the price of securing French agreement.[46] The Chancellor subsequently condemned the Prime Minister's soft line towards the Paris Government as 'contrary to everything we as a Party and Government have professed',[47] whilst MacDonald for his part observed that Snowden's activities at the Conference gave him 'a great problem in diplomatic handling'.[48] The conflict between the two men was no secret to foreign representatives at the London Conference, complicating an already difficult situation, particularly since the French delegation was profoundly suspicious of Snowden. The Chancellor and MacDonald also clashed sharply over the negotiations with the USSR during the summer of 1924. Snowden did not share the hope of many senior figures in the Labour Party (including MacDonald) that an agreement with Russia would increase trade and reduce unemployment, and his natural prudence made him sceptical about the wisdom of issuing an official guarantee for a loan that the Soviet Government hoped to raise in the City. He was particularly critical of the vague phraseology of the draft treaty negotiated by Arthur Ponsonby, who dealt with the day-to-day negotiations, brusquely observing to the head of the Soviet delegation that 'no Government could take the responsibility of presenting to Parliament such a document'.[49] However, whilst the Chancellor had the support of a number of other ministers, including J.H. Thomas, MacDonald eventually put his weight behind the agreement and insisted that the loan guarantee should go ahead.[50] Snowden, like Henderson, ultimately found it difficult to identify an effective strategy to advance his own views on foreign policy when they came into direct conflict with those of a Prime Minister who was determined to assert himself. The same was true of many other ministers. Even the Service ministers were forced to accept such controversial decisions as the scaling back of development at the Singapore Naval Base, despite claims from some of their departmental advisers that it might be seen as proof that Britain lacked the will to defend its imperial position in the Far East. MacDonald's position as Prime Minister gave him a degree of authority and power that he would not have possessed had he held the post of Foreign Secretary alone.

The Foreign Office and the 1924 Labour Government

When the Labour Government took office in 1924, many on the left of the political spectrum were convinced that the British diplomatic establishment was drawn from a narrow social elite determined to frustrate popular demands for a more open style of government. The Foreign Office inherited by MacDonald was certainly staffed almost entirely by men who had enjoyed the kind of 'exclusive upbringing' and 'still more exclusive training' against which the Prime Minister had once railed so passionately in his pamphlets and articles.[51] Of the seven career diplomats who served as ambassador in

1924, three were educated at Eton and a fourth at Harrow; the others had attended more modern foundations such as Cheltenham. Of the seven men listed with the rank of Counsellor in the 1924 *Foreign Office List*, four had been educated at Eton whilst another went to Harrow.[52] The situation was not markedly different among junior officials. Although the precise relationship between education and privilege was a complex one, even such rudimentary evidence shows clearly that the Foreign Office remained a defining institution of the British Establishment during the 1920s, with the result that a career there continued to command greater social *cachet* than a post in one of the Home departments. Nevertheless, although the Foreign Office was still a bastion of social exclusiveness in 1924, the previous chapters have shown that its members had for some years found it difficult to translate their status into more direct influence on the foreign policy-making process. The relationship between social privilege and power was more complex and dynamic than realised by at least some critics of traditional diplomacy.

MacDonald had no experience of running a department of his own at the time he decided to combine the posts of Prime Minister and Foreign Secretary. Viscount Haldane and Henderson were the only members of the first Labour Cabinet who had experience of high office before 1924. The Prime Minister's private diary shows that he spent a good deal of time carrying out the routine duties that every Foreign Secretary was expected to perform. On one day alone in September 1924, for example, he received the US ambassador and the Turkish minister, as well as discussing a loan for Germany with the Governor of the Bank of England. He was then forced to wade through several boxes of dispatches, noting sadly in his diary that 'the long day's concerns epitomise what distresses British ministers have to bear'.[53] MacDonald travelled abroad on a number of occasions, visiting Paris to take part in discussions with French ministers on a range of issues, as well as becoming the first British premier to address the League Assembly in Geneva. He also devoted a good deal of time and energy to receiving foreign visitors, often at Chequers, where he believed that the informal atmosphere was more conducive to successful negotiations. MacDonald undoubtedly struggled to master the endless flow of material that came daily into the Foreign Office. Lord Curzon had found the scale of his duties as Foreign Secretary almost intolerable. His successor had to carry them out while simultaneously dealing with the myriad complex issues that he was required to address in his capacity as Prime Minister.

It has been suggested that MacDonald responded to the problem of his high workload by following a carefully crafted strategy predicated on developing an effective 'partnership' with his Foreign Office officials, in which the Prime Minister sought to promote a coherent process of long-term policy planning, whilst avoiding the trap of becoming submerged in 'overwhelming' detail.[54] It is in fact hard to find compelling evidence that MacDonald really made a coherent effort to establish a new policy-making regime during his nine months in charge at the Foreign Office. The documentary evidence suggests that he was less diligent at reading dispatches and departmental memoranda than his predecessor. He certainly minuted official papers far less assiduously than Curzon. The Prime Minister was in reality forced to focus his energies on broad issues of foreign policy for the simple reason that he lacked the time to pay attention to questions of detail. He was as a result unable to exercise the same level of control over the Foreign Office as Curzon, whose penchant for ferreting out the minor lapses of officials during his time as Foreign Secretary had played a significant part in fuelling their distaste for the 'Very Superior Person'.

MacDonald treated his staff with much greater consideration than his predecessor, prompting one of them to observe ruefully that 'It is odd we should have had to wait for the Labour Party to give us a gentleman'.[55] The mutual respect was doubtless strengthened by the fact that there was a fair degree of agreement over important questions of policy. MacDonald's willingness to take a reasonably positive line towards the French accorded with the instincts of most senior officials. Although his critical rhetoric on such questions as alliances and the balance of power sat uncomfortably with the 'official mind' of the Foreign Office, most senior staff were shrewd enough to realize that MacDonald tended in practice to take a sober view of questions relating to European security, instinctively supporting a policy based on a judicious mixture of isolation and involvement. The Prime Minister came to office convinced that his Party could achieve its fundamental objectives by working through the established institutions of government, and that in doing so it would gain public trust and secure its position as the natural successor of the Liberal Party. Although MacDonald did consider establishing a new diplomatic 'Sandhurst' to train future generations of Foreign Office clerks and diplomats, there is little evidence that he had many doubts about the quality of the advice offered to him by officials.[56] He developed a high opinion of Eyre Crowe, the indefatigable Permanent Secretary at the Foreign Office, and encouraged him to take a full part in international negotiations and conferences.[57] Crowe for his part frequently made recommendations about policy to the Prime Minister. MacDonald also established good relations with other senior officials, including William Tyrrell and J.D. Gregory, even though both men were deeply suspicious of the political values espoused by the new Labour Government. MacDonald kept up an extensive personal correspondence with many ambassadors in post abroad. Lord D'Abernon in Berlin regularly sent the Prime Minister extracts from his diary dealing with important political developments, whilst Lord Crewe in Paris wrote frequently on subjects ranging from French attitudes towards Germany through to his own health.[58] Other ambassadors such as Ronald Graham in Rome and Charles Eliot in Tokyo also sent private letters to Number 10, offering the kind of sensitive observations and comments that they would not necessarily have wanted to include in an official dispatch. Critics of MacDonald have often claimed that he became too immersed in the values and culture of the British establishment in the years following his rise to power, showing a degree of deference to individuals and institutions that was quite at odds with the radical socialism of his earlier years. The Prime Minister certainly showed no great desire to marginalise the diplomatic establishment in 1924, despite its traditional *bête noir* status for many on the left of British politics, but his desire to work within existing institutions and procedures was above all a reflection of his confidence that he could do so without losing sight of his fundamental objectives. It was characteristic of MacDonald's whole approach to government in 1924.

Whilst MacDonald succeeded in establishing a good working relationship with his officials, the same was not true of the two other ministers most closely associated with the Foreign Office in the 1924 Labour Government. Lord Parmoor (Lord President of the Council with particular responsibility for League affairs) was an erstwhile Conservative whose views on foreign policy were conditioned by his deep Christian commitment to an internationalism that found little echo among senior Foreign Office staff. He noted in his memoirs that senior officials there were 'not cordial' towards him, something which he ascribed to the 'antagonism between the supremacy of the Foreign Office and the rising spirit of the new international movement in Geneva'.[59] His private comments were still sharper, and by August 1924 he was complaining to MacDonald that senior Foreign Office staff had 'steadily opposed me' and 'made my position a very difficult one'.[60] Arthur Ponsonby's experiences were equally bleak, despite his initial hopes that he might have a 'real say' in policy.[61] Many senior officials made no secret of their distaste for an erstwhile diplomat who had made his public reputation through repeated attacks on the British diplomatic establishment.[62] Ponsonby in any case always found it difficult to carve out a precise role for himself, since MacDonald was not consistent in the way he delegated business to his Under-Secretary, something that became particularly apparent during the course of the Anglo-Soviet negotiations that took place in the summer of 1924. Ponsonby was at first far more optimistic than MacDonald about the prospect of making fundamental changes to the way in which the new Government dealt with foreign affairs, lobbying hard to introduce procedural changes that were designed to promote greater outside scrutiny of Foreign Office business. In April 1924 he proudly told the House of Commons that the Government would in future lay all treaties and agreements before Parliament for twenty-one days in order to provide an opportunity for 'examination, consideration and if need be discussion'.[63] There was, though, no systematic attempt by ministers to overhaul the diplomatic machine itself. Many Labour ministers were surprised on taking office to find that their officials were like 'polished instruments, waiting on [them] hand and foot, seemingly acquiescent in any policy'. [64] Their brief experience of government served to confirm in the minds of many of them that a Labour Government could operate through the established bureaucracy.

The greatest tension between members of the Foreign Office and their

political masters came to the fore when policy towards Soviet Russia was
under review, since it was the one area on which senior officials strongly disagreed with the Prime Minister himself. Eyre Crowe refused to take part in
the negotiations that took place with the delegation that arrived in London
to discuss a possible treaty, and later boasted that 'the Foreign Office as a
department was free from all responsibility for the treaty which rested
entirely with Ponsonby'.[65] In reality, though, Foreign Office officials *were*
closely involved in the complex preparations for the Anglo-Soviet Conference, although the Board of Trade and the Treasury also played a major part
given that the talks revolved heavily around detailed financial questions.[66]
J.D. Gregory of the Northern Department argued in March that, since the
Foreign Office had the greatest responsibility 'for the defence of British
interests abroad', it should take the lead in co-ordinating the activities of the
various government departments involved in the talks.[67] Both Gregory and
Owen O'Malley, another Foreign Office official, were appointed members of
the main British delegation. Ponsonby certainly organised the talks in a way
that sometimes ran counter to normal diplomatic protocol, most notably
when he arranged a series of face-to-face meetings between members of the
Soviet delegation and representatives from the Association of British Creditors of Russia. He did not, though, systematically ignore the views of the
Foreign Office in the way that Gregory subsequently implied in his
memoirs. Nor is there much substance to the claim that a group of left-wing
MPs outside the formal British delegation 'exercised a powerful influence
throughout the negotiations'.[68] Indeed, as the talks slowly ground to a halt
during the summer, there were many voices in the Labour movement who
considered that Foreign Office officials were actually taking advantage of
their privileged position in order to sabotage negotiations.[69] It was in reality
the sheer complexity of the issues under discussion, along with the scale
of the differences between the two sides, which led to the lack of progress in
the talks. It was only when negotiations appeared to be on the point of
breaking down, in early August, that a group of Labour backbenchers took a
controversial initiative that seems to have played a part in saving the talks
from collapse.

MacDonald, the left and foreign policy

There is still some uncertainty about the exact sequence of events that took
place following the threatened breakdown at the Anglo-Soviet Conference in
early August, over the issue of compensation for owners of property nationalised by the Bolsheviks. A number of left-wing backbenchers, including
E.D. Morel and A.A. Purcell, certainly offered Ponsonby their services as
intermediaries with members of the Soviet delegation. On the day following
the announcement that the negotiations faced stalemate, Ponsonby was then
able to inform the House of Commons that an agreement had now been
reached with the Soviet delegation. Purcell and Morel both unashamedly

viewed the Anglo-Soviet talks through the prism of radical socialism, subsequently arguing that 'The foes of the Anglo-Russian Treaty are to be found among those who are the bitterest opponents of the rights ... and of the aspirations of the British working class'.[70] Whilst ministers were anxious to avoid this kind of language, preferring to emphasise the sober economic benefits of an agreement, the obscure circumstances surrounding the *volte-face* helped to promote the idea that the Labour Government was in thrall to its left-wing backbenchers. This impression received added credence when it became clear that the treaty agreed with the Soviet delegation included a loan guarantee that MacDonald had previously said would not be offered (and which Snowden bitterly opposed primarily on the grounds of financial rectitude). Conservative spokesmen complained that – in an ironic echo of the Labour Party's traditional commitment to open diplomacy – the Government had failed to keep Parliament properly informed of developments in the Soviet talks.[71] The air was heavy with innuendo in a Commons adjournment debate on 7 August, helping to pave the way for the famous series of 'red scares' that destabilised the Government throughout its final weeks, culminating in the celebrated affair of the Zinov'ev Letter widely blamed in the Labour movement for the scale of the election defeat in October.

It is true that MacDonald and Ponsonby were both reluctant to speak much in public about the Anglo-Soviet talks that took place in London during the spring and summer of 1924, although it could be argued that advocates of open diplomacy had always been primarily concerned with the *outcome* rather than the *process* of negotiations. Once he came to office, MacDonald certainly came to recognise the value of a 'relative freedom of action in foreign affairs', which meant that he did not have to seek approval for 'every move' either from his fellow ministers or from a wider public.[72] The Government's commitment to table all international agreements in Parliament for twenty-one days ruled out the kind of secret treaties that had been commonplace before 1914, but it did not require ministers to provide detailed accounts of negotiations that were actually underway. Nor was MacDonald particularly forthcoming when addressing the House of Commons about foreign affairs, and the tone of his speeches was on the whole less frank than the one subsequently adopted by Sir Austen Chamberlain, when he sought to carry the House of Commons with him during the protracted talks that led to the Locarno agreements of 1925. MacDonald had in his earlier days campaigned vigorously for reforms designed to allow Parliament to exercise closer control over foreign affairs, but once in office he increasingly believed that detailed oversight by the Legislature was incompatible with effective diplomacy.

The cautious tone that characterised MacDonald's remarks about foreign affairs in Parliament was in part inspired by the difficult political situation facing his government. The Conservative Party was by some distance the largest party in the House of Commons, and its spokesmen were only too eager to take advantage of any issue that might undermine the Government. The Labour Party itself contained a number of left-wing MPs who were reluctant to offer unconditional support to a Government they feared was losing touch with its grassroots. MPs drawn from the Independent Labour Party, who included many with a particular interest in foreign affairs such as Noel Buxton, displayed a particularly striking degree of independence. Many activists in the Labour movement still doubted whether the assorted constitutional doctrines concerning ministerial responsibility were sufficient to ensure effective public accountability. Whilst the Party had already established its credentials as a moderate socialist party committed to promoting change within the parliamentary system, its extra-parliamentary origins in the trade union movement still indelibly informed its culture and mode of operation. The structure of the Party Conference, along with the close links between individual MPs and particular unions, bound the Government to the wider movement in a way that had no parallel in the other two main parties. The Party leadership itself had shown as recently as 1920 that it was ready on occasion to endorse extra-parliamentary action to influence policy, when it supported moves by the dockers to prevent the shipment of munitions to Polish forces involved in a war with Bolshevik Russia.[73] By contrast, rank and file Labour MPs had few real opportunities to influence the foreign policy of the 1924 Labour Government. The Prime Minister certainly paid lip-service to the importance of listening to the opinion of his backbenchers, but as Fenner Brockway subsequently noted, he made little real effort to engage with the various deputations that called on him from time to time to discuss the issue.[74] Nor did he pay much attention to the various party committees that discussed international questions. The role played by backbenchers such as Morel and Purcell during the final hours of the Anglo-Soviet negotiations was the exception rather than the rule in the formulation of foreign policy in MacDonald's first government.

There were in fact tensions between the Labour Government and other sections of the Labour movement on a whole range of international issues throughout 1924. The Government's refusal to make big cuts in defence expenditure won it plaudits from *The Times*, but cost it the support of many of its back-bench MPs, who wanted a moral gesture to kick-start arms reductions across Europe. The cautious record of the MacDonald Government on colonial questions led to claims in journals such as the *Socialist Review* and the *New Leader* that ministers were abandoning the principles that they had once espoused. The same pattern was visible in many of the most contentious areas of foreign policy proper. The Geneva Protocol caused divisions at all levels of the Party, which was hardly surprising given the contrasting views about the value of the League, whilst the slow pace of the Russian negotiations in the spring and summer of 1924 created considerable tension between left and right. The Miners Conference that met in August 1924 demanded an end to all reparations and war debts, even though the Government had already made it clear that such a course of action was diplomatically impossible given the concerns of the French on the whole issue.[75] MacDonald doggedly refused to respond to his more radical critics. The Prime Minister was determined to use his first term in office to show that a Labour Government could govern without being distracted by internal divisions within the Labour movement, and his refusal to countenance demands for a more distinctively socialist foreign policy was at least partly a reflection of his desire to prove that ministers were not 'wild men' seeking to push through a thoroughgoing social and political revolution. It also reflected his understanding that radical changes in the international arena were likely to prove more elusive than many on the left of his party believed.

MacDonald also went to some length to distance himself from many of his erstwhile colleagues in the Union of Democratic Control, the organisation which had for ten years served as the most prominent radical pressure group for reform to traditional patterns of diplomacy.[76] The Prime Minister had established good relations with many socialists across Europe during his lengthy political career, but once in office he made it clear that he was reluctant to use these unofficial channels to break the diplomatic deadlock over such thorny issues as German reparations and the French occupation of the Ruhr. He responded with little enthusiasm when the veteran UDC activist E.D. Morel wrote to him in late January offering to help the new Government 'officially or unofficially, privately or publicly'.[77] He reacted equally cautiously when J.A. Hobson advised him to seek a Parliamentary resolution supporting a more open style of diplomacy, replying firmly that there was no Parliamentary time for such a move.[78] When H.N. Brailsford offered to arrange a meeting between the Prime Minister and the French socialist Léon Blum, in order to discuss Anglo-French affairs, MacDonald replied that he would probably be out of town at the time Blum was in London.[79] In the middle of February, a member of MacDonald's private office noted that the Prime Minister was unable to meet a member of the Hungarian left-wing opposition, on the grounds that 'In his official capacity he has to conduct negotiations through the usual channels' and could not be 'official and unofficial at the same time'.[80] MacDonald's commitment to diplomatic propriety showed how far he had distanced himself from his earlier rhetoric. Although he was ready to engage in a personal diplomacy that smoothed away some of the rigidities of traditional diplomatic discourse, he showed little desire to engage in the kind of far-reaching changes favoured by many on the left of the Labour movement.

MacDonald's relationship with the most significant foreign affairs 'pressure group' of the 1920s, the League of Nations Union, was also a difficult one. The Prime Minister broke with recent tradition by refusing to serve as the LNU's Honorary President, and gave his staff orders not to trouble him with any correspondence originating from the organisation. MacDonald's suspicion of the Union was partly rooted in his scepticism about collective security, at least as it was conceived by some of the League's more fervent supporters such as Robert Cecil, who helped to author the Draft Treaty of Mutual Security that was rejected by the Labour Government in the summer of 1924. Although most senior figures in the Labour movement were committed to the principle of an 'internationalist' foreign policy, ministers in the 1924 government were concerned that the French government was trying to subvert the ideals of collective security, by using the League to extract binding guarantees to defend the post-Versailles *status quo*. They were therefore perennially anxious about making any agreements that might limit the freedom of the British government to determine how it would respond in any particular situation. MacDonald did not share the Liberal internationalism espoused by most of the LNU's leaders, which assumed that complex international problems could be resolved if they were mediated through the kind of international regime they believed was emerging in Geneva.[81] Although the Prime Minister was reconciled to the idea that the League could play a useful role in developing international stability, he was not keen to see it become the main focus of international politics, at least until he was certain that it could genuinely serve as a genuine focus for arbitration rather than an adjunct to French security policy. It was ironically a position that echoed that expressed by many Conservative politicians in the 1920s.

Conclusion

The attacks that were made on the 'old diplomacy' before and during the First World War helped to delegitimise traditional diplomatic institutions and increase popular support for the League of Nations. For those on the left of British politics, however, the assault on the old diplomacy had always encompassed something more than a simple desire to establish a new international organisation charged with facilitating fresh patterns of multilateral agreement. Most prominent members of the UDC, for example, had been equally concerned about introducing administrative and political changes to rein in the supposed independence of the Foreign Office. The critique of traditional diplomacy put forward by many members of the Labour Party, including MacDonald and Ponsonby, was part of a broader critique of the social and political *status quo*. The appointment of a minority Labour Government was therefore a moment of truth for political leaders whose ideas on international politics had previously been articulated in the form of a critical rhetoric rather than a sustained consideration of the practical difficulties inherent in promoting real change.

Although it is hard to define the precise character of MacDonald's socialism, which was perhaps more radical than sometimes acknowledged,[82] by the time he became Prime Minister he was unambiguously committed to a reformist domestic programme that was designed to foster change through the prism of the existing political and administrative system. The same was true in the international arena. His diplomatic vision was by 1924 rooted in a powerful if ill-defined sense that establishing the right atmosphere between governments was more likely to prevent war than complex bilateral or multilateral agreements. Whilst he came to office with a number of well-defined views on particular policy issues, such as the need to extend *de jure* recognition to the Soviet government, MacDonald did not have a definite international agenda beyond a strong commitment to help maintain and strengthen peace in Europe. The Prime Minister was partly (if unwittingly) responsible for setting in motion the negotiations that led up to the drafting of the Geneva Protocol, but he always viewed the League of Nations as a useful addition to the international landscape, arguing that its 'real force ... is moral rather than material'.[83] The paradoxical result was that MacDonald showed himself to be decidedly lukewarm about the most far-reaching attempt made since the end of the First World War to change the texture of global politics. In his final weeks in office he was ready to acknowledge in private that the best he could hope to achieve in the international arena was to 'keep my hands absolutely free so as to take advantage of any change that may take place in the general orientation of international policy'.[84] Such a cautious *credo* owed little to the rhetoric of the Second International and far more to the kind of pragmatic culture characteristic of the Foreign Office.

MacDonald's readiness to build a good working relationship with his Foreign Office staff reflected his belief that a Labour Government could introduce major changes across the whole gamut of public policy without making fundamental changes to the existing institutions of government. The debacle surrounding the publication of the Zinov'ev Letter in the days before the October General Election created the impression in some quarters that Foreign Office officials had actively conspired against the Labour Government, seeking to damage its reputation by leaking material they knew would be damaging to ministers at a time of great political sensitivity. The most recent works on the subject have in fact shown that the premature release of the Zinov'ev Letter to the press was the consequence of a breakdown in communication between senior officials and MacDonald (who was visiting South Wales at the time).[85] Whilst the precise role of the British intelligence services in the whole affair remains ambiguous, there is no evidence of a systematic Foreign Office plot to embarrass the Prime Minister, despite the bitter opposition of a number of senior officials towards the policy of seeking accommodation with Moscow. Many of the outlandish assertions made on all sides following the publication of the Zinov'ev Letter owed more to the febrile political atmosphere of the time than to a considered review of the facts of the situation. Although MacDonald certainly bypassed the Foreign Office on occasion,[86] officials never felt they were excluded from the foreign policy-making process in the way that had been the case when Lloyd George was at Number 10. The chorus of praise for MacDonald among Foreign Office staff is hardly evidence of irreconcilable differences and tensions.

MacDonald's dual tenure as Prime Minister and Foreign Secretary undoubtedly gave him considerable opportunity to dominate the foreign policy-making process. He kept intact the Cabinet Secretariat, which had markedly strengthened the position of Number 10 over the previous few years, and made extensive use of the indefatigable Hankey when dealing with foreign affairs.[87] The Prime Minister's control of the Foreign Office also gave him easy access to expert advice from officials who had an intimate knowledge of international affairs, as well as the opportunity to exercise 'hands-on' control over the complex web of communications that bound together London both with its embassies abroad and with foreign governments. Perhaps most importantly, MacDonald enjoyed the advantage of setting the pattern of discussion in Cabinet over foreign affairs, which gave him considerable opportunity to determine the boundaries to other ministers' involvement in debate about the whole arena of international relations. On these considerations alone, then, it might be tempting to suggest that the Prime Minister was able to obtain exactly the kind of freedom in dealing with foreign affairs that had always been of such concern to critics of traditional diplomacy. There were, though, always a number of powerful constraints on MacDonald's independence. His decision to hold two major offices of state meant that he sometimes found it difficult to master the huge range of complex questions that came before him. Nor could the Prime Minister ignore altogether the views of his ministerial colleagues on foreign affairs, for fear of undermining the Cabinet's precarious unity. MacDonald's first taste of office showed him that the hopes and aspirations of opposition would always have to be mediated through a mundane set of political and administrative realities. It was a lesson that was subsequently learnt by generations of Labour politicians.

4 Austen Chamberlain at the Foreign Office (1924–29)

Introduction

When Austen Chamberlain died in the spring of 1937, his colleagues in the House of Commons honoured their late colleague with a glowing set of tributes.[1] Stanley Baldwin told the House that 'I have had nothing but kindness and consideration from him through all the changes and chances of political life'. The Prime Minister went on to praise Chamberlain as 'a great Parliamentarian who never said 'anything derogatory about a man'. Clement Attlee, speaking in his capacity as Leader of the Labour Party, agreed that the Commons had lost 'one of its most distinguished members', who had been inspired throughout his life by a 'single-minded devotion to what he thought was right'. Lloyd George recalled that Chamberlain was one of 'the fairest and most chivalrous as well as one of the most effective of Parliamentary antagonists', who had 'never once delivered a foul blow'. Even James Maxton of the Independent Labour Party, a man who by his own admission usually delighted in dissenting from the views of his Parliamentary colleagues, noted that he was happy on this occasion to endorse everything that had been said in the Chamber.

Whilst there was genuine warmth in many of the tributes paid to Chamberlain, a close look shows that their authors focused as much on his *character* as his *achievements*. By the time of his death, the view was widespread that the erstwhile Foreign Secretary had 'always played the game and always lost it' – an aphorism attributed variously to Churchill, Balfour and Birkenhead.[2] J.L. Garvin, editor of the *Observer*, spoke dismissively of Chamberlain as an 'essentially mediocre' man, who never had the vision or ability to achieve anything substantial during his long political career.[3] Even the author of a favourable *Times* editorial was forced to concede that his subject had lacked 'fire'.[4] The Treaty of Locarno, which Chamberlain himself identified as his greatest achievement, had come to be seen as virtually irrelevant by the time of his death, in the wake of the German re-occupation of the Rhineland in March 1936.[5] There was therefore a faint but unmistakable sense among those who spoke about Chamberlain that this 'gentleman in politics' had failed to make the sort of impact that might have been expected after so lengthy a career.

Austen Chamberlain's reputation has been partly obscured by comparison with his father and half-brother, a perennial risk for those fortunate (or unfortunate) enough to belong to a celebrated political dynasty.[6] Joseph Chamberlain was one of the most colourful and influential politicians in late Victorian and early Edwardian Britain, an architect of civic activism, who later went on to become one of the standard-bearers of imperialism. Although he never became Prime Minister, his titanic presence helped to influence the tone of British political life for a generation. Neville Chamberlain's political career was also more spectacular – or perhaps notorious – than that of his half-brother. He exercised considerable influence on defence and foreign policy when he served as Chancellor of the Exchequer in the first half of the 1930s, before subsequently becoming the principal standard-bearer of appeasement during his time as Prime Minister. Austen Chamberlain's public reputation during his lifetime was by contrast one of almost stifling dullness. His long ministerial career marked him out as one of the most enduring figures in the British political establishment during the first few decades of the twentieth century, but it was only on rare occasions that he managed to emerge from a grey cocoon of anonymity, attracting the kind of attention that was automatically accorded to his more colourful and charismatic colleagues such as Churchill and Birkenhead.

Chamberlain was a vastly experienced politician by the time he arrived at the Foreign Office in November 1924, following the defeat of the short-lived Labour Government in the election that took place the previous month. He was first elected to the House of Commons in 1892 as a Liberal Unionist, at a time when his father's political career was still at its height. He entered the Cabinet as Postmaster-General in 1902, becoming Chancellor of the Exchequer the following year, and he remained at the Treasury until the election of Campbell-Bannerman's new Liberal administration two years later. During the long Liberal ascendancy that preceded the First World War, Chamberlain became one of the most prominent Unionist politicians, although he lost out in the race to replace Balfour as party leader in 1911, in part because his background as a Liberal Unionist made him unacceptable to many leading Tories. He later served as Secretary of State for India in the Lloyd George wartime coalition, resigning when a critical report concluded that the Indian authorities had seriously mishandled the disastrous Mesopotamian campaign. The incident did little to damage Chamberlain's reputation, however, and he soon returned to the government. At the start of 1919 Chamberlain went back to the Treasury, becoming Conservative leader in 1921, before forfeiting the post and his ministerial role in the political upheavals that resulted from the collapse of the Lloyd George government in the autumn of 1922. His appointment as Foreign Secretary two years later was no real surprise, since he had acted as opposition spokesman on foreign affairs during the previous few months, although it came as a blow to Lord Curzon who had himself hoped to return to the Foreign Office.

Chamberlain seldom showed much sustained interest in the diplomatic intricacies of foreign affairs before arriving at the Foreign Office in 1924. His long ministerial career had, however, provided him with a solid understanding of how British foreign policy was made, as well as the broader strategic and financial context that shaped Britain's relations with the wider world. Whilst he never fully shared his father's passionate belief in the need for closer economic and political ties between Britain and the white dominions, the Foreign Secretary noted in his very first speech after taking office that 'The first thoughts of any Englishman on appointment to the office of Foreign Secretary must be that he speaks in the name, not of Great Britain only, but of the British Dominions beyond the seas, and that it is his imperative duty to preserve in word and act the diplomatic unity of the British Empire'.[7] He subsequently devoted much of his time at the Foreign Office to developments in areas such as China, where growing instability seemed to pose a potential threat to the whole British position in the Far East. Chamberlain was, though, also well-versed in European affairs when he arrived at the Foreign Office. He had spent a year in Paris after graduating from Cambridge, taking courses at the École des Sciences Politiques, and mixing with writers associated with the *Revue des Deux Mondes*, and although he spent much of the subsequent year in Germany, attending lectures in Berlin, he always remained at heart an instinctive Francophile.[8] Chamberlain's first few weeks in office undoubtedly served to convince him that Britain's own security interests required close involvement in Europe, most notably to help improve the appalling state of Franco-German relations.[9] His 'commitment to Europe' was nevertheless always governed in a large part by a shrewd recognition that stability on the continent was necessary to allow the country to focus effectively on securing its global interests.[10] Austen Chamberlain was as firmly convinced as any of his colleagues that Britain was a global rather than a European power.

Chamberlain arrived at the Foreign Office with an open mind about the policies he wanted to pursue, although he left it firmly committed to the principles and practices embodied in the Locarno treaties. The new Foreign Secretary shared the characteristic British scepticism about the wisdom of basing foreign policy on a grand framework of values and objectives. During his time in office, however, he developed a clear set of assumptions that informed his view both of diplomacy and his own role as Foreign Secretary. Chamberlain told the House of Commons in the spring of 1925 that:

> I profoundly distrust logic when applied to politics, and all English history justifies me. Why is it that, as contrasted with other nations, ours has been a peaceful and not a violent development ... It is because instinct and experience alike teach us that human nature is not logical, that it is unwise to treat political institutions as instruments of logic, and that it is in wisely refraining from pressing conclusions to their logical end that the path of peaceful development and true reform is really found.[11]

This characteristically Burkean analysis of the political process dictated Chamberlain's view of such organisations as the League of Nations, which he feared was in danger of being hijacked by 'enthusiasts' who did not understand that it could only succeed by 'proceeding tentatively' on a path of 'gradual evolution'.[12] The Foreign Secretary firmly believed that international politics would for the foreseeable future be organised around the independent sovereign state, and was convinced that traditional diplomatic practices and procedures could find an accommodation even between governments that were divided by deep ideological divisions and conflicting national interests. Although the Foreign Secretary did not for one moment share the hopes of those 'enthusiasts' who believed in the possibility of transforming the character of the international system, he did firmly believe that an active and effective diplomacy could protect Britain's national interests and advance the cause of international peace. Chamberlain was described by one of his early biographers as a 'practical idealist',[13] a phrase that neatly captures the mixture of pragmatism and optimism that informed much of his behaviour whilst at the Foreign Office.

Chamberlain's impact on the foreign policy-making process fluctuated considerably between 1924 and 1929. It is as a result difficult to endorse uncritically the view of one distinguished scholar that his 'rise to the foreign secretaryship re-established foreign office power at a stroke', although it is certainly true that the influence of the Foreign Office was higher at the end of Chamberlain's tenure than it was at the start.[14] The new Foreign Secretary's long political career gave him considerable prestige and authority within the Conservative Party, which was bolstered by his reputation as a competent administrator and a 'safe pair of hands', whilst his performances in the House of Commons were generally agreed to be effective if lacking in inspiration. Chamberlain's political *nous* was, by contrast, more questionable. His failure to win the Unionist leadership in 1911 showed that he was not universally trusted across the party, whilst the political crisis of 1922 placed him at odds with a majority of Conservative backbenchers. Although he commanded a good deal of respect across the political spectrum, there were always those who, like Arthur Balfour, regarded him as a 'bore'.[15] Chamberlain was, in short, regarded with respect rather than affection or admiration. The previous chapters have suggested that an effective foreign secretary needed more than simple respect if they were to exercise a dominant influence on the policy-making process. They also needed the energy and personality to win others across to their point of view. Austen Chamberlain worked hard to put his own stamp on British foreign policy during the years between 1924 and 1929, but he sometimes found it difficult to find ways of defeating opposition both from within the government and beyond.

Chamberlain, the Cabinet and the Foreign Office

Chamberlain was deeply committed to the view that the institutions and practices of traditional diplomacy represented the best means of defending Britain's national interests. When Winston Churchill wrote to him from the Treasury at the start of 1926, asking for economies in running the diplomatic establishment, Chamberlain replied firmly that 'the success of diplomacy depends upon personal influences exercised not only by the Secretary of State himself and responsible officials in London, but by the Ambassadors and Ministers and members of their staffs'. He went on to note that 'Much of the most valuable information I get comes in letters which recount conversations held when some foreign minister receives hospitality from a member of the Embassy staff or offers that hospitality in return'.[16] The Foreign Secretary thought highly of the British civil service, noting in a letter to one correspondent that 'The longer I remain in public life, the more I wonder how the ministers of other countries get on'.[17] It is therefore not surprising that his attitude towards his senior officials was strikingly different from Lord Curzon's. Whilst Curzon had belittled or ignored his staff, Chamberlain treated them as a valuable source of information and advice.[18] His private correspondence with senior members of the Foreign Office was informal and even whimsical in tone, quite unlike the autocratic epistles that emanated from the pen of Curzon, and was perhaps rather at odds with Chamberlain's own austere public persona.[19] The Foreign Secretary frequently convened meetings of officials in his room to discuss important issues of policy, a practice that allowed staff down to the level of Head of Department to contribute to debate in a way that was almost unthinkable in the years between 1919 and 1924. He also corresponded at length with ambassadors and ministers in post abroad, treating their views as a vital source of evidence, to be taken into account when making decisions about policy.[20] His staff reciprocated by showing a loyalty to Chamberlain that they had never offered to Curzon, repeatedly paying tribute to his industry and accessibility.[21] Some outsiders believed that the Foreign Secretary was inclined to act as little more than a mere cipher for his officials. There was, though, little truth in such a charge. Chamberlain had been contemptuous of Curzon's failure to establish his 'weight' in directing British foreign policy. He was determined that he would not be dominated either by his officials or his ministerial colleagues.[22]

The Foreign Secretary spent his first few weeks at the Foreign Office cloistered with his officials trying to master the intricacies of the international situation.[23] Whilst there was no unified Foreign Office 'view' on most major international issues during the 1920s, senior officials generally remained committed to defending the entente with France as a key measure in ensuring European security. Both Eyre Crowe, who served as Permanent Secretary until his early death in 1925,[24] and his successor, William Tyrrell, placed great importance on the London–Paris axis. The same was true of

Lord Crewe, the ambassador at Paris during the Locarno negotiations, although Lord D'Abernon in Berlin was predictably an advocate of closer Anglo-German relations.[25] Neither Chamberlain nor his senior advisers developed a clear view about the best way of promoting European security during the Foreign Secretary's first few weeks in office, but there was general agreement among them that 'We live too close to [Europe's] shores to escape being affected by the insecurity of the European situation'.[26] The instinct of most officials, and of Chamberlain himself, was to search for some new agreement that could assuage French security fears and prevent any future German threat to European security. It was not, though, a view that was shared by many members of the Cabinet.

The Foreign Office's influence on policy depended critically, of course, on the texture of the relationship between the Foreign Secretary and other senior figures in the government. Chamberlain established a good working relationship with Stanley Baldwin. Although the two men were never personally close, they were both instinctive Francophiles, who nevertheless recognised that European security depended on reintegrating Germany into the international system. Their private correspondence was usually informal and friendly, if not particularly warm in tone. The Prime Minister told Chamberlain at the end of 1926, a year when his own attention had been focused on the upheavals surrounding the General Strike, that 'It has been a great comfort throughout this year to feel that I never need worry about foreign affairs and to feel perfect confidence in the judgement and wisdom of the Foreign Secretary'.[27] Chamberlain for his part noted several months earlier that whilst he had at one stage placed little faith in Baldwin, the Prime Minister had come to show 'a quiet confidence and self-reliance of which at the earlier time there was little sign. He is now a great figure in the country'.[28] Chamberlain also appreciated the support Baldwin usually gave him in Cabinet when foreign affairs were under discussion. The Prime Minister's famously 'hands-off' style of management nevertheless provided prominent ministers such as Churchill (Chancellor of the Exchequer) and Birkenhead (Secretary of State for India) with an opportunity to exert their own influence during discussions over foreign policy.[29] Baldwin's readiness to take a back seat when foreign policy was under review had the paradoxical effect of both weakening and strengthening the position of his Foreign Secretary.

Baldwin's second Cabinet was, like his first, full of ministers who were determined to make their own mark on foreign policy, either because they had strong views on the subject, or because they believed that it was part of their departmental remit. Churchill's move to the Treasury provided him with considerable influence on many aspects of Britain's international relations. His determination to cut naval expenditure encouraged him to put pressure on Chamberlain and other ministers to improve relations with Japan, or at least to confirm that war was unthinkable,[30] whilst his lingering anti-communism led him to take a key role in agitating for a diplomatic break with Moscow in 1926–27. Leo Amery at the Colonial Office came into conflict with Chamberlain over a whole host of imperial issues, particularly over the Far East, and vigorously questioned the wisdom of involving Britain too closely in the emerging architecture of European security. Lord Birkenhead generally shared Churchill's 'die-hard' instincts about European and imperial affairs, whilst his tenure at the India Office led him to look with grave anxiety at potential Soviet incursions into central Asia. Other ministers such as the Home Secretary William Joynson-Hicks ('Jix') also reacted with scepticism to many of Chamberlain's proposals on policy – particularly those that involved some kind of formal commitment to uphold the European *status quo*. Some of the Foreign Secretary's sharpest disagreements were with Robert Cecil, Chancellor of the Duchy of Lancaster, who had special responsibility for League of Nations affairs prior to his resignation in 1927. Cecil was critical of the government's decision not to ratify the Geneva Protocol early in 1925, whilst his relationship with Chamberlain was complicated by uncertainty about the precise allocation of responsibility between them for managing League business. He was at times successful in winning over his colleagues, perhaps most notably in 1926, when he persuaded them to force the Foreign Secretary to take a more positive attitude towards the admission of Germany to the League,[31] but he generally found his position a dispiriting one. Although his eventual departure from office took place over the specific question of policy towards the Naval Disarmament Conference of 1927, it was in reality the consequence of several years of frustration in the face of his colleagues' repeated refusal to place the League at the heart of their foreign policy.

The struggle to determine foreign policy continued to take place in a number of different settings, ranging from the full Cabinet and the Committee of Imperial Defence, through to inter-departmental committees and informal conversations in the corridors. It also frequently 'spilt out' into a more public domain. Churchill and Birkenhead, in particular, were astute at using confidential briefings to the press in the hope of advancing their own ideas within government, as well as sometimes contributing articles under their own names.[32] The two men also used high-profile speeches to arouse public support for the positions they defended in Cabinet. Chamberlain's private letters were full of angry references to articles in the press attacking his policies, not least because he suspected that they were sometimes prompted by other ministers, but he made little sustained effort to exercise his own influence on leading journalists and newspaper editors. The rest of this chapter examines Chamberlain's dogged attempts to direct Britain's relations with the wider world during his time at the Foreign Office, focusing as before on the network of relationships that governed his power and influence within the core executive and beyond, with particular reference to two major areas of British foreign policy: the Locarno treaties of 1925, and the formulation of policy towards Soviet Russia during 1924–27. Whilst it is not practical to provide a detailed analysis of two such complex policy areas in the space available here, it is possible to examine the problems faced by the Foreign Secretary when seeking to promote his chosen policies in the face of opposition both within government and beyond. Chamberlain proved remarkably adept at guiding both his Cabinet colleagues and the broader political elite towards accepting the principle that Britain should offer a binding commitment to maintain the territorial *status quo* in western Europe against any attempt to overthrow it by force. He found it much harder to mobilise support for the policy of cautious engagement that he sought to pursue when dealing with the USSR.

Locarno and the question of European security

The Baldwin government that came to office at the end of 1924 quickly decided to reject the Geneva Protocol, on the familiar grounds that it might limit Britain's freedom of manoeuvre at times of international crisis, although the Cabinet did not take a final decision on the subject until March 1925. Such a course of action was, though, bound to renew the long-standing fears of the French government about a potential future threat to its security from Germany.[33] The government in Berlin was for its part enraged by the decision in January to delay the first phase of allied withdrawal from the Rhineland (the schedule of which had originally been agreed at Versailles). The British government's decision to reject the Geneva Protocol so soon after coming to power inevitably raised the broader question of its attitude towards the League of Nations. Chamberlain regularly attended meetings of the League Council and Assembly during his time at the Foreign Office, but he remained sceptical about any proposals designed to make the League the pivotal institution of international politics. In an address to the student body of Glasgow University, in 1926, he warned against the danger of allowing 'our zeal for good causes to outrun our discretion', and pointedly reminded his audience that the League was an 'international and not a super-national' institution.[34] He went on to note that it could only work if the great powers were in agreement. The Foreign Secretary believed more or less from the moment he arrived in office that Britain needed to operate *both* through the League *and* through traditional diplomatic channels in order to secure the kind of international agreements capable of promoting European security. The Locarno agreements that were eventually signed in October 1925 were the logical outcome of such a position.[35]

A sub-committee of the Committee of Imperial Defence was set up in December 1924 to discuss the future of British policy towards the continent, and by the start of the following year it had become clear that the service departments were willing at least to contemplate the offer of some kind of security guarantee to France, particularly since Germany was still identified as the most likely future enemy in any war.[36] The Cabinet Secretary Maurice Hankey was also reluctantly coming round to the view that some form of guarantee to France might be the best way of promoting European stability,[37] whilst there was certainly considerable support within the Foreign Office for such a course of action. In January, Crowe wrote a draft pact for the CID sub-committee, to be signed by Britain, France and Belgium, that was based on the assumption that Britain would fight to protect the other two countries if there was a danger of seeing their Channel or North Sea ports pass into the hands of another power.[38] Other senior officials, including Tyrrell, broadly supported such a proposal (although one or two of his colleagues did caution against basing policy on an uncritical acceptance of the dangers of Prussian militarism).[39] Chamberlain himself endorsed as 'the considered view of the Foreign Office' a memorandum written by Harold Nicolson in February 1925, which argued that 'The first hope of stability in Europe lies in a new *entente* between the British Empire and France'.[40] The situation changed rapidly during this period, though, as a complex series of international and domestic developments posed a major challenge to Chamberlain's preferred policy of re-enforcing the entente with France.

Towards the end of January, the German Foreign Office approached the British government through the ambassador in Berlin, Lord D'Abernon, proposing a mutual security pact 'guaranteeing [the] present territorial status' in western Europe.[41] The proposal was largely the work of the German Foreign Minister Gustav Stresemann, although D'Abernon himself had played a significant role in encouraging such a move.[42] The clumsy German manoeuvres that followed the initial proposal caused a good deal of uncertainty and irritation in both London and Paris, since the two governments feared that Berlin was trying to drive a wedge between them.[43] Chamberlain nevertheless acknowledged in a letter to Lord Crewe in Paris that the German 'memorandum itself and the spirit which it discloses . . . are the most hopeful sign I have yet seen'.[44] The development of Chamberlain's own views on European security during the first few weeks of 1925 remains clouded in some confusion. Richard Grayson has suggested in his admirable study of Chamberlain's foreign policy that the Foreign Secretary was not irrevocably committed to a pact with France and Belgium alone, but was instead always open to some kind of scheme along the lines of the one suggested in the German memorandum.[45] It certainly appears that Chamberlain's ideas were fluid and uncertain. The Foreign Secretary was committed to addressing French fears over Germany, but he was flexible in deciding how best to achieve such a goal, telling Lord Crewe in the middle of February that he could see advantages in German involvement in a pact that offered France a guarantee over the security of their common border.[46] A number of his Foreign Office advisers, most notably Eyre Crowe, were by contrast more sceptical about the wisdom of agreeing to a mutual security pact that included Germany.

The discussions about European security that took place within the Cabinet and the CID during February and March revealed a good deal of confusion and uncertainty among ministers. It is tempting, but almost certainly wrong, to suggest that Chamberlain took the position of defending the cause of European commitment against colleagues who were by instinct strongly isolationist. The pattern was in reality more complex. At a CID meeting in the middle of February, Balfour appeared to warn against any form of European commitment, whilst other ministers such as Birkenhead and Amery were ready to contemplate some form of British guarantee to preserve the *status quo* in the west of the continent.[47] Over the next few days, Worthington-Evans at the War Office wrote a paper broadly supporting the idea of a pact with France, a position that was vigorously opposed by Samuel Hoare at the Air Ministry.[48] Winston Churchill favoured a more staunchly isolationist stance than most of his colleagues, writing to Chamberlain on 23 February that the government should not commit itself 'beyond the limits of human foresight',[49] although he was ready to contemplate some kind of British guarantee of the Franco-German border if the two countries were themselves able to come to an agreement.[50] The discussion was equally confused when the issue came to Cabinet at the start of March. A meeting on 2 March agreed that Britain should under no circumstances ratify the Geneva Protocol or agree to any kind of pact with France and Belgium, but held the door open to a broader pact including Germany as a means of dealing with 'the present state of insecurity and tension in Europe'.[51] Yet just two days later, a number of ministers seemed to have had second thoughts. Curzon and Balfour had already privately approached Chamberlain to urge him against making any public commitments during his forthcoming visit to Geneva,[52] and the Cabinet that met on 4 March watered down its previous decision to consider a pact including Germany on the grounds that it was 'beyond what public opinion ... at home or in the Dominions would accept'.[53] Ministers nevertheless also agreed, somewhat contradictorily, to authorise Chamberlain to tell the French that the British government would use its best endeavours to ensure that any proposals of the kind put forward by Germany 'should not fail for want of British concurrence'. It is difficult to interpret the complex debates about European security that took place in late February and early March in terms of such rarefied concepts as 'policy initiation'. The disagreements within the CID and Cabinet were seldom clear-cut divisions between individuals with well-defined views about the best way of promoting European stability. Chamberlain's own views oscillated as he sought to find ways of promoting French security that would be acceptable both to his fellow ministers and to Paris, whilst his ministerial colleagues also changed their position, as they reflected on the likely response of public opinion to any kind of British commitment to defend the *status quo* in Europe. The struggle to define Britain's policy towards Europe during these critical days and weeks took the form of an ongoing series of skirmishes and compromises rather than a clear-cut struggle to promote a particular position.

The same complex pattern continued into the middle of March, when

Chamberlain left on a trip to Paris and Geneva. There has been some disagreement among scholars about the nature of the divisions within Cabinet
during this period,[54] but it appears that tension between Chamberlain and
his Cabinet colleagues was once again rooted as much in confusion as it was
in a well-defined disagreement over policy. A meeting of ministers that took
place on 11 March in response to a request by Chamberlain from Geneva for
guidance vigorously rejected an Anglo-French pact, even if it formed part of
a more comprehensive plan to integrate Germany into a new West European
security architecture, but it seems that ministers may have been labouring
under some misapprehension about the Foreign Secretary's actual
intentions.[55] Nevertheless, the letter that Crowe sent to the Foreign Secretary after the meeting of ministers, bitterly attacking participants for their
'wooly-headed pronouncements' against any form of British involvement in
Europe,[56] certainly alarmed the Foreign Secretary. He subsequently
telegraphed to Crowe asking him to tell the Prime Minister that 'if the discussion reported by you really represents the intentions of the Cabinet, I
have been placed in a wholly false and intolerable position'.[57] Chamberlain's
remarks showed that he was ready at least to contemplate threatening resignation in order to defend his view that Britain should become involved in
establishing some kind of new European security architecture.

The furore created by the meeting of ministers on 11 March soon faded
away, though, and when Chamberlain returned to London in the third week
of March the climate was 'much friendlier'.[58] Baldwin made strenuous efforts
to soothe his Foreign Secretary, although Chamberlain himself was never
quite sure where he stood with 'the sphinx', and doubted whether the Prime
Minister was willing to back him unequivocally.[59] By the time he attended a
Cabinet meeting on 20 March, the Cabinet was ready to authorise the
Foreign Secretary to tell Parliament that the German Government's proposals for a mutual security pact represented 'the best basis for reaching a
settlement of security'.[60] Once again, it is probably unwise to interpret this
outcome as a clear victory for Chamberlain against the isolationists. The
views of most ministers had been in flux throughout the previous month.
The series of decisions that paved the way for the British government to
enter negotiations for some form of mutual security pact emerged from a
policy-making process that was incremental and *ad hoc* in character. The
Foreign Office itself subsequently enjoyed a fair amount of freedom in the
diplomatic manoeuvres that led up to the Locarno agreements of October
1925, although a number of ministers continued to view the process with a
good deal of concern.[61] Chamberlain kept the Cabinet informed about developments, although his briefings were quite infrequent, and he sought
approval before taking any decision that was likely to prove particularly
controversial.[62] He was also happy for the Cabinet to establish *ad hoc* committees to decide how best to respond to initiatives coming from the French
or German governments.[63] The Foreign Secretary continued to exert considerable energy to secure the support of ministers whom he knew to be

concerned about committing Britain to the defence of the existing borders of western Europe,[64] recognising that his latitude in discussions with the French and German governments was ultimately governed by the extent to which his Cabinet colleagues were ready to support him.

Chamberlain was determined to play the role of honest broker during the course of the international negotiations that led up to Locarno,[65] although he made little secret that he found the French government much easier to deal with than its German counterpart, rarely even meeting with the German ambassador in London. Whilst he met with French politicians in person on a number of occasions, he normally preferred to work through Lord D'Abernon when dealing with the German government. The relationship between the two men remained, though, rather strained. The Foreign Secretary's relationship with Lord Crewe and his staff at the Paris Embassy was by contrast much warmer, in part because he met them more frequently during his trips to the French capital. Senior British officials at the Paris Embassy were themselves often suspicious of the British ambassador in Berlin, believing that he underestimated German strength and did not pay enough attention to French security fears.[66] Despite these potential tensions, though, the diplomatic machine operated fluently enough in the months leading up to the formal negotiations that began at Locarno in October. Members of the British diplomatic establishment skilfully headed off demands that they considered unacceptable, such as the French government's desire for a formal arbitration treaty, and the German government's demand for major concessions over colonies. Chamberlain himself not only played the role of an honest broker between Paris and Berlin; he was also remarkably effective at managing the tensions and differences that periodically threatened to erupt among British politicians and officials.

The events leading up to the Locarno agreements inevitably attracted a good deal of parliamentary and public attention throughout 1925, and whilst the details of the various negotiations were kept secret, a mixture of press leaks and official disclosures meant that the various participants could never hide behind a veil of secrecy in the way that had often happened before 1914. Chamberlain had sat in the House of Commons for more than thirty years at the time he became Foreign Secretary, which meant that he was generally astute at deciding how best to approach the Chamber. Although his somewhat old-fashioned demeanour and laboured oratory were not necessarily conducive to winning the enthusiastic support of MPs, his frankness and sincerity impressed even his critics.[67] The House of Commons was sharply divided about the whole question of international security during the first few months of Baldwin's second administration, and the fact that the Locarno agreements eventually attracted widespread support in Parliament is at least in part testimony to the Foreign Secretary's political skills. Chamberlain's strategy in dealing with the House of Commons throughout 1925 was very clear. At the beginning of March he committed himself to taking the House of Commons into his 'fullest confidence' in order to win all-party support for a 'national policy'.[68] In speech after speech the foreign secretary worked hard to persuade MPs to accept his view that 'the dominant enemy in Europe to-day is the sense of insecurity which reigns everywhere'.[69] He also repeatedly attacked the idea of isolation 'as a dream and nothing more', and argued that some form of British engagement with the security architecture of western Europe was necessary to bring stability to the continent.[70] The Foreign Secretary was being characteristically honest when he declared his intention of being open with the House of Commons. His speeches were usually as frank as was possible without committing a clear breach of diplomatic protocol.

Chamberlain's decision to promote his chosen policy so doggedly reflected his conviction that achieving continental stability was a major British national interest, and he was shrewd enough to recognise that his policy could not be successful unless he succeeded in changing fundamentally the way in which most of his fellow countrymen viewed Britain's place in the world. He went to great lengths to counter rumours that he was pursuing a 'personal policy', insisting that he had the full support of the Cabinet.[71] The debate in Parliament that took place on 18 November, after agreement had finally been reached at Locarno, showed that Chamberlain had been remarkably successful in winning over the House of Commons to his policy of constructive engagement. Both Lloyd George and MacDonald broadly supported the agreements (although they did raise certain doubts about issues ranging from the reaction of the dominions through to the impact on disarmament). The most serious opposition came from left-wing MPs who opposed a Pact that they believed was based on the implicit threat of force rather than a clear commitment to peaceful arbitration,[72] along with a number of Conservatives who remained committed to the virtues of splendid isolation. Chamberlain had, in the course of a few months, managed to isolate most of his critics both in Cabinet and in Parliament, winning widespread support for his belief that 'We are too near the Continent to rest indifferent to what goes on there'.[73] It was a remarkable achievement given the deep-seated suspicion of continental engagement that was evident across large sections of both the Conservative and Labour parties.

Chamberlain recognised that discussion of foreign policy in the press could have a major impact on public and parliamentary opinion, and both his private correspondence and Foreign Office files suggest that he monitored reports in the major newspapers with some care. Whilst *The Times* had been sharply critical of the Lloyd George government in general, and Lord Curzon in particular, Chamberlain generally received a good press from the newspaper. The new foreign editor, Harold Williams, 'put his greatest energies behind Chamberlain's Locarno policy', and encouraged the paper to take a more positive attitude towards Germany.[74] During the months between March and October, *The Times* consistently supported the 'hopeful and important negotiations' being conducted by the Foreign Secretary,[75] running leading articles arguing that the 'main interest' of Britain was 'that peace in

Europe should be made secure for many years'.[76] The paper praised Chamberlain for expressing his views 'admirably' in Parliament, and repeatedly discounted rumours that he was pursuing a 'personal policy with the rest of the Cabinet looking helplessly and unwillingly on'.[77] There is little evidence, though, to suggest that Chamberlain had particularly close personal ties with senior figures on *The Times* (although the paper did of course traditionally enjoy good contacts with senior members of the Foreign Office).[78] Although he conducted a regular correspondence with H.A. Gwynne of the *Morning Post*, reporting on conversations he had held with leading politicians from other countries, the Foreign Secretary seldom made any sustained attempt to influence press coverage of international developments.

The *Manchester Guardian* and the *Daily News* were rather more non-committal than the *Times* in their response to the news that the British government was trying to negotiate a security pact designed to promote European stability, although they supported the agreements that were eventually signed at Locarno in the autumn. The Beaverbrook *Daily Express*, by contrast, launched a furious campaign in May 1925 against a pact that might commit Britain to a war 'involving the lives of our sons and even our grandsons, and putting them in imminent peril of death'.[79] Chamberlain recognised that such reports could whip up anxiety among a public frightened of any move that might drive Europe once again to the brink of oblivion, which doubtless helps to explain why he went to such trouble to express in Parliament his view that a security pact offered the best way of preventing a future war. He was also concerned that Labour MPs or even backbenchers from his own party might use public anxieties in an effort to mobilise opinion against the negotiations. The Foreign Secretary was nevertheless confident by the end of June that he had 'won the battle' to persuade both public and parliamentary opinion of the wisdom of some kind of agreement to guarantee the frontiers of western Europe.

The most important pressure group concerned with the Locarno negotiations was of course the League of Nations Union, which had broadly supported the Geneva Protocol, even continuing to campaign for ratification once Chamberlain announced that the British government had no intention of approving it. The Foreign Secretary became increasingly irritated by the LNU's activities in the first half of 1925, particularly since the language in some of its publications seemed to imply that he was not sufficiently committed to the principles enshrined in the League Covenant. Chamberlain even threatened to resign from the organisation at one stage, and refused to address LNU meetings on the grounds that it might appear he was supporting a policy that the government had already decisively rejected. Since the LNU leadership was largely drawn from the confines of the British establishment, the Foreign Secretary could not afford to ignore its views altogether, but the organisation remained in essence an 'outsider group' with little influence on policy. Despite its high level of popular support, Chamberlain was determined that his pragmatic policy of promoting European security by a series of regional pacts would not be sabotaged by those who continued to believe that the League could transform once and for all the character of the international political system. Although he went to great lengths to stress that the Locarno agreements were consistent with the system of collective security centred on Geneva, they owed more to a traditional diplomatic mindset which assumed that relations between sovereign states represented the defining characteristic of the international system.

The significance of the Locarno agreements has, as noted earlier, been endlessly discussed by historians. A.J.P. Taylor famously noted in *The Origins of the Second World War* that Locarno 'ended the First World War; its repudiation eleven years later marked the prelude to the Second'.[80] Chamberlain himself placed great emphasis on 'the spirit of Locarno' throughout his time as Foreign Secretary, believing that the understandings he helped to broker in 1925 had played a vital role in changing the political climate of Europe. Whilst it is difficult to arrive at a final judgement on the vexed question of whether the guarantees offered by Britain at Locarno were part of a deeper 'commitment to Europe', or instead part of a strategy designed to allow the country to turn its face away from the continent by stabilising the situation there, it is hardly controversial to suggest that London's reluctance to become involved in any guarantee of the *status quo* in central and eastern Europe was to have major consequences in the following decade. The chaotic and uncertain debates that took place in London about a possible British commitment during the opening months of 1925 starkly reveals how important issues of policy could be the result of uncertainty and compromise rather than clear thinking. It nevertheless remains true that the Locarno accords might not have come about without Chamberlain's skilful efforts to overcome the various domestic and international obstacles to any form of European security pact.

Chamberlain and British policy towards the Soviet Union

Although Chamberlain was generally successful at moulding British policy towards western Europe in the period leading up to the Locarno agreements, he was less effective at promoting his chosen policy towards Soviet Russia, failing to prevent the downward spiral that culminated in a breach in diplomatic relations between London and Moscow in May 1927. The Baldwin government moved quickly on coming to office to announce that it had no intention of recommending to Parliament the Anglo-Soviet treaty recently negotiated by the MacDonald administration.[81] Some members of the new Cabinet hoped to go a good deal further. Churchill wrote to Chamberlain shortly after the election suggesting that the government 'should revoke the [*de jure*] recognition of the Soviet Government which was decided on by MacDonald'.[82] Several of his colleagues also favoured some form of dramatic action. Chamberlain resolutely opposed such pressure, supported at this stage by Baldwin, but the exchange with Churchill signalled that policy towards Russia would soon become one of the most contentious issues for the new government.

Chamberlain's attitude towards the USSR was remarkably consistent throughout the period between the 1924 election and the break in diplomatic relations that took place in 1927. He was loath to allow Anglo-Soviet relations to distract him from the task of securing international stability in the western part of Europe. Although he was horrified by the violence set in motion by the 1917 Revolution, the Foreign Secretary was determined not to allow ideological antipathies to become the driving force behind British policy towards the Soviet Union. In speech after speech he sought to pursue a course between Conservative diehards and left-wing Labour MPs, praising instead a middle position that sought to use the sober language of diplomacy to manage tension between the British and Soviet governments.[83] His views dovetailed with those held by many senior officials at the Foreign Office. A memorandum drafted in the Northern Department within days of the election warned that a break in diplomatic relations would give the Soviet government 'a great deal of advertisement and fresh material for propaganda'.[84] William Tyrrell, who replaced Eyre Crowe as Permanent Secretary in the spring of 1925, despised the Bolshevik regime, but he still shared the Foreign Secretary's scepticism about the wisdom of ending diplomatic relations with Moscow, fearing that such a move would drive Germany and Russia closer together. The same was true of J.D. Gregory, who served as the Assistant Under-Secretary responsible for supervising the Northern Department, which dealt among other countries with the USSR. The two men only began to revise their opinions at the end of 1926, when continued attempts by the Soviet government to exert its influence in China led them to consider whether the benefits of maintaining diplomatic relations with Moscow were not outweighed by the costs.

The main Cabinet critics of Chamberlain's cautious policy towards Soviet Russia were Churchill, Birkenhead and Joynson-Hicks. Churchill was of course a veteran critic of Moscow, a position inspired by his passionate belief that the Soviet government posed an active threat both to domestic order and to the tranquillity of the colonies.[85] Birkenhead was a long-standing opponent of any form of idealism in foreign policy,[86] and repeatedly argued that the Soviet challenge could only be met by a forceful and determined response from the British government. As Secretary of State for India, he was also particularly exercised by the potential challenge of the USSR in Asia, although he was if anything even more concerned about the Soviet government's efforts to promote labour unrest in Britain. Birkenhead launched some of the fiercest attacks on unions for accepting 'red gold' during the turbulent summer of 1926, and rejoiced in the collapse of the General Strike in May as a victory over Soviet infiltration. Joynson-Hicks at the Home Office was equally concerned about the challenge posed to domestic order by possible Soviet agitation. The three men together formed a natural caucus within Cabinet in support of a tougher policy towards Moscow. Since Churchill and Birkenhead, in particular, were also adept at mobilising support in the press, the 'die-hard' critics were well placed to mount a challenge to Chamberlain's ability to determine policy towards the USSR.

Although the Locarno negotiations dominated the minds of British foreign policy-makers for much of 1925, Soviet policy towards the Middle East and China continued to command a good deal of attention. Chamberlain and his officials fretted about possible Soviet designs on Persia and Afghanistan,[87] whilst Birkenhead angrily demanded from the India Office that the government should respond forcefully to subversive activities that he believed were designed to destroy the British Empire. A handful of individuals in the Eastern Department of the Foreign Office believed that Soviet activities were provocative enough to warrant a fierce reaction, but the Foreign Secretary and his most senior officials generally favoured a more restrained response. In July 1925, Chamberlain informed the Prime Minister that a diplomatic rupture with Moscow would create domestic tension and foster the impression that the ongoing negotiations for a mutual security pact were secretly directed against the USSR.[88] Although the Foreign Secretary was wary of circulating papers about Soviet affairs to the Cabinet, for fear of compromising intelligence sources, he made sure that ministers were kept informed of major developments. He was also keen to share responsibility for any decision about the future of diplomatic relations with Russia, asking the Prime Minister to establish a special Cabinet committee to discuss the issue.[89] As Baldwin was in any case inclined to allow members of the Cabinet to engage in wide-ranging discussion about domestic and foreign policy, the critics of Chamberlain's policy of polite *hauteur* towards the Soviet government always had ample opportunities to pursue their case.

The labour disturbances of 1926 profoundly affected domestic attitudes in Britain towards the USSR, particularly as many senior figures in the Conservative Party automatically (and not altogether unfairly) assumed that Soviet agents had played a significant part in promoting unrest. The government in Moscow was certainly anxious to promote the influence of communists in the trade unions, providing money direct to the mineworkers' union, although the real roots of the labour crisis were in fact always domestic in origin. The Zinov'ev Letter was still fresh in the public mind, which made it easy for the 'die-hards' to make a plausible case that labour unrest was orchestrated from Moscow as part of its campaign to promote world-wide revolution via the Comintern. The General Strike in May provoked a major review of Britain's relations with Soviet Russia. Chamberlain acknowledged that the Soviet government was engaged in propaganda activities that directly breached the commitments it had made in the 1921 Trade Agreement, but he doubted whether they had much real effect on developments within the labour movement. Ministers such as Birkenhead were by contrast furious about 'Russian infiltration, Trade Unionist tyranny, Red

Flag demonstrations and Socialist Sunday Schools'.[90] Churchill was implacable in his determination to avoid 'compromise of any kind' with the strikers,[91] serving as the main architect of the government newspaper *The British Gazette* that was produced during the emergency, whilst Joynson-Hicks at the Home Office played a major role in co-ordinating the Government's response to the strike. Both men shared Birkenhead's concern that the Soviet government would take advantage of the labour unrest to mount new propaganda campaigns. These fears were echoed far beyond the Cabinet. In the weeks following the collapse of the strike, a number of national newspapers began a strident campaign demanding an end to diplomatic relations with Moscow. The *Daily Mail* ran editorials attacking 'Moscow's Stranglehold on Our Miners',[92] and also pointedly criticised the 'strange tenderness' of Chamberlain's pronouncements on the Soviet Union.[93] There were in addition numerous attacks on the Soviet government from Conservative MPs in Parliament, condemning the 'Russian menace' as 'second to none in importance and peril'.[94] Although it is not entirely clear to what extent 'diehard' ministers actively sought to orchestrate the campaign, both Churchill and Birkenhead made use of their contacts with the press and sympathetic MPs to increase pressure on the Cabinet to adopt a harsher line on Anglo-Soviet relations.

Chamberlain worked hard throughout the summer of 1926 to persuade his colleagues that the moment was not opportune for the rupture of diplomatic relations. The whole issue was discussed in depth at a Cabinet meeting on 16 June, following the circulation of a memorandum by Joynson-Hicks, which argued that the Foreign Office was inconsistent in supporting diplomatic relations with Moscow whilst simultaneously acknowledging that the Soviet government directed the subversive activities of the Comintern.[95] Chamberlain's response, which he repeated a few days later in Parliament, was the same one that he had repeatedly put forward throughout the previous eighteen months: namely, that a break in relations would introduce a new and complicating factor into European politics that might undermine international stability. The Foreign Secretary managed to prevail over his Cabinet critics during the discussions that took place in the second half of June, largely because he received support from both Baldwin and a number of other senior ministers, but he was realistic enough to know that the ideological zeal of his critics would not be assuaged for long by worthy lectures on the fragility of European security. He wrote to his sister a few days after the critical Cabinet meeting noting that for now 'the Prime Minister and Cabinet are with me [but] ... I do not know whether it will be possible to forebear indefinitely'.[96] Ministers such as Churchill and Birkenhead were certainly not prepared to allow the matter to drop either in Cabinet or in public, and the *Daily Mail* and the *Morning Post* also continued their campaign for a change in policy. As long as the subject remained so politically charged, the Foreign Secretary faced a constant struggle to defend his cautious policy against his Cabinet critics and their supporters in the press.

Chamberlain's critics not only sought to assert themselves in full Cabinet; they also made use of the various Cabinet committees to promote their chosen policy. Churchill and Birkenhead were particularly exercised about the threat posed by the USSR to Indian security. Since strategic policy was made 'on the margins of power and responsibility of several elements in government',[97] a whole range of ministers and officials were able to insist that they should be involved in discussions about countering the Soviet challenge in Asia. The General Staff in London had already concluded by the end of 1925 that 'Moscow is bent on permeating Afghanistan with Russian influence', and were planning how best to counter any possible aggression against the country.[98] Birkenhead raised the question of Indian defence before the CID in June 1926, at a time when he was of course agitating for a break in diplomatic relations with Moscow, arguing that the Soviet government was trying to surround India with 'a circle of Bolshevik states'. He therefore believed that the British government should make a public declaration that any encroachment on Afghanistan would be treated as a *casus belli*.[99] Although the Government in India was decidedly sceptical about such a policy,[100] it commanded a good deal of support from the Chiefs of Staff in London.[101] Chamberlain for his part predictably opposed the views of Birkenhead, telling the CID in July that 'he did not think it at all possible to contemplate a war with Russia in order to prop up Afghanistan'.[102] Whilst his views commanded general support within the Foreign Office, a number of ministers including Samuel Hoare and Churchill sided with Birkenhead, although few firm decisions were actually made on the subject prior to the final break with Moscow in May 1927. The debates that took place over Anglo-Russian relations both in the Cabinet and the CID during the summer of 1926 had, though, broadened the network of individuals and departments involved in dealing with policy towards the USSR. Chamberlain subsequently found it even harder to defend his policy in the face of pressure both from within and beyond the heart of government.

The Foreign Secretary faced an almost impossible task in staving off pressure for a break with Moscow during the year following the general strike. Newspapers such as the *Daily Mail* continued to campaign for an end to diplomatic relations, and a number of public meetings took place at which speakers angrily called for the expulsion of the 'red bandits' from London. Conservative MPs like Oliver Locker-Lampson used their position to keep up pressure on ministers in the House of Commons. A handful of ministers including Balfour still supported the Foreign Secretary's moderate line over Russia, but they were less vocal than opponents such as Churchill and Birkenhead, who were confident that they commanded popular support in their campaign to overturn Chamberlain's policy. Baldwin continued to support his Foreign Secretary, but the Prime Minister's relaxed style of managing his Cabinet meant that he made little sustained effort to counter the efforts of die-hard ministers to seek a change in policy. The crisis that exploded in China at the end of 1926 undermined Chamberlain's position still further, since it was widely assumed that the Soviet government was orchestrating the protests that erupted against the western powers there. The Foreign Secretary himself doubted whether attacks on western businesses and missions in China were really the direct consequence of Soviet agitation,[103] but such a restrained opinion met with little support at a time when ministers were concerned about a possible repeat of the Boxer Rebellion, and Birkenhead noted wistfully that he wanted to see 'this Bolshevik-inspired rabble confronted by real troops'.[104] Chamberlain himself eventually came to support a tougher policy towards China than the one recommended by his advisers, but the development of the crisis in the Far East undoubtedly played a significant part in weakening his control over policy towards Soviet Russia during the opening months of 1927.

Chamberlain's long-standing policy towards the USSR was always vulnerable to the charge of contradiction. The Foreign Secretary never denied that the Soviet government had consistently behaved in a way that broke the rules of traditional diplomacy, arguing instead that although the British government had the right to end diplomatic relations with Moscow, it should resist such a course of action on the grounds that it would foster a degree of international instability that might threaten Britain's own national interests. Such a policy represented an admirably sober attempt to base foreign policy on a realistic appraisal of the international situation, but Chamberlain found it hard to prevail in a political environment where attitudes towards the Soviet Union were the product of ideology and emotion rather than cool diplomatic calculation. He rather undermined his own position in January 1927 when he announced to Cabinet that the Foreign Office planned to send a Note of Protest to the Soviet government, following its discovery that the authorities in Moscow had been tampering with the diplomatic bags of foreign powers.[105] Chamberlain remained confident during the following weeks that Baldwin remained opposed to any attempt to break off diplomatic relations,[106] but he was forced to acknowledge that the eventual dispatch of the Note a few weeks later 'carries us a stage further towards a breach'.[107] A few days earlier, the Cabinet had already agreed that 'if the present policy of the Russian Soviet Government was continued, a breach of relations in the next few months is almost inevitable'.[108] The Foreign Secretary found it harder than ever to justify maintaining diplomatic relations with Russia when his own department had taken the initiative in protesting about the Soviet government's breaches of diplomatic protocol.

The raid by the Metropolitan police on the headquarters of the Soviet trade organisation Arcos, that took place on 12 May 1927, was simply the final spark that led to the decision to expel Soviet officials from London. Over the previous few weeks, intelligence sources had produced new evidence about Soviet espionage activities in Britain, culminating in a claim that an Arcos employee had illegally obtained a secret military training manual.[109] Jix authorised the raid without informing Chamberlain, despite the likely diplomatic consequences, a move that was almost certainly inspired by the Home Secretary's desire to present his colleague with a *fait accompli*. Although the missing manual was not found during the raid, the British government still went ahead with the expulsion of Soviet diplomats, citing numerous documents showing that Soviet officials had engaged in activities that were incompatible with their official status.[110] Chamberlain made no sustained attempt to oppose the decision in Cabinet, although some more junior members of the Foreign Office continued to argue that without 'further proof' there were only 'very flimsy reasons for breaking off diplomatic relations'.[111] The Foreign Secretary strongly defended in Parliament the Cabinet's decision to expel Soviet diplomats, even though such a move reflected a clear defeat for his long-standing view that maintaining diplomatic links with Moscow represented the best means of exercising leverage on the government there.[112] In reality, of course, the decision to expel the Soviet mission was the culmination of many months and years of pressure, and the Arcos raid was the occasion rather than the cause of the Cabinet's decision on 23 May 'that the Russian Trade Agreement should be terminated' and Soviet representatives expelled from Britain. The dispatch of the Note of Protest a few weeks earlier had created a political momentum that was destined to undermine the lingering viability of the Foreign Secretary's policy towards the USSR. Chamberlain's struggle to defend his chosen policy during the years before the Arcos raid reveals a good deal about the strength and weakness of his position. Although he was able for thirty months to face down calls for a break with Moscow by insisting that international diplomatic considerations should take primacy over domestic political pressures, he was unable to defend his policy indefinitely in the face of determined opposition from a number of his Cabinet colleagues buoyed up by support from the right-wing press. The Foreign Office 'view' could not survive in the face of such pressure.

Conclusion

A brief review of some of the other major issues faced by Chamberlain during his time at the Foreign Office appears to confirm that his influence on the foreign policy-making process fluctuated according to the particular issue under discussion. British policy towards China proved to be an issue of concern throughout the life of the second Baldwin government, given Britain's extensive financial interests in the region, along with the strategic vulnerability of Hong Kong and other imperial possessions in the Far East.[113] The civil war between Nationalists and Communists complicated the issue still further. During his first two years in office, the Foreign Secretary gave British officials in both London and China considerable latitude in dealing with the region, although he was more closely involved when broader questions about naval developments in the Far East were under review, given his determination to defend the cause of a 'strong navy' as a vital component of imperial security.[114] The situation changed during the crisis that developed towards the end of 1926, when the Kuomanting effectively seized control of the customs at Canton, following the previous failure of an international conference that had been called to discuss the vexed question of tariffs. The Foreign Secretary and his officials were ready to consider making unilateral concessions to the Chinese by allowing them greater control over tariff policy, although Chamberlain himself initially wanted any change in policy to be carried out in tandem with the other powers. There was, though, considerable resentment in Cabinet against what was seen as too weak a Foreign Office line. Leo Amery at the Colonial Office accused the Foreign Office in September 1926 of lacking 'spirit', and made it clear that he thought the Foreign Secretary was too preoccupied with European affairs at the expense of developments in Asia and elsewhere.[115] It is certainly true that members of the diplomatic establishment were inclined to favour a cautious policy towards China during the second half of the 1920s, since they were intensely conscious of Britain's military weakness in the region, a position that subsequently became still more pronounced during the Far Eastern crisis of 1931–32. In November 1926, Victor Wellesley, the Deputy Under-Secretary in London with particular responsibility for the Far East, wrote a paper on 'British Policy in China', urging that London should be ready to make concessions on the vexed question of tariff policy, even at the cost of breaking with the other powers over the issue.[116] Chamberlain himself worked hard to persuade his sceptical colleagues that Britain should pursue a moderate policy that met the 'legitimate aspirations of the Chinese nation'.[117] Miles Lampson, the senior British representative in China, spoke for many in the Foreign Office when he noted early in 1927 that he saw his role as reconciling 'the protection of our vested interests with the satisfaction of legitimate Chinese national aspirations'.[118]

Many of Chamberlain's Cabinet critics were by contrast inclined to see the growing disorder and anti-British sentiment in China as evidence of Bolshevik agitation in the region. It has already been seen that the crisis that erupted in the final weeks of 1926 played a major role in hardening attitudes towards the USSR. Diehard ministers like Jix believed that the 'Chinese leaders are Bolshie in heart', and the Home Secretary made it clear that he placed no faith in the 'F.O. theory that China will get rid of her Bolshevik advisers as soon as she gets her freedom'.[119] China completely dominated the Cabinet agenda in the first few weeks of 1927, as it seemed that Nationalist forces might seize control of Shanghai, the focus of Britain's main financial interests. The Chiefs of Staff favoured preparations for military intervention in the region, a position predictably supported by ministers such as Jix and Birkenhead, and in the middle of January ministers agreed to send a sizeable force of 13,000 men to the region. Chamberlain himself supported the move, but the strong impression remained among several of his colleagues that the Foreign Office had been 'weak and timid' over the previous few months.[120] Even Chamberlain's half-brother Neville later observed that the Foreign Office had been remiss at dealing with the situation. The Foreign Secretary had once again found it hard to assert his chosen policy on an issue where passions ran high both in the Cabinet and beyond, although in the event the expulsion of Soviet 'advisers' from China a few months later seemed to prove his case about the essentially indigenous nature of the unrest there.

Chamberlain was more successful in asserting himself in the formulation of policy towards the USA, a subject that continued to be intimately bound up with the vexed question of naval rivalry.[121] The Foreign Secretary showed little sustained interest in the more technical aspect of defence questions throughout his time in office, although he was alert to the broader strategic context that shaped the development of British foreign policy both in Europe and beyond. Chamberlain was in general an advocate of a 'strong' navy, which he believed was critical for imperial security, but he backed Churchill at the Treasury in his struggle to cut the naval estimates for 1925–26. The Foreign Secretary was by instinct wary of allowing the service ministries to take the lead in defining Britain's security needs. Following the failure of the 1927 Naval Conference to secure any agreement between the USA, Britain and the other naval powers,[122] a sharp division emerged between the Admiralty and the Foreign Office over the whole matter of belligerent rights. Chamberlain and his senior advisers, including Esmé Howard at the Washington Embassy, placed high priority on securing some form of agreement with the American administration, believing that tension and division between the two countries weakened Britain's global position. The Foreign Secretary was therefore ready to contemplate making concessions on belligerent rights as the price of securing some kind of agreement. The Admiralty, by contrast, remained resolutely opposed to such concessions, a position predictably supported by Hankey in the Cabinet Office. The struggle to determine the pattern of British policy towards the USA was fought out in Chamberlain's final years in office both in the full Cabinet, and in Cabinet committees such as the Belligerent Rights Sub-Committee, where debate took place about the possible form of an Anglo-American arbitration treaty. The question at issue was, as the leading scholar of Chamberlain's policy towards the USA has pithily suggested, whether 'foreign policy be snipped and trimmed to accommodate naval requirements, or should diplomatic interests predominate'.[123] Chamberlain and the Foreign Office eventually gained the upper hand in the conflict, whilst hard-line opponents of the policy of including belligerent rights in any arbitration treaty found themselves in a minority both in committee and in the full Cabinet. The 'blue-print' that emerged from this tortuous process was therefore inspired primarily by the Foreign Office position that policy towards the USA should be based on broad political principles rather than a narrower consideration of naval 'equivalence' alone. The Foreign Secretary proved himself adept at forcing the question at critical moments, most notably in December 1928, when he took the issue to Cabinet in an effort to impress on ministers that the whole question of belligerent rights could not be divorced from broader political questions about Anglo-American relations.[124] In the event, though, the whole issue proved somewhat academic, since the Baldwin government fell from office before detailed naval talks could begin, and it was left to its successor to pick up the challenge of naval disarmament.

A review of the other issues dealt with by Chamberlain whilst Foreign Secretary would serve only to flesh out the argument presented in the previous pages. Brian McKercher's illuminating essay on Chamberlain's time as Foreign Secretary is undoubtedly correct in arguing that the Foreign Office exercised greater influence on policy during the second half of the 1920s than in the years immediately following the end of the First World War.[125] Stanley Baldwin was no Lloyd George, and during his time at Number 10 there was never any question of there being 'two Foreign Offices', each with its own distinctive objectives and policies. Senior officials in Chamberlain's Foreign Office were able to rest assured that their views were given due weight by a Foreign Secretary who valued their skills and advice. It is nevertheless too sweeping to refer to Chamberlain restoring Foreign Office influence at 'a stroke' (as McKercher suggests in his essay). The different policy-making landscape of the post-war world meant that it was harder than ever to divorce diplomacy from the wider strategic and financial environment. Baldwin's second Cabinet was full of ministers who were convinced that it was both their duty and right to exercise their influence on British foreign policy, whilst the Prime Minister's consensual style of running Cabinet made all areas of policy subject to collective scrutiny. Although Austen Chamberlain certainly played an important role in directing British foreign policy in the second half of the 1920s, he never enjoyed anything approaching the independence and freedom enjoyed by Sir Edward Grey twenty years earlier.

5 Arthur Henderson at the Foreign Office (1929–31)

Introduction

The appointment of Arthur Henderson as Foreign Secretary in the minority Labour Government that came to office in 1929 created considerable tension in the higher reaches of the Party hierarchy. Ramsay MacDonald was at first inclined to appoint J.H. Thomas to the post, but his hand was forced when Henderson made it clear that he was unwilling to accept any other position. The Prime Minister even considered taking the Foreign Office himself once again, but his experience five years earlier had convinced him that 'such dual posts were too much for the power of any man'.[1] He therefore decided to appoint Thomas as Lord Privy Seal, allowing Henderson to take the position that 'he had set his heart upon'.[2] Although Henderson and MacDonald had for years been the two most powerful figures in the Labour Party, there were important personal and ideological differences between them. MacDonald was by instinct and aptitude a far more cerebral figure than his Foreign Secretary, whose mind was described somewhat unfairly by Beatrice Webb as 'a clumsy instrument'. She was nevertheless sensitive to the fact that Henderson possessed 'a shrewdness in his judgement' that had allowed him to play a critical role in the development of the Labour Party during its first quarter century.[3] Nor was Henderson only interested in domestic issues. As a member of Lloyd George's War Cabinet he had played a major role in preparations for the controversial international socialist conference in Stockholm, as well as making a high profile visit to Petrograd in 1917 to persuade the Russian socialist parties to support the continued participation of their country in the war. In the years following the end of hostilities, he helped to establish the 'Hands-Off Russia' campaign that was designed to stymie any attempt by the British government to overthrow the new Bolshevik regime in Moscow. Henderson wrote a number of pamphlets on foreign policy during the years after 1918, which reflected both his strong commitment to the League and his dislike of the Paris peace settlement.[4] He was also of course a central player in the tentative moves by the first Labour Government to negotiate the Geneva Protocol in 1924. Henderson was inclined to look with some scepticism on the activities and demands of the

French government, widely identified within the Labour Party as an obstacle to attempts to build a genuinely new international order capable of overcoming the kind of national enmities that had erupted in 1914. Although he was sensitive to the fact that the League's origins made it vulnerable to the charge that it was little more than an organisation designed to police the peace treaties, Henderson always remained fundamentally optimistic about its potential to prevent a repetition of the events that had plunged Europe into war in 1914.

The socialist internationalism manifested by Henderson's enthusiastic leadership of the 'Hands-Off Russia' campaign had long faded when he took charge at the Foreign Office, by which time there was not a great deal to distinguish his views from those of League of Nations Union activists like Robert Cecil and Gilbert Murray. The new Foreign Secretary was an active member of the Wesleyan Methodist Church, which was strongly committed to the maintenance 'of international rights and general peace',[5] and his instinctive internationalism was forged as much by his religion as his socialism. Henderson was confident that the League offered the best hope of establishing a system of global security that would allow individual states to disarm confident in the knowledge that such a move would not make them vulnerable to attack. It is of course easy with the benefit of hindsight to ridicule such a position, but in 1929 the challenges of Manchuria and Abyssinia still lay far in the future. The new Foreign Secretary was in any case realistic enough to understand that effective collective security would not be achieved easily. Any utopian tendencies in his world-view were reined in by a shrewd recognition that international agreement of any kind always required patient negotiation and a readiness to compromise.

Henderson was Foreign Secretary in a minority government whose members were never certain how long they could remain in office.[6] There were also deep personal tensions between its leading members. The political situation was made more uncertain by the economic crisis that erupted in the wake of the Wall Street crash of 1929, and Philip Snowden at the Treasury was determined to use his position to influence British policy on such questions as reparations and war debts, given the increasingly precarious status of the public finances. Although there was always a certain disjunction between the domestic and foreign policies of the 1929–31 Labour Government, ministers nevertheless remained deeply sensitive to the demands of financial stringency. The fundamental problem faced by the second Labour Government in the international arena was the familiar one of seeking to defend global interests with limited resources. British policy towards Egypt, for example, was based on the search for a *modus vivendi* that would allow Britain to defend its strategic interests in the Suez Canal zone whilst limiting its costly military presence elsewhere in the country. British policy towards the United States was largely predicated on reaching an agreement on naval questions that would secure Britain's relative position whilst holding out the prospect of lower defence spending. Henderson himself was confident that a robust system of collective security of the kind he hoped to promote would not only make a future war less likely, but would also serve to reduce wasteful expenditure on armaments that could be better spent on more socially deserving causes.

Henderson and the Foreign Office

The prospect of a Labour government created far less political frisson in 1929 than five years previously, although the Party's manifesto still espoused a surprisingly radical rhetoric that firmly committed it to the construction of socialism in Britain. *Labour and the Nation* also committed the party to unstinting support for the League of Nations, as well as specific policies such as the restoration of diplomatic relations with Moscow and adherence to the so-called 'Optional Clause' (reviewed later), which provided for compulsory arbitration of international disputes by the International Court of Justice. Henderson's ironic suggestion to senior Foreign Office staff on coming to office that he was confident of their loyal support, despite 'the Bolshevik character of the present Administration', was made in the sure knowledge that his audience knew perfectly well that the new Government was deeply committed to the normal constitutional process.[7] Henderson's deputy Hugh Dalton nevertheless insisted on circulating copies of *Labour and the Nation* to senior Foreign Office officials, so that they would be in no doubt about the priorities of the new Government. Dalton himself later wrote that ministers had not required Foreign Office staff to 'invent' a foreign policy in 1929, arguing instead that the role of officials was to work out 'in practicable detail the solution of particular problems in the light of the general principles' laid down for them by politicians.[8] His claim was too simplistic. Although senior figures in the Labour Party had devoted a great of time to thinking about international politics in the 1920s, they still had to face the difficult problem of applying their ideals to a whole array of actual problems.

The constitutional position set down by Dalton shortly after the fall of the second Labour Government inevitably failed to capture the complexity of the foreign policy-making process during the period 1929–31. Foreign Office officials were not in practice reduced to the role of executing decisions made by their political masters, for the simple reason that such a clear division of labour was not possible. It is nevertheless true that Henderson and Dalton were both confident about their own judgements on foreign affairs. Henderson's Private Secretary, Walford Selby, later noted that his chief was an 'expert decentraliser' who deliberately chose to concentrate on major matters of policy leaving his staff to deal with more marginal issues.[9] The surviving Foreign Office correspondence confirms that Henderson was not particularly assiduous at reading the vast correspondence that came across his desk, a trait that led one of his senior officials to label the Foreign Secretary as 'constitutionally lazy',[10] but was in reality a reflection of his determination to make up his own mind on important issues. Henderson himself believed that his staff were 'all right so long as they're doing their routine',[11] but he was not impressed by their capacity to think imaginatively about international affairs, suspecting that the prevailing mood in the Foreign Office was sceptical about the policies set down in *Labour and the Nation*. The Foreign Secretary frequently lost his temper with his officials, even bawling them out on occasion in public, but most of them adapted without difficulty to such behaviour.[12] Whilst Henderson could on occasion be extremely acerbic, he was never viewed by his officials with the kind of fear that Curzon had attracted during his time at the Foreign Office.

Henderson's most difficult relationship was with Sir Ronald Lindsay, who served as Permanent Secretary prior to his departure for the Washington Embassy early in 1930. Lindsay was sceptical about the wisdom of signing the Optional Clause, fearing it would represent a major constraint on Britain's freedom of international manoeuvre, a position that was shared by many other officials and senior representatives of the armed forces. Both Henderson and Dalton were irritated by opposition to a policy they believed was a necessary adjunct of their declared commitment to collective security. They were also irritated by Lindsay's supposedly 'disloyal' tendency to deal direct with MacDonald on various questions of foreign policy,[13] although such a practice was in fact less unusual than they seemed to imagine. The personal relationship between Henderson and Lindsay's replacement as Permanent Secretary, Sir Robert Vansittart, who also enjoyed good relations with MacDonald, was by contrast much warmer. Vansittart nevertheless subsequently wrote that his chief was 'a very good man without being a very good Secretary of State',[14] questioning his judgement on a number of issues, ranging from the restoration of diplomatic relations with Moscow through to the use of information derived from secret intelligence sources. Such differences in turn masked a more fundamental distinction between the two men over international affairs. Vansittart remained instinctively wedded to the view that balance of power politics held the key to promoting British security both in Europe and beyond,[15] and whilst he entertained some hopes that the League might help to promote international security, he shared the prevailing Foreign Office view that Geneva was above all a location in which more traditional forms of international politics could be played out. The Foreign Secretary, by contrast, remained hopeful that the panoply of League meetings and institutions could provide the foundation for a new pattern of international relations that would in time supersede the conventions and practices of the past. Vansittart's own views on international affairs were increasingly dominated in the early 1930s by his anxiety about the potential threat to Britain should Germany ever break free from the shackles of Versailles, a view that he outlined with characteristic and colourful fluency in his celebrated 'Old Adam' series of papers.[16] The Permanent Secretary's manifest ability and outgoing personality meant that he commanded considerable respect among his colleagues, and he was without doubt the dominant official at the Foreign Office throughout the 1930s, but his influence on policy remained limited as long as Henderson was still in office. The Foreign Secretary was inclined to think of post-Versailles Germany in terms of its current weakness rather than its potential strength, and he was confident that 'the German question' could be resolved through the mechanisms of collective security. Although Vansittart's previous service as Principal Private Secretary to Baldwin and MacDonald provided him with an impressive array of contacts across the British political elite, it took some time for him to develop his own distinctive style, later characterised by Anthony Eden as 'a relentless, not to say ruthless, worker for the views he held strongly himself'.[17]

Henderson's dislike of the more bureaucratic and ceremonial elements of his job, when combined with the numerous demands on his time, also influenced his relations with British representatives in post abroad. The Foreign Secretary wrote very few personal letters to individual ambassadors and ministers, which removed an important channel of communication that had traditionally helped to keep those in the field abreast of opinion in London. Many of them, by contrast, continued to send in letters containing material that was for one reason or another considered unsuitable for a formal dispatch. Most ambassadors still assumed that it was part of their job to offer advice on questions of policy, more often than not emphasising the importance of the bilateral relationship between the British government and the government to which they were accredited. Before his death at the end of 1929, Esmé Howard in Washington stressed the importance of closer relations with the United States,[18] whilst Horace Rumbold in Berlin repeatedly advised the Foreign Secretary to support the government of Heinrich Brüning on the grounds that it was preferable to any likely alternative.[19] Some ambassadors, including William Tyrrell in Paris and George Grahame in Madrid, also maintained an extensive private correspondence with the Prime Minister, which gave them an alternative channel of influence on the foreign policy-making process in London. Since Henderson was not a particularly assiduous reader of telegrams and dispatches,[20] it is difficult to determine what use he made of the mass of material that arrived daily in Foreign Office from missions abroad. Once again, though, there seems to be some substance to Dalton's claim that the Foreign Secretary was not greatly inclined to pay much attention to the views of his advisers on important issues of policy, instinctively preferring to place more trust in his own experience and judgement.

Dalton himself was scathing in his analysis of the quality of the British diplomatic establishment, and his diary contained numerous unflattering judgements about the quality of individual officials. He condemned Alexander Cadogan (a future Permanent Secretary) as 'a sad stick' and William Strang (then a comparatively junior official but also subsequently Permanent Secretary) as 'competent but a bit squirmy'.[21] He was particularly critical of senior officials like Victor Wellesley (Deputy Under-Secretary) and George

Mounsey (an Assistant Under-Secretary), arguing that their long tenure in London ('home-stickers') meant that they were no longer in touch with developments abroad.[22] Dalton had more time for Vansittart ('a sound fellow'), although he still condemned the Permanent Secretary for preferring words to actions.[23] Foreign Office staff for their part laboured under no illusion about Dalton's attitude towards them, deeply resenting his efforts to play a central role in the day-to-day life of the Office. They were also concerned about the anomalous position of Robert Cecil, who was installed in the Foreign Office by Henderson as 'a kind of additional civil servant', charged with helping to coordinate British policy in London and Geneva.[24] Nor were they much happier about the role played by Henderson's Parliamentary Private Secretary, Philip Noel-Baker, an erstwhile academic and pacifist with a passionate commitment to disarmament. The presence of men like Dalton and Cecil in the Foreign Office represented a more or less conscious attempt on the part of the second Labour Government to ensure that the government's declared foreign policy objectives did not become bogged down in a welter of bureaucratic obfuscation and delay. Senior members of the British diplomatic establishment, for their part, sometimes feared that their professional *amour propre* was not always treated with due respect by their political 'masters'.

Henderson and the Cabinet

Henderson's time at the Foreign Office was made more difficult by his poor relationship with Ramsay MacDonald, the consequence of personal and political tensions that could be traced back over many years.[25] The Prime Minister remained deeply concerned with foreign affairs on his return to office, even though he decided against taking the Foreign Office himself for a second time, and he made it clear from the outset that he intended to keep Anglo-American relations in particular under his personal control. In practice, though, MacDonald also intervened across the whole range of foreign policy during the lifetime of the second Labour Government. The Prime Minister and Henderson were fundamentally at odds on the whole question of collective security and the League of Nations, a difference that had already been apparent five years earlier during the life of the first Labour Government, when it had been clear that Henderson's support for the Geneva Protocol ran far deeper than MacDonald's. MacDonald's views on foreign affairs had become more conventional than ever by the late 1920s, and he had apparently reconciled himself to the impossibility of securing any fundamental reordering of international politics, although he remained genuinely committed to the cause of disarmament. The Prime Minister's attitude towards the Optional Clause was at best lukewarm, despite the Labour Party's election pledge to support it, in part because he was concerned that the issue should not be allowed to cause a split between Britain and the Dominions. The Foreign Secretary had to fight hard both in the full Cabinet and Cabinet committee to win ministerial support for signing the Optional Clause with only a small number of reservations.[26] Although the most sustained opposition came from the service departments, most notably the Admiralty, MacDonald's refusal to offer unequivocal support inevitably made it harder for the Foreign Secretary to win the bureaucratic battle.[27] The same was true when Henderson came into conflict with Philip Snowden over international financial questions, although since the Prime Minister disliked his Chancellor at least as much as his Foreign Secretary, he was usually content to allow the two men to squabble with one another. MacDonald also tried to prevent Henderson from exerting much influence over the talks that took place at the London Naval Conference in 1930, in part because naval disarmament was so central to the course of Anglo-American relations, in which the Prime Minister took a particular interest. According to one senior member of the Labour Party, MacDonald was not averse to inspiring press attacks on Henderson,[28] a charge which if true would seem to suggest a degree of political spite, given that the Prime Minister possessed the authority to confront his Foreign Secretary in a more direct fashion.

Henderson's relationship with other senior ministers was also on occasion difficult. Philip Snowden was determined, as in 1924, to assert himself on questions of international finance, leading to the emergence of sharp divisions between the Foreign Secretary and Chancellor at the first Hague Conference on reparations in 1929. When the international financial crisis subsequently reached its peak, in the summer of 1931, Henderson pursued a course of action that was almost entirely at odds with the one favoured by the Treasury. The Foreign Secretary's deep commitment to disarmament and arbitration also frequently brought him into conflict with the service ministries. He was particularly critical of the First Lord of the Admiralty, Albert Alexander, who attracted opprobrium from both Henderson and Dalton for his uncritical readiness to follow the counsel of his service advisers.[29] Nor did Henderson enjoy good relations with J.H. Thomas, who had of course himself wanted the Foreign Office, but was instead appointed Lord Privy Seal before subsequently taking over at the Dominions Office. The Foreign Secretary did, though, generally co-operate quite well with Lord Passfield at the Colonial Office on the vexed questions of Egypt and Palestine. Despite his powerful personality and considerable political acumen, Henderson often preferred not to fight too directly in Cabinet for his chosen policies, preferring to take a subtler and less direct approach.[30] Dalton wrote in his diary that the Foreign Secretary proved himself to be an adept international negotiator during his time at the Foreign Office, combining patience and determination in order to secure his chosen objective.[31] He adopted a similar tactic with his Cabinet colleagues, making use of his long experience of internal Labour Party politics to judge how best to win support among ministers for his proposals.

Both Henderson and Dalton looked with suspicion on Sir Maurice Hankey, who exercised a good deal of influence on MacDonald, recognising that he had little instinctive sympathy with many of the policies they wanted to promote. The Cabinet Secretary was deeply sceptical about the decision to sign the Optional Clause, echoing the demands of the Admiralty for an extensive range of 'opt-outs' on such matters as belligerent rights. He also remained as doubtful as ever about the potential of the League of Nations to serve as the foundation for a new international order, and feared that it might simply serve to limit the freedom of the British government to decide under what circumstances it wished to fight. Henderson himself was schooled enough in the Byzantine politics of the Labour Party to understand that the struggle to determine policy took place as much in the myriad of Cabinet committees as it did in the full Cabinet itself. He regularly attended the meetings of the Committee of Imperial Defence, although he was not a particularly active contributor to the proceedings there, and sat on the numerous Cabinet committees established to deal with such questions as British policy towards Palestine and Egypt. The Foreign Secretary was also inevitably involved in debate about a whole range of domestic questions, as well as remaining General Secretary of the Labour Party, an activity that commanded a great deal of time, and was probably responsible for the perception in some quarters that he was inclined to neglect his duties at the Foreign Office. Many of those who worked with Henderson paid tribute to his energy – remarkable for a man who was heading for his late sixties by the time he took charge at the Foreign Office – and which allowed him to manage the competing demands of his time with surprising ease.

The reaction of the press to the election of the second Labour Government was far more muted than in 1924, whilst the decision by many Beaverbrook and Rothermere publications to devote their energy during 1929–30 to promoting imperial preference rather diverted their attention away from attacks on MacDonald and his colleagues.[32] The worsening economic situation did, though, eventually lead to calls in newspapers such as the *Manchester Guardian* for a National Government, a view subsequently endorsed by Geoffrey Dawson of *The Times*, despite his initial opposition to such a move. The Prime Minister himself dealt more skilfully with the press during his second administration than in 1924, although there were still strict limits to the support he was able to count on from Fleet Street. His appointment of Henderson to the Foreign Office came as a surprise to most editors and correspondents, who seemed to find it hard to imagine the new Foreign Secretary flourishing in a milieu so far removed from the one in which he had spent most of his working life. Henderson himself was not particularly adept at handling the press, with the result that he faced sharp attacks from time to time, perhaps most notably on his policy towards Egypt in 1929, reviewed in more detail below. He was by contrast generally able to rely on the warm support of the LNU, whose leaders welcomed the support of a man whose views on international relations bore a striking relation to their own.[33] He was also usually able to depend on a high level of support among the rank and file of the Labour Party, which helped to swell his influence within government, although Henderson himself paid little sustained attention to the various resolutions and policy documents produced by the Labour Party during his time at the Foreign Office. The impact of Party opinion was once again felt most strongly on the question of Russia. The Foreign Secretary was committed to the restoration of diplomatic relations with Moscow, as were his colleagues, but the complex financial and diplomatic questions involved forced them to take a more cautious line than many of the Party's grassroots members.[34] Whilst many Labour activists blamed the Foreign Office for the delays in reaching agreement with the Soviet government, reflecting their traditional suspicion of the denizens of 'the Box', in reality the Board of Trade and the Treasury also played a major part in urging caution about the terms on which diplomatic relations should be resumed.[35] The return of British diplomats to Moscow at the end of 1929 only came about following six months of hard bargaining.

The following pages examine Henderson's role in formulating the British response to a number of important international developments during the life of the second Labour Government: the dismissal of Lord Lloyd as High Commissioner in Egypt; the management of reparations and war debts; and the events surrounding the London Naval Conference of 1930. Each of these developments provided the Foreign Secretary with a distinct series of challenges, requiring him to identify ways of ensuring that his own views received a hearing within the whirlpool of the policy-making process. The tension between Henderson and other senior Cabinet ministers repeatedly placed important constraints on his ability to mobilise support. The Foreign Secretary nevertheless generally proved shrewd enough to find ways of ensuring that his voice was always heard when important international questions were at stake.

Henderson and the making of foreign policy during the second Labour Government

Ministers in the second Labour Government showed little desire to reform the British diplomatic establishment, despite the long-standing distrust expressed by many party members about the culture and operation of traditional diplomacy. Henderson and Dalton were confident of asserting themselves in the face of any qualms expressed by their professional advisers over the wisdom of placing collective security and disarmament at the heart of British foreign policy. Whilst the Foreign Secretary was happy to see Sir Ronald Lindsay leave the Foreign Office for the United States at the start of 1930, given their disagreement over such matters as the Optional Clause, the erstwhile Permanent Secretary was himself keen to take up residence at the Washington Embassy. The dramatic resignation of Lord Lloyd as High Commissioner in Egypt in July 1929 was, by contrast, a more complex business.[36] Lloyd was known to be critical of the new government's determination to negotiate a treaty clarifying the ambiguous semi-colonial relationship between Britain and Egypt, and his forced departure from office was seen by many in the Conservative Party and the national press as a vindictive act of political spite. In reality, though, whilst there was a certain degree of symbolism in Lloyd's dismissal, reflecting ministers' determination to assert their chosen policy, the High Commissioner had been at odds with the Foreign Office in London long before the Labour government was returned to power.

Lloyd's position as High Commissioner in Cairo, which he first took up in 1925, was decidedly ambiguous. Although the British government had announced as early as 1922 that it planned to intervene less frequently in future in the internal affairs of Egypt, British officials resident in the country continued to play a major role in the administration throughout the following years. As a result, Lloyd's belief that he was not simply 'a common-or-garden ambassador' did not just reflect the personal grandiosity of a man who had previously been a long-serving Governor of Bombay.[37] The High Commissioner took a different view of Anglo-Egyptian relations from most members of the diplomatic establishment even when Austen Chamberlain was still in charge of the Foreign Office. He was intensely wary of any reduction of the British military and civilian presence in Egypt, arguing that such a withdrawal was likely to compromise the security of the Suez Canal and the Sudan, as well as undermining orderly government across the country. The Foreign Office was by contrast more inclined during the second half of the 1920s to take a 'liberal' view of policy towards Egypt, predicated on running down the British presence except in areas of particular sensitivity and importance. Sir Nevile Henderson, who served as Lloyd's deputy in Cairo, noted in his memoirs that he did not see 'eye to eye' with the High Commissioner on many subjects,[38] whilst officials in the Egyptian Department in London were convinced of the need to reduce the British presence in Egypt. Chamberlain himself never developed a good personal relationship with Lloyd, writing to his sister in October 1927 that 'Lord Lloyd does not heartily accept my policy and my principal advisers would wish me to get rid of him'.[39] Vansittart, who was himself close to Lloyd, noted in his memoirs that a cabal of officials in London were convinced that the dismissal of the High Commissioner was necessary in order to promote a viable Egyptian policy.[40]

The dislike of Lloyd expressed by many members of the Foreign Office stemmed in part from real differences over policy, but it also reflected resentment at the activities of an 'outsider' who was not a career member of the Diplomatic Service. The diplomatic establishment seldom welcomed others 'muscling in' on important jobs that they believed should be held by one of their own number. Lloyd's biographer suggests that Labour ministers including Henderson deliberately took advantage of these tensions on coming to office in order to engineer a crisis that allowed them to assert their authority, whilst officials in London also put pressure on the Foreign Secretary to take decisive steps. Ronald Lindsay repeatedly told Henderson that Lloyd had never been 'completely in harmony' with the Egyptian policy laid down by London over the previous few years, and made no secret of his desire to see the High Commissioner removed, a view that was echoed by other senior officials including William Tyrrell.[41] Following consultation with MacDonald, who drafted some of the relevant telegrams in person, Henderson informed Lloyd that his perusal of the files on Egypt had raised doubts whether the High Commissioner's views could be reconciled 'with those of either my predecessor or myself'. He therefore asked him to return to London for consultation.[42] There was something disingenuous about the Foreign Secretary's implication that Lloyd's position had become untenable simply because of disagreements over policy. In a painful face-to-face interview that took place after the High Commissioner returned home, Henderson reputedly told him that 'the fact is there are certain members of my party who don't like you',[43] clearly suggesting that the reasons for Lloyd's dismissal were indeed partly a consequence of crude political calculation.

Lloyd's dismissal predictably roused fury in some quarters, even though Henderson made a masterly speech in the House of Commons, defending the government's action in the face of charges that it might deter other British representatives from speaking with 'candour' in the future. The sacking of the High Commissioner signalled ministers' determination to assert their right to make policy, but the Prime Minister and Foreign Secretary were able to make such a bold move secure in the knowledge that they could point to Lloyd's long-standing disagreements with the Chamberlain Foreign Office as evidence that they were not acting out of political vindictiveness. In the months that followed, though, Henderson and MacDonald's views on Egypt began to diverge, whilst at least some of the Foreign Secretary's own officials came to question the way in which he handled the negotiations with the Egyptian government that opened in London in the spring of 1930.[44] The Prime Minister commented adversely in his diary on a number of occasions about Henderson's handling of Egyptian affairs,[45] and Dalton subsequently wrote in his memoirs that the Foreign Secretary was forced at one point to threaten resignation in order to assert his right to conduct Egyptian business as he thought best.[46] The tactic seems to have worked, and Henderson was largely successful in facing down his domestic critics during the talks over a new treaty.[47] His eventual failure to reach agreement with the Egyptian representatives who came to London early in 1930 was primarily the result of problems created by the complicated political situation in Cairo, rather than a consequence of any sustained opposition from within the British government.

It was noted earlier that there was almost perpetual tension between Henderson and Snowden throughout the life of the 1929–31 Labour government, a conflict that was based both on a clash of personality and more concrete disagreements over policy. The Hague Conference on reparations that assembled just a few weeks after the MacDonald administration took office was summoned to discuss changes to the pattern of German reparation payments, in the light of the recent Young Report, as well as setting down a corresponding timetable for the withdrawal of allied forces from the Rhineland. Snowden made it clear in a paper circulated to the Cabinet in the middle of July that he was opposed to the changes proposed by the Young Committee, which effectively required Britain to accept a disproportionate share of a proposed reduction in reparation payments by Germany.[48] The Cabinet supported his views,[49] giving some credence to the Chancellor's subsequent claim that the tough line he pursued at the Hague Conference had received prior sanction from his fellow ministers. On the first day of the Conference, Snowden made a characteristically trenchant speech in which he argued that although the British government was ready to consider a settlement that would 'wipe the slate clean of all international debts and reparations', as long as they existed Britain would insist on 'being fairly treated in this matter'.[50] A few days later, he followed up this performance with an even more acerbic intervention, condemning a proposal by the French Finance Minister as 'grotesque and ridiculous', a charge that predictably aroused the fury of the French delegation. Dalton condemned the Chancellor for 'yelling insults at foreigners',[51] whilst Henderson was infuriated at an outburst that threatened to prevent agreement among members of the political commission who were discussing the evacuation of the Rhineland. The whole situation was made still more complex when a message from the Prime Minister urging the need for compromise was inadvertently transmitted to the Hague *en clair*, thereby revealing the deep split among members of the British delegation, and potentially weakening their bargaining position in talks on both financial and political questions.[52]

Henderson was profoundly unhappy at the prospect that disagreement over a comparatively small sum of money – around two million pounds – might endanger a political agreement that he believed would do much to help the pacification of Europe. He therefore devoted a huge amount of energy to smoothing away the tensions raised by the Chancellor's speech, playing a central role in the Political Commission that he chaired, and which eventually came up with an agreed formula governing the withdrawal of allied troops from the Rhineland.[53] Snowden's outburst was motivated in part by his genuine concern over the financial implications for Britain of the Young Report, but it also reflected his long-standing belief that the French represented the main obstacle to peace. The splits in the British delegation at the first Hague Conference starkly revealed the extent of divisions over foreign affairs within the second Labour Government, as well as providing a dramatic illustration of the way in which the management of international financial questions had the potential to check the power of the Foreign Office. They also revealed the scale of the personal tension between the Foreign Secretary and the Chancellor of the Exchequer. MacDonald shrewdly noted in his diary a few weeks after the end of the Conference that the two men had 'laid in a vast store of ill-will for each other', a development that exercised a profound influence on their relationship over the following two years.[54]

The disagreements between the departments headed by Snowden and Henderson showed themselves on a number of other occasions during 1929–31. There was a degree of tension over the question of personnel appointments in the Foreign Office (including that of Vansittart as Permanent Secretary).[55] The Treasury also looked askance at proposals to establish a new economic section within the Foreign Office, fearing that such a development might usurp its own influence and expertise in international affairs.[56] The role of financial questions in provoking discord within the government was particularly pronounced during the crisis of 1931, when Henderson found himself at odds with both Snowden and MacDonald over the whole question of reparations and war debts. The proposal by President Hoover in June 1931 for a one-year moratorium on the payment of reparations and war debts, in response to yet another financial crisis in Germany, was welcomed by the British government both as a response to the immediate situation and as a possible long-term foundation for resolving the whole issue. Snowden's deep-seated francophobia meant that he was predictably unconcerned by the likely reaction of the French government to a proposal to end German reparation payments, telling the Cabinet in early July that he hoped Paris would put aside its concerns and act on the President's initiative.[57] The Treasury was also, of course, deeply sensitive to the likely impact of the failure of the German banking system on the health of Britain's financial institutions. Henderson similarly welcomed the Hoover proposal, but was more sensitive to the fact that French reservations might undermine the prospect of agreement for an international moratorium on debt payments,[58] and was subsequently inclined to seek firm concessions from Berlin as a *quid pro quo* for international financial support. The Cabinet for its part repeatedly authorised the Prime Minister, the Foreign Secretary and the Chancellor to act on the whole issue as they thought best. This complex international and domestic situation provided the background to a determined attempt by Henderson to promote his own views on policy in the middle of July in virtual defiance of his two most senior colleagues.[59]

Henderson travelled to Paris on 14 July to discuss a range of international issues, including the agenda for a visit that he was shortly scheduled to make to Berlin in company with the Prime Minister. On the day after his arrival, though, MacDonald telephoned Henderson asking him to cancel the projected trip to Berlin, since the Prime Minister now intended to convene a major international conference in London on the financial crisis. French politicians were perturbed at such a prospect, fearing that it might create pressure for a more conciliatory policy towards Germany, and the Foreign Minister Aristide Briand questioned the idea of a London conference in a meeting with his British counterpart. The records of the meeting show that Henderson made no effort to defend MacDonald's proposal for a Conference, instead suggesting that the Prime Minister should still accompany him on a visit to Berlin in order to 'sound the German government'.[60] The Foreign Secretary's subsequent telegram to London, along with a general summary of events that he wrote a few days later, concealed the fact that he had flouted the Prime Minister's wishes.[61] MacDonald nevertheless continued to insist on his proposals for a London Conference, prompted in large part by the deep anxiety of the financial authorities at the scale of sterling withdrawals from the City.[62] Snowden added to the pressure by telegraphing the Foreign Secretary in Paris to emphasise that the financial authorities were convinced that Germany could never obtain financial stability 'so long as reparation liabilities are insisted upon'.[63]

Henderson knew that the kind of 'revisionist' proposals favoured by the Treasury would cause immense anxiety to the French government, making the international situation still more difficult, and it was presumably for this reason that he decided to invite German representatives to visit Paris in order to discuss the crisis. MacDonald was infuriated by his Foreign Secretary's action, both because he sought no prior approval, and because the move threatened to undermine plans for the London Conference. The Prime Minister made it clear to the French government that he was unwilling to send any senior British representatives to Paris to discuss financial matters, and emphasised that Britain would not take part in any loan to Germany, given the impossibility of restoring the German economy without a fundamental review of reparations. Hidden beneath these complex machinations was a struggle to determine the direction of British policy. Henderson believed that the financial crisis could only be resolved if the French were given some incentive to offer financial assistance to Germany, in return for political concessions on such questions as the German-Austrian Customs Union, whilst Snowden and (increasingly) MacDonald were convinced that no real improvement could take place without agreeing to a wholesale reform of reparations. Snowden's instinct had always been to bully the French into changing their policy. Henderson was by contrast enough of a diplomat to recognise that Britain needed to respond to the perennial concern of Paris in all matters relating to Germany. His 'personal diplomacy' involved a considerable degree of dissimulation, and there is little doubt that he was stretching his authority and independence to the limit, but the Foreign Secretary was in reality a shrewder judge of the diplomatic and political realities underlying the financial crisis than his colleagues back in London.

The events surrounding the London Naval Conference that assembled early in 1930 highlighted a series of disagreements within the second Labour Government over the best way of approaching vital questions of international security. The process once again showed the problems faced by Henderson when trying to assert himself in the policy-making process. Ministers were committed to supporting the various attempts to promote disarmament that had been under way at Geneva since 1925,[64] which were widely seen across the Labour Party as a vital component of the search for collective security. There was, though, also a more practical reason to support efforts to control the level of international armaments: namely, the desire to place limits on the build-up of military forces that might be used to challenge Britain's global interests. During the months before the second Labour Government came to power, senior figures in the Foreign Office had become sharply critical of the service departments' sustained opposition to proposals for arms limitation. Ronald Lindsay even went so far as to suggest in March 1929 that their objections should be 'brushed aside' in order to allow the Foreign Office to put forward 'a serious programme' outlining a framework for international agreement on disarmament.[65] MacDonald for his part returned to office determined to improve relations with the United States, a prospect that had become somewhat more feasible following Herbert Hoover's recent accession to the Presidency in place of Coolidge, but the Prime Minister was also firmly committed to maintaining a strong Royal Navy.[66] MacDonald's determination to play the decisive role in Anglo-American relations in general, and naval disarmament in particular, placed considerable constraints on the ability of other ministers to exercise a decisive influence on developments. Although Henderson repeatedly sought to use his position during 1929–30 to support naval disarmament, a position that ironically for once placed him on the same side of the debate as Snowden, his direct influence on the policy-making process was always limited.

MacDonald worked feverishly in the weeks after coming to office in an effort to identify the broad outlines of a possible deal with the United States government over naval disarmament. Henderson was by contrast not personally much involved in the detailed exchanges that took place between London and Washington during the summer of 1929, which focused on such convoluted questions as how best to compare different classes of cruiser. His views in practice seem to have broadly echoed those of the Foreign Office's leading naval expert – Robert Craigie – who believed that Britain required an agreement with the United States in order to prevent the emergence of 'a definite American naval superiority'.[67] Henderson did not accompany MacDonald on his trip to the United States in October 1929, during which the Prime Minister continued his search for some kind of understanding with Washington, reflecting the Foreign Secretary's marginal role both in Anglo-American affairs in general and questions of naval disarmament in particular. MacDonald was delighted by his reception in America, believing that his trip had done much to improve the tone of relations between London and Washington,[68] although a close inspection reveals that the concrete results were less striking than the Prime Minister believed.[69]

It had been agreed prior to MacDonald's American visit that a five-power naval conference should be summoned in London early in 1930, comprising representatives from the United States, Britain, Japan, France and Italy. Henderson served on the Cabinet Committee that discussed preparations for the Conference,[70] and was also a member of the main British delegation, which was given considerable independence by the Cabinet to decide how best to handle the negotiations.[71] During a meeting of the Cabinet Committee, on 9 January, the Foreign Secretary vehemently argued that a sustained effort should be made to use the Conference to promote real disarmament rather than to secure simple agreement on complex questions of parity between the various navies,[72] but his proposals were viewed at the time with scepticism both by senior naval representatives and by the Prime Minister himself. A few days later, though, MacDonald used a press conference to announce that he was willing to consider a freeze on battleship construction (a move already favoured by the American delegation).[73] MacDonald's sudden change of heart was probably due as much to the influence of Snowden as Henderson, for the Chancellor was determined to seize any opportunity to reduce the costs of naval construction,[74] but the Foreign Secretary's intervention certainly reflected his determination to counter the navy lobby's influence on the negotiations. Henderson was also vocal throughout the first few months of 1930 on the question of French and Italian naval disarmament, which proved in the event to be a particularly intractable problem given Italy's determination to assert its right to equality with its neighbour to the west. He was initially sceptical about calls for some kind of Mediterranean Pact, which was desired by the French as a means of increasing their security, pointing out in a meeting of the British delegation that the League Covenant and the Kellog Pact already provided the kind of 'definite guarantees' sought by Paris. MacDonald shared his Foreign Secretary's views, and was as determined as ever to avoid extending any kind of British guarantee to France beyond those inherent in Britain's existing treaty commitments.[75] Henderson, though, subsequently became more sympathetic to French security concerns, and privately made clear that he was ready to consider strengthening the League Covenant in a way that would make for a more binding British commitment,[76] but he was unable to persuade his colleagues to re-consider their earlier position. The French and Italians in any case proved unable to reach an agreement, with the result that the London Conference concluded in April only with a three-power agreement between Britain, the United States and Japan. Henderson worked hard over the year that followed to search for agreement between France and Italy, but he was never able to bridge the gap between them, and became increasingly frustrated by the refusal of the French to give serious consideration to any proposals that might reduce the country's military strength.

One historian of the London Naval Conference has noted that 'MacDonald retained complete control over the negotiations'.[77] Another has suggested that the Conference paved the way for the restoration of the Foreign Office as *primus inter pares* in foreign policy-making (including policy towards the United States).[78] The two statements are not in fact so contradictory as they might at first appear. Despite the Prime Minister's determination to act as a pivotal figure in both Anglo-American relations and naval disarmament questions, his views were not so far removed from those of the Foreign Office in general, and the Foreign Secretary in particular. Henderson and MacDonald both believed in the importance of improving relations with Washington following the débacle of the Coolidge Conference of 1927. The two men also favoured disarmament both as a matter of principle and as a way of controlling defence expenditure without weakening Britain's international military position. It would therefore be unwise to assume that the Prime Minister's determination to take the lead in relations with the USA and on naval disarmament necessarily represented a straightforward 'defeat' for Henderson. The Foreign Secretary and his senior staff were broadly happy with the direction of policy on both these issues in 1929–30, even though Henderson himself believed that a more determined attempt could be made to lower the level of naval armaments, whilst senior Foreign Office officials like Craigie actually played an important part in framing British proposals at the London Conference. The Foreign Secretary was under the circumstances reasonably pleased with the outcome of the talks that took place in the first few months of 1930.

Conclusion

Arthur Henderson played an important role in the complex political machinations that led to the disintegration of the Labour Government in August 1931, becoming leader of the Labour Party following his refusal to support MacDonald in the formation of a National Government designed to deal with the financial crisis.[79] A few months later he became Chairman of the Geneva Disarmament Conference, playing a tireless if ultimately futile role in seeking to forge an agreement between the major powers to reduce worldwide expenditure on armaments. The article on Henderson published in one of the best-known collections of essays on inter-war diplomacy was included in the section dealing with 'fighters for lost causes', a judgement that was presumably designed to emphasise his ultimate failure to promote collective security and international disarmament.[80] There is undoubtedly some justice in this verdict. The descent of Europe into the turmoil of the 'low dishonest decade' of the 1930s starkly illustrated the futility of the various attempts that had been made since 1918 to institute a new diplomacy that would prevent national rivalries from ever again exploding into war. Arthur Henderson was, though, always a practical utopian. His prosaic temperament and long experience in the bruising world of Labour Party politics prevented him from falling prey to the more visionary fancies of the pacifists and romantics, who hoped that the mere creation of new international institutions could automatically break down older patterns of international rivalry. Collective security and disarmament were for Henderson always ideals that needed to be worked for by the familiar processes of lengthy negotiation and compromise. It was for this reason that he proved able to bounce back from the numerous setbacks and disappointments he faced in the final years of his life.

Henderson adjusted remarkably well to the rarefied atmosphere of the Foreign Office and its arcane procedures when he took charge there in the summer of 1929, managing to assert himself without alienating the men who worked for him, despite his occasionally ferocious outbursts of temper. The man who had started his working life as an apprentice in a Newcastle engineering works never felt particularly comfortable with the more ceremonial aspects of his job, but nor was he overwhelmed by the complexity of the problems with which he was forced to deal. Whilst Foreign Office staff often resented the activities of Dalton and Cecil, they were surprisingly relaxed when confronted by a Foreign Secretary who could be decidedly blunt in speech, and did not always make much effort to conceal his belief that his officials were out of touch with the demands of a changing world. The real opposition to many of the policies favoured by Henderson came not from within the Foreign Office but from his own ministerial colleagues. The Foreign Secretary's passionate support for collective security and disarmament was entirely in accord with the promises outlined in *Labour and the Nation* before the 1929 election. The position he took on most of the major controversies that confronted him when in office were in line with the spirit of that document. Henderson was convinced that Britain's national interests could best be promoted by fostering a new spirit of internationalism, embodied in the League, which would in time provide new mechanisms for resolving disagreements and tensions without resort to war. It was Ramsay MacDonald, by contrast, who seemed to feel most reservations about offering unconditional support for a strong League of Nations. Despite his earlier radicalism in matters of international politics, the Prime Minister increasingly articulated the kind of realist view that had long been espoused by his Cabinet Secretary and by many leading Conservative politicians, based on support for a strong navy and a desire to prevent Britain from accepting commitments that might impose constraints on her freedom of manoeuvre in times of crisis. Arthur Henderson had many of the skills required to thrive at the Foreign Office. He could master a brief effectively. He possessed the authority and acumen needed to hold his own in the various disagreements about international affairs that divided ministers in the second Labour Government. He was a shrewd administrator who had the confidence to delegate minor matters to his officials. There may have been something idealistic in the Foreign Secretary's long-standing hope that it would in time be possible to change the character of international politics, but he always took a decidedly hard-headed view of the policy-making process itself, recognising the limits it placed on his ability to advance his chosen objectives. It was for this reason that he was so adept at doggedly pursuing his objectives whilst remaining sensitive to the constraints under which he operated.

6   Sir John Simon at the Foreign Office (1931–35)

Introduction

Five men served as Foreign Secretary between the collapse of the Labour Government in the summer of 1931 and the outbreak of the Second World War eight years later. The Liberal peer Lord Reading was only at the Foreign Office for a few weeks at the start of Ramsay MacDonald's first coalition government. Sir John Simon served there from the autumn 1931 until the summer of June 1935, whilst Sir Samuel Hoare's brief tenure of office ended in his resignation from office just six months later, in the wake of the political storm that erupted following publication of his agreement with the French premier Pierre Laval over the future of Abyssinia. His successor Anthony Eden also resigned from office, in February 1938, ostensibly because he no longer felt able to support Neville Chamberlain's search for improved relations with Mussolini's Italy and Hitler's Germany. Lord Halifax, who took over at the Foreign Office following Eden's resignation, was at first happy to support the Prime Minister's policy, but he too became increasingly critical of Chamberlain's handling of foreign affairs in the months following the Munich crisis of September 1938. The Foreign Office proved to be even more of a poisoned chalice in Auden's 'low, dishonest decade' than was the case in the 1920s.

The vast literature on appeasement that has appeared over the past forty years or so has shown the danger of making glib judgements about British foreign policy in the 1930s. British policy-makers faced huge constraints on their freedom of action throughout the decade, ranging from the country's economic and military weakness, through to the dominions' caution at the prospect of being dragged into a European war. The rise of the Nazi regime in Germany posed a fundamental challenge to the international framework set up at Versailles and Locarno, whilst the growing political instability in central and south-eastern Europe created a political vacuum that Berlin and Rome were both determined to fill. In the Far East, Japan's determination to assert itself as the dominant regional power threatened long-standing British interests in the region. The global economic malaise that fuelled regime change across much of Europe itself became part of the warp and woof of international conflict, as disagreements over such issues as tariffs and access to raw materials became important sources of global tension. Nor was it easy for successive British governments to identify effective strategies for dealing with these problems. The perennial political instability in Paris often rendered France an uncertain ally, and the growing isolationist ethos in the USA made it difficult to secure reliable support from Washington. To make matters worse, the failure of the League of Nations to respond effectively to Japan's aggression towards China in 1931–32 demonstrated graphically the impotence of the system of collective security established at the Paris Peace Conference more than a decade earlier. British governments throughout the 1930s continued to face the unenviable problem of exercising a high degree of international responsibility without the commensurate power. The men who headed the Foreign Office during these years all too often found themselves being held responsible for damaging international developments which were often far beyond their control.

Few foreign secretaries have attracted so much criticism from their contemporaries as Sir John Simon, who headed the Foreign Office between 1931 and 1935. Nor has posterity been much kinder to him, despite the sterling efforts of his biographer.[1] Simon was one of the targets of Cato's celebrated polemic against the 'Guilty Men' of appeasement,[2] and he has ever since been indelibly associated with Britain's failure to respond to the challenge of the dictators in the years before the Second World War, not least because of the policies he implemented as Foreign Secretary during the first half of the 1930s. It is, though, difficult to see how any individual could have dealt successfully with such threatening developments as Japan's aggression in the Far East and Nazi Germany's increasingly flagrant repudiation of the Versailles settlement. The poor state of Britain's defences and finances in the first half of the decade denied the country the resources to respond effectively to a series of global challenges, each of which could plausibly be presented as a threat to vital national interests. Diplomacy alone could not cope with problems that demanded a more co-ordinated response cutting across departmental boundaries. Any assessment of the charges made against Simon during his time at the Foreign Office must therefore take into account the circumstances under which he laboured. Would any other individual have been able to devise a more effective way of dealing with the international situation in the early 1930s? And, equally pertinently, could any other minister have identified strategies for mobilising the weight of the government machine behind such policies? Such counterfactual questions must of course remain without definitive answer, but the following pages suggest that a cruel dilemma faced all those charged with directing Britain's relations with the wider world in the 1930s. Whilst an effective response to the increasingly dangerous international environment required close co-operation among a number of government departments, the complex character of such a bureaucratic-political process actually made it harder to formulate imaginative and appropriate policies. Although the phenomenon was not a new one, it became more pronounced than ever during the first half of the 1930s.

Simon suffered from incessant press attacks throughout his time at the Foreign Office. Liberal papers such as the *Manchester Guardian* and the *News Chronicle* censured him for not responding robustly enough to Japanese aggression against China. Conservative papers like the *Daily Express* and the *Daily Mail* accused him of failing to provide a strong lead in foreign affairs. Only J.L. Garvin of the *Observer* proved to be a reliable supporter. There were a number of press campaigns for Simon's resignation, most notably during the crisis caused by Germany's withdrawal from the Disarmament Conference in October 1933, and again in the spring of 1935 following Berlin's announcement of its intention to reintroduce conscription. His position was made more vulnerable by the political complexion of the first National Government, formed by Ramsay MacDonald in the summer of 1931, in the wake of the collapse of the second Labour Government. As leader of the Liberal Nationals, Simon often found himself isolated in a government dominated by Conservatives and led by an erstwhile socialist, a dilemma that became still more pronounced after the withdrawal of the Samuelite Liberals in September 1932 over imperial preference.[3] He was as a result seldom able to rely on the wholehearted support of his Cabinet colleagues during the bleak times when he faced a mauling in the press.

Simon was by background a distinguished lawyer, who first entered Parliament in the Liberal landslide of 1906, before being appointed Solicitor-General at the age of just thirty-seven. He subsequently entered the Cabinet as Attorney-General in 1913, and was appointed Home Secretary two years later, before resigning shortly afterwards over the introduction of conscription. In the 1920s he played a part in the various political machinations that witnessed the Liberal Party's decline from its erstwhile political pre-eminence into a series of ill-tempered factions divided by personality and ideology. It is no easy matter to identify with any precision Simon's views on international issues during the 1920s. During the years before he came to office, his occasional pronouncements on foreign affairs usually reflected the characteristic Liberal belief in the virtues of collective security, along with suspicion of such supposedly outmoded phenomena as balance-of-power politics.[4] He was certainly not well-versed in the intricacies of British diplomacy when he arrived at the Foreign Office in November 1931, in place of Lord Reading, although the new Foreign Secretary did have the advantage of being a good linguist. His chairmanship of a Commission reviewing Indian government in the late 1920s had given him extensive insight into questions of imperial administration, but little real opportunity to expand his knowledge of international politics or the problems of imperial defence. His appointment to the Foreign Office was predictably well received by such stalwarts of the League of Nations Union as Robert Cecil and Gilbert Murray, who believed that Simon shared their instinctive internationalism and anti-militarism, but fate decreed that the new Foreign Secretary never had the luxury of a honeymoon period in which to master the details of his new job. He was instead immediately confronted by the conflict between Japan and China that had erupted a few weeks earlier, in September 1931, following an alleged incident of sabotage against the Japanese controlled South Manchurian railway (the so-called Mukden incident). The international response to the Far Eastern crisis of 1931–32 starkly revealed both the fragility of collective security and the limits of British power in a region six thousand miles from home. Simon quickly became a scapegoat for the British government's failure to respond more robustly to Japanese aggression against China, thereby damaging his reputation and weakening his authority throughout his remaining years at the Foreign Office.

Simon and the Foreign Office

Simon probably travelled abroad more frequently during his time in office than any previous British Foreign Secretary, attending countless international conferences and League meetings, as well as visiting numerous capitals for bilateral talks. Although he was confident of dealing with the resulting fatigue, he feared that his absence from London was 'not good for our foreign policy'.[5] It certainly made it difficult for him to establish an effective relationship with his Foreign Office advisers. Simon was not a popular figure with members of the British diplomatic establishment. Nor was he viewed as an effective minister. Anthony Eden (who served as his junior minister) noted that Simon found it difficult to delegate effectively,[6] whilst Austen Chamberlain heard that he was poor at giving 'direction' to his officials, who consequently found it hard to fathom 'what he is at or what they should try for'.[7] Simon's aloof personality did nothing to help matters. Although his awkward manner concealed a degree of shyness, as well as an innate decency, it was certainly not calculated to win the loyalty of his staff. The texture of his relationship with Sir Robert Vansittart remains particularly opaque. Simon mentioned his Permanent Secretary just once in his (admittedly uninformative) memoirs.[8] Vansittart, by contrast, wrote a surprisingly affectionate account of his erstwhile chief.[9] Vansittart continued to interpret his role as that of expert adviser and principal channel of advice to the Foreign Secretary. He was also confident enough to provide Simon with advice about how best to deal with the Cabinet during discussions of foreign affairs.[10] The Permanent Secretary's own views on the international situation were as ever dominated by his fear of Germany, which became still stronger following Hitler's rise to power in 1933, and he continued to write numerous memoranda and minutes suggesting possible ways of responding to the threat. Simon was for his part generally more confident that judicious concessions to Berlin might encourage governments there to adopt a more moderate line abroad. Vansittart always feared that his political master lacked the determination to defend the Foreign Office's position in Cabinet, and it was partly for this reason that he felt impelled to fight so hard for his chosen policies in settings such as the Defence Requirements Committee, along with the other inter-departmental committees on which the Foreign Office was represented. His fears were echoed by officials such as Ralph Wigram, the politically astute First Secretary at the Paris Embassy, who returned to London to take charge of the Central Department.[11] Although there were growing divisions within the Foreign Office during the first half of the 1930s about how best to deal with the deteriorating international position, there was nevertheless widespread agreement among officials that Simon was too inclined to shelter behind the principle of collective responsibility in order to avoid taking difficult decisions himself. There was also a pervasive sense that he lacked the imagination and skill to devise an effective foreign policy.

Austen Chamberlain told one of his sisters in August 1933 that Simon was unpopular with British ambassadors abroad since he failed to provide them with clear instructions or advice.[12] He added that the Foreign Secretary never sent private letters to heads of British missions. This second claim was not in fact true. Simon wrote fewer private letters to British ambassadors than most of his predecessors, but this was largely because he was so often away from London, and he certainly read the correspondence sent to him by ambassadors such as Francis Lindley in Tokyo and Ronald Graham in Rome. Chamberlain's critical views of Simon were partly based on information that he received from William Tyrrell, ambassador to Paris and a long-time Chamberlain confidante, who made little secret of his deep loathing of Simon.[13] Chamberlain's own dislike of Simon was in any case so intense that his opinions cannot necessarily be trusted.[14] There is nevertheless considerable evidence that the supposed drift of British diplomacy under Simon irritated many senior diplomats in post abroad. Even the normally emollient Alexander Cadogan, who was based in Geneva for much of the early 1930s, noted ruefully in a letter to Eden in January 1933 that 'To navigate difficult seas you must have both a chart and a captain. I had hoped to get the latter, but you know the difficulties that have arisen there'.[15]

Eden's own relationship with Simon has been obscured down the years by the younger man's subsequent use of his voluminous memoirs to attack the 'appeasers', among whom he numbered his erstwhile chief.[16] In reality, as will be seen in a later chapter, Eden's status as a supporter of the League and a strident critic of the dictators was more ambiguous in the first half of the 1930s than he later suggested.[17] His appointment as substitute head of the British delegation at the Disarmament Conference, at the start of 1933, nevertheless provided him with an opportunity to bolster his reputation among League enthusiasts back in Britain.[18] MacDonald first pointed out the need for such an appointment, arguing that Simon could not provide the British delegation with the necessary continuity,[19] a view accepted by the Foreign Secretary, who added that his frequent presence at Geneva also had the unfortunate effect of encouraging representatives from other countries to look constantly to Britain for a lead. The Prime Minister was initially reluctant to select Eden for such a post, arguing that he lacked the requisite political weight, but the Foreign Secretary was quite happy at the prospect and even noted that he was ready to accept the younger man as a kind of 'Assistant Foreign Secretary'.[20] Nor does Simon seem to have been unduly perturbed when Eden was appointed Lord Privy Seal at the end of 1933, although he was always angered by rumours that the younger man might soon be appointed as his successor. The extensive private correspondence between Simon and Eden was generally good-natured, perhaps surprisingly so on the part of the younger man, and gives little evidence of any fundamental and sustained difference on policy. Eden preferred to reserve his most barbed comments for his diary. The younger man was not averse to using his close relationship with Stanley Baldwin to by-pass Simon, perhaps most notably at the start of 1933, when he proposed to the Conservative leader that Britain should compile a draft disarmament convention in order to advance progress at the Disarmament Conference in Geneva. By the time of the eventual German withdrawal from the Conference, in October 1933, Eden had made a powerful impression on many of his Cabinet colleagues for his skilful handling of League business,[21] which contrasted all too easily with the Foreign Secretary's apparent failure to give a dynamic lead to Britain's relations with the rest of the world.

Simon and the Cabinet

There was some truth in Vansittart's claim that Simon placed greater emphasis on the views of his ministerial colleagues than on those of his official advisers – although it is of course possible to construct a perfectly good constitutional rationale for such a position. The Foreign Secretary spent much time in Cabinet discussions of foreign affairs outlining problems rather than setting down clear recommendations, preferring instead to seek his colleagues' advice about how best to proceed. His approach frequently attracted criticism from other ministers. MacDonald repeatedly condemned Simon for lacking 'clear views' and demanding instructions.[22] Neville Chamberlain believed that he was 'temperamentally unable to make up his mind'.[23] Eden complained that the Foreign Secretary never fought to defend his position in Cabinet, a view echoed by William Ormsby-Gore.[24] Such charges have done a good deal to damage Simon's reputation, painting him as an indecisive figure, lacking the flair and determination to respond to the problems confronting him. In reality, though, many of the issues on which the Foreign Secretary sought advice were questions of such critical importance that they fully merited prolonged discussion at the highest level of government. Several members of the Cabinet were, moreover, only too ready to push their own ideas on a whole range of international questions. Any serious attempt to deal with the complex economic, military and diplomatic threats facing Britain in any case demanded a degree of inter-departmental co-ordination that made it difficult for any single minister or department to offer a clear and unequivocal lead on policy. Simon's biographer has rightly pointed out that any evaluation of the Foreign Secretary's performance should keep in mind the sheer scale of the problems he faced.[25] It is equally important to remember that his ability to direct policy was constrained by the domestic political and bureaucratic environment in which he operated.

Simon was isolated in the first National Government, commanding a small group of some thirty-five MPs that was of no particular importance given the huge size of the government's majority following the election of October 1931.[26] Walter Runciman was the only other Liberal National in the Cabinet. Although the ideological odyssey of Simon and his party had taken them far from mainstream Liberalism, he still lacked the personal contacts and rapport with other ministers that could have helped him to secure greater support in Cabinet. Many senior Conservatives looked on Simon's appointment to the Foreign Office with a distinct lack of enthusiasm (although Neville Chamberlain initially praised him as 'very sound').[27] Nor was Simon successful at establishing a good working relationship with Mac-Donald. The Prime Minister's private diary shows that he thought little of his Foreign Secretary's abilities, although his criticism of Simon's performance was not always fair, given that he managed to complain simultaneously that the Foreign Secretary demanded too much guidance *and* failed to follow Cabinet instructions.[28] MacDonald's correspondence also shows that he was himself determined to play a major role in setting the course of British foreign policy.[29] Simon for his part seemed surprisingly ready to accept such incursions. At the end of 1932, after he had been in office for more than a year, he rather touchingly told MacDonald that 'A Foreign Minister ought to be in constant personal touch with the Prime Minister, and certainly no-one holding my office has ever had more reason to be grateful for constant help and encouragement and guidance in difficulty than I'.[30]

Simon's relationship with Stanley Baldwin, who was as Conservative leader a figure of great authority in the National Government, was also on occasion very strained. Baldwin's interest in international affairs grew perceptibly during the 1930s, most notably on defence questions, and he was deeply (and perhaps wrongly) impressed by evidence that the electorate was becoming more concerned about the threat of war. Like many ministers in the National Government, he interpreted the Labour victory at the celebrated East Fulham by-election of autumn 1933 as evidence that public opinion would oppose any foreign policy predicated on large-scale British rearmament.[31] Baldwin was also convinced that recent developments in armaments technology, most notably the development of long-range bombers, would make any future conflict far more terrible than the war of 1914–18, a view articulated in his famous claim in Parliament in November 1932 that 'the bomber will always get through'. Simon's relationship with Neville Chamberlain at the Treasury was perhaps even more critical in determining the Foreign Secretary's influence on foreign policy. Chamberlain's portfolio made him a central figure in international financial negotiations of the kind that took place at Lausanne in the summer of 1932, where he headed the British delegation that agreed to a settlement effectively ending German reparation payments,[32] and Simon himself was perfectly happy to accede to the Chancellor on an issue that was of such clear concern to the Treasury.[33] Nor did Simon play much part in preparations for the Ottawa Conference that was held in the autumn of 1932, where agreement was reached on future economic relations between Britain and the empire, although on this occasion the Foreign Secretary did express some concern at the prospect of the Foreign Office being excluded from discussion of 'world relations in the economic field'.[34] Chamberlain became increasingly determined to assert himself in the international arena during Simon's last two years in office. He pushed hard for a *rapprochement* with Japan in 1934, in order to reduce expensive defence commitments in the Far East, and took the lead in proposing a new European security agreement in the wake of the final collapse of the Disarmament Conference. The Chancellor's low opinion of the Foreign Office was reflected in his increasingly poor opinion of Simon himself, and his determination to drive forward British foreign policy was a direct consequence of his conviction that the Foreign Secretary and his officials had no real sense of how to deal with the international crisis confronting them.

The service ministers also played a large part in discussions about international developments. Lord Londonderry at the Air Ministry was a particularly vocal critic of proposals drafted by the Foreign Office on disarmament. Whilst many ministers, including Baldwin and Simon, argued during the early stages of the Disarmament Conference that an international agreement to eliminate military aviation would promote British security, Londonderry repeatedly warned that such a move would make it harder to take 'police action' to enforce order within the far-flung Empire.[35] He was a particularly bitter critic of Eden, whom he accused on several occasions of wilfully ignoring Cabinet instructions.[36] Lord Hailsham at the War Office and Eyres-Monsell at the Admiralty similarly found themselves at odds with the Foreign Office over disarmament. Several other ministers also played a significant role from time to time in the formulation and execution of British policy on broad issues of foreign affairs. Herbert Samuel, for example, served as a delegate both at the Disarmament Conference in Geneva and the Lausanne Conference on reparations, before his departure from the government in October 1932. Nor, of course, was discussion on international affairs confined to the full Cabinet. One of the most striking developments of the 1930s was the growing importance of Cabinet committees in the formulation and review of foreign policy, manifested most obviously in the second half of the decade by the establishment of the Foreign Policy Committee. During the first half of the 1930s, the CID and its subcommittees continued to provide an important setting for discussion on defence matters. The pessimistic reports of the Chiefs of Staff Committee on such matters as Britain's military position in the Far East played an important part in informing discussions within the full Cabinet. A significant role was also played by *ad hoc* committees such as the Far Eastern Committee, set up at the start of 1932 to deal with the crisis created by Japan's aggression towards China, and the Committee on German Rearmament that was first convened in November 1934. The discussions in the Defence Requirements Sub-Committee, established in the autumn of 1933 to make recommendations about the future configuration of Britain's defence efforts, touched repeatedly on broader questions of diplomatic strategy. The Ministerial Disarmament Committee was also of particular importance throughout the early 1930s. The Committee was originally set up in 1932 to prepare for the Disarmament Conference, and played an important role in reviewing progress there, but it subsequently became an important setting for more general discussions about international security (including, ironically, questions of rearmament).[37] The Foreign Office was naturally represented on all these committees, which provided an important setting for securing effective inter-departmental co-ordination, but they also provided a new set of potential bureaucratic constraints on Simon and his officials. The complexity of the committee structure presided over by Maurice Hankey was less and less conducive to dynamic policy-making, and ministers who attacked Simon for failing to provide a decisive lead on foreign policy consistently underestimated the extent to which the process of departmental co-ordination actually served to make it harder to devise a clear policy.

Simon became Foreign Secretary at a time when public concern about international affairs was on the rise, prompted by fears of a possible future war and the palpable failure of the League of Nations to respond effectively to the crisis in the Far East. The Foreign Secretary's rough treatment in the press was partly the result of the fact that he lacked a natural 'constituency' of supporters there. The Liberal Nationals were too conservative for the taste of publications like the *Manchester Guardian* and too liberal for publications like the *Daily Mail*.[38] The press attacks that were regularly made upon Simon naturally weakened his already fragile authority within the Government. Nor was he a popular figure among the lobbies and pressure groups that sought to influence the foreign and defence policy of the National Government. Leading activists in the League of Nations Union were disappointed by Simon's failure to support more decisive action in response to Japanese aggression in 1931–32.[39] Members of the burgeoning if inchoate peace lobby were also disappointed by the failure of the Disarmament Conference to make any striking advances following its opening in February 1932, and Simon became a natural target for their wrath, particularly among those on the left of the political spectrum associated with organisations such as the Union of Democratic Control. The Foreign Secretary even became the target of claims that he owned large shareholdings in armament firms, which was rumoured to account for his supposed reluctance to support such moves as a ban on the private manufacture of armaments. There was in fact no truth in the allegations, but Simon was eventually forced to launch a slander action to prevent them from spreading any further.[40] Such experiences turned him into a harsh critic of the peace movement in all its various guises.[41] Simon never managed to establish the kind of popular profile that might have helped to strengthen his hand within government, and the fact that he was unable to draw on the support of a large party organisation or a significant section of the press made it hard for him to combat the frequent charge that he was an ineffective Foreign Secretary.

The remaining part of this chapter focuses on two of the most important problems faced by Simon during his time at the Foreign Office – the crisis in the Far East and the quest for European security – in order to assess in more detail his role in the policy-making process. During his first two years in office, Simon shared the general view that Britain was too weak to risk war against Japan, and he faced little real pressure within government to take a tough line with the government in Tokyo. The situation was somewhat different when British policy towards the Disarmament Conference was under discussion, but Simon's views on the subject still corresponded quite closely with those of political 'heavyweights' such as Baldwin and MacDonald, who offered him support when the service ministers attacked the Foreign Office for being too quick to promote the principle of 'qualitative disarmament'. In the period following the withdrawal of Germany from the Disarmament Conference, though, Simon found himself increasingly torn between conflicting advice about how best to deal with developments both in the Far East and in Europe. He vacillated when faced with disagreement over the wisdom of seeking an understanding with Japan, and found it difficult to identify new ways of ensuring European security when it became clear that the Nazi regime was unwilling to seriously consider disarmament. It was against this background that he faced a fresh chorus of calls for his dismissal in the spring of 1935, shortly before MacDonald finally handed over the reins of power to Baldwin.

Simon at the Foreign Office, 1931–33

Britain's diplomatic relationship with Japan seldom topped the Foreign Office agenda in the decade following the Washington Naval Conference of 1921–22, although anxiety about imperial security in the Far East was of course a pervasive concern throughout the whole inter-war period. The British government reacted in a decidedly ambivalent manner to the Mukden incident of September 1931, when Japanese troops used an incident of sabotage on the Southern Manchurian railway as a pretext for extending their military presence in the region. There was some anxiety in London at the prospect of Tokyo strengthening its control over a region that remained formally subject to Chinese sovereignty, but sympathy for the nationalist government was strictly limited, given both its past hostility to Britain and its failure to create the political stability required to safeguard British economic interests in the region.[42] The economic crisis at home in any case dominated the attention of ministers in the closing months of 1931, with the result that it was only when fighting broke out in the more economically important region around Shanghai early in 1932 that the Far East really came to the top of the political agenda.[43] In the weeks immediately following Simon's appointment as Foreign Secretary, in November 1931, the Foreign Office enjoyed considerable latitude in deciding how to react to the challenges posed by the Mukden incident and its aftermath. Most senior members of the British diplomatic establishment were reluctant to support any action that might antagonise Japan during the Far Eastern crisis of 1931–32. Francis Lindley, the ambassador in Tokyo, sent numerous dispatches and telegrams back to London warning against any action that would provoke the Japanese government.[44] He was particularly critical of any attempts by the League to impose sanctions, fearing that such a move might provoke Tokyo to pursue a still more aggressive policy.[45] Miles Lampson, British ambassador in China, took a more balanced view of the situation, but his counsels were of limited influence in the Foreign Office. Sir Victor Wellesley, the Deputy Under-Secretary with particular responsibility for Far Eastern Affairs, staunchly defended Lindley against the charge that he was unduly sympathetic to the government in Tokyo.[46] He also repeatedly argued that Britain's weak military situation in the Far East, when combined with the inherent instability of the Chinese government, meant that 'from a material point of view we have nothing to gain and much to lose by antagonising Japan'.[47] Sir John Pratt, a veteran member of the Consular Service who acted as adviser to the Far Eastern Department, took a similar line in a whole series of memoranda and minutes.[48] Vansittart was less involved in the day-to-day handling of developments in the Far East, but he too was sensitive to the danger of creating a formidable adversary in a region where Britain had little military leverage. There were a few dissenting voices questioning this prevailing wisdom. The case of Lampson has already been mentioned, whilst Allan Leeper at the League of Nations Department in London favoured a tough line at Geneva towards Japan.[49] Sir Ronald Lindsay in Washington warned that too supine a response by the British government to developments in the Far East would alienate the US administration. Such counsels were not, though, powerful enough to challenge the widespread consensus among senior members of the diplomatic establishment that Britain should react with caution to calls for a strong international response to Japanese aggression against China.

The advice that Simon received from his ministerial colleagues was similarly unequivocal in opposing any policy that might promote a clash with Japan, and the records of the full Cabinet and its Far Eastern Committee show that ministers were consistently wary of any moves in Geneva that might require Britain to use military force against Japan.[50] The Foreign Secretary's long-standing commitment to collective security meant that he was more sensitive than some ministers to the potential consequences should the League fail to respond effectively to the Far Eastern crisis, but he was nevertheless sensitive to the underlying military and diplomatic realities. Like other ministers, he received CID memoranda warning that economic sanctions were unlikely to prove effective and that Britain was in no position to take military action.[51] It was for this reason that he spent a great deal of time and effort at Geneva trying to discourage the League from taking any action that might provoke the government in Tokyo.[52] Nor was the Foreign Secretary under any illusions that the United States would join Britain in military action, bitterly telling his Cabinet colleagues that 'America always leaves us to the difficult work vis-à-vis Japan'.[53] MacDonald and Simon were, though, both anxious to make every effort to avoid 'slighting the American point of view',[54] which explains their decidedly clumsy response to a proposal in January 1932 by the US Secretary of State, Henry Stimson, urging non-recognition by the two governments in response to any forcible change to the *status quo* in the Far East. Stimson subsequently condemned the British government in his memoirs of taking too weak a stand over Japanese aggression in the Far East,[55] but it was in reality the Secretary of State himself who clung to the illusion that rhetoric and diplomacy could alone force Tokyo to take a more cautious line. Simon and his colleagues knew that strong words were of little value without the necessary determination and wherewithal to follow them up with deeds.

Simon was not, then, the principal architect of Britain's cautious response to Japan's 'forward' policy in the Far East in the months following the Mukden incident, and his understanding of the factors constraining Britain's response broadly echoed that of other ministers and senior diplomats.[56] The same was true in the period following the publication of the celebrated League Report (the Lytton Report) on the conflict in the Far East in October 1932. Simon continued to argue that 'we must not involve ourselves in trouble with Japan', telling the League Assembly in December that he was unwilling to ascribe sole responsibility to Tokyo for the events of the previous fifteen months. The speech predictably received a negative press in papers such as the *Manchester Guardian*, as well as among the stalwarts of the League of Nations Union, but the sentiments uttered by Simon were broadly in line with those held by most of his ministerial colleagues and senior officials. Nor can the Foreign Secretary be held primarily responsible for the farce of the short-lived arms embargo on Japan and China introduced by Britain in March 1933, following renewed Japanese aggression, since he himself had profound doubts about the wisdom of such a move (although he was remiss in not spelling out his concerns to the Cabinet with more force).[57] Simon's tenure of the Foreign Office meant that he was an obvious scapegoat for popular frustration about the National Government's failure to pursue a more vigorous policy in the Far East during its first eighteen months in office. Critics saw his hesitant performance at Geneva, combined with his failure to identify bold solutions to the crisis, as evidence of a lack of determination and imagination. In reality, though, they simply reflected the stark truth that there was neither the international nor the domestic will to pursue a firmer policy towards Japan.

The second issue that repeatedly exercised Simon during his first two years in office was the World Disarmament Conference that opened at Geneva in February 1932, following many years of detailed preparation. The Conference proved to be a source of international disagreement and controversy from the moment it convened. There were even sharp disagreements about who should act as chairman (Arthur Henderson was eventually selected much to the chagrin of MacDonald). Philip Noel-Baker subsequently blamed the Foreign Office for the Conference's failure, suggesting that the Foreign Secretary was never prepared to take any decisive step that might have cost him his job.[58] Such a charge was not fair. Noel-Baker never really grasped the sheer technical complexity involved in any negotiations about arms reductions, despite his long-standing involvement with disarmament policy. Nor did he recognise the extent to which the whole question was bound up with broader questions of European security. The German government was determined, in the words of the Chancellor Heinrich Brüning, that the Conference should 'solve the problems of general disarmament on the basis of equal rights and equal security for all peoples'.[59] The French government was by contrast as steadfastly opposed as ever to any change that might bolster Germany's position and threaten France's security. Simon was in no position to resolve such conflicting demands, whilst divisions within the British government in any case placed real limits on his freedom of manoeuvre. Cabinet discussion prior to the Conference showed that many ministers hoped that international disarmament could offer a cost-effective way of promoting British security, but the defence ministers and their military advisers were always wary of proposals that might weaken the country's already fragile defences.

There was in fact a profound tension in British policy on armaments questions throughout the period before Germany's final withdrawal from the Disarmament Conference in October 1933. The Cabinet's agreement to scrap the Ten Year Rule in March 1932, which took place with Simon's concurrence, showed that ministers accepted the warning by the Chiefs of Staff that Britain's defences had been allowed to slide into a dangerous condition.[60] At the same time, though, they were reluctant to increase expenditure immediately, accepting the Treasury's view that 'sound finances and a healthy trading position' were equally important for national security.[61] Many ministers therefore looked to the Disarmament Conference as a means of reducing international tension whilst simultaneously strengthening Britain's position vis-à-vis the major continental countries.[62] Ministerial discussion on preparations for the Conference, in January 1932, focused on the abolition of submarines and a reduction in the size of capital ships. There was also considerable debate about the far more sensitive question of air disarmament.[63] Robert Cecil was convinced that the Cabinet had failed to devise any coherent policy when the Conference opened in February, and it certainly appears that Simon and his colleagues subsequently reacted to events as much as they moulded them, although there was probably little alternative given the complexity of the problems under review.[64] The opening weeks of the Conference showed the scale of the task ahead. The French delegation put forward plans that would have effectively provided the League with a military force, capable of providing a real guarantee of international security. Their German counterparts repeated their claim for equality of status. Simon concentrated on calling for 'qualitative' disarmament – in effect the abolition of certain kinds of offensive weapons rather than simple numerical limits – a position that had already been sketched out both in the full Cabinet and in the Disarmament Committee. A good deal of the activity at Geneva took place in the myriad expert committees established to review developments in a particular area, the proceedings of which often became bogged down in complex debates about the offensive or defensive character of particular categories of weaponry. Simon himself was profoundly sceptical about the activities of the experts,[65] a view that was shared by many of his officials,[66] but the Foreign Secretary did devote a huge amount of his time throughout 1932–33 to searching for ways of resolving the complex issues that divided the leading powers. He took part in numerous meetings in Geneva with members of the other main national delegations and, when in London, the Disarmament Conference frequently dominated both his dealings with foreign representatives in the capital and his correspondence with British diplomats in post abroad.

Eden condemned Simon in his memoirs for failing to take opportunities to push the Disarmament Conference forwards, most notably in the spring of 1932, when Brüning put forward a proposal based on a modest increase in Germany's military capacity.[67] In reality, though, the French government was never likely to accept such a proposal without some kind of (politically impossible) British guarantee of French security. Nor can Simon really be held responsible, as Noel-Baker subsequently argued, for failing to respond more enthusiastically to President Hoover's dramatic proposals in June 1932 for the abolition of offensive weapons and sharp cuts in all other categories. Hoover's plan failed to grasp fully the security fears of the major European powers, and would in any case have had a particularly severe impact on the Royal Navy. Simon himself was in fact rather more positive about the proposals than many of his colleagues, warning that Britain might be 'missing a great opportunity' by failing to respond positively, but the Cabinet was unwilling to engage with the plan in any meaningful fashion.[68] The sharpest Cabinet divisions in the summer of 1932 took place over the future of military aviation. The Foreign Secretary had by May become an advocate of the abolition of military and naval aircraft, and the Foreign Office took the lead in putting forward proposals for such a policy, a position that attracted the strong support of Baldwin and a number of other ministers. The prospect provoked Londonderry and the Air Ministry into furious opposition.[69] The

Cabinet was reluctant to dismiss altogether the Air Ministry's fears that abolishing military aircraft would make it impossible to carry out 'police actions' to maintain colonial order, leaving Eden to lament in his diary that an important chance had been missed to improve the atmosphere at Geneva.[70] The temporary withdrawal of the German government from the Conference in July, following its refusal to support even Simon's modest proposed alternative to the Hoover plan, in any case showed the impossibility of securing any kind of agreement there. The crisis nevertheless provided another dent in the Foreign Secretary's credibility, prompting MacDonald to write in his diary in late September that Simon had become deeply unpopular at Geneva.[71]

Simon continued to face sharp disagreement at home in the autumn of 1932 on the best way of securing Germany's return to the conference table. At the end of September, the Minister of War Lord Hailsham 'absolutely smashed' a Foreign Office suggestion that the powers ought to agree to scrap all categories of weapons forbidden to Germany by Versailles, leaving Simon and advisers in considerable disarray.[72] Acting on the advice of Neville Chamberlain, Simon then began to work on a confidence-building measure designed to make concessions to Germany over a period of time, following proof of its readiness to act as a 'good neighbour'.[73] The Foreign Secretary subsequently announced in the House of Commons that the British government was ready to acknowledge in principle the validity of Germany's claim for equality of treatment, and the following month Berlin was persuaded to return to Geneva. Whilst the move probably helped to restore Simon's public standing,[74] developments in the first few weeks of 1933 made the issues before the Disarmament Conference more intractable than ever. Hitler's appointment as Chancellor at the end of January signalled the birth of a regime that was never likely to be satisfied simply by removing the shackles of Versailles in favour of equal treatment in matters of armaments. There was as a result always something unreal about the debates and discussions that took place at the Disarmament Conference between the start of 1933 and Germany's eventual withdrawal in October. Simon was less involved than before in the day-to-day details of the Disarmament Conference, following Eden's appointment as substitute head of the British delegation, and he was clearly becoming increasingly sceptical about the possibility of agreement.[75] The Foreign Secretary nevertheless continued to attract blame for failing to find solutions to problems that nobody had any real idea how to address.

Eden used his new position at Geneva to push for a more positive British policy towards disarmament, writing to Baldwin in February 1933 that the only way ahead lay in the production of a complete Draft Convention for consideration by the Conference.[76] He apparently neglected to tell Simon about his proposal until two days later, one of a number of occasions on which he unashamedly by-passed the Foreign Secretary in an effort to win support of senior ministers for his ideas. Eden took the lead composing the

Draft Convention,[77] which eventually received cautious Cabinet approval, with the result that Simon and MacDonald arrived in Geneva in March to present the document and lobby for its acceptance by the other governments represented there. Both men were, however, decidedly sceptical about the prospects of success,[78] which doubtless explains why they subsequently accepted an invitation from Mussolini to visit Rome to discuss a possible four-power security pact. Simon's ill-health in the summer of 1933 meant that he became further removed than ever from day-to-day developments in Geneva, where proceedings soon became bogged down again despite Eden's best efforts to drive the talks forward. In May, it was the Junior Minister's turn to find himself placed in a difficult position, when the Cabinet in London steadfastly continued to oppose any move that might abolish bombing for police purposes. Simon returned to the fray three months later, travelling to Paris to discuss possible ways forward with the French Foreign Minister Edouard Daladier, following which he drew up draft proposals requiring all the major powers to reduce their forces to a common level following a four-year trial period, in which Germany would be expected to show its good faith on matters of armaments.[79] The Foreign Secretary himself had no great confidence in his plan, which was at least partly a gesture designed to ensure that Britain did not receive the blame for the possible break-up of the Conference, but on 14 October 1933 he outlined its main provisions to the Secretariat of the Disarmament Conference. A few hours later, the German government took advantage of the occasion to announce that it intended to withdraw both from the Conference and the League, on the grounds that the other major powers were still refusing to offer equality of treatment in the immediate future.

Germany's withdrawal from the Disarmament Conference and the League did immense damage to Simon's public reputation, and weakened his already fragile position within the Cabinet, even though it is unclear whether the situation could in fact have been handled any more effectively. The Foreign Secretary himself was not unduly perturbed by developments, since he had already lost faith in the Conference, and was hopeful that developing closer relations with Italy could provide a means of countering any German threat in the near future. He nevertheless instructed his officials to draw up renewed proposals for the Disarmament Conference, in the hope of persuading public opinion that the British government was not responsible for the impasse in Geneva.[80] He also argued strenuously in Parliament that Britain remained committed both to the League and disarmament. The Foreign Secretary nevertheless faced a chorus of press criticism following the German government's decision to leave Geneva. The *Times* attacked Simon for being too ready to respond to the concerns of the French government.[81] Other newspapers openly discussed the possibility of his imminent departure from office. Simon's colleagues also felt that the Foreign Secretary's response to the crisis had been inadequate, and rejected the new proposals drawn up by the Foreign Office in the wake of the German withdrawal setting down possible strategies for the future.[82] MacDonald criticised Simon in his diary for his 'unwillingness to face up to the international situation'.[83] Chamberlain speculated on the need for a new man at the Foreign Office.[84] The complaints of Simon's colleagues focused primarily on the Foreign Secretary's failure to identify a positive way forward in the wake of the German withdrawal. The lengthy discussion that took place in Cabinet around this time showed, though, that other ministers had few clear ideas about how to proceed beyond setting down a series of vague *desiderata*.[85] Simon again found himself in the uncomfortable position of being held responsible for failing to resolve problems that were by their very nature insoluble.

Simon at the Foreign Office, 1934–35

Simon only recovered slowly from the health problems he suffered in the summer of 1933, and there were times during his last eighteen months in office when he found it hard to cope with the demands of his job, a situation that was made worse by the constant criticism he faced in the press. The two most intractable problems facing him during this period were the continuing vulnerability of British interests in the Far East and the growing threat to European security posed by Nazi Germany. Whilst there was a reasonable consensus within the Cabinet over policy towards Japan until the spring of 1933, the situation began to change rapidly in the final months of the year, with the result that Simon increasingly found himself caught up in a battle to determine the course of British diplomacy towards the Far East. The catalyst was the publication of a report by the Chiefs of Staff in October 1933 that set down the priorities for British defence, arguing that the threat to Britain's interests in the Far East remained greater than the threat in Europe.[86] Neville Chamberlain, mindful of the enormous costs that would be involved in strengthening British defences in the region, responded by urging the Cabinet to consider a new understanding with Japan, which would allow the British government to limit its defence spending in the region and focus instead on threats closer to home.[87] The Defence Requirements Committee that met soon afterwards, and was dominated by Vansittart, Fisher and Hankey, similarly focused on the German threat in making its recommendations for increased defence expenditure early in 1934.[88] There was nevertheless a sharp division between Vansittart and Fisher about Japan, which was reflected in a broader disagreement between the Foreign Office and the Treasury over policy towards the Far East throughout 1934. Whilst Fisher predictably endorsed Chamberlain's call for some kind of agreement with Tokyo, most senior Foreign Office officials remained sceptical about the wisdom of seeking any formal understanding with Japan, even though many of them did not initially share Vansittart's view that the major threat to British interests was to be found in Europe.[89] Vansittart's own opposition to any understanding with Tokyo was rooted in his anxiety that such a move would upset the global balance of power.[90] He was afraid that an Anglo-Japanese understanding might make the Japanese government confident enough to pursue a more aggressive policy towards the Soviet Union, which would in turn encourage Stalin and the other Soviet leaders to seek agreement with Germany, in order to concentrate on the threat from the east. Such a series of moves would then allow Berlin greater opportunity to focus on its ambitions in central Europe. It was for this reason that Vansittart gave serious thought in 1934–35 to possible strategies for improving Anglo-Russian relations, despite the recent debacle of the Metro-Vickers affair,[91] in the hope that such a strategy could offer a long-term guarantee against a renewed German challenge either in the east or the west of the continent.[92]

Simon appeared to waver on the whole question of British policy towards the Far East throughout 1934, apparently torn between the advice of his Permanent Secretary and the views of his most assertive Cabinet colleague. On 14 March he expressed few strong views in Cabinet when Chamberlain argued that 'we should decline to align ourselves with Washington' at the forthcoming Naval Conference,[93] to be held in London later in the year, but just a few days later he approved the circulation of a Foreign Office memorandum arguing against any kind of Non-Aggression Pact with Tokyo on the grounds that it might alienate the United States and China.[94] His uncertainty lingered throughout the summer, as the Treasury continued to press for an agreement with Japan in order to justify a reduction in the ambitious defence programme submitted by the Defence Requirements Committee.[95] Simon himself was ready on occasion to respond to overtures from the Japanese government suggesting that Tokyo might be ready to discuss a possible non-aggression pact,[96] noting in early August that the Cabinet (which in practice mainly meant Chamberlain) was pressing for some such policy.[97] Vansittart and most other senior officials at the Foreign Office, with the partial exception of Robert Craigie, Head of the American Department, remained wary of such a course of action. By the start of September, Simon was clearly uncertain how to act. On 7th September he informed Chamberlain by letter that his proposals for an accommodation with Japan failed to meet the objections laid down by the Foreign Office six months earlier,[98] but less than two weeks later he told the Chancellor at a private luncheon that he might be ready to reconsider his views. A difficult meeting between Vansittart, Simon and Chamberlain then took place at the end of September, at which the Chancellor and the Foreign Secretary agreed to draft a joint memorandum on Far Eastern policy for the Cabinet.[99] Chamberlain was, however, appalled at the draft subsequently produced by the Foreign Office, believing that it was far too negative in discussing the potential benefits of an Anglo-Japanese agreement, and he only agreed to circulate it to Cabinet following extensive rewriting.

The whole issue of a rapprochement with Japan in fact became somewhat academic when the opening of the Naval talks in London in October showed that there was no real scope for agreement, since the Japanese were deter-mined to reject the 3:5:5 ratio established at the Washington Conference in favour of one that would offer something closer to naval parity with Britain and the United States.[100] The conflict between the Treasury and the Foreign Office during the previous few months had nevertheless revealed a funda-mental disagreement about how best to defend Britain's global interests with limited resources. It was a struggle that continued over the next few years, as the Treasury's caution over the cost of rearmament became one of the main factors shaping the policy of appeasement.[101] Chamberlain and Fisher favoured a strategy that sought to build better relations with Japan in order to allow for lower overall defence expenditure, focused on threats to Britain's security in Europe, and the two men were ready to risk any con-comitant alienation of the United States. Vansittart and most of his senior colleagues were by contrast afraid that such a move would undermine the delicate balance of international power in a way that might actually increase Germany's freedom of manoeuvre in Europe. Although the Permanent Secretary and his staff were content to support moves to improve relations with Japan, given the vulnerability of Britain's interests in the Far East, they were reluctant to agree to any kind of formal pact. Simon's failure to take a consistent position in the whole controversy largely accounts for the fact that the issue was allowed to drag from late 1933 until the autumn of the following year. The Foreign Secretary seemed to find it difficult to make up his mind about the best course for British policy in the Far East. As a result, he constantly found himself torn between the different courses of action that were pressed upon him.

A similar uncertainty plagued Simon when he confronted the worsening situation in Europe during 1934–35. The Foreign Secretary never took such an alarmist view as Vansittart of the threat posed to Britain by Nazi Germany, although his comments on dispatches arriving in London from Berlin show that he had no illusions about the nature of Hitler's regime. He told the Cabinet in March 1934 that Germany was always likely to direct its energies to the south and east,[102] although he was shrewd enough to realise that Berlin's growing confidence meant that the British government might have to pay more attention 'than we have yet done to French demands for security'.[103] During his final eighteen months at the Foreign Office, the policy favoured by Simon was effectively predicated on making limited con-cessions to Germany, particularly on armament questions, whilst at the same time ensuring that Britain remained on good enough terms with Rome and Paris to deter Berlin from embarking on an adventurist foreign policy. The Foreign Secretary was concerned to secure good relations with Mussolini, particularly in the wake of the murder of the Austrian Chancellor Dollfuss in July 1934, since he believed that the Italians alone could rein in German ambitions in central Europe (a region where he believed Britain should 'keep out of trouble ... at all costs').[104] There was a strong diplomatic logic behind such a policy. Even Vansittart was not averse to making limited concessions to Germany. It is of course easy in the light of subsequent events to ridicule the notion that Hitler's ambitions were ever likely to be satisfied by easing the strictures of Versailles, but such an idea commanded considerable support across much of the political and diplomatic establishment during the 1930s, even among those who later led the chorus of attacks on the supposedly immoral policy of appeasement.

Simon's views on rearmament during 1934–35 reflected both his lingering liberal internationalism and his reluctance to endorse fully his Permanent Secretary's *realpolitik* view that rapid action was required to strengthen Britain's defences in order to guarantee its security. It has already been suggested that Simon had few clear ideas about the way forward in the weeks following Germany's withdrawal from the Disarmament Conference. He placed little hope in the Foreign Office proposals forwarded to Paris and Germany in January 1934 for a renewal of talks, but told Eric Phipps in Berlin that they should be pursued 'however slender the chance of agreement'.[105] The Foreign Secretary believed that 'time is on Germany's side' as far as rearmament was concerned, and he remained convinced that Britain's best course was to seek to place some limits on the process, without going so far as to alienate Berlin to the point where it paid no heed whatsoever to international opinion. Simon was involved in the complex discussions that took place throughout the summer of 1934 on the implementation of the Defence Requirement Committee's proposals for major increases in military expenditure, but he remained a somewhat peripheral figure in the bad-tempered debates about the allocation of funds between the various service ministries.[106] The formal suspension of the Disarmament Conference in the spring of 1934 led him to become a reluctant supporter of rearmament, particularly in the light of the numerous memoranda compiled by the Service ministries and the Foreign Office purporting to show the scale of Germany's military build-up.[107] He endorsed the conclusions of the Cabinet Committee on German rearmament that was set up in November 1934, and in a Parliamentary debate the same month sharply attacked the forthcoming LNU Peace Ballot, accusing its organisers of naivety and mischief-making.[108] Despite some claims to the contrary, it seems clear that the Foreign Secretary broadly supported the White Paper that was eventually issued in March 1935 setting out increases in defence spending in the years ahead.

The attacks on Simon by his own Cabinet colleagues went on throughout 1934, reflecting ministers' frustration at his failure to identify a new strategy for promoting European security in the wake of Germany's withdrawal from Geneva. Chamberlain continued to intrude in areas that normally lay within the purview of the Foreign Secretary. The Chancellor's proposal for a new European Security Pact, which was discussed at length in the Disarmament Committee and the Cabinet in the spring and summer of 1934, represented a clear attempt to drive forward policy in a way that would meet

the Treasury's determination to constrain defence spending whilst simultaneously advancing international security.[109] Simon did seek to claim credit for
arranging the plebiscite on the future of the Saar that took place early in
1935, presenting a detailed plan to Cabinet in late November,[110] but even in
this case the Chancellor played an important role in ensuring that the plan
to provide an Anglo-Italian force to supervise voting actually won Cabinet
approval.[111] The confusion and uncertainty of the international environment
that subsequently dominated Simon's final six months in office, in the first
half of 1935, made it impossible for the Foreign Secretary to do much to
salvage his reputation.

The White Paper on Rearmament issued in March 1935 signalled the
government's readiness to address some of the weaknesses highlighted by
the Defence Requirements Committee. Two months earlier, Simon had
taken a leading role in the conference with French ministers about how best
to react to the German military build-up. He presented a paper to Cabinet
in early January, demanding that the British negotiating team be given the
'flexibility' to respond to any proposals made by the French delegation,[112]
which in the event took the form of a French proposal for an Air Pact
between the Locarno Powers.[113] The German government predictably welcomed the prospect of such a Pact, which would in effect have recognised
the air force it had been illegally developing for some years. Berlin also held
out the possibility of a high-level Anglo-German meeting, a proposal to
which Simon responded enthusiastically, particularly as the prospect of a
visit to Moscow by a senior British politician was also currently under
review.[114] The Foreign Secretary eventually decided under Cabinet prompting to visit Berlin with Eden, leaving the younger man to proceed to the
USSR alone, but the preparations descended into farce when the publication
of the Defence White Paper led the German government to postpone the
trip on the pretext that Hitler was suffering from a bad cold. The diplomatic
situation was made still more difficult a few days later, when Berlin
announced the reintroduction of conscription. Simon was nevertheless determined to press ahead with the trip, authorising a Note to Berlin asking
whether his visit was still desired, a move he took without prior consultation with Paris or Rome. He also wrote a paper for his colleagues setting
down his view that a refusal to go ahead would achieve little, and 'destroy
finally any prospect of agreeing about anything'.[115] A few days later he presented an agenda for his talks to the Cabinet.[116] Simon's behaviour over the
German visit can certainly be presented as compelling evidence of 'appeasement', in the light of the clear breach of the Versailles Treaty signalled by
the reintroduction of conscription, although the logic behind the trip can
perhaps be reconciled with the 'dual' character of British policy towards
Berlin outlined earlier. The Foreign Secretary and most of his Cabinet colleagues had for some time accepted that changes to Versailles would be
required if there was to be any realistic prospect of an agreement with
Germany. Nor, it should be added, was there much sustained opposition to

Simon's trip among his fellow ministers, with a few exceptions such as Ormsby-Gore,[117] although there were widespread doubts about his ability to negotiate effectively once he arrived there. The Foreign Secretary's decision to press ahead with the Berlin visit in the face of Hitler's provocations may have been unwise, but it was certainly not taken in the teeth of unified opposition from his Cabinet colleagues.

Simon travelled to Berlin in the hope of impressing on Hitler the benefit of an Eastern European Security Pact, but the German dictator was predictably unwilling to make any promises on issues such as Austria, instead raising the prospect of the return of his country's colonies taken after the First World War.[118] He also reacted positively to the possibility of an agreement that would allow Germany a navy that was 35 per cent of the size of the British navy. The Foreign Secretary returned from Berlin still inclined to the view that Britain should continue to engage constructively with the German government, rather than adopt a policy based solely on rearmament and the development of a Rome–Paris–London axis. The same was true of his Cabinet colleagues. The two cabinets that met on 8 April in preparation for the talks with the French and Italian governments at Stresa urged the need to establish solidarity with France and Italy without alienating Berlin.[119] The Stresa Pact itself was less a formal agreement with definite objectives than a symbolic representation of the concern about Germany felt by the governments in London, Paris and Rome. MacDonald led the British delegation, a decision that apparently reflected widespread anxiety in some quarters at the prospect of Simon acting as the lead negotiator. Both the Prime Minister and the Foreign Secretary were determined to gain Mussolini's co-operation and goodwill, which doubtless helps to explain why they failed to demand explicit guarantees about the burgeoning crisis in Abyssinia, a decision that was soon to return to haunt the British government.[120] MacDonald observed in his diary that the Stresa Pact was really just the logical culmination of developments that had been taking place for some time,[121] a position echoed by Simon, who was anxious that it should not be seen as evidence that Britain had now abandoned any idea of seeking co-operation with the German government. Although the Anglo-German Naval Agreement of spring 1935 was largely prompted by the Admiralty's desire to limit any future threat to Britain's global role,[122] it too reflected Simon's long-standing willingness to endorse a degree of German rearmament, in the hope that it would prevent Berlin from pursuing an even greater military build-up.[123]

Simon's relations with his own official advisers became increasingly difficult during his last year or so in office, although the situation was complicated by the continuing lack of consensus within the Foreign Office about how best to respond to the changing international situation. Vansittart had still not entirely given up hope of securing some kind of deal with Germany over rearmament in the first half of 1934, but once it became clear that no agreement was possible, he began to advocate the development of a strong

London–Paris–Rome axis. It was a position that was supported by most of his colleagues such as Ralph Wigram and Allan Leeper, although some like Robert Craigie and Orme Sargent remained hopeful that it might yet prove possible to prevent a return to the crude *Macht Politik* of an earlier age.[124] Vansittart placed particular emphasis on the importance of preventing any German threat to Austrian independence, fearing that an *Anschluss* would greatly strengthen the Nazi regime and bolster its 'overweening superiority complex'.[125] The Permanent Secretary's commitment to building close relations with Paris and Rome also explains why the Foreign Office responded so positively to the French offer of an Air Pact early in 1935, a position that infuriated Hankey and the Chiefs of Staff, who complained bitterly that they were not consulted about the military implications of such a move.[126] Vansittart was predictably a strong advocate of the Stresa Pact, placing far more emphasis than the Foreign Secretary on the possibility that it might serve as a genuine cornerstone for containing Germany.[127] He had become far more critical of Simon by the start of 1935, fearing that the Foreign Secretary was becoming too inclined to consider concessions to Berlin, particularly in the period leading up to his controversial visit in March. It certainly appears that Simon deliberately neglected to consult his Permanent Secretary fully about the preparations for his trip. Although the term was not yet in vogue, Vansittart was undoubtedly concerned that his political master was too ready to seek to resolve the challenge of Germany via a policy of appeasement.

Conclusion

During the weeks leading up to his departure from the Foreign Office, in June 1935, Sir John Simon had become so unpopular among Conservative backbench supporters of the National Government that there was a veritable campaign for his departure. Churchill told his wife in May that 'everyone of every party, official and political, wants to get rid of Simon'.[128] His sentiments reflecting a prevailing feeling in Cabinet and beyond that the Foreign Secretary had failed to guide British foreign policy through the maze of problems that threatened European and global security. There was some justice in a number of the charges made against Simon. Although the Foreign Secretary's legal expertise made him effective at analysing and dissecting problems with forensic skill, he always found it much harder to identify and recommend a definite course of action. Nor did he always find it easy to piece together the complex linkages between the various problems that he was forced to confront during his time in office, and there may have been some justice in Hankey's jibe that the Foreign Secretary 'has few ideas and will always eat out of the hand of a fertile mind like MacDonald's'.[129] Nevertheless, as has been suggested throughout this chapter, any assessment of Simon's time at the Foreign Office must take into account the circumstances under which he was forced to operate. Most of the crises that erupted during his time in office were beyond his control. The legacy of more than a decade of low defence expenditure, when combined with the economic and financial crisis that erupted in 1929, meant that the resources available to the British government were simply too meagre to respond effectively to the challenges that developed in the early 1930s. The long-standing British reluctance to authorise any continental commitment beyond the vapid generalities of Locarno prevented any Foreign Secretary from offering the kind of guarantees that might have exercised a tangible influence on the development of international politics in Europe, whilst the continuing support of domestic public opinion for the chimera of collective security placed real limits on the country's freedom of international manoeuvre. Although it is certainly possible to condemn members of the National Government for overestimating the constraints under which they laboured during the early 1930s,[130] any serious charge against Simon cannot simply focus on his failure to solve the international crises that confronted his country during his years at the Foreign Office. It must also consider the skill with which he played the hand that was dealt him.

British foreign policy during the early 1930s was as ever governed by a mixture of financial, military and political factors. Although it has been argued in previous chapters that 'diplomacy' was never a discrete function, divorced from broader strategic and economic considerations, the linkages became closer than ever during the first half of the 'low, dishonest decade'. Simon himself always identified the Cabinet and its committees as the principal arena for debate about foreign policy. It was for this reason that he was inclined to offer his ministerial colleagues a range of proposals for discussion, rather than making a clear recommendation, a *modus operandi* that played a large part in fomenting the idea that he was indecisive and easily swayed by others. In reality, though, the sheer complexity of the international environment faced by Britain in the early 1930s, when combined with the political sensitivity of foreign and defence policy, meant that the Foreign Secretary could never offer the kind of clear and unambiguous guidance that ministers seemed to crave. There was, moreover, something hypocritical about much of the criticism that was directed at Simon's supposed indecisiveness, given the determination of many other ministers to assert their own position when international affairs were under review. Simon lacked the political resources to assert himself effectively in this complex decision-making environment. As a Liberal National in a coalition government he was unable to rely on the sort of informal networks and friendships that might have helped him to win more enthusiastic support from his colleagues. Nor did he have the kind of personality that would have allowed him to impress himself on other ministers. Simon often took the blame for policies that were actually approved by the Cabinet as a whole. Although he never developed the breadth of vision required to think imaginatively about the perils facing his country, he was unfortunate enough to serve as Foreign Secretary at a time when both domestic and international politics conspired to make his position more uncomfortable than any of his immediate predecessors.

7   Sir Samuel Hoare at the Foreign Office (1935)

Introduction

History has not been kind to Sir Samuel Hoare. Although he served at the Foreign Office for just six months, his time there ended in chaos and resignation, when it became clear that public opinion was infuriated by the Anglo-French plan he co-sponsored with the French Prime Minister Pierre Laval in an effort to resolve the crisis created by the Italian invasion of Abyssinia in October 1935. The pact was widely held by British public opinion to undermine the moral authority of the League of Nations as a vehicle of collective security, by making too many concessions to Mussolini in order to secure peace, and it has subsequently come to play an important role in the whole mythology of appeasement. The situation in 1935 was, however, a good deal more complex than has sometimes been realised. Hoare's resignation attracted a wide range of responses from his contemporaries. For some – including most ministers – it was a price that had to be paid by the Foreign Secretary for sponsoring an unpopular policy that did not have prior Cabinet sanction. For others, ranging from members of the Labour Party through to activists in the League of Nations Union, Hoare was a scapegoat who paid the price when public opinion rebelled against the Cabinet's cavalier attitude towards collective security. Hoare himself represented his resignation as a matter of principle, which he felt bound to carry out once he realised the gulf that separated him from his Cabinet colleagues. Such wide-ranging responses show the problems of attempting to use the niceties of constitutional theory to explain the complex realities of domestic politics. Hoare was both the architect and the victim of the crisis that erupted in December 1935.

Almost two decades after leaving the Foreign Office, Samuel Hoare wrote in his memoirs that he never wanted to become Foreign Secretary in the summer of 1935. Having spent the previous four years at the India Office, he believed that he would be better placed to serve as the new Viceroy, helping 'to turn the Government of India Act into a living All-India Federation'. He nevertheless accepted Baldwin's request to replace Simon as Foreign Secretary, taking up residence in a 'vast and draughty' office with 'the atmosphere of a pretentious hotel lounge'.[1] He soon came to miss the intimate atmosphere of his small study in the India Office, as well as the Indian Office officials, who were by tradition less assertive and less quarrelsome than their counterparts in the Foreign Office. The circumstances surrounding Hoare's appointment remain somewhat obscure, and the new Foreign Secretary may in fact have been less reluctant to accept the post than he subsequently implied, given that experience in such a high profile role would help to advance his ambition of one day becoming Prime Minister.[2] Baldwin, for his part, was at one stage considering Anthony Eden for the Foreign Office, and Hankey was so convinced that Eden would be promoted that he even telephoned to offer his congratulations. In the event, though, Baldwin called the junior minister into his office and bluntly informed him that 'Sam [Hoare] is going to the Foreign Office and I want you to stay on and help him there'.[3] Eden reluctantly agreed. Although he served his new chief loyally in the six months that followed, the circumstances surrounding Hoare's appointment still rankled many years later when he composed his memoirs.

Hoare's long years in government had won him considerable respect among his colleagues at the time he became Foreign Secretary, but he lacked a strong political base or a well-defined group of backbench supporters within the Conservative Party. Baldwin's decision to appoint Hoare to the Foreign Office was taken following consultation with Neville Chamberlain and Geoffrey Dawson of *The Times*, who both believed that the erstwhile head of the India Office had the necessary combination of *gravitas* and competence to meet the demands of the post. The appointment was not, though, met with any enthusiasm by Austen Chamberlain, who made little secret of the fact that he believed he could do the job better himself. Hoare later admitted that pressure of work meant that he had not given much attention to European affairs while at the India Office,[4] with the result he was not well-versed in the problems that had exercised the Foreign Office so intensely over the previous few years. He subsequently observed ruefully in his memoirs that few inter-war foreign secretaries could claim to have made much of a success of their time in office, pointing out that Henderson had failed to tie up 'the ragged ends that irritated the world', whilst Chamberlain had 'faded into obscurity' following the 'golden dawn' of Locarno.[5] Hoare also wrote a good deal in *Nine Troubled Years* about the constraints placed on British foreign policy during the 1930s by the scale of disarmament that had taken place since 1918, which meant that successive governments were forced to become 'hesitant and opportunist' in the face of an increasingly turbulent world.[6] He argued that ministers had been forced to give particular attention to the pacific instincts of public opinion, manifested a few years earlier in the East Fulham by-election, and highlighted in 1935 by the results of the celebrated LNU Peace Ballot.[7] Hoare was sharply critical of the Peace Ballot in *Nine Troubled Years*, suggesting that it promoted 'pacifist influences', although in reality the ballot probably just manifested widespread public support for the chimera of a system of collective security that could by some mysterious process be reconciled with the achievement of universal disarmament. It is too easy to dismiss the chapters in Hoare's memoirs on his time as Foreign Secretary simply as an attempt to rewrite history and justify his conduct. The author took great pains in his research for the book, which is altogether more satisfying than many other works of its kind,[8] and an examination of the documents relating to his tenure of the Foreign Office shows that he was genuinely concerned *at the time* about the constraints placed on Britain's freedom of international manoeuvre in 1935. Although Hoare had little recent experience of international affairs when he arrived at the Foreign Office, he was certainly no novice in dealing with complex international questions. He headed the shadowy British Intelligence Mission in Russia during the First World War, and was closely involved in moves to establish the new Czechoslovak state that came into being in 1919. He also served at the Air Ministry during the 1920s, which gave him some insight into defence questions. The fundamental problem confronting British foreign policy during Hoare's time at the Foreign Office in the second half of 1935 was finding a way of remaining loyal to the League, or at least to be seen as remaining loyal to the League, whilst at the same time discouraging it from taking any action that might drive Mussolini into the arms of Hitler. The problem was insoluble. Samuel Hoare made some serious misjudgements during his time at the Foreign Office, but he was in large part a victim of the various dilemmas he outlined so lucidly in his memoirs.

The basic story of the Abyssinia crisis itself can be told very briefly.[9] Following a clash between Italian and Ethiopian troops at the end of 1934, the British and French governments desperately sought to find a way of satisfying Mussolini's territorial demands on a fellow League member, whilst preserving the prestige of the League intact. In June 1935, the British government tried to 'appease' fascist Italy by sending Eden to Rome with a plan that granted Mussolini at least some of his demands on Abyssinia, in turn compensating Abyssinia with the small port of Zeila in British Somaliland. Mussolini's predictable refusal of the offer was followed by months of anguished and largely fruitless negotiations between Rome, Paris and London. In September, Hoare made a speech to the League Assembly in Geneva that was widely interpreted as evidence that Britain was firmly committed to the principle of collective security, and would impose economic sanctions on Italy in line with the procedure set down by the Covenant. The long-awaited start of the Italian invasion three weeks later put added pressure on League members to take decisive action. The prospect of imposing a sanction on the export of oil to Italy raised particular problems for the British government, however, since many ministers feared that Mussolini might respond with a 'mad dog' attack on Royal Navy warships in the Mediterranean. The transparent desire of Pierre Laval's government in Paris to avoid conflict with Italy, for fear of losing a possible ally against

Germany, also meant that the British government could never be sure what support they would receive if war actually broke out in the Mediterranean. The Hoare–Laval Pact negotiated in Paris on 7–8 December met many of the principal Italian demands over Abyssinia, in an apparent attempt to ensure that Mussolini would not break irrevocably with the British and the French. Although it was put forward under the pretext of being no more than a formal recommendation to the League, the Pact quickly ran into trouble when public opinion in Britain concluded that the principle of collective security was being sacrificed. Hoare's resignation took place less than two weeks after news of it was first leaked to the French press.

Hoare, the Foreign Office and Abyssinia

Hoare's lack of detailed knowledge about the main diplomatic problems of the day when he arrived at the Foreign Office meant that he lacked a clear vision of the direction in which he wished to guide British foreign policy. He therefore relied a good deal on his officials for advice. The Foreign Secretary hinted in his memoirs that he found it difficult to come to terms with the culture of the Foreign Office, finding many of his officials less deferential and more divided than those he had left behind at the India Office: 'Everyone seemed to be over-excited. There appeared to be no generally accepted body of opinion on the main issues. Diametrically opposed views were pressed upon me, and sometimes with the intolerance of an *odium theologicum*'.[10] Hoare did, though, establish a good working relationship with Vansittart, who in turn rejoiced that he at last had 'a Foreign Secretary I can work with'.[11] The Foreign Secretary relied heavily for counsel on his Permanent Secretary. The two men met frequently to discuss Foreign Office business in the informal surroundings of their own homes, in Cadogan Gardens and Denham respectively, as well as in the more formal setting of Whitehall. Vansittart helped to draft many of Hoare's speeches, including his celebrated address to the League Assembly in September, and his resignation speech in December. The correspondence between the two men was distinguished both by its informality, which would have been unthinkable in the days of Curzon, and by the Permanent Secretary's unashamed readiness to press his opinions on policy. Hoare was reasonably diligent in reading the massive Foreign Office correspondence that came across his desk, complete with minutes and memoranda composed by officials. The officials who staffed the Abyssinian Department in 1935, including Maurice Peterson and Patrick Scrivener, contributed numerous well-informed and shrewd comments on the development of the crisis in East Africa. Lancelot Oliphant, the Assistant Under-Secretary responsible for supervising the Department, was also a prolific author of minutes on incoming documents. Hoare, though, seems instinctively to have preferred to receive advice on most matters through Vansittart, who was of course able to view and comment on all the most important dispatches and memoranda, although the Foreign Secretary also expressed great admiration for officials such as Ralph Wigram of the Central Department. Nor was he a great fan of the kind of informal discussion and *ad hoc* committees that subsequently became the hallmark of the Foreign Office under Eden and Halifax, which tended to reinforce his Permanent Secretary's role as the major conduit for official advice. Although it would be too simplistic to suggest that Hoare accepted Vansittart's views uncritically, he welcomed his Permanent Secretary's clear advice and 'singleness of purpose' at a time when so many senior figures in the British establishment had few ideas how to cope with the turbulent international environment.[12] It is striking that the Foreign Secretary seems to have paid little attention to voices in the Foreign Office counselling caution in the fraught days leading up to his departure in December to negotiate with Laval.[13]

Vansittart's own thoughts on the Abyssinian imbroglio focused on the need to avoid any conflict with Italy that might make the European situation more threatening. The basic framework that governed his response to the developing crisis was set down in a note he sent to Hoare before a Cabinet meeting on 19 June, which discussed the approach Eden should take on his forthcoming visit to Rome.[14] Vansittart argued that the destruction of the League and the Stresa Front, which would be a likely consequence of a major war over developments in east Africa, should be avoided at all costs. This was partly because Italy would then be more inclined to 'throw herself into the arms of Germany', and partly because a conflict over Abyssinia would destroy once and for all the system of collective security on which British public opinion placed so much importance. It was for this reason that Vansittart proposed that the Abyssinian government should be encouraged to cede territory to Italy, in return for the British handing over the port of Zeila to Addis Ababa (a move that he acknowledged in one of his minutes was tantamount to buying off Mussolini). Hoare minuted that he was 'most grateful' for Vansittart's note, and made extensive use of its arguments when trying to convince his Cabinet colleagues that the British government should attempt to satisfy Italian demands.[15] The Hoare–Vansittart policy that evolved over the following months rested on the assumption that both domestic opinion and European security required Britain to prevent the collapse of the League, even if this meant accepting an outcome that would grant Mussolini much of what he wanted. The Foreign Secretary subsequently noted in his memoirs that he had pursued a 'dual policy', designed to resolve the Abyssinian crisis via direct negotiations with Rome, whilst at the same time ensuring that Britain played its part in the League's attempt to resolve the crisis through the mechanisms of collective security. His critics, along with many later historians, have suggested that this policy was simply duplicitous.

Hoare followed the usual practice of keeping up a semi-private correspondence with ambassadors and other senior diplomats in the most important posts. His most extensive correspondence was predictably with Sir Eric

Drummond, the erstwhile Secretary-General of the League of Nations, who had since taken over as British ambassador in Rome. Drummond consistently urged the Foreign Secretary to take a positive line when dealing with Mussolini – a position that on occasion earned a rebuke from Hoare – who fretted on a number of occasions that 'we have sometimes let the Italians get away with their case more easily than they deserved'.[16] The ambassador placed little faith in the League's ability to take effective action against the Italian government, a position that he acknowledged was 'very sad' for someone of his background, although he firmly rejected the idea that the Embassy was too pliant in its dealings with the Italian government.[17] Few other ambassadors were quite so outspoken as Drummond in urging a particular policy upon Hoare, although Sir Percy Loraine in Constantinople also set down his recommendations on policy with considerable force. Sir George Clerk in Paris, who played a key role in liaising between the British and French governments, was more restrained than Drummond in pushing his own views. Hoare nevertheless kept Clerk abreast of the dilemmas faced by the British government, sometimes expressing frustration at the impossible situation in which he found himself. In a letter written in late August, when tripartite talks between Britain, France and Italy were already deeply bogged down, he noted that both the Cabinet and the country were determined to stick to the Covenant and avoid war: 'You will say that these feelings are self-contradictory. At present, at least, the country believes they can be reconciled. Most people are still convinced that if we stick to the Covenant and apply collective sanctions, Italy must give in and there will be no war. You and I know the position is not as simple as that'.[18] Since Hoare was only in office a few months, he did not have the time to develop a stable working relationship with senior British representatives posted abroad, but the tone of his correspondence makes it clear that he was inclined to treat them as confidantes rather than functionaries. Even so, whilst their dispatches and letters were read with care at the Foreign Office, none of them were able to exercise a decisive influence on the development of British policy during the Abyssinian crisis.

The continued presence of Anthony Eden at the Foreign Office – now elevated by Baldwin to full Cabinet rank as Minister for League Affairs – inevitably created problems. Eden was disappointed not to become Foreign Secretary himself, and he was honest enough to acknowledge in his memoirs that he expected to find it hard to 'usefully play second to a strong chief'. Since Baldwin declined to set down any clear guidelines about the division of the work between the two senior Foreign Office ministers,[19] they were forced to put in place an *ad hoc* set of arrangements that neither man found entirely satisfactory.[20] Hoare himself told Austen Chamberlain that 'it is in practice impossible to distinguish between League of Nations questions and questions dealing with general foreign affairs',[21] whilst MPs professed some confusion about the correct target for their questions on international relations. Eden played a central role in many of the key negotiations that took place over Abyssinia in the second half of 1935, in London and Paris, as well as in Geneva. In his memoirs he wrote at length about his unhappiness at the direction taken by Hoare and the rest of the Cabinet throughout the crisis, arguing that they did not place enough emphasis on promoting an effective League response to Italian aggression in East Africa. The Minister for League Affairs was, though, considerably less remote from the decision-making process than he subsequently implied.

Eden's frequent absences in Geneva certainly made it difficult for him to keep up with developments back home, but when he was in London he normally paid a full part in the key committees and meetings that took place there. He complained bitterly in his memoirs that Hoare pursued an inconsistent policy during the Abyssinian crisis, particularly in the early autumn, when the Foreign Secretary appeared to take a far more cautious line than was consistent with his earlier Geneva speech pledging Britain's support for collective security.[22] It is, though, hard to record a strong and sustained note of disagreement in Eden's extensive correspondence with Hoare.[23] The Minister for League Affairs certainly took a more robust line than the Foreign Secretary in the weeks following the outbreak of hostilities in east Africa, on 3 October, when ministers in London became anxious that Geneva was moving too quickly to impose sanctions on Italy.[24] One of Eden's most astute biographers is nevertheless right to suggest that his subject frequently expressed contradictory and inconsistent views on the Abyssinian crisis, and was by no means a consistent opponent of making concessions to Rome.[25] He was involved in the initial discussions about the proposal he took to Mussolini in June, offering the transfer of some Abyssinian territory to Italian control,[26] and seems to have endorsed the decision to send Maurice Peterson of the Foreign Office to Paris in October to seek a compromise peace that by definition would require some degree of appeasement of Mussolini's ambitions in Africa.[27] Eden in fact had few coherent ideas about how best to resolve the fundamental dilemma facing the makers of British policy in the second half of 1935 – that is the need to sustain the credibility of the League whilst preventing it from pursuing measures that might drive Mussolini towards Hitler. Nor, it should be added, is it clear that he was entirely ignorant of the likely outcome of Hoare's critical meeting with Laval in early December. It will be suggested below that the Foreign Secretary made no effort to conceal his desire to reach agreement with the French Prime Minister on joint proposals to end the war in east Africa during the days leading up to his fateful trip to Paris. Since Eden was in London during this period, it seems unlikely that he can have been completely unaware that the Foreign Secretary hoped to secure an Anglo-French agreement that was almost certainly bound to involve a surrender of Abyssinian territory to Italy.

Hoare, the Cabinet and Abyssinia

Hoare's resignation in December 1935 came about after a number of his Cabinet colleagues made it clear that they believed his presence in the government had become a political liability. Previous post-war foreign secretaries such as Curzon had on occasion lost the confidence of their fellow ministers, but none had faced the kind of opposition that emerged at an extraordinary Cabinet meeting on 18 December, when minister after minister threatened to resign unless the Foreign Secretary left office. This naturally raises the question as to whether Hoare was ousted for pursuing a policy that was never approved by the Cabinet, or was instead the victim of the British government's failure to formulate an effective response towards the Abyssinian crisis. And, perhaps more contentiously, was he simply abandoned by his ministerial colleagues in December for pursuing a course of action about which none of them had previously expressed any grave doubts and to which they could be judged to have given their tacit approval? The political machinations of December 1935 cast interesting light both on the role of the Foreign Secretary and the constitutional conventions governing ministerial responsibility.

Marked differences had already appeared in Cabinet over the Abyssinian crisis by the middle of 1935, and although the debate shifted in the following months according to the vagaries of circumstances, the pattern remained broadly intact.[28] Some ministers, perhaps most notably Eden and William Ormsby-Gore, were instinctively inclined to support some form of League action against Italy.[29] Others, including Service ministers such as Eyres-Monsell at the Admiralty, were by contrast deeply concerned about the prospect of any conflict with Italy given the vulnerability of British forces in the Eastern Mediterranean. Hoare was content for the Cabinet to act as the focus for key decisions on foreign policy during his six months in office, circulating numerous papers, and providing ministers with detailed oral briefings about diplomatic developments. Before his fateful meeting with Laval in December, he showed no wish to assert his independence or pursue a particular policy without references to his colleagues. During August and September 1935, when only a few full Cabinet meetings took place, the Foreign Secretary tried to keep in close contact with both the Prime Minister and other ministers who had a particular interest in foreign affairs. Indeed, Hoare wrote bitterly to Chamberlain in the middle of August complaining that he did not receive *enough* advice from some of his colleagues, describing how at a recent meeting with Baldwin the Prime Minister 'would think about nothing but his holiday and the necessity of keeping out of the whole business [of Abyssinia] almost at any cost'.[30] Such a charge was not really fair. Less than two weeks earlier, Baldwin had chaired a group of ministers and officials in Downing Street which discussed the line to be taken by Anthony Eden in the forthcoming talks on the crisis in Paris between France, Britain and Italy.[31] And, a few days after the Foreign Secretary wrote to Chamberlain, Baldwin returned specially from his holiday to preside over a small meeting of ministers and a special Cabinet devoted to the results of the recent tripartite talks in Paris.[32] Although Baldwin's 'hands-off' style of Cabinet management continued to be interpreted by some around him as lack of 'grip', the Prime Minister actually monitored the ominous international situation with some care, well aware that it was likely to influence both public opinion and the general election that he planned to call within the following few months.

Whilst Hoare was happy to keep all his ministerial colleagues informed about developments in Abyssinia, his closest confidante throughout the crisis was Neville Chamberlain. It was seen in the previous chapter that Chamberlain repeatedly used his position at the Treasury to involve himself in a whole range of international issues when Simon was at the Foreign Office, and the Chancellor was by the second half of 1935 increasingly confident that he had both the knowledge and ability to master the intricate problems involved in framing British foreign policy. He told his sister in July that one of Hoare's recent speeches took a line that 'was suggested by me'. A few weeks later he wrote about one ministerial meeting on Abyssinia that 'I have as usual greatly influenced policy'.[33] Hoare for his part told Chamberlain in September that 'I value your praise more than all the others put together'.[34] The two men were generally agreed on policy throughout the second half of 1935, supporting League sanctions on Italy, whilst favouring a continuing dialogue with Rome designed to identify any possible way out of the crisis.[35] Chamberlain was, predictably, also Hoare's strongest Cabinet supporter in the crisis that erupted after details of the Hoare–Laval Pact were leaked to the press.

The Service ministers were, as noted, instinctively wary of any policy that might bring Britain into conflict with Italy. It was a position echoed by Maurice Hankey, along with most of the CID sub-committees with a strong military presence.[36] This scepticism was most pronounced at the Admiralty, where there was a long-standing irritation that supporters of the League expected the Royal Navy to become the policeman of the world, despite not having the resources to play such a role effectively. Eyres-Monsell repeatedly warned the Cabinet that British ships in the Mediterranean might be vulnerable to attack given their lack of effective anti-aircraft guns, and noted that any build-up in the region risked weakening Britain's position in the Far East. Such advice echoed the views put forward at the Chiefs of Staff sub-committee.[37] Serving naval officers were wary of the consequences that would ensue if the British government decided to use military force to meet its obligations under Article 16, although there was general agreement that Italy would be defeated if Mussolini was foolish enough fight. Admiral A.E. Chatfield wrote to Vansittart on 8 August, before the imposition of League sanctions on Italy, warning against the danger of 'precipitated hostilities with Italy until we are more ready. It would be a serious business if the great League of Nations, having at last agreed to act together, was able to be flouted militarily by the nation whom it was trying to coerce'.[38] When the League finally agreed to impose limited economic sanctions, and was beginning discussion of a possible oil sanction, the Admiralty continued to sound a voice of caution even as it responded to directives to increase the British naval presence in the Mediterranean. Such caution inevitably provided an important backdrop to discussions in London, as well as British participation in the debate about sanctions at Geneva on bodies such as the Committee of Five and the Committee of the Eighteen, which were convened to discuss possible courses of action. Hoare's subsequent lament about the difficulty of conducting diplomacy at a time of military weakness was not just a convenient fiction constructed in his autobiography. They instead formed an important part of the environment dealt with by policy-makers throughout the crisis.

The Abyssinian crisis erupted at a time of virtually unprecedented public interest in foreign affairs, manifested both in the Peace Ballot and the General Election that took place in November.[39] The desire of ministers to prevent a humiliating climb-down by the League was governed by their anxiety about the impact of such a development on public opinion, as well as by their concern over the future of European security.[40] Hoare himself, whilst well aware that he was not a popular figure in Parliament, went to considerable lengths to mobilise support across the political establishment in favour of government policy. In the second half of August, for example, he spoke frankly about the unfolding crisis with influential backbench Conservative MPs such as Churchill and Austen Chamberlain, as well as with the leaders of the Liberal and Labour parties (Samuel and Lansbury), along with Robert Cecil from the League of Nations Union.[41] He also kept in close contact with important figures in the press including Geoffrey Dawson and Lord Beaverbrook, who had for a long time served as a kind of patron to Hoare, providing him with the support that helped his rise up the political hierarchy.[42] The Foreign Secretary's own correspondence and minutes, like those of his Cabinet colleagues, make it plain that he recognised the extent to which the League had become something of a talisman among public opinion. Cabinet minutes relating to the Abyssinian crisis show that ministers were convinced that public opinion was deeply concerned by developments in east Africa.[43] As a result, their speeches on foreign affairs during the General Election campaign in October almost invariably contained laudatory references to the principle of collective security, a move deliberately designed to counter charges by Labour candidates that the recent White Paper on defence proved that the Baldwin government planned to institute a rearmament programme on a scale that would raise tension across Europe.[44] Although the impact of popular opinion on the Baldwin government's foreign policy must to some extent remain speculative, the prevailing sense that support for the League was a political imperative undoubtedly played a part in undermining the coherence of British policy during the Abyssinian crisis.

The Foreign Secretary and his colleagues were determined that their response to the Abyssinian crisis should be co-ordinated with the French government, even though many of them shared Eden's sense that Paris was a 'thieves' kitchen', whose denizens could never be trusted to behave in a straightforward and trustworthy manner.[45] Ministers and senior officers alike regarded French co-operation as vital both for implementing sanctions and in countering any military strike by Italian forces in response to punitive measures by the League. Laval was, however, deeply distrusted in London, where general opinion held that the French Prime Minister would under no circumstances risk war with Mussolini. There were also dark suspicions that the Italian dictator was offering bribes in order to exercise undue influence over a section of the Paris political elite. The French government was itself deeply inconsistent throughout the crisis, desperately seeking a way of keeping on terms both with London and Rome. Laval firmly aligned himself with Britain in the tripartite talks that took place in Paris in August,[46] but the moment they were over he hinted that France might not be able to back up its words with deeds, helping to create an atmosphere of crisis back in London. Two months later, in October, the French Prime Minister caused deep consternation when he informed George Clerk at the Paris Embassy that British naval deployment in the Mediterranean could be seen as provocative by Rome, with the result that France was reluctant to make its ports available in the case of an Italian attack on British forces. Although Laval repeatedly affirmed his country's commitment to collective security, both Hoare and Eden feared that he would never be ready to accept an open break with Mussolini, which under the circumstances meant that it was almost possible to see how the League could deal effectively with the situation in East Africa. Even the staunchly Francophile Vansittart speculated about whether it was not time to seek a new policy that did not rely so much on the co-operation of the French.[47]

Hoare's own attitude to collective security seemed to waver during the six months he was in office. It is certainly difficult to reconcile the Foreign Secretary's enthusiastic support for collective security in his September speech to the League Assembly in Geneva, in which he committed Britain to 'an unwavering fidelity to the League', with his behaviour in Paris three months later. The Foreign Secretary had little time for the enthusiasts of the League of Nations Union, later condemning their meetings as 'semi-religious services' that were 'throughout inspired by a spirit of emotional revivalism'.[48] And, whilst public opinion both at home and abroad was deeply impressed by his Geneva speech, Hoare himself noted just four days after delivering it that 'I do not pretend to be optimistic about the future', suggesting he was not entirely convinced by the shibboleths he had so recently uttered.[49] Hoare was certainly perturbed by the enthusiastic reaction to his speech, which was approved in advance by Baldwin and Chamberlain, fearing that some members of the audience had interpreted it as a British commitment to take unilateral action if necessary to prevent Italian aggression. Given all these uncertainties and ambiguities, it has been suggested that the Foreign Secretary's commitment to collective security was little more than a cynical piece of diplomacy designed to assuage public opinion, which was eventually abandoned once the election was over and public opinion no longer had to be assuaged.[50] There is no doubt a certain truth in this analysis, but there is also evidence to suggest that Hoare's commitment to collective security ran deeper than sometimes recognised, making his behaviour in Paris on 7–8 December all the more inexplicable. At a Conference of Ministers on 21 August, he joined with Eden in advising their colleagues that public opinion required them 'to operate through the regular League of Nations procedure'.[51] In September he told the Cabinet that he would favour 'moderate sanctions' against Italy once it began armed operations in east Africa.[52] Although he took a more cautious line in October in the immediate wake of the outbreak of hostilities in east Africa, by November Hoare was warning Hankey against the dangers of 'letting down the League', even though the General Election was now out of the way and ministers could afford to be more relaxed about public opinion. The Foreign Secretary also made it clear that he was ready to consider an oil sanction on Italy, something desperately opposed by Hankey and the Chiefs of Staff, who were afraid that such a move would trigger an attack by Italy in which France 'cannot be relied upon to help us'.[53] The agreement Hoare eventually negotiated with Laval certainly damaged the League's authority, perhaps fatally, but by seeking a solution to the Abyssinian conundrum that was acceptable to Italy it could also be seen as an attempt at resolving a crisis that was threatening to overwhelm the League. Vansittart constantly pressed on Hoare the need to find some way of keeping the League intact whilst avoiding a breach with Italy. The Hoare–Laval Pact should perhaps be seen as a doomed attempt to combine these irreconcilable *desiderata*.

Crisis and resignation

Perhaps the most critical question surrounding the Hoare–Laval Pact concerns the extent to which the Foreign Secretary was acting on his own initiative in his talks with the French Premier in Paris on 7–8 December. The record remains ambiguous. In the last week of November, Maurice Peterson telegraphed London from Paris with some draft proposals for a possible Anglo-French plan to end the fighting in Abyssinia, suggestions which were circulated to the Cabinet.[54] At Cabinet on 2 December, Hoare once again warned against any course of action that was not based on the principle of collective security, arguing that public opinion would be appalled if the government reneged on the pledges that had been given in the recent election campaign. He went on to suggest that ministers should agree to an oil sanction in principle, although he urged that it should not be implemented until military preparations for a possible Italian attack in the Mediterranean were further advanced. The Foreign Secretary also noted that he was about to visit Paris where he would 'see M. Laval and . . . try and press on peace talks with him'. The Cabinet debated the whole issue at great length, and Baldwin characteristically allowed every minister present to express their opinion on the issues before them. The defence ministers reiterated that Britain's military weakness indicated the need for a cautious policy, and secured a general agreement that 'we ought not to face hostilities unless they were absolutely forced upon us'. A decision on an oil sanction was effectively deferred, and the Foreign Secretary was instructed to continue his search for peace if there was 'a reasonable prospect of a settlement'. The Cabinet did not therefore provide Hoare with a detailed mandate to negotiate a settlement with Laval, but it clearly did authorise him to continue his search for a peaceful outcome to the crisis. Ministers also tellingly noted that they hoped the Foreign Secretary would take 'a generous view of the Italian attitude'.[55]

The Cabinet records for the meeting on 2 December make it clear that ministers knew Hoare intended to 'press on peace talks' during his stay in Paris. Hoare wrote on 2 December to Clive Wigram, the King's Private Secretary, that he thought the next few weeks would provide 'a period of intensive negotiations for a settlement. We intend to go all out for bringing the conflict to an end'.[56] On 5 December, he told a meeting of the Dominions High Commissioners in London that he hoped to reach agreement with Laval on joint proposals. On the same day he reassured Eden that he had no intention of committing ministers to a policy they were not happy to support, a statement he repeated in a conversation with Baldwin the following day, suggesting that the Foreign Secretary believed he had their support and goodwill.[57] Eden and Chamberlain subsequently denied that ministers had any sense of the kind of deal Hoare was contemplating,[58] but it is hard to find any evidence that the Foreign Secretary made a sustained attempt to cover up his hopes of reaching a settlement. It is therefore tempting to assume that at least some of Hoare's colleagues were burying their heads in the sand, refusing to face up to the harsh truth that any peace plan was bound to be unfavourable to Abyssinia, whilst others simply did not think through in a coherent manner the complex issues before them.

Hoare and Laval agreed during their talks in Paris on 7–8 December to recommend terms to the League that effectively rewarded Italy for its aggression in east Africa, providing it with large swathes of Abyssinian territory and virtual economic control over the rest of the country.[59] Although the negotiations were chaotic and disorganised, both the Foreign Secretary and Vansittart were happy with the agreement they reached.[60] There is little doubt, though, that ministers back in London were genuinely taken aback when Maurice Peterson arrived on the morning of 9 December with a copy of the agreement. MacDonald noted in his diary that it appeared 'a pretty bad climb-down'.[61] Eden later recalled that he was only kept from resignation by the knowledge that he could not make a sensible judgement without more information about Hoare's motives in 'agreeing to such proposals before consulting us'.[62] The Foreign Secretary himself travelled on to

Switzerland following the conclusion of his talks with Laval where, as fate decreed, he broke his nose in a skating accident and was instructed by his doctor not to return home. Hoare's absence from London in the week following his fateful meeting with Laval undoubtedly added to the confusion among his colleagues. Ministers attending the Cabinet that met on the evening of 9 December had not yet had time to study the terms in detail, with the result that their discussions were clouded in confusion and uncertainty.[63] Eden warned those present that 'some features of the proposals were likely to prove distasteful' to members of the League. Others fretted that the terms negotiated by Hoare seemed very much like 'rewarding the aggressor'.[64] The Cabinet nevertheless concluded after lengthy discussion to 'support the policy of the Secretary of State for Foreign Affairs'. The unambiguous nature of this conclusion needs to be borne in mind in the light of later developments. No minister chose to resign in the wake of the Cabinet's decision, even though the evidence does suggest that a good number of them were perturbed *at the time* about Hoare's actions. In failing to do so, they could be seen in effect to be 'absolutely and irretrievably responsible' for the policy set in motion by the Foreign Secretary.[65] As was subsequently pointed out in Parliament, ministers could have chosen to reserve their judgement until they had received more information.

The conventions relating to the collective responsibility of the Cabinet for government policy should perhaps be understood less as unambiguous rules framing the political process, and more as an uncertain set of principles that are subject to the vagaries of conflicting interpretation and political manoeuvre. The response of ministers to the crisis that erupted once the general character of Hoare's agreement with Laval became known revealed this process in action. The public reaction to the leaked terms of the Hoare–Laval Pact was largely hostile. *The Times* insisted on 11 December that any agreement should not 'give Italy ... more than general goodwill would have helped her to obtain by peaceful means'. Other papers such as the *Daily Mirror*, the *Daily Express* and the *News Chronicle* took an even more negative line. MPs from all parties received numerous letters complaining that the Government had cynically abandoned the principles that ministers articulated during the recent election campaign. The Cabinet meetings held on 10 and 11 December showed that ministers were becoming increasingly nervous about the burgeoning public opposition to the Hoare–Laval Pact. As a result, Eden was given considerable latitude in deciding what line to take during his forthcoming trip to Geneva, apparently in an effort to provide him with a chance to distance the British Government from the agreement.[66] Nevertheless, telegrams were sent to Addis Ababa and Rome on 11 December commending the terms to the two governments,[67] a factor that critics of the government made much of in the Commons debate that followed Hoare's resignation, since it provided evidence that ministers had effectively endorsed the Pact. The speeches in Parliament on 10 December highlighted ministers' confusion about the situation. A good deal has been written about Baldwin's curious statement to MPs that his lips were 'not yet unsealed', and that he would in due course be able to explain recent developments in such a way 'that not a Member would go into the Lobby against us'.[68] The Prime Minister was in fact doing little more than playing for time, hiding behind the fact that the terms of the agreement had not been officially published, and he soon came to regret his words, which provided a field day for cartoonists. Eden argued in a brave but unconvincing speech that news of the Paris talks should have come as a 'surprise to no-one',[69] since Britain and France were simply attempting to facilitate the League's search for a peaceful solution to the crisis. Both Baldwin and Eden were careful to avoid as far as possible the whole question of collective responsibility for the agreement, but in private ministers were clearly struggling to reconcile the pressures upon them. When Vansittart returned to London on 12 December, unaware of the scale of the furore,[70] ministers were already beginning to blame the Permanent Secretary and his political master for the situation in which they found themselves.

Hoare was still too ill to attend Cabinet meetings when he returned to Britain on 16 December, but he was soon plagued by a series of visits from his ministerial colleagues desperately seeking some way out of their dilemma. Neville Chamberlain served as the chief intermediary between Hoare and the Cabinet during these critical days, although the Chancellor had already told one of his sisters on 15 December that Government MPs were already convinced that the Foreign Secretary could not survive.[71] On 17 December, Chamberlain reported to the Cabinet that Hoare intended to defend his action in seeking an agreement with Laval during the forthcoming Commons debate, taking the line that the League had to face 'the realities of the situation', news which caused enormous consternation among ministers.[72] The Foreign Secretary was of course in an impossible position. If he failed to defend the agreement he negotiated in Paris then he would be forced to admit a major error of judgement that made his continued presence at the Foreign Office impossible. If he chose to defend himself, then as a member of the Cabinet he effectively associated his colleagues with an unpopular policy. Although the Cabinet had effectively assumed collective responsibility for Hoare's policy on 9 December, during the following ten days ministers started to speak and act in a way that assumed the constitutional aspect of the crisis was one that touched primarily on the Foreign Secretary's own individual situation. MacDonald noted in his diary on 15 December that he would consider resignation unless the Government disassociated itself from the Hoare–Laval Pact, apparently oblivious to the fact that he was himself a member of a Cabinet that had agreed to support the policy just six days earlier.[73] Whilst the National Government had received a massive majority in the November General Election, the anxiety among its backbench supporters was serious enough to threaten a major political crisis. Hoare's resignation therefore appeared as a tempting prospect to ministers, since it offered a way of diverting blame away from the Cabinet and on to an individual minister. The logic of politics meant that the Hoare–Laval Pact had to be packaged as an act of ministerial misjudgement rather than collective folly.

The Cabinet that met on 18 December was appalled when Chamberlain informed them that Hoare was still convinced of the 'rightness of his action', even though he accepted that in the light of public opinion the Government would not be able to 'adhere to his plan'.[74] A public pronouncement along these lines would clearly not distance the Government sufficiently from events in Paris on 7–8 December. Baldwin began proceedings by noting that Hoare – who was still not well enough to attend Cabinet – must feel as though he was 'on trial'. The ensuing discussion showed that he was. The Minister of Health Kingsley Wood said he was 'apprehensive' about Hoare's proposed speech. Cunliffe-Lister then upped the stakes by warning that he would have to resign if Hoare made a speech along the lines indicated. Other ministers including William Ormsby-Gore and Walter Elliot took a similar position. Lord Halifax added that Hoare's continued presence in the Cabinet would gravely weaken the 'moral authority' of the government, a pronouncement that carried great weight given the speaker's prestige within the British political establishment. It soon became clear that the Foreign Secretary did not have enough support to continue in office. Although Baldwin was reluctant to commit himself at this meeting, the Prime Minister made no sustained attempt to save Hoare. Ministers instead once again dispatched Chamberlain to inform Hoare of their views and, following a further visit, the Foreign Secretary duly tended his resignation.

The Commons debate that followed Hoare's resignation illuminated the complex relationship between constitutional theory and political practice, as all the main participants attempted to exonerate themselves and present their actions in the best possible light.[75] The Foreign Secretary himself stood up in the House on 19 December, his nose still heavily bandaged, in order to make a personal statement explaining his decision to resign. He was forthright in his defence of his actions in Paris two weeks earlier, telling his listeners that 'my conscience is clear ... looking back at the situation I was placed in a fortnight ago, I say to the House that I cannot honestly recant. I sincerely believe that the course I took was the only course under the circumstances'. He argued – with some justification – that his policy towards the Abyssinian crisis had always been predicated on an attempt to remain loyal to the League whilst simultaneously searching for any opportunity 'to find a peaceful settlement to this hateful controversy'. He went on to add that his resignation was due above all to his recognition that 'I have not got the confidence of the great body of opinion in the country, and I feel that it is essential for the Foreign Secretary, more than any other Minister in the Government, to have behind him the general approval of his fellow-countrymen'. By taking such a line, Hoare refused to acknowledge that his resignation could be seen as any acknowledgement of fault on his part. He pointedly said almost nothing about his relationship with his ministerial colleagues during the crisis, limiting himself to a throwaway comment that he had been 'pressed on all sides' to go to Paris in early December.

In the debate that followed, Clement Attlee, Leader of the small Labour opposition group of MPs, immediately focused on the vexed question which Hoare had said little about: namely, the Cabinet's role in recent developments. He began by noting pointedly that whilst the erstwhile Foreign Secretary had explained the reasons for his departure from office, 'we have not yet had an explanation as to where the Government as a whole stand in this matter'. He went on to criticise the decision to send Hoare to Paris given his already parlous state of health, and demanded to know whether the Foreign Secretary had been given detailed instructions or had instead been 'given a free hand' or 'told just to go and do his best'? Attlee then pointed out that details of the agreement between Hoare and Laval had been sent back to London on the morning of 9 December, and enquired whether ministers had endorsed it at the Cabinet held later that day, adding that if so 'I cannot see why the late Foreign Secretary is the only one resigning'. He also tellingly pointed out that the dispatch of a telegram to Addis Ababa two days later, urging the Emperor to accept the Hoare–Laval Plan, seemed to prove that the Cabinet had accepted responsibility for the agreement. Attlee was not of course privy to all the discussions that had taken place over the previous ten days, but his speech shrewdly pulled together all the available information to make a convincing case that Hoare's resignation should not represent the end of the crisis. He may, though, have overplayed his hand. By raising the question of the position of the Prime Minister and the Cabinet, he encouraged Conservative backbenchers, led by Austen Chamberlain, to rally to the Government in the debate that followed.

Baldwin struggled to respond to Attlee's charges in a speech that even close colleagues acknowledged was unconvincing. The Prime Minister defended the Cabinet's decision to accept the terms negotiated by Hoare on the grounds that its members felt they had no choice but to trust the judgement of their absent colleague. He went on to admit that he had been at fault in not recalling the Foreign Secretary back to London once the depth of the crisis became clear. He hinted – though without much conviction – that much of the confusion had been caused by the 'real difficulty' in maintaining effective communication between Paris and London. Most strikingly of all, the Prime Minister made no real attempt to counter the claim that the Cabinet had made a collective decision to accept the terms of the Hoare–Laval Pact on 9 December. In a response to an intervention by one MP, he acknowledged that 'The responsibility was that of myself and my colleagues, and it is the responsibility of each and all of us. I think that everyone who has had Cabinet experience will admit that that is the position'. Baldwin was, in fairness, anxious not to heap all the blame for the crisis on Hoare. In taking such a line, though, he did nothing to shelter his Government from further assault. Opposition MPs lined up to attack the weakness of the Prime Minister's position. Stafford Cripps argued that Baldwin should now be speaking from the back benches. Another Labour MP expressed his amazement that Hoare should be 'thrown to the wolves', given that the Prime Minister accepted that 'he and the rest of the Government are equally responsible for the terms which have aroused so much condemnation'. Hugh Dalton pithily suggested that 'His Majesty's Government are collectively responsible for what has been done wrong'. Both Baldwin and Neville Chamberlain, who spoke later in the debate, effectively based their defence on the fact that the Government had been flexible enough to change its position when the full extent of public hostility to the Hoare–Laval Pact became clear. It was a weak case. Hoare himself had accepted that the terms he negotiated in Paris were no longer viable prior to the Cabinet on 18 December, but he had still been forced to leave office by his colleagues.

Conclusion

Hoare received many letters of sympathy following his departure from the Foreign Office. Leo Amery praised his resignation speech and attacked Baldwin for deserting his Foreign Secretary.[76] Rex Leeper from the Foreign Office applauded Hoare for standing by his convictions.[77] Journalists including Malcolm Muggeridge and Victor Gordon-Lennox added their commiserations.[78] There was a good deal of cynicism in the press about the events surrounding the Foreign Secretary's departure. The *Daily Express* expressed the sentiment of much of Fleet Street when it noted acidly on 20 December that 'Belief is widespread among primitive men that the wrath to come may be averted by sacrificing one transgressor to the powers of darkness'. It was a shrewd judgement, for Hoare's fellow ministers certainly hoped that their colleague's resignation would calm the storm raging around them. Most ministers nevertheless expected that the erstwhile Foreign Secretary would soon return. Baldwin noted in Parliament on 19 December that he hoped to see Hoare return to the front bench in a short time. Even George V expressed a hope that he would soon be back in office.[79] There was a general recognition within the political establishment that Hoare's supposed *faux pas* was not serious enough to end his political career.

It has often been argued that constitutional conventions relating to collective and ministerial responsibility have grown weaker in the period since 1945, and that ministers no longer take them as seriously as their predecessors. There is almost certainly some truth in this analysis, but the operation of such conventions has always of necessity been a vexed and uncertain process. The political calculations surrounding the resignation of Sir Samuel Hoare as Foreign Secretary certainly casts doubt on any lingering illusion that there was a constitutional golden age in which politicians acted according to a clear set of well-understood rules. The events of December 1935 illustrate both the 'messiness' and the contingency of the political process. Politicians necessarily reacted to events in the wake of the Hoare–Laval agreement largely on the basis of short-term political considerations rather than in response to the potential constitutional implications of the situation. Indeed, until the debate in the House of Commons on 19 December, few members of the Government really grasped that there was a constitutional as well as a political aspect to the crisis they faced. Once Attlee and other Labour politicians sought to suggest that the Hoare–Laval debacle raised important questions of principle, though, the Government's supporters rallied round and prevented a political crisis from becoming a constitutional one that could threaten the Prime Minister's continued tenure of office.

There will probably always be some doubt about the exact circumstances surrounding Hoare's fateful visit to Paris in December 1935. Neither the official records nor the private papers provide a definitive answer to the question of whether the Foreign Secretary really believed that he was acting in accord with his instructions. There is, though, a great deal of evidence to suggest that ministers knew that he intended to seek an agreement with Laval as soon as possible. If they did not, then they were at the very least remiss in failing to follow up the numerous statements in which Hoare alluded to his intentions. It is true that the Cabinet minutes for 2 December do not show that ministers gave the Foreign Secretary detailed instructions for his forthcoming visit to Paris, although they can certainly be read to suggest that he was only required to seek further advice should he fail to reach agreement. The minutes for the meeting on 9 December, by contrast, specifically record that the Cabinet accepted responsibility for the agreement Hoare had just reached in Paris. It may well have been that ministers extended too much trust to the Foreign Secretary. It may also be that Hoare's judgement was clouded by his illness and by his comparative lack of experience in the intricacies of diplomacy. None of these considerations were, however, relevant to the constitutional nature of the crisis. In the event, of course, political realities triumphed over constitutional niceties, since the Baldwin government was able to rely on massive support in the House of Commons to secure its position. The intricacies and vagaries of British political life meant that a potential question of collective responsibility could be passed off as a matter for an individual minister alone.

8 Anthony Eden at the Foreign Office (1935–38)

Introduction

Anthony Eden was just thirty-eight when he took charge of the Foreign Office at the end of 1935, but he was in many ways better prepared to carry out the job than any of his recent predecessors. He had served as Parliamentary Private Secretary to Austen Chamberlain during the 1920s, speaking on foreign affairs in the House of Commons and attending League meetings at Geneva,[1] before subsequently serving as the Junior Minister at the Foreign Office in the National Government that came to power in 1931. Eden's involvement in the Disarmament Conference during the years that followed made him one of the most prominent faces of British foreign policy abroad, and by the time he entered the Cabinet as Minister for League Affairs in 1935 he had also established a strong domestic reputation for his grasp of international politics. As a result, his appointment in place of Samuel Hoare just a few months later came as no great surprise, although *The Times* predicted that Austen Chamberlain was the most likely candidate.[2] Baldwin himself had made it clear some years before that he regarded Eden as a 'potential Foreign Secretary', although in the event he seemed decidedly unenthusiastic when it came to appointing him to the job, noting somewhat ungraciously that since Chamberlain was too old for the post 'it looks as if it will have to be you'.[3] The new Foreign Secretary never entirely forgave the Prime Minister for taking such an offhand approach to his appointment.

Eden's standing at home rested in part on his good looks and suave dress sense, both of which helped him to stand out in the grey world of the 1930s political establishment. His reputation as a staunch defender of the League of Nations and collective security also increased his popularity at a time when such recent events as the East Fulham by-election and the Peace Ballot seemed to have demonstrated the depth of public concern about a future war. It is not altogether clear to what extent Eden deliberately sought to exploit his personal popularity as a way of strengthening his political position, but his high profile certainly made his dramatic resignation from the Foreign Office in February 1938 all the more worrying for the Chamberlain government. Behind the Foreign Secretary's debonair public image, though, lay another and altogether more troubled personality. Eden was without doubt deeply affected by the responsibility of dealing with the momentous issues that faced him throughout the 1930s. A number of his Cabinet colleagues and senior Foreign Office advisers were concerned that his judgement was prone to desert him at times of crisis.[4] Any serious effort to make sense of the circumstances surrounding the Foreign Secretary's departure from office in 1938 cannot afford to ignore the way in which complex personal tensions and human frailties contributed to the process.

It has sometimes been suggested that Eden's commitment to the League of Nations was a reflection of his experience as a soldier on the First World War battlefields, which claimed the lives of two of his brothers.[5] In reality, though, he looked at the League with some caution throughout the 1920s, opposing the Geneva Protocol, and fretting about the possible constraints on Britain's freedom of manoeuvre implied by the country's involvement in the mechanisms of collective security. It was only in the early 1930s that he began to develop his reputation as the foremost proponent of the League within the National Government. His experience of the endless complexities of the Geneva system during his time as a junior Foreign Office minister seems, paradoxically, to have persuaded him that the institution offered the best hope for preventing Europe from sliding back towards the cataclysm of 1914. Even the débâcle of the Disarmament Conference was unable to shake his faith in the League, and he spent a good deal of time and energy during these years in trying to ensure that Geneva remained a central focus in world politics. Although he was ready to trim his views during the Abyssinian crisis, when it became clear that the Cabinet was reluctant to take the lead in imposing sanctions on Italy, there was genuine passion in his repeated demands that Britain should be 'firm in support of the League of Nations'.[6] Such words often sounded like empty rhetoric on the lips of his colleagues. When Eden voiced them they had the patina of truth.[7]

Eden was convinced throughout the 1930s that Britain had a vital role to play in stabilising the situation on the continent. In a speech to the Conservative Association in Fulham, in the spring of 1935, he attacked those who believed that the country's involvement in European affairs would damage the unity of Empire (a view that still commanded widespread support on the right of the Party).[8] He continued to articulate these themes in his speeches throughout his first year of office, arguing that Britain's wealth and prestige imposed on the country a duty to promote international order on the continent.[9] The fallout of the Hoare–Laval Pact, along with the remilitarisation of the Rhineland in March 1936, undoubtedly made it harder for the Foreign Secretary to maintain the League at the heart of his vision of the future European order. Although Eden still used the language of 'collective security' – and genuinely hoped that the League could play a positive role in stabilising the international situation – he recognised that new strategies were required to deal with the numerous threats to world peace that emerged during his time at the Foreign Office. The remilitarisation of the Rhineland showed that Hitler was prepared to take decisive action to challenge the European *status quo*, whilst the continued pace of German rearmament raised inevitable questions about Berlin's future intentions towards Austria and Czechoslovakia. The intervention by outside powers in the Spanish Civil War, which erupted in 1936, showed how easily unrest in one part of Europe could undermine the stability of the whole continent. Nor were the challenges confined to Europe. The Japanese invasion of the Chinese mainland in 1937 highlighted the continuing vulnerability of British interests across the Far East. Eden's time at the Foreign Office was therefore spent facing the familiar dilemma of deciding how best to meet these challenges at a time when Britain's nascent rearmament programme had not yet yielded the results required to allow the government to take a firm diplomatic line in Europe and beyond. During his time in office he increasingly came to favour a form of 'collective security' predicated on the establishment of closer relations between the various states threatened by the rise of the dictators.

Eden's resignation from Neville Chamberlain's Cabinet in February 1938 has of course helped to secure his reputation as one of the most prominent anti-appeasers. He carefully cultivated this reputation in the years that followed, portraying himself in his memoirs as a consistent critic of appeasement,[10] but the reality was a good deal more complex. It has been seen in previous chapters that appeasement was for much of the 1930s an incremental response to a complex and uncertain international environment. British foreign policy after 1933 rested on a more or less articulated belief that it would be impossible to take an assertive line abroad until the rearmament programme began to bear fruit, and there is not much evidence to suggest that Eden systematically distanced himself from these assumptions during his first eighteen months in charge at the Foreign Office (when Baldwin was still Prime Minister). It was only when Chamberlain subsequently sought to elevate this *ad hoc* approach to international affairs into a more systematic and determined search for agreement with the dictators that Eden became really uneasy about 'appeasement'. And even then, it should be said, his fears always focused on Mussolini's Italy rather than Nazi Germany or Japan. This was due in part to the scale of Italian involvement in the Spanish Civil War, which faced the Foreign Secretary with one of his main challenges during his time at the Foreign Office, but it also reflected a personal animosity that went back to his difficult meeting with the Italian dictator in June 1935. Eden later denied that his policy towards Italy was influenced by his personal dislike of Mussolini,[11] but there is little doubt that the Italian dictator became something of a *bête noir* for him, in the same way that Nasser was to do two decades later during the Suez crisis. The rest of this chapter examines some of these developments in more depth, focusing in particular on Eden's relationship with Chamberlain following the latter's appointment as Prime Minister in May 1937. The conflict between the two men during the months leading up to the Foreign Secretary's resignation was in part the result of differences over the direction of policy, but it also reflected deep-seated tensions and disagreements about the foreign policy-making process itself. Eden's growing reservation about Chamberlain's search for an under-standing with Hitler and Mussolini was exacerbated by his sense that the Prime Minister was operating in a way that undermined the position of the department he headed. Like Curzon fifteen years earlier, he came to resent the way in which Number 10 attempted to set the direction of British foreign policy.

Eden and the Foreign Office

Eden was of course thoroughly familiar with the personnel and procedures of the Foreign Office when he took charge there at the end of 1935. He battled hard to maintain control over appointments and promotions, strongly resist-ing pressure from the Treasury to become involved in the process, thereby showing himself to be deeply imbued with the departmental ethos which assumed that members of the diplomatic establishment had their own dis-tinctive expertise that set them apart from the rest of the Civil Service.[12] The Foreign Secretary established a strong *esprit de corps* with his officials, treating them as experts who could offer valuable advice in formulating the recom-mendations he made to Cabinet on foreign policy. Although he was reason-ably diligent in reviewing the official papers that were put before him, Eden often preferred to discuss matters face-to-face with staff, believing that such informal meetings provided the best way of thrashing out difficult prob-lems. Senior officials including Orme Sargent, George Mounsey, Lancelot Oliphant and Robert Craigie were all regularly involved in the detailed reviews of policy that took place when the Foreign Secretary was in London. Eden also placed considerable store on the opinions of Ralph Wigram, who headed the Central Department until his early death in 1936, along with those of his successor William Strang. Eden's devoted Private Secretary, Oliver Harvey, played a particularly significant role as an informal political confidante and 'sounding board'. The Foreign Secretary had clear (if usually unexpressed) views about the calibre of the men who worked for him, prais-ing the work of the Central and Southern Departments, but privately lam-basting officials in the Far Eastern Department for failing to respond imaginatively to the crisis created by Japan's aggression against China.[13] Eden was particularly close to Lord Cranborne, who served as his junior minister, and resigned with the Foreign Secretary in February 1938. Whilst the two men occasionally disagreed over such issues as the raising of sanc-tions on Italy, in the summer of 1936,[14] they held similar views on most major international developments. Cranborne also proved popular among the permanent Foreign Office staff, integrating well into the organisation's structures and *modus operandi*, as well as playing a significant role in the debates about policy that took place there during 1936–38.

Eden's relationship with his two most senior officials was, ironically, rather more problematic. Alexander Cadogan, who was appointed senior Deputy Under-Secretary in the Foreign Office in 1936, before replacing Vansittart as Permanent Secretary at the start of 1938, was more inclined than the Foreign Secretary to support some form of *rapprochement* with Hitler and Mussolini. Cadogan's unpublished diary for 1937 shows that he disagreed with his political master on a number of issues, most notably on policy towards Spain during the Civil War, and believed that Eden's judgement was at times in question.[15] He also felt excluded from decisions over policy. Cadogan's personal relationship with Eden was, however, reasonably good despite these differences (the two men had worked closely together in Geneva in the early 1930s where they had established a considerable degree of mutual respect). The same was not true of the Foreign Secretary's relationship with Vansittart. The criticism Vansittart faced during the Abyssinian crisis had seriously damaged his authority, whilst Eden in any case found him a difficult man to work with, hinting in his memoirs that the Permanent Secretary was too inclined to pursue his own policy regardless of the instructions of ministers.[16] Vansittart was more cautious than Eden about taking any action that might drive Mussolini into the arms of Hitler, given that he identified Germany as the real threat to British security, and he was therefore more inclined to favour good relations with Rome than his political master. It was for this reason that Eden made a concerted (if eventually unsuccessful) attempt to get rid of his Permanent Secretary at the end of 1936, by persuading him to become ambassador in Paris.[17] Vansittart was eventually 'kicked upstairs' at the start of 1938 to the ill-defined post of Chief Diplomatic Adviser, a move brought about by Neville Chamberlain, who was convinced that the Permanent Secretary was using his influence and vast array of contacts to undermine the Prime Minister's policy of improving relations with Berlin.[18]

Eden followed his predecessors in maintaining a private correspondence with the heads of major British diplomatic missions abroad, designed to supplement the more formal channels of communication such as dispatches and telegrams. The Foreign Secretary looked with scepticism on letters and dispatches received from Eric Drummond (subsequently Lord Perth) in Rome, since the ambassador had long since acquired a reputation in the Foreign Office as a zealous advocate of better Anglo-Italian relations. He was more inclined to pay attention to the views of the ambassador in Berlin, Sir Eric Phipps, a strong critic of the Nazi regime who opposed any concessions to Hitler on the ground that they would only whet his appetite for further adventures.[19] Phipps's views did, though, undergo a marked metamorphosis following his transfer to the Paris Embassy early in 1937, and by the time of the Munich crisis in the autumn of 1938 he had become a strong advocate of Chamberlain's appeasement policy.[20] During the period when Eden was still in office, though, Phipps's views on policy were seldom far removed from those of the Foreign Secretary. He was, for example, perturbed by the scale of Italian intervention in Spain, believing that a victory for the Franco government would pose real problems for British interests in the region, and he even briefly considered resigning himself in the wake of Eden's departure from office.[21] Phipps only really became one of Chamberlain's 'ambassadors of appeasement' in the months following Eden's departure from office,[22] when his views became increasingly influenced by pessimistic voices in the French political elite who suggested that their country was too weak to risk a confrontation with Germany.

The most controversial ambassadorial appointment made during Eden's time as Foreign Secretary was that of Sir Nevile Henderson, who replaced Phipps in Berlin, having previously been posted in South America.[23] Eden observed in his memoirs that 'It was an international misfortune that we should have been represented in Berlin at this time by a man who, so far from warning the Nazis, was constantly making excuses for them ... More than once ... I had to warn him against the recurring habit of interpreting my instructions in a fashion too friendly to the Nazis.'[24] Henderson undoubtedly felt that he had a special mission to improve Anglo-German relations, writing in his own memoirs that he was convinced 'that the peace of Europe depended upon the realisation of an understanding between Britain and Germany'.[25] Shortly before departing to take up his new post, he had been invited to a lengthy meeting with Neville Chamberlain – who was still Chancellor of the Exchequer at the time – at which the future Prime Minister 'agreed that I should do my utmost to work with Hitler and the Nazi Party as the existing Government in Germany'.[26] Henderson worked hard to improve Anglo-German relations from the moment he arrived in Berlin, helping to ensure the go-ahead of Lord Halifax's controversial visit to the country in November 1937,[27] and throughout his time in Germany he seems to have taken Chamberlain's words as an express permission to play a role that went beyond the one normally expected of an ambassador. Eden rebuked him on a number of occasions for speaking without proper authority, most notably in the summer of 1937, when in a meeting with the Austrian Minister in Berlin he appeared to support the principle of Austro-German union.[28] The maverick qualities of the ambassador also raised fears among many Foreign Office officials. Eden may, though, have exaggerated his concern about Henderson's activities when writing his memoirs. It will be seen in the following pages that the Foreign Secretary was himself by no means averse to some form of bilateral deal with Germany during his time in charge at the Foreign Office. Nor did he seem as concerned at the time by Henderson's close relationship with Chamberlain as he later implied. Some of the personal schisms and tensions that later became part of the appeasement legend were rather less clear-cut when viewed from a contemporary perspective.

Eden and the making of foreign policy under Baldwin

Eden experienced differences with some of his ministerial colleagues even before Chamberlain became Prime Minister, complaining bitterly in his memoirs that Baldwin failed to offer him full backing in Cabinet,[29] although it is not clear that such a charge was entirely fair.[30] Although there were times when the Foreign Secretary found it difficult to persuade ministers to approve his recommendations, such disagreements represented part of the normal ebb and flow of political debate at the heart of government. There was in reality something close to a Cabinet consensus on the main lines of foreign policy throughout Eden's first eighteen months at the Foreign Office. Most ministers supported the process of British rearmament set in motion following the report of the Defence Requirements Committee, and the subsequent white paper on defence, whilst hoping at the same time to promote a general 'appeasement' that would avoid any return to the balance of power politics of the period before 1914. Such a position was, though, susceptible to many different interpretations when applied to actual developments. If there was a striking difference between Eden and some of his colleagues, it was that the Foreign Secretary was more inclined to believe that Britain was in a position to take a tougher line towards Berlin and Rome without driving Hitler and Mussolini into a united axis of opposition. In his final months in office, in particular, he was also more interested than most of his colleagues in promoting a form of 'collective security' designed to mobilise international support to prevent further expansion of the two main European dictator states. It was only following his resignation, though, that Eden really became a more definite advocate of a general alliance designed to rein in the ambitions of the European dictators.

A number of brief case studies of foreign policy-making during the last eighteen months of Baldwin's third government can illustrate some of these points in a little more depth. Eden's reaction to German's remilitarisation of the Rhineland in March 1936 was not strikingly different from the reaction of other ministers, who were all painfully aware that public opinion and the poor quality of Britain's air defences would make it difficult to take a firm line with Berlin.[31] A few days after German troops entered the Rhineland, the Foreign Office drafted a paper noting that discussion had already taken place in London about possible talks on the zone's future, with the result that recent events had not in fact 'produced a result [that] we were not prepared ultimately to contemplate'.[32] In the frantic talks that took place in the following days with representatives of the French and Belgian governments, Eden counselled caution and warned against any rash response to Hitler's move.[33] Although some ministers did write privately to the Prime Minister warning against the danger of allowing the French to dictate British policy,[34] there is little evidence that Eden's colleagues were seriously concerned that the Foreign Secretary would commit them to a policy they were not happy to support. Baldwin and Eden both favoured talks between the

French and British military staffs in the wake of the crisis, a policy that was supported by most ministers with the exception of a small number including John Simon and Kingsley Wood, who were concerned that such a development would make the tense international situation still more difficult. There was also general support among ministers for the Foreign Secretary's diligent effort to clarify and reassert the status of the Locarno treaties in the wake of Hitler's challenge. The remilitarisation of the Rhineland certainly provoked a crisis atmosphere both at home and abroad, but Eden's instinctive response echoed that of most members of the Cabinet. He was reluctant to risk war on a matter that was not generally regarded as a vital British interest and on which it would be difficult to mobilise public support.

Eden's position on sanctions following the Hoare–Laval débacle was somewhat tougher, reflecting his deep-seated distrust of Mussolini and Italian foreign policy, a theme that had been central to his thinking on international relations since at least the opening months of the Abyssinian crisis. At the end of February 1936 he proposed to ministers that they should agree to an oil sanction designed to put pressure on Italy to come to some form of agreement over the future of Abyssinia. A number of ministers agreed with him, citing the pressure of public opinion, whilst others such as Walter Runciman at the Board of Trade (who was like Simon a Liberal National)[35] were opposed on the grounds that such a move might damage British trade. Although the oil sanction was never implemented, given the difficulty of securing support in Geneva, Eden continued to favour the maintenance of the measures that had been imposed the previous year.[36] Most ministers were, however, vacillating on the subject by the spring of 1936, doubting the value of sanctions, but anxious about a hostile public response should they decide to end them.[37] Neville Chamberlain brought the issue to a head in a speech in early June when, without consulting other ministers, he described the maintenance of sanctions as 'the very midsummer of madness'. The Chancellor acknowledged in a letter to one of his sisters that he had made a 'blazing indiscretion', but defended himself by arguing that someone had to 'give a lead' on the issue.[38] Eden's public and private reaction to Chamberlain's speech was surprisingly muted.[39] This may simply have represented hard-headed recognition on his part that a majority of his colleagues wanted sanctions removed, a position that echoed the advice of many of his officials, one of whom noted rather acidly that the Foreign Secretary was unable to give an 'intelligible answer' when asked to explain the purpose of maintaining them intact.[40] At the same time, though, there is little evidence that Eden was prepared to expend much energy campaigning for the maintenance of sanctions. He certainly encouraged the Foreign Office to move quickly once the decision had been taken to end them.[41] The Foreign Secretary did nevertheless continue to fight for the principle that Britain should defend the League and 'build our future policy on the basis of its continued existence'.[42] Eden also resisted pressure from Chamberlain and a number of other ministers to seek an amendment to Article 16 of the

Covenant, which set down that if any League member resorted to war 'in disregard of its covenants ... [it would] *ipso facto* be deemed to have committed an act of war against all other Members of the League'.[43] The Foreign Secretary was ready to admit that the Abyssinian crisis had shown up the League's shortcomings, but he continued to resist calls from some of his colleagues for a radical rethinking of its role and operation.

The Spanish Civil War posed Eden with his greatest challenge during his time as Baldwin's Foreign Secretary, causing him to become 'very jumpy', as he sought to deal with an intractable conflict that created enormous international and domestic tension.[44] The Foreign Secretary played a key role in the creation of the Non-Intervention Committee, based in London, which was established to prevent outside interference in the Spanish *imbroglio*. In practice, though, the German, Italian and Soviet governments made little effort to hide their involvement in the conflict, and the practical impact of the Committee was limited. A number of ministers, including Samuel Hoare, made no secret of their concern that a victory for the Government forces in Spain might increase the influence of the USSR in western Europe, a position that was echoed by numerous leading Conservatives outside the Cabinet including Churchill.[45] Hankey also endorsed this position, noting that the challenge of bolshevism in France and Spain might even force Britain to 'throw in our lot with Germany and Italy'.[46] Eden devoted considerable effort both at home and abroad to promoting the non-intervention effort, believing that it offered the best means of preventing the victory of Franco, which he feared would be followed up by further German and Italian pressure elsewhere in Europe. At the start of 1937, he wrote a Cabinet paper calling for the British fleet to take the lead in preventing volunteers and war material from being shipped to Spain, and suggested that France and Portugal should be asked to redouble their efforts to stop supply by land.[47] The reaction of his colleagues in the face of such proposals was very cautious. Hoare, who had by now returned to office at the Admiralty, argued that such an operation would be technically difficult. Duff Cooper at the War Office warned that it would make European war more likely.[48] There were also doubts within the Foreign Office about Eden's proposal. Whilst a meeting of senior officials agreed that Eden's paper should be recommended to Cabinet, Cadogan for one thought it rather a 'hare-brained scheme'.[49] Although many senior members of the British political establishment mused privately that a victory for Franco would be less damaging than a victory for Soviet-backed government forces, Eden remained more fearful of an extension of Italian and German influence in the western Mediterranean. It was for this reason that he was even tempted in 1937 to allow the Popular Front government in France to provide the Republicans in Spain with military supplies, despite the fact he had previously put pressure on Paris to follow a policy of strict neutrality. Eden was undoubtedly more sensitive than most members of the Cabinet to the passionate views of the British left on the Spanish Civil War, and his support for non-intervention was partly inspired by a shrewd recognition that it was less likely to cause domestic division than any other policy.[50] On this issue, more than any other during the life of the third Baldwin government, the Foreign Secretary found himself taking a position that set him apart from most of his ministerial colleagues.

The perennial tensions involved in co-ordinating foreign policy with defence and economic policy were as sharp as ever during Eden's first eighteen months at the Foreign Office. The Board of Trade's support for the end of sanctions against Italy was largely motivated by its fear over the economic consequences of the embargo. The Treasury continued to exercise considerable influence on the pattern of British rearmament, motivated in large part by its concern over the possible implications for the public finances, whilst Chamberlain unashamedly sought to exercise his influence on a whole range of international questions.[51] Eden nevertheless worked hard to maintain good relations with his Cabinet colleagues during his time at the Foreign Office under Baldwin, and the usual *ad hoc* arrangements for securing inter-departmental co-ordination continued to function, although not always without difficulty. The co-ordination of foreign and defence policy continued to pose a particular problem. Despite Eden's strong commitment to the British rearmament programme, he was not in fact particularly interested in the detailed complexities of strategy and procurement that obsessed the Chiefs of Staff and the various defence ministers. He seldom attended meetings of the Committee of Imperial Defence, preferring to be represented by one of his officials, which meant that he was often unfamiliar with the vast array of issues that came within its purview. To make matters worse, the defence ministers were not represented on the new Foreign Policy Committee that was set up by the Cabinet in April 1936, and whilst Baldwin normally chaired both the Committee of Imperial Defence and the Foreign Policy Committee, the situation was not conducive to integrating discussion of foreign policy with discussion of military matters. Nor were matters much improved by the appointment of Thomas Inskip as Minister for the Co-ordination of Defence in the spring of 1936, since the uncertain nature of his remit led him to focus his attention primarily on narrow technical issues rather than broader questions of strategy. There was a widespread perception within government that the Foreign Office's role in the second half of the 1930s was to 'buy time' until successful rearmament allowed for a more assertive response to international challenges. During Eden's time at the Foreign Office, though, the institutional arrangements were never really put in place to facilitate the development of a well co-ordinated response to the array of international problems facing Britain.

One of Eden's biographers has suggested there was already tension between the Foreign Secretary and other members of the Cabinet by the final months of 1936, since he favoured a more 'leisurely' approach to the problems of improving relations with Germany and Italy than most of his colleagues.[52] It is, though, important not to overstate the differences between Eden and other ministers during the time when Baldwin was still at Number 10. The Foreign Secretary was certainly not implacably opposed to improving relations with Berlin and Rome, even if he considered the matter less urgent than some of his colleagues. He was for example ready to contemplate with some equanimity a deal with Berlin that would return to Germany some of its former colonies as part of a broader political agreement.[53] The foreign policy of the Baldwin government during its last eighteen months was the outcome of the usual process of discussion and disagreement. The Foreign Secretary was certainly not always able to get his way, but he suffered no constraints that were not part of the normal 'checks and balances' of Cabinet government. Although it is possible to identify sharp differences of opinion amongst ministers over foreign policy during the eighteen months before Chamberlain replaced Baldwin at Number 10, they should not be seen as the inevitable harbingers of Eden's dramatic departure from office in February 1938.

Eden and the making of foreign policy under Neville Chamberlain

Neville Chamberlain was well versed in the intricacies of international politics when he arrived in Number 10 in May 1937. Nor did he suffer from any doubts about his mastery of the subject. He told one of his sisters at the height of the Abyssinian crisis two years before that he had 'as usual greatly influenced policy',[54] whilst a few months later, after Eden had moved to the Foreign Office, he proudly described how he had 'taken the lead all through' a recent conference with French ministers.[55] There is little evidence that Chamberlain seriously dissented from the main lines of the foreign policy pursued by the third Baldwin government, and when he became Prime Minister he echoed the familiar mantra that rearmament and careful diplomacy 'will carry us safely through the danger period' created by the growing power of Germany.[56] Chamberlain did, though, differ from his predecessor in two important ways. He was in the first place more willing than Baldwin to make a sustained effort to improve relations with Rome and Berlin, in order to secure the kind of European pacification that had been dreamt of by British governments since 1919. He was also ready to involve himself personally in detailed negotiations with foreign powers. Eden for his part at first welcomed Chamberlain's appointment, believing that the new Prime Minister would offer him more effective support than his predecessor, but the potential for conflict between the two men quickly became apparent in the weeks and months that followed.

Chamberlain was politically astute enough to understand how to mobilise the formidable political powers available to a British Prime Minister. As Chancellor of the Exchequer he had shown himself adept at asserting himself within the complex array of inter-departmental and Cabinet committees where much of the daily work of government was carried out. His arrival at Number 10 gave him the opportunity to intervene on a far greater scale. Chamberlain never shared Baldwin's instinctive belief that government should be run by allowing ministers autonomy in the running of their departments. The Lloyd George era had shown the potential power of Number 10 to act as the driving force across a whole swathe of public policy, and Chamberlain quickly sought to establish his office as a key actor in the foreign policy-making process. The new Prime Minister was wary of the elaborate edifice of Cabinet committees developed by Maurice Hankey over the previous two decades, believing that it placed a drag on dynamic policy-making, but he was ready to make use of the system to strengthen his own position. As chairman of the Committee of Imperial Defence and the Foreign Policy Committee he was uniquely placed within government to oversee the formation of foreign and defence policy. Chamberlain was also well placed both by his position and his experience to dominate the Conservative Party, helping him to limit the impact of Conservative critics of his foreign policy such as Churchill and Boothby, thereby ensuring parliamentary support even at such critical times as Eden's resignation and the Munich crisis.[57] His reach also extended well beyond Westminster and Whitehall. During his time as Prime Minister, Chamberlain was adept at using the Number 10 Press Office that had been set up a few years earlier both to mute criticism of his policies and to mobilise support for appeasement in newspapers such as *The Times*.[58]

The new Prime Minister also gave a significant role to Sir Horace Wilson, whose formal title of Chief Industrial Adviser did little to hint at the wide-ranging nature of his duties. Wilson played a significant role in the execution of British foreign policy under Chamberlain, travelling with the Prime Minister on his visits to Hitler in September 1938, and acting as an important liaison between the Foreign Office and Number 10. It is, however, important not to overestimate his part in the development of Chamberlain's foreign policy, which was exaggerated by some of the early critics of appeasement. Lord Halifax later recalled that he found Wilson 'extremely helpful' in keeping the Foreign Office and Number 10 informed of one another's activities during his time at the Foreign Office.[59] Eden's comments on Wilson in his memoirs are also comparatively subdued. Although Chamberlain discussed foreign policy with Wilson on a regular basis, the Chief Industrial Adviser was above all an agent rather than an architect of policy. Nevertheless, whilst he was never the *éminence grise* that has sometimes been suggested, his position showed how the Prime Minister was able to make use of his advisers at Number 10 to extend the reach of his power across government. The role of another of these informal agents, Sir Joseph Ball, will be considered in more detail below.

It would be misleading to suggest that Eden and Chamberlain were at daggers drawn throughout the eight months leading up to the Foreign Secretary's resignation, but the Prime Minister's desire to adopt a more 'hands-on' approach to foreign policy meant that the possibility of disagreement was present from the start. Eden had resented Baldwin's lack of interest in foreign affairs, but he was at least secure in the knowledge that the Prime Minister was unlikely to take any major initiative running directly contrary to the wishes of his Foreign Secretary. Chamberlain, by contrast, sought to use his formidable political power to direct foreign policy in a manner that quickly came to irritate Eden. The new Prime Minister had looked askance at the Foreign Office for a number of years, dating back at least as far as the dispute over policy towards Japan in 1934, and from the moment he came to office he suspected that senior officials (particularly Vansittart) were opposed to his policy of establishing better relations with Berlin and Rome. In early August he noted in a letter to his sister that the Foreign Office was 'jealous' of anyone who trespassed on areas they considered their own private domain, and a few days later he expressed anxiety that they would deliberately miss opportunities to improve relations with Mussolini.[60] As the weeks passed, his comments became sharper. By the autumn the Foreign Secretary himself was becoming a focus of discontent in the Prime Minister's correspondence.[61] Eden subsequently implied in his memoirs that the growing tension between Chamberlain and himself in the second half of 1937 was largely due to a clear difference over policy towards Hitler and Mussolini. Whilst there was some truth in his claim, though, the real situation was rather more complicated than it appeared in the pages of *Facing the Dictators*.

The interventionist role played by Italy during the Spanish Civil War certainly confirmed Eden's long-standing suspicion of the fascist regime in Rome, and made him deeply reluctant to enter negotiations about possible *de jure* recognition of Italian rule in Abyssinia. Chamberlain for his part arrived in Number 10 happy to consider such a prospect as part of a long-term programme for improving relations between Britain and Italy. In the months after he came to office, the Prime Minister made use of an elaborate secret channel to the Italian government, the main actors in which were Sir Joseph Ball, an erstwhile MI5 agent who had subsequently become Head of the Conservative Research Department, and Adrian Dingli, a London barrister who served as Legal Counsellor to the Italian Embassy.[62] In the middle of July, Ball sent Dingli to Rome, from where he returned with a message that the Italian government would welcome a move to improve relations between the two countries. The Italian ambassador in London, Dino Grandi, subsequently saw Eden to request an interview with Chamberlain that eventually took place on 27 July. At this meeting, Chamberlain composed a friendly letter to Mussolini noting that the British government was ready 'at any time to enter upon conversations with a view to clarifying [the] misunderstandings and unfounded suspicions' that had dogged Anglo-Italian relations over the previous two years.[63] It is still not clear whether the Prime Minister was entirely aware of all the the convoluted circumstances that led up to his meeting with Grandi, but he certainly neglected to show his letter to Eden on the grounds that the Foreign Secretary would probably 'object to it', a sure indication that he was ready to marginalise the political head of the Foreign Office.[64] There were in fact considerable differences within the Foreign Office over policy towards Italy during the second half of 1937. When Miles Lampson, by now the ambassador in Cairo, wrote to the Foreign Office in July arguing that Mussolini's ambitions posed a threat to Britain's vital interests in North Africa, both Orme Sargent and Vansittart minuted that his 'Italophobia' was exaggerated, a position that reflected both men's instinctive convictions that it was Germany which posed the real threat to British interests in Europe.[65] Eden's minutes make it clear, though, that he profoundly distrusted the intentions of the Italian government. In an early draft of a Cabinet Paper on Anglo-Italian relations, he noted despairingly 'that many of my [Cabinet] colleagues believe we can reach, and that fairly soon, a state of relations with Italy that will justify our relaxing our rearmament effort', adding that 'Italian policy is too untrustworthy for this to be possible'.[66] He also tartly criticised internal Foreign Office memoranda that took too 'soft' a line on Italy, noting that any positive moves by the British government to improve relations with Rome were always seen in the Italian capital as 'a sign of weakness'.[67] When Halifax briefly took charge of the Foreign Office, in August 1937, the Foreign Secretary wrote him a private note urging that Britain should 'go slow' on Anglo-Italian *rapprochement*.[68] Chamberlain for his part grew increasingly frustrated by Eden's reluctance to support talks with Italy. At the end of August he told his sister that 'We can't go on for ever refusing recognition [of Italian control of Abyssinia] . . . and it seems to me that we had better give it while we can still get something in return for it'.[69] In September he complained that Eden 'has never really believed in Musso's sincerity', and a few weeks later criticised the Foreign Secretary for being too easily provoked by the Italian dictator's anti-English rants.[70] The Treaty of Nyon, signed by the powers in September 1937, briefly held out the prospect of some kind of accommodation with Italy over foreign intervention in Spain, but its manifest failure meant that the whole question of Anglo-Italian relations remained an important source of tension between the Prime Minister and the Foreign Secretary.[71]

There were also differences between Chamberlain and Eden over policy towards Germany in the second half of 1937, although they were not as sharp as the younger man subsequently implied in his memoirs. Eden looked with a degree of equanimity throughout 1936 and 1937 at the possibility of an agreement with Hitler on the colonial question, a subject that was perennially discussed as a possible way of securing 'an appeasement of the political situation' in Europe.[72] Nor did he initially oppose the celebrated visit by Lord Halifax to a hunting exhibition in Germany in the autumn of 1937, which both Halifax and the Prime Minister favoured as a way of making informal contact with key members of the German government.[73] Oliver Harvey recorded in his diary that Eden was profoundly unhappy at the prospect of the visit, but the Foreign Secretary's initial reaction was in reality more equivocal, and Harvey himself acknowledged that a number of Foreign Office staff actually favoured some kind of an approach to Hitler.[74] Eden's real concern was to dampen public expectations of the trip, which he feared might create undue pressure for an early agreement when news about it was leaked to the press. Following Halifax's return from his trip, in which he had meetings with Hitler and Goering,[75] Eden and his senior officials were happy to draft a paper setting down the course of possible future negotiations with Germany over the colonial question. The Foreign Secretary did, however, remain determined that any agreement should form part of a broader understanding in which Berlin offered guarantees not to use force to change the *status quo* in Europe.[76] It would be wrong to imagine that the Halifax visit represented a deliberate attempt to marginalise the Foreign Secretary and drive policy forward in a way that he did not approve. Eden was concerned that Halifax should not be seen to be 'forcing himself on Hitler',[77] but he was not implacably opposed to the principle of establishing the kind of contacts with Berlin that might help to pave the way for future negotiations. Harvey was convinced that an anti-Eden cabal had emerged in Cabinet by the final weeks of 1937 – based around Hoare, Simon and Halifax – as well as the Prime Minister himself. He also speculated in his diary about the possibility of Eden's resignation, noting that the Foreign Secretary was increasingly frustrated by his position.[78] Harvey's impressions were not, though, always accurate. Eden's views on vital questions of foreign policy were given a proper hearing both in Cabinet and the Foreign Policy Committee in the final weeks of 1937, but a majority of ministers instinctively favoured a determined search for better relations with Berlin and Rome. The Foreign Secretary was not the victim of a 'cabal'. He simply faced a situation in which his views placed him in a minority.

The starkest disagreement between Eden and the Prime Minister emerged over the government's response to a message from President F.D. Roosevelt in January 1938, proposing an international meeting to promote disarmament and secure equal access to raw materials for all countries.[79] In an exchange of letters in early January, Eden had already suggested to Chamberlain that Britain should seek to develop better relations with the United States, as a means of countering the dictator states both in Europe and the Far East. The Prime Minister by contrast stubbornly insisted on the need to press ahead with attempts to secure an understanding with Rome. It also seems that Chamberlain was by this stage once again making use of his 'secret channel' to push ahead with talks.[80] Eden was on holiday in the south of France when Roosevelt's message arrived in London, and Cadogan (who had just replaced Vansittart as Permanent Secretary) told Chamberlain direct about the receipt of the message. The Prime Minister was unenthusiastic about the President's proposal, which risked complicating his own attempts at improving relations with Berlin and Rome, and he sent a cool response expressing concern that such a move might cut across his own attempts to improve the political situation. When Eden returned from holiday he was appalled to hear of Chamberlain's reply. Although the details of Roosevelt's plan were admittedly extremely vague, the Foreign Secretary believed that greater American involvement in global affairs could play an important role in securing international peace, not least by changing the psychological and military balance of power against the dictator states. The eruption of fighting in the Far East in 1937 had once again highlighted the vulnerability of British interests in the region, and the United States alone had sufficient naval power to help Britain counter the Japanese threat.[81] American involvement of the kind proposed by Roosevelt was also likely to make a strong impression in Europe. In a series of tense meetings in the Foreign Policy Committee, on 19–21 January, Eden persuaded his colleagues to take a more positive response to the American proposal, and delay any unconditional *de jure* recognition of Italian sovereignty over Abyssinia (which was certain to alienate Roosevelt and weaken the President's tentative plans to increase his country's global engagement). It is still not clear how Eden was able to win over his colleagues on the Committee, particularly since a majority of them initially expressed little support for his position. He certainly threatened resignation on the issue at one stage,[82] although as Chamberlain pointed out this was unrealistic given that the President had asked the British to keep details of his proposals secret. The Foreign Secretary's ministerial colleagues may, however, have been concerned enough at the prospect to accept Eden's insistence that *de jure* recognition should be dependent on a broader settlement of outstanding problems, particularly the status of Italian 'volunteers' fighting with Franco's supporters in Spain. In the event, however, the Foreign Secretary's efforts proved to be in vain. The administration in Washington itself procrastinated over the next few weeks, and Roosevelt himself eventually decided to withdraw his earlier proposals so as not to interfere with any British initiative.

Winston Churchill later noted that the disagreement over Roosevelt's initiative was the main reason for Eden's resignation,[83] but the fact he did not resign for another month suggests that the situation was rather more complicated. The Foreign Secretary's decision to leave the Cabinet in February was in reality the consequence of a number of factors. In late January, he was ready to consider a new proposal by Chamberlain offering colonial concessions to Germany in return for guarantees in Europe, although he insisted on some definite way of ensuring that Berlin was held to any deal. Eden was also ready to consider negotiations with Rome, although he remained unaware of the existence of Chamberlain's 'secret channel', later noting that he would have resigned at once had it come to his attention. At the end of January, the Foreign Secretary discussed policy towards Italy with French officials at Geneva, and on his return to London insisted that there was 'no reluctance on our part' to begin conversations.[84] The Foreign Secretary was, though, reluctant to offer *de jure* recognition without some definite form of *quid pro quo*, a position that was in fact at odds with the one he had himself taken just a few weeks earlier in a correspondence with Chamberlain, when he argued that such a move should only be taken 'on its merits'.[85] In the second week of February, the situation became more complex still, when it became clear that Neville Chamberlain's sister-in-law, who was visiting Rome, had shown Mussolini and his Foreign Minister Count Ciano letters from the Prime Minister expressing a strong desire to push ahead with nego-tiations. Chamberlain never intended his sister-in-law to act in so indiscreet a manner,[86] but Eden was appalled when he found out about the situation, writing to Chamberlain on 8 February that such 'unofficial diplomacy does place me in a most difficult position'.[87] Eden also noted that he believed Italy was over-extended and weak, with the result that Britain could afford to take a tough line in any conversations. The Prime Minister agreed that Italy was not in a strong position, but once again warned against the danger of giving 'the impression that we do not want to have conversations at all'.[88]

The differences between the two men deepened over the next ten days, as Eden became more irritated than ever at Chamberlain's attempts to forge ahead with the Italian conversations. Although he was not aware of the secret channel to Rome,[89] the Foreign Secretary was convinced – correctly – that Number 10 was waging a press campaign in favour of talks.[90] Eden remained determined that the Italian government should offer some kind of concession to British demands for the withdrawal of Italian volunteers from Spain prior to substantive talks, whilst the Prime Minister remained content for the subject to form part of the actual conversations. On the evening of the 17 February pro-Government MPs meeting at Westminster expressed support for a strong line towards Italy, a move that undoubtedly encouraged Eden to stick to his view that negotiations with Italy should proceed with caution. Recent research has suggested that Chamberlain's use of the secret channel intensified during late January and early February, with the result that the Prime Minister was by now deeply concerned that evidence of his role would be made public, which doubtless made him more sensitive and defensive over the whole issue. The tension between Chamberlain and Eden during their celebrated meeting with Dino Grandi on 18 February has become the stuff of diplomatic legend. The Italian ambassador subsequently told Count Ciano in Rome that during the meeting 'Chamberlain and Eden were not a Prime Minister and a Foreign Minister discussing with the Ambassador of a Foreign Power a delicate situation of an international char-acter. They were – and revealed themselves as such to me in defiance of all established convention – two enemies confronting each other, like two cocks in a true fighting posture'.[91] Grandi was asked at one point to leave Eden and Chamberlain alone so that they could discuss matters further, during which time a sharp exchange took place between the two men. Eden recalled that the Prime Minister was 'more vehement than I have ever seen him before', accusing the Foreign Secretary of missing 'chance after chance' to improve relations with Italy. Eden for his part stubbornly continued to oppose the opening of talks without more substantial evidence of Italian goodwill.[92] Chamberlain later noted in a letter to his sister that he realised 'the time had come when I must make my final stand and that Anthony must yield or go'.[93] The events of the next few days proved that the Prime Minister was in the stronger position to assert his will.

Several ministers wrote accounts of the critical Cabinet meetings that led up to Eden's resignation.[94] At the meeting on 19 February, Chamberlain began by explaining with masterly understatement that he 'did not quite agree' with the Foreign Secretary on policy towards Italy, and went on to suggest that 'the present occasion' provided a rare opportunity to show Mussolini 'that he might have other friends beside Herr Hitler'. The Prime Minister also suggested that an agreement with Italy would allow lower defence expenditure and help to improve the public finances. Eden for his part argued that starting talks with Italy without firm guarantees over the withdrawal of volunteers from Spain involved 'real risks', and would 'be regarded as another surrender to the Dictators'. He also made it clear that he believed Italy and Germany had already reached some kind of secret deal over the future of Austria, with the result that it would in practice prove impossible to detach Mussolini from Hitler, something that the Prime Minister still believed was possible. In the discussion that followed, most ministers backed Chamberlain's position, although a few like Malcolm Mac-Donald (Secretary of State at the Dominions Office) and Lord Zetland (Secretary of State at the India Office) were reluctant to see talks with Italy go ahead without some prior concessions. Simon supported the Prime Minister unequivocally. Halifax acknowledged that Eden had made some good points, but expressed concern 'lest we should postpone too long and lose our opportunity'. Hoare argued it was the last chance to prevent Europe from being 'divided into two camps'. Inskip suggested that failure to pursue the conversations would make war more likely. When it became clear that most ministers favoured starting the talks with Italy, Eden responded that he was unwilling to carry out such a policy, adding that if his colleagues 'decided against his view, he hoped they would find someone else to help them carry through this decision'. The Foreign Secretary's statement seems to have come as a genuine shock to most of his colleagues, who were appalled at the political damage that would result from such a development, particularly as few of them believed that the disagreement involved 'a matter of principle'.[95] It is still not clear whether Eden's resignation threat was a tactical manoeuvre designed to force his colleagues to accept his position. He had threatened to resign on at least one previous occasion, during the debates that took place in the Foreign Policy Committee over the Roosevelt telegram, suggesting that the Foreign Secretary understood that such a move could strengthen his hand when dealing with other ministers. He was certainly ready to wait and see whether a possible compromise formula, briefly sketched out at the meeting on 19 February, could be refined at a further Cabinet to be held the following day, suggesting that the Foreign Secretary was not yet irrevocably set on leaving the government.

The proceedings were even more convoluted at the Cabinet meeting on 20 February, particularly as the papers were by now full of the crisis.[96] Before the Cabinet met, Chamberlain called for Eden in person and made it quite clear that he believed resignation was unavoidable. He also infuriated the Foreign Secretary further by noting that he had received information suggesting the Italian government was ready to agree to Eden's earlier proposals for the withdrawal of their 'volunteers' from Spain, a development of which the Foreign Office knew nothing. The Cabinet that met in the afternoon was horrified to learn that the two men believed there was no alternative to Eden's departure, and ministers tried feverishly to identify a course of action that would allow the Foreign Secretary to stay in the Cabinet. During a brief adjournment, several ministers led by Halifax came up with a formula that would allow negotiations to begin on the basis that there would be no final *de jure* recognition of Italian control over Abyssinia until there was clear evidence that the Spanish problem had been satisfactorily resolved. Eden was unwilling to be convinced, making it clear that his 'difference of outlook' with the Prime Minister went beyond the question of the Italian conversations, citing in particular the problems created by Roosevelt's initiative the previous month. Chamberlain for his part made no effort to persuade his Foreign Secretary to remain.[97] On the evening of 20 February, Eden sent his letter of resignation, citing not only disagreement with the Prime Minister over the Italian conversations, but also 'a difference between us in respect to the international problems of the day and ... the methods by which we should seek to resolve them'. In his resignation statement in the House of Commons the following day, the erstwhile Foreign Secretary focused on differences between himself and his colleagues over policy towards Italy, although he alluded obliquely to the difficulty created by Chamberlain's rejection of Roosevelt's message the previous month. He said nothing about policy towards Germany. Eden made a concerted effort to present his resignation as one of principle, warning against 'too keen a desire on our part to make terms with others rather than that others should make terms with us', language that was music to the ears of those Conservative MPs who had become increasingly perturbed by the direction of the government's foreign policy. Some of the press backed the Foreign Secretary's apparent stand against 'appeasement'. Others, including *The Times*, which was by now the standard-bearer of a positive policy towards the dictators, thought the conflict was 'tragically unreal' and involved no real point of principle.[98] The Conservative 'anti-appeasers' in Parliament were surprisingly restrained during the debate that took place in the House of Commons following Eden's resignation statement, indicative perhaps of the lingering strength of traditional political loyalties.[99] The Labour leader Clement Attlee had no such inhibitions, and predictably seized the occasion to pour scorn on the government's whole approach to foreign affairs.[100]

Eden's correspondents reacted in different ways to his decision to resign. From the Foreign Office, Cadogan neatly avoided passing judgement on the rights and wrongs of the case, noting that 'I am convinced that you have done right because you have remained true to *yourself*'.[101] Oliphant thanked Eden for being 'a wonderful chief'.[102] Many ambassadors in post abroad responded with shock.[103] Oliver Harvey wrote passionately that 'our generation, the war generation ... have been forced by events [to be] far wiser than our elders and betters', but still found themselves in the invidious position of being excluded 'from any influence on policy'.[104] Most of Eden's ministerial colleagues wrote in kindly terms, paying homage to his personal integrity, but expressing little support for his views, confining themselves instead to rather patronising suggestions that he should take a holiday to recover his spirits.[105] From beyond the ranks of government and officialdom, Churchill roundly demanded that Eden should not spare the feelings of ministers, but do 'full justice to your case' in order to win round public opinion in favour of a tougher foreign policy. Despite the concern of his colleagues, the Foreign Secretary's resignation did not in fact destabilise the government, in part because Ball skilfully orchestrated a careful campaign designed to mute criticism in the press. Eden's departure from office merely allowed Chamberlain to consolidate his control over the foreign policy-making process in the months that followed.

Conclusion

Why did Anthony Eden resign from the Foreign Office? It is tempting to follow the lead provided by his resignation statement to the House of Commons and assume that the decision was the consequence of a major disagreement with Chamberlain over policy. The disagreements between the two men was not, though, as complete as Eden later implied in his memoirs. Eden was prepared during his time at the Foreign Office to consider bilateral conversations with Germany that would effectively trade colonies for guarantees in Europe. He also shared Chamberlain's pessimism about maintaining intact the *status quo* in the Far East. The Foreign Secretary was at times even ready to contemplate *de jure* recognition of Italian control over Abyssinia. Nor is it necessarily wise to accept Oliver Harvey's assertion that Eden was seriously considering resignation as early as the autumn of 1937 because he was so frustrated at his position. In an exchange of letters that took place between Chamberlain and Eden a few weeks later, at the start of 1938, the Prime Minister wrote to his Foreign Secretary noting his regret that 'the more active interest in foreign affairs that I have shown has almost inevitably led to malicious suggestions that I was usurping your place'. He then went on to outline his understanding of their official relationship:

> *You* are the Foreign Secretary and on you must fall the chief responsibility for the conduct of foreign affairs. If they fail, the chief blame must be yours: if they succeed, the chief credit must also accrue to you.

> My part is to help in any way I can: by suggestion, by warning, by support and if necessary by defence. As PM I must always regard foreign affairs as of the first importance. In present circumstances they overbear everything else. Therefore they must take up a large part of my thoughts . . . But I feel that our partnership has been fruitful during the past few months. We have made no serious mistakes and we have certainly achieved some notable successes.[106]

Eden's reply written a few days later, shortly before the arrival of Roosevelt's message, was striking for its lack of bitterness or anger:

> I know, of course, that there will always be some who will seek to pretend that the Foreign Secretary has had his nose put out of joint, but that is of no account beside the very real gain of close collaboration between Foreign Secretary and Prime Minister which, I am sure, is the only way that foreign affairs can be run in our country.[107]

Such sentiments do not tally easily with Harvey's diary entries. If Eden was already so angry at Chamberlain's incursions into the realm of foreign policy that he was already close to resignation, then he failed to take a heaven-sent opportunity to express his concern. Lord Halifax, who played a central role in trying to forestall Eden's resignation, gave what may be the most convincing verdict on the Foreign Secretary's departure from office when he described it in his private notes as:

> The cumulative result of a good many different things: partly subconscious irritation at Neville's closer control of foreign policy; partly irritation at his amateur incursions into the field through Lady Chamberlain, Horace Wilson, and his own letter to Mussolini; partly Anthony's revulsion from Dictators, which I have always told him was too strong inasmuch as you have got to live with the devils whether you like them or not; and partly, as I have also often told him, his excessive sensitiveness to the criticism of the left'.[108]

In the complex and messy world of politics, clashes of principle are often submerged in the chaos and confusion of events, only coming to the fore when fatigue or personal conflict suddenly make it impossible to conceal them any longer.

Whilst it may be impossible to trace the smooth linear development of a well-defined division between Chamberlain and Eden, it is possible to identify certain clear differences between the two men over such issues as the Italian conversations and the Roosevelt telegram. Harvey was convinced that a small clique in the Cabinet were 'jealous' of Eden and actively trying to determine the course of foreign policy regardless of his preferences.[109] Harvey's virulent language suggests, though, that a number of Eden's closest advisers were at times inclined to fall into something approaching a siege mentality. Halifax was certainly convinced that Cranborne acted as a major influence in egging Eden on towards resignation during the critical debates in Cabinet on 19–20 February.[110] It is worth recalling that not all senior members of the Foreign Office felt so passionately as Harvey and Cranborne about questions of policy, and many 'anti-appeasers' such as Vansittart and Sargent were convinced that Germany rather than Italy posed the main threat to Britain, with the result that they were inclined to favour a more positive policy towards Rome. A number of British ambassadors in key European posts, including Henderson and Drummond, broadly sympathised with Chamberlain. It is also important to remember that a majority of the Cabinet agreed with the Prime Minister's views on foreign affairs. Only a handful of ministers such as Walter Elliot and Malcolm MacDonald actively supported Eden's preferred policy at the Cabinet meeting on 19 February. Most of those present expressed a clear wish for the start of conversations with Italy. It would therefore be wrong to treat the Foreign Secretary's resignation as a victory for 'Prime Ministerial power' or even as a triumph for a small Cabinet clique surrounding Chamberlain. The Cabinet had a collective responsibility for decision-making, and a large majority favoured a policy that Eden felt unable to accept. As Eden himself later noted in his memoirs, a minister had no option but to resign if he could not accept responsibility for a policy he disagreed with.[111]

Eden's position showed how difficult it was for a Foreign Secretary to advance his views when the Prime Minister and his colleagues did not share them. His diary suggests that he often found Cabinet discussion of foreign affairs 'tiresome'. He certainly resented the intervention of ministers like Kingsley Wood who 'knows nothing but speaks much'.[112] Eden's greatest potential asset when defending his views in Cabinet was probably his reputation both with the public and among a section of the younger Conservative backbench MPs, but it was no easy task to make use of this diffuse popularity within the heart of government. The most effective weapon Eden had at his disposal was the threat of resignation, since this would undoubtedly damage the government's standing both in the country and in Parliament, but such a threat was a blunt instrument that could not be easily deployed. It seems likely that the vague talk of resignation between Harvey and Eden in the autumn of 1937 was an essentially private if rather melodramatic response to the routine frustrations faced by a minister who does not see eye-to-eye with all of his colleagues. Eden did seriously consider resignation over Roosevelt's initiative in January 1938, but was stymied by the fact that he could hardly justify such a dramatic act by referring to a move that the President had asked to be kept secret. When he finally threatened to resign at Cabinet on 19 February, his words undoubtedly had the effect of galvanising his colleagues to find some way to prevent him carrying through his threat. Oliver Stanley from the Board of Trade even suggested that the consequences of such a development would be so dire that ministers should accede to Eden's position in order to keep him in the Cabinet. However, since Chamberlain had already decided that 'Anthony must yield or go', there was never any real chance of a compromise. Once the Prime Minister was ready to face the political fall-out from Eden's departure, both from his own backbenchers and from the opposition, the Foreign Secretary was effectively powerless to do anything further to prevent the start of the Italian conversations.

There remains, of course, the whole question of Chamberlain's use of Ball and Dingli to keep in contact with the Italian Embassy in London and the government in Rome. Parallels have often been made between Chamberlain's treatment of Eden and Lloyd George's treatment of Curzon in the early 1920s.[113] There is certainly a mass of evidence to show that Chamberlain did repeatedly make use of Ball as an informal channel to the Italian Embassy, despite Ball's subsequent claim to the contrary.[114] Eden himself consistently maintained that he had no knowledge of the contacts, although it is clear from his memoirs that he suspected Ball of being involved in attempts by Downing Street to brief the press in favour of Anglo-Italian talks.[115] In a letter sent to the historian F.S. Northedge, in 1966, the erstwhile Foreign Secretary wrote firmly that neither he nor the Foreign Office had any knowledge of Ball's links with the Italian Embassy (a position that was later confirmed by Cadogan).[116] Eden's ignorance appears surprising given that rumours of the activities of Ball and Dingli were rife among the press *corps* in London, but there is no reason to question his claim that he had no definite knowledge of the situation. Chamberlain for his part probably at first viewed the secret channel as a useful means of pushing forward the policy of improving relations with Rome rather than as a mechanism for deliberately bypassing Eden. Halifax hinted many years later that the Prime Minister was sometimes given to a 'well-intentioned stupidity' in handling foreign affairs that could on occasion backfire and cause problems.[117] By the end of 1937, though, as the differences between Eden and Chamberlain over Italy became starker, the Prime Minister did become more inclined to circumvent his Foreign Secretary. He was also increasingly ready to use the Press Office at Number 10 to provide briefings designed to promote his own views on policy. The fact nevertheless remains that if Eden was indeed ignorant of the secret channel then there is no reason to suppose it played a major factor in his resignation. He left office because he was unable to persuade the Cabinet to share his growing concern that the search for agreement with Hitler and (above all) Mussolini would fail to secure peace in Europe. The Foreign Secretary was in this sense an anti-appeaser, willing to challenge the view that military weakness and public reluctance made it impossible for Britain to pursue a resolute foreign policy. Even the briefest glance at his two years in office suggests, though, that Anthony Eden was never so consistent or coherent a critic of the policy of appeasement as he later implied.

9 Lord Halifax at the Foreign Office (1938–39)

Introduction

The events that took place in Europe during the eighteen months before the outbreak of the Second World War continue to exercise a powerful hold on the popular imagination, with the result that the *Anschluss*, the Munich agreement and the guarantee to Poland remain the stuff of countless television programmes and examination curricula. British foreign policy during the climactic years of appeasement has also attracted a huge amount of scholarly attention. For critics of appeasement, the period between the *Anschluss* and the German occupation of Prague in March 1939 was marked by the British government's continued failure to take the kind of decisive measures that might yet have reined in Hitler's long-signalled *drang nach osten*. For other scholars, by contrast, such a judgement ignores the constraints under which ministers laboured when dealing with the challenges posed by the dictator states during the final years of the 'low dishonest decade'. The man who served as Foreign Secretary during this period – Edward Wood, 3rd Viscount Halifax – has perhaps surprisingly avoided the worst of the vitriol directed at 'the guilty men' of appeasement. He came out comparatively unscathed in Cato's celebrated attack on the *Guilty Men*. Winston Churchill was also quite sparing in his criticism, despite claiming in *The Gathering Storm* that Halifax's approach towards foreign affairs closely resembled that of Neville Chamberlain.[1] Halifax's manifest level-headedness commanded widespread respect across the Conservative Party in the late 1930s, even though he had previously played a controversial role as Viceroy of India in setting the country on the path towards greater self-government. His emollient if austere manner also meant that he grated less on opposition politicians than the more acerbic Chamberlain, which perhaps explains why his name was often mentioned as a possible Prime Minister by those who believed that Britain required a genuinely national government to deal with the international crisis. Halifax was, in short, a living incarnation of the *gravitas* and common sense that were widely held by his contemporaries to be the hallmark of the ideal inter-war foreign secretary.

Viscount Halifax was by background a natural *habitué* of the British political establishment, the scion of a wealthy landed family, who was educated at Eton and Oxford before being elected as MP for Ripon in 1910 at the age of just twenty-nine. His decision to stand as a Conservative was not the consequence of any strong ideological commitment, but rather a tacit recognition that the contemporary Liberal Party no longer represented the Whig values to which his family had traditionally been committed. Halifax did, though, inherit from his father a piety that went far beyond the niceties of conventional religious observance.[2] His devout Anglo-Catholicism, when combined with his passionate love of hunting, led the Churchill family to christen him with the derisory soubriquet of 'the Holy Fox'. His religious convictions do not, though, seem to have exercised a decisive impact on his attitude towards international politics.[3] At a time when a growing number of Christians insisted that their faith imposed a duty to renounce war, Halifax instinctively viewed the injunctions of the Sermon on the Mount as a transcendent ethic that could not be applied in a simple and unproblematic manner to real human problems.[4] Although his most recent biographer is right to point out that Halifax remained enough of a Whig to believe that international conflict could prove amenable to the process of rational negotiation, there was a marked pessimism in his temperament that led him to take a sceptical view of the potential for radical change to the human condition.[5]

Halifax was firmly committed to the general direction of Chamberlain's foreign policy when he took charge at the Foreign Office in February 1938. He recognised that Britain was not yet equipped – militarily, financially or psychologically – to fight a major war that could lead to widespread devastation at home and the destruction of the Empire abroad. In the wake of the remilitarisation of the Rhineland, in the spring of 1936, he had already signalled his desire to avoid 'exclusive alliances' in favour of a policy that would allow Germany to 'play the part of a good European'.[6] It was with this in mind that he had made his celebrated 'hunting' trip to Berlin in November 1937, in the hope that it would facilitate the kind of contacts that would make it possible to develop a better understanding between Britain and Germany. The Foreign Secretary also recognised that public opinion in Britain was at best uncertain in its attitude towards the prospect of using force to deter the dictator states. Halifax's support for 'appeasement' before the Munich crisis was in essence a pragmatic response to the pressures of domestic and international politics, and there were already occasions during his first few months in office when it became clear that he was prepared to support a more robust policy towards the dictator states than the Prime Minister. Halifax was always essentially a realist in matters of international politics. In the period before the Czechoslovak crisis he was inclined to believe that British interests could best be upheld by seeking some form of accommodation with the dictator states. In the months after Munich, by contrast, he came to the view that Britain was involved in a zero-sum game that demanded a more concerted effort to counter the ambitions of Berlin, Rome and Tokyo.

The rest of this chapter focuses on Halifax's handling of foreign policy during his first eighteen months at the Foreign Office – that is before the outbreak of war in September 1939 – with particular reference to the critical developments that took place in Europe during the period. The sheer complexity of the international environment created an endless series of challenges that made it difficult for policy-makers in London to pursue a well-thought out course of action. It is nevertheless possible, as suggested above, to identify a marked shift in Halifax's views on international politics in the wake of the Czechoslovak crisis of September 1938. The following pages will also question any lingering notion that Neville Chamberlain was the sole architect of British foreign policy during 1938–39. Although the Prime Minister found himself increasingly at odds with his Foreign Secretary in the wake of the Munich crisis, he never sought to isolate Halifax in the way that he had marginalised Eden during the latter's final months at the Foreign Office. Nor did he ride roughshod over the views of his Cabinet ministers. Chamberlain was far more than *primus inter pares* in the foreign policy-making process, but he seldom sought to impose his views in cases where there was clearly large-scale opposition to his proposals. The Prime Minister has rightly received much of the 'flak' for the failures of British policy in the months leading up to the Second World War. Even a brief glance at the documentary record suggests, however, that both the real and the constitutional responsibility more often than not lay with the Cabinet as a whole.

Halifax and the Foreign Office

The members of the diplomatic establishment who served Halifax during 1938–39 were divided about the best way of dealing with the challenges facing Britain in the months before Munich. The ambassadors in Berlin and Rome – Henderson and Perth – remained convinced that improved bilateral relations between Britain and the countries to which they were posted represented the best way forward. The same was broadly true of Robert Craigie in Tokyo.[7] Eric Phipps in Paris also became a strong supporter of appeasement during the months leading up to the Munich crisis, often incurring the wrath of Foreign Office 'hawks' such as Vansittart and Sargent, although his views fluctuated considerably during the final year of peace.[8] Basil Newton in Prague was generally sceptical about the long-term viability of the Czechoslovak state, and entertained considerable doubts about whether its preservation should become a major foreign policy objective of the British government.[9] In London, Cadogan proposed that Berlin should be asked to spell out in detail its international *desiderata*, in order to facilitate negotiations for a final settlement of outstanding Anglo-German questions.[10] Vansittart (who was by now 'promoted' to the ill-defined post of Chief Diplomatic Adviser) by contrast continued to favour an uncompromising line towards Germany throughout the spring and summer of 1938, and even remained hopeful that Mussolini might yet somehow be brought back into the anti-Nazi fold. Orme Sargent also wanted the British government to take resolute steps to prevent Germany from dominating Europe, although he was more inclined to hope that this could be achieved by means of a strong Anglo-French alliance alone. Most other senior officials held views somewhere between these extremes. The months following the Munich agreement tended to reduce the differences among officials working in London.[11] Cadogan gloomily noted in his diary after the German occupation of Prague in March 1939 that 'the whole situation ... is turning out ... as Van predicted and as I never believed it would',[12] and the Permanent Secretary himself became a supporter of a 'containment' policy predicated on offering guarantees to the smaller European states and securing an alliance with the USSR. It was a position broadly endorsed by most of his Foreign Office colleagues in London in the final year before the outbreak of hostilities, although a number of senior diplomats in post abroad continued to cling to the hope of achieving some kind of understanding with the dictators in order to avoid war.

There was a striking symmetry between the development of the views of Cadogan and Halifax about the European situation in the eighteen months before the outbreak of war, reflecting a broader pattern of personal sympathy between the two men. They met together almost daily, including weekends when Halifax was not away in the country hunting, and often walked to work together through St James's Park discussing the latest crisis to confront the Office. Vansittart's anomalous position by contrast continued to pose numerous problems, and he repeatedly complained both about his exclusion from the circulation list of important documents and his limited access to the Foreign Secretary.[13] Nor, unlike Cadogan, did he regularly attend meetings of the intermittently influential Foreign Policy Committee. The Foreign Secretary followed Eden's practice in preferring to work face-to-face with officials rather than communicating via memoranda and minutes. *Ad hoc* meetings were regularly called to discuss particular problems. Meetings on important issues relating to Germany typically included Halifax, Cadogan, Sargent, Strang, Vansittart and, on occasion, William Malkin (the Foreign Office Legal Advisor). When Italy was under review, Maurice Ingram from the Southern Department usually took part in the deliberations, whilst Laurence Collier was a discretely influential figure whenever policy towards the USSR was the subject for discussion. Oliver Harvey was also frequently present, along with a shifting cast of other officials, who were consulted when they were deemed to have expertise that was likely to be of particular value. Halifax valued the advice that he received from his official advisers, but he always remained confident enough to articulate his own views on the major problems that confronted him during his time at the Foreign Office. He was an experienced politician who understood that at a time when international questions dominated the domestic political agenda, the real struggle to set the direction of policy was likely to take place in the

Cabinet rather than at the Foreign Office. If there was a decline in the institutional influence of the Foreign Office on foreign policy during 1938–39 – and there probably was – it was above all due to the fact that the questions it dealt with had become far too sensitive for ministers to leave to officials.[14]

Halifax's junior minister during his time at the Foreign Office was Rab Butler, who had been a junior minister at the India Office when his new master served as Viceroy in Delhi. Butler spoke warmly of Halifax in his memoirs;[15] Halifax did not mention Butler in his own reminiscences. The reasons for this curious lacuna are not altogether clear, but the relationship between the two men was certainly much more distant than the one that existed between Eden and Cranborne during 1935–38. Harold Nicolson speculated in his diary that Butler was never so ardent an appeaser as his contemporaries believed, but there is little real evidence to support such a view, and his differences with Halifax over policy in the wake of Munich were almost certainly a factor in damaging the relationship between the two men.[16] Although Butler played a significant role in the negotiations for a Soviet alliance that took place in the summer of 1939, he was like Chamberlain always sceptical about the value of an agreement with Moscow. Butler paid a warm tribute in his memoirs to the officials he worked with whilst at the Foreign Office, but like a number of his predecessors he struggled to integrate himself into its organisational culture and procedures. Nor did he ever become a real confidante of the Prime Minister, despite the marked symmetry of their views on international politics. Whilst Butler was the Foreign Office spokesman on foreign affairs in the House of Commons, given that Halifax sat in the Lords, he was not being unduly modest when he wrote in his memoirs that he was never 'a prime mover in the complex and dramatic events' that took place during 1938–39.[17]

Halifax, the Cabinet and the pattern of policy-making

Halifax was a well-respected figure in the upper reaches of the Conservative Party when he became Foreign Secretary in February 1938, but it is not easy to discern the exact character of his relationship with Neville Chamberlain. Even so well placed an observer as Rab Butler found it difficult to make up his mind whether there were any fundamental differences between the two men over foreign policy. Butler suggested in his memoirs that Halifax played a major role in encouraging the Prime Minister to take a tougher line towards Germany in the period after Munich,[18] but in a private minute written at the time he implied that the two men had usually been in close agreement on policy.[19] Chamberlain certainly admired his Foreign Secretary's diligence and competence,[20] as well as recognising that he could not afford to alienate so senior a political figure, whilst Halifax for his part respected the probity of the Prime Minister. The relationship was therefore in large part one of equals – in as much as a Prime Minister can ever deal with one of his ministers on such terms – and it is difficult to accept the verdict of one scholar that 'Chamberlain had only to speak for Halifax to fall loyally into step'.[21] Chamberlain did, though, continue to take a 'hands-on' role in foreign policy throughout the period, writing at length to British ambassadors in post abroad, and personally drafting telegrams to foreign governments. He also attended numerous meetings with foreign leaders and representatives in London, as well as travelling to Italy with Halifax in January 1939 for discussions with Mussolini. Most famously, of course, Chamberlain flew to Germany on three occasions in September 1938 to discuss with Hitler ways of preventing a European war over Czechoslovakia – his celebrated 'Plan Z'. The Prime Minister continued to take great pains throughout 1938–39 both to mobilise political support for his foreign policy and to marginalise its opponents. He persistently refused to appoint critics of appeasement such as Churchill and Eden to the Cabinet, despite intense pressure from some quarters of the Conservative Party. He also used his control of the party apparatus to limit attacks from within its ranks (although he found it increasingly hard in the final months of peace to muffle the unease about the international situation expressed by many Conservative MPs).[22] The Prime Minister also made the News Department at Number 10 the primary focus for government attempts to manage news coverage of its policies,[23] a strategy that was broadly successful, at least until the spring of 1939. Despite repeated criticism of the government's foreign policy both from the Labour Party and from Conservative anti-appeasers on the backbenches, the Chamberlain government proved reasonably adept at managing the political fall-out of the international crises that dominated Halifax's first year as Foreign Secretary.

It would be wrong to suggest that Chamberlain and Halifax were the only figures in a position to influence debate in Cabinet on foreign affairs, either before or after the Munich crisis. Christopher Hill has shown that the Cabinet enjoyed a good deal of opportunity to discuss foreign policy in the months leading up to war,[24] with the result that there were occasions when the Prime Minister was forced to bow to the views of his ministers, even when he disagreed with them. Halifax himself does not seem to have resented Chamberlain's personal involvement in the conduct of foreign affairs, subsequently denying both in public and private that the Prime Minister ever interfered unduly with his conduct of policy.[25] He was, though, understandably riled when announcements emanated from Number 10 that had not been cleared in advance with the Foreign Office.[26] There is little doubt that the Foreign Secretary found himself increasingly at odds with Chamberlain over the direction of foreign policy in the final twelve months before the outbreak of war. Although it would be misleading to talk of a well-defined struggle to define the course of foreign policy in the wake of the Czechoslovak crisis of September 1938, the Foreign Secretary undoubtedly became more willing than before to contemplate forceful policies to rein in the expansionist policies of Germany and Italy.

The pattern of ministerial involvement in the foreign policy-making process fluctuated as always according to the constellation of circumstances and personalities involved. During the crisis of September 1938, an inner Cabinet composed of Chamberlain, Hoare, Simon and Halifax met regularly to discuss developments.[27] Following the conclusion of the crisis, though, the meetings of the inner Cabinet became less frequent.[28] The Foreign Policy Committee (FPC) grew in importance as a location for decisions about foreign policy during 1938–39, meeting numerous times between the resignation of Eden and the outbreak of war. Its members spent a good deal of energy reviewing documents drafted by the Foreign Office, and a number of papers and telegrams emanating from officials there wilted under close questioning in the FPC. The most significant decisions of the Committee were, though, usually referred to the full Cabinet for approval. Even the briefest review of the relevant material shows that the decisions and recommendations of the FPC were often 'unpicked' and reconsidered in detail at the full Cabinet. The state of Britain's armed forces naturally continued to loom large in the minds of all those with any responsibility for the conduct of foreign affairs, and Halifax himself diligently attended meetings of the Committee of Imperial Defence whenever possible. Chamberlain was determined to change the culture of the CID following Hankey's retirement in 1938, in order to make the system more dynamic and less of a 'clearing house for all the many plans of rearmament',[29] but his efforts achieved little of substance. The CID system still struggled to provide a coherent institutional framework for co-ordinating Britain's strategic policy in the period leading up to the outbreak of war. Nor were matters much improved by the best efforts of successive Ministers for Defence Coordination, whose role continued to be defined in a narrow manner that prevented them from providing an effective focus for integrating the policy-making process. The Treasury under Simon continued to question the wisdom of huge increases in defence expenditure, fretting about the impact on the public finances and the civilian economy, but the critical character of the international situation, when combined with Warren Fisher's failing health, probably served to reduce Treasury influence on foreign and defence policy in the two years before the outbreak of war.[30] The Chiefs of Staff as ever took a pessimistic view of Britain's military position, and their warning that Britain could do nothing to stop a German take-over of Czechoslovakia heavily influenced British policy towards central Europe in the months before Munich. The warnings of some of the dominions that they might not be able to come to Britain's aid if the country became involved in a European war also became a potent factor in the various Cabinet debates that took place on international developments during 1938–39. Halifax himself was deeply sensitive during his first six months in office to the various constraints faced by Britain when responding to developments abroad. The following pages examine how he sought to promote his views on the best way of dealing with the crisis in central Europe that erupted just a few weeks after he came to office.

Halifax and the Czechoslovak crisis

The German *Anschluss* with Austria that took place in March 1938 came as no great surprise to the Cabinet or the Foreign Office. Chamberlain fretted that the German government's action would make 'international appeasement' harder to achieve, but he was reluctant to accept that recent events in central Europe required a fundamental reconsideration of his policy.[31] He was not alone in taking this view. Cadogan went so far as to rejoice a few weeks after the *Anschluss* that 'Austria's out of the way', suggesting to Henderson in Berlin that it would be easier to begin meaningful negotiations with Berlin now that an unwelcome distraction had been resolved.[32] Halifax's own response was similarly low key, perhaps echoing the divisions among his officials,[33] and he praised Chamberlain for refusing to be rushed into any ill-considered response to Hitler's action.[34] The *Anschluss* did nevertheless raise important questions about the integrity of the Czechoslovak state, whose German-speaking Sudeten minority was already agitating for greater autonomy or even transfer to the Reich. The French government was committed by treaty to defend Czechoslovakia against invasion, as indeed was the Soviet government, but Halifax and Chamberlain were both opposed to offering any formal British guarantee (a possibility that had been discussed and rejected when Eden was still in office). They were also reluctant to pledge that Britain would come to France's aid should the country become embroiled in war with Germany as a result of its obligations in central Europe. In a Cabinet meeting on 14 March, the Prime Minister and Foreign Secretary both warned their colleagues about the danger of making 'threats that could not be carried out', pointing out that Britain lacked the forces to intervene effectively in the region.[35] Their views were bolstered by a Chiefs of Staff report submitted a few days later, which made it clear that Britain lacked the military wherewithal to breathe life into any guarantee, and fuelled ministers' perennial fear about British vulnerability to a German attack from the air.[36] Halifax told ministers that whilst the report was 'an extremely melancholy document ... no Government could afford to overlook it', and recommended that the British government should put pressure on Prague to make concessions to secure a settlement with its Sudeten minority. He also warned the Foreign Policy Committee that Britain should be careful not to give Germany the impression that she was being encircled by hostile powers.[37] The Foreign Secretary made no attempt to conceal the ignominious character of the course of action he proposed, frankly describing it to his colleagues as 'a disagreeable business which had to be done as pleasantly as possible.[38]

Halifax's grim realism was questioned by some of his colleagues. Hore-Belisha at the War Office expressed concern at Cabinet on 16 March about Britain's failure to confront the dictators, despite his first-hand knowledge of the indifferent state of the country's military preparations.[39] His unease was echoed by a number of his colleagues at a Cabinet meeting on 22

March, who were anxious that public opinion would resent 'having to knuckle under to the Dictators for lack of sufficient strength', but after lengthy discussion ministers broadly accepted the Chamberlain–Halifax line that 'a policy of bluff would be dangerous'.[40] On 24 March the Prime Minister made a speech in the House of Commons in which he ruled out any form of guarantee to Czechoslovakia on the grounds that it 'would automatically remove' the government's right to decide whether to go to war. He added, though, that 'if war broke out it would be unlikely to be confined to those who have assumed [binding] obligations',[41] a policy deliberately designed to keep Berlin guessing about Britain's likely response to any further advance in central Europe. Halifax took a similar line in the House of Lords. Both men subsequently worked hard to avoid offering 'anything which could be construed as a commitment over Czechoslovakia' during the meetings that took place with French ministers in early May.[42] The 'guessing' policy represented a logical response to the various pressures facing the Cabinet, seeking to offer a measure of deterrence, whilst at the same time preventing the British government from being put in a position where its bluff could be called. To its critics both at home and abroad, though, such a policy could all too easily appear as little more than a muffled announcement that Britain had disinterested itself from the future of central Europe.

Chamberlain told his sister that he found Halifax a 'comfort . . . to me' in the crisis that followed the *Anschluss*, and was relieved that he had not had to deal with Eden 'in these troubled times'.[43] The two men were also in accord over the crisis that erupted in the middle of May, when rumours began to circulate that German troops were poised to move across the Czechoslovak border.[44] The Foreign Secretary and the Prime Minister instructed Henderson to tell the German government that Britain might not be able to remain aloof from any war over the future of Czechoslovakia,[45] a decision that was apparently not approved in advance by the Cabinet or the Foreign Policy Committee. Much of the British press subsequently credited the government's firm line for winning the war of nerves and preventing an invasion. Halifax and Chamberlain, by contrast, drew the somewhat paradoxical conclusion that the May crisis showed the need to put still more pressure on the Czechoslovak Prime Minister Eduard Beneš to come to terms with the Sudeten minority. Halifax told Cabinet on 25 May that he was inclined to the view that Czechoslovakia should become a neutral state, terminating its alliances with France and Russia, in order to free the French from a potentially embarrassing obligation to defend the country against a German attack. He was even ready to consider in private the possibility that the Sudeten Germans should be allowed to secede from the country and join the Reich instead. Chamberlain added that his mind had been moving 'in the same direction' over the past few days (which was hardly surprising given the degree of consultation between the Prime Minister and Foreign Secretary).[46] Chamberlain had long rejected Churchill's call for a Grand Alliance to contain Germany, on the grounds that no possible alliance would in practice be strong enough to protect Czechoslovakia,[47] whilst Halifax warned that the German government was likely to behave still more aggressively if it perceived that it was being encircled by hostile powers.

The Foreign Secretary's commitment to some kind of *rapprochement* with Germany ran deep during his first few months in office. Although he was perfectly well aware of the character of the Nazi regime, he told Henderson following the *Anschluss* that 'Hitler's racial ambitions are not necessarily likely to expand into international power lust',[48] noting a few weeks later that despite the current problems 'I do not think we ought to give up the idea of getting on terms with [Germany]'.[49] It is easy with the benefit of hindsight to condemn such naivety, but such views were of course compatible with the traditional Foreign Office position that domestic developments in other countries were of concern only to the extent that they had a direct impact on the international environment. Halifax's own advisers in London were themselves uncertain about how to deal with the burgeoning international crisis in the spring and summer of 1938. Cadogan repeated his long-standing advice that the German government should be encouraged to set down its *desiderata* in order to facilitate a peaceful compromise of the Sudeten crisis, a stance that reflected his conviction that Hitler's ambitions could still be managed within the usual patterns and procedures of diplomacy.[50] Members of the Central Department, including Strang, generally favoured putting pressure on the Benes government to make concessions,[51] a position put even more strongly by Robert Hadow, a First Secretary who had recently returned to London from the Prague Mission, and who became one of the strongest 'appeasers' within the Foreign Office.[52] Even Orme Sargent, normally a fierce critic of those who favoured a soft line towards the dictator states, noted at the end of April that Benes should be told to 'do his damndest' to come to an agreement with Konrad Henlein (leader of the Sudeten Germans).[53] Vansittart predictably continued to oppose any course of action that might weaken resistance to Nazism, but many senior Foreign Office staff at least grudgingly recognised that Britain was not in a position to exert much leverage on developments in central Europe. Halifax's support for Chamberlain's policy towards Czechoslovakia in the months before Munich might not have been universally popular among his officials – but nor was it conducted in the face of a united wall of opposition.

The Prime Minister and Foreign Secretary were also broadly agreed on policy towards Italy, and following Eden's resignation the two men moved quickly to revive the conversations with Italy, despite the country's continued involvement in the Spanish Civil War.[54] The talks themselves took place in Rome between Ciano and Perth, but Halifax took the lead in Cabinet and Foreign Policy Committee when discussing the principles that should inform the British negotiating position. The agreement was eventually initialled in the middle of April, although Chamberlain was forced to make it clear in Parliament in the face of criticism that firm evidence of the withdrawal of Italian forces from Spain was 'a pre-requisite' for final *de jure* recognition of the Italian conquest of Ethiopia.[55] There were, however, some areas of policy on which Chamberlain and Halifax disagreed even before the watershed of Munich. The Foreign Secretary was more ready than Chamberlain to use British resources to oppose expansion by the dictator states in areas where such policies had a realistic chance of success. At a meeting of the Foreign Policy Committee, in June, Halifax defended a Foreign Office paper calling for Britain to use its economic and financial power to resist further German advances in south-east Europe. Chamberlain queried the proposal on the (somewhat contradictory) grounds that it was not clear whether Germany actually wanted to extend its influence in the region and that Britain could not in any case do anything to prevent it. After a number of sharp exchanges between the Prime Minister and the Foreign Secretary, it was eventually agreed to establish a committee charged with identifying ways of promoting British economic influence in south-eastern Europe, a move that probably represented a partial victory for Halifax.[56] The two men also clashed on the subject of offering financial help to the Chinese government in order to assist its resistance to Japanese forces. Although the Foreign Office was generally inclined to play down the potential threat from Japan during this period, the Foreign Secretary argued that the Chinese were effectively 'fighting the battle of the western nations in the Far East', and warned that Britain might be seen as being 'afraid to act' unless the government took some positive action in the form of a loan. A number of his colleagues were by contrast deeply reluctant to approve a course of action that could be seen as provocative to the Japanese, citing in evidence the generally cautious views of Sir Robert Craigie in Tokyo, whose telegrams and dispatches were regularly circulated to Cabinet. Chamberlain himself was inclined to support critics of the proposal, arguing that Britain was 'not in a position . . . to defend ourselves' in case of a Japanese attack on British interests in the region. The difference was resolved when Halifax himself somewhat unexpectedly changed his mind – doubtless in part due to his recognition of the scale of opposition – citing fears that imperial defence would be weakened if the Royal Navy had to deploy a large proportion of its ships in the Far East.[57] Such disagreements between the Foreign Secretary and the Prime Minister were, however, the exception rather than the rule in the months before Munich. Chamberlain and Halifax for the most part worked in harmony during the spring and summer of 1938, their cooperation fostered by their shared view about the best way to respond to developments in Europe.

Halifax and policy-making during the Munich crisis

The final stages of the Czechoslovak crisis of September 1938 witnessed the emergence of sharp divisions between Halifax and Chamberlain, which in turn both echoed and amplified frictions among other members of the Cabinet. When news of German troop movements in the east of the country began to trickle back to Britain in the final days of August 1938, it appeared that an invasion of Czechoslovakia might be imminent. The dispatch of the Runciman Mission a few weeks earlier, charged with securing agreement between the Prague government and its Sudeten minority, had at first raised hopes in London that it might yet be possible to secure a peaceful solution to the crisis. By the time of an emergency meeting of ministers on 30 August it was clear, though, that Runciman was unlikely to find any common ground between Benes and Henlein.[58] Halifax once again repeated to his colleagues his familiar claim that Britain could not exert much influence on developments in central Europe, and warned against the position of Conservative backbenchers such as Robert Boothby, who had suggested that a German invasion of Czechoslovakia could be averted by declaring such a move as a clear *casus belli*. The Foreign Secretary told his colleagues that 'He would feel extremely uneasy at making any threat if he was not absolutely certain that the country would carry it out', and proposed instead that the Cabinet should continue to pursue the policy of keeping Hitler guessing about British intentions. Most of his colleagues accepted this position. Whilst a few ministers such as Duff Cooper and Stanley expressed anxiety about the wisdom of discouraging the French government from standing up to Germany, most remained committed to the general policy pursued by the Foreign Secretary and the Prime Minister over the previous few months.[59] The Cabinet met on numerous occasions during the frantic days of the September crisis, and ministers were usually given an opportunity to express their views, with the notable exception of Chamberlain's decision on 13 September to put 'Plan Z' – his personal visit to Hitler – into action without their prior approval. The Prime Minister himself engaged in a process of almost continuous consultation with an inner Cabinet of Halifax, Hoare and Simon. Horace Wilson also played a significant role during the crisis, travelling with Chamberlain to Germany, and making a solo trip to see Hitler in the wake of the second 'summit' meeting at Godesberg. Cadogan in London was closely involved in decision-making throughout September – these 'awful' days as he referred to them in his diary[60] – meeting regularly with Chamberlain and Halifax to discuss developments. Vansittart was also consulted with some frequency, despite his close contacts with Churchill and other critics of government policy, as were senior diplomats at the major British missions abroad. William Strang as Head of the Central Department accompanied Chamberlain on all three of his trips to Germany. Few other members of the diplomatic establishment in London were in a position to exercise much sustained influence on the principal decision-makers, although senior officials at the Berlin Embassy (most notably Henderson and his deputy Ivone Kirkpatrick) were closely involved in every aspect of the Prime Minister's visits to Hitler. Both the pace and critical character of developments in September 1939 meant that ministers took a 'hands-on' approach to the management of the crisis, with the result that the decision-making process was firmly located within the Cabinet in general and the inner Cabinet in particular.

The prospect of Hitler's scheduled speech at Nuremberg on 12 September roused particular anxiety among British policy-makers in London during the preceding days, since they were afraid that the Fuehrer would commit himself so far over Czechoslovakia as to make some form of German military intervention unavoidable. Halifax had instructed Henderson in early August to seek an interview with Hitler at Nuremberg, in order to caution him of the likely consequences of any military action,[61] but in the days leading up to the speech both the Prime Minister and the Foreign Secretary oscillated on how firm the warning should be.[62] They were however eventually persuaded by the ambassador not to authorise an 'ill-timed and disastrous' message that would only serve to enrage the Fuehrer,[63] a recommendation that predictably aroused the fury of Vansittart, who believed that a firm statement represented the best way of deterring a German attack. Hitler's Nuremberg speech was in the event less inflammatory than feared. It nevertheless became clear the following day that some French ministers, including the Prime Minister Edouard Daladier and the Foreign Minister Georges Bonnet were – despite their recent bold declarations to the contrary – desperate to avoid a situation in which their country would be forced to honour its guarantee to Czechoslovakia. As one distinguished historian of the period has put it, 'Bonnet was as eager to be restrained as the British were to restrain him'.[64] The pace of rearmament had been no more impressive in France than in Britain over the previous few years, and the two men knew that the weakness of their country's armed forces was likely to be cruelly exposed by a conflict with Germany.[65] It was against this background that Chamberlain decided on 13 September to put Plan Z into effect, sending a telegram to Berlin announcing his intention to visit Hitler in person, in order to find 'a peaceful solution' to the crisis.[66] When the Prime Minister had first told Halifax about his 'daring' plan earlier in September it 'took [the Foreign Secretary's] breath away',[67] but there is no evidence that he made any attempt to oppose such a course of action. Vansittart at the Foreign Office was predictably hostile. Cadogan was cautiously positive. Simon and Hoare also approved the plan. When Chamberlain informed the Cabinet of Plan Z on 14 September, he prefaced his remarks with the hope that ministers would not feel he had 'gone beyond his proper duty in taking this action', and felt impelled to stress that he had already discussed it at length with the inner Cabinet. His decision was generally approved of – 'a magnificent proposal' as one of them described it – although some ministers like Stanley were anxious that it should 'not lead us further along the road to complete surrender'.[68] On the following day, Chamberlain duly left by air for the journey to Hitler's remote alpine retreat at Berchtesgaden, where the two men talked at length for two days about the crisis in central Europe. The Prime Minister was cautious not to commit himself to any particular course of action during this 'summit' meeting, but he nevertheless tentatively offered a personal opinion that 'I had nothing to say against the separation of the Sudeten Germans from the rest of Czechoslovakia, provided that the practical difficulties could be overcome'.[69] Such a statement was, as both men knew full well, a major concession that effectively signalled the British government's potential readiness to disinterest itself from a change in the *status quo* in central Europe.

Chamberlain's failure to consult the full Cabinet before implementing Plan Z was uncharacteristic. Most of its members were excluded from the small circle of officials and ministers who reviewed day-to-day developments throughout the September crisis, but the Prime Minister usually sought his colleagues' views on a regular basis, a fact not always recognised by those who subsequently criticised him for disregarding the advice of those around him. Chamberlain noted in a letter to his sister that developments on 13 September had convinced him that he could not risk delaying the implementation of his plan for another twenty-four hours.[70] His decision to take Horace Wilson rather than Halifax with him to Germany was apparently accepted without qualms by the Foreign Secretary. William Strang travelled with the Prime Minister, who was of course also able to call on the advice of the British Embassy in Berlin, so Chamberlain was not entirely divorced from the views of the diplomatic establishment (although Henderson's own views were by now of course very different from those of his colleagues back in London).[71] The Prime Minister was convinced that his trip's success would depend on its dramatic impact both on the Fuehrer and on public opinion back home. His meeting with Hitler was intended as a kind of theatrical *coup*, symbolising the critical character of the international crisis, and the dreadful costs that would result if no solution could be found. Chamberlain's decision to leave Halifax in London was therefore not intended as a snub, but rather as a deliberate attempt to create the political momentum required to avert war. The formulation and implementation of Plan Z nevertheless symbolised the Prime Minister's conviction that he alone had the vision and prestige to carry out such an audacious 'divergence from British diplomatic practice'.[72] It is hard to imagine that Eden would have been as relaxed as Halifax at being side-lined at such an important moment in history.

Chamberlain optimistically informed the Cabinet on his return to Britain that Hitler's determination to incorporate the Sudeten Germans in the Reich represented the limit of his territorial ambitions in Europe, adding that the 'acceptance of the principle of self-determination is not abject surrender'. Most ministers agreed that Britain had little alternative but to accept a change to the *status quo* in central Europe, although some ministers including Stanley and Duff Cooper remained deeply unhappy about the situation. Stanley even went so far as to suggest that if Britain was faced by a choice between surrender over Czechoslovakia and war then 'we should fight'. Halifax unequivocally backed the Prime Minister, arguing that Britain should only ever go to war in defence of 'the great moralities which know no geographical boundaries' (state sovereignty evidently not being one of the great moralities). Whilst he was unhappy about offering a guarantee to the rump Czechoslovak state, the Foreign Secretary grudgingly accepted that there was no alternative if the Czechs were to be persuaded to cede territory peacefully.[73] At a series of meetings that took place with French ministers in London over the following two days, agreement was reached on a proposal to be submitted to Prague calling for the transfer to the Reich of areas with a large German population. The two governments also agreed to offer Czechoslovakia some kind of 'general guarantee against aggression' to replace its existing treaties.[74] The government in Prague eventually accepted these Anglo-French proposals under enormous pressure from London and Paris, in the forlorn hope that such a move might limit future German demands.

The relationship between Chamberlain and Halifax became more complex when the Prime Minister visited Godesberg on 22–23 September to put the Anglo-French proposals to Hitler in person, accompanied once again by Wilson and Strang, along with Henderson and Kirkpatrick from the Berlin Embassy. Although Chamberlain's instructions from the Cabinet offered a certain amount of latitude, there was a general consensus that the Prime Minister should refuse to consider possible Polish and Hungarian claims on Czechoslovak territory (which dated back to the Paris Peace Conference), nor agree to a rapid German advance into areas likely to be transferred to the Reich. On arrival in Godesberg, though, Hitler quickly raised both these issues with the British premier, demanding that the transfer of Sudeten areas to the Reich should take place within a few days, a timetable that would have made any kind of orderly transition quite impossible. The rumblings of concern that had been audible in the Cabinet after Chamberlain's previous visit grew much louder when the Prime Minister reported back by telegram on the new situation. Halifax, Simon and Hoare were perturbed at reports of renewed German troop movements near the Czechoslovak border. They therefore authorised dispatch of a telegram to Prague stating that His Majesty's Government could no longer 'take responsibility' for advising the Czech government not to mobilise. Chamberlain in Germany sought to have the telegram delayed, but it was nevertheless sent out on the evening of 23 September.[75] The Prime Minister was himself appalled at Hitler's demands, but his colleagues back home were clearly concerned that he might be ready to make too many concessions in his eagerness to reach some kind of agreement. On the evening of 23 September, a group of ministers dined at the Foreign Office to discuss the situation, after which Halifax drafted a telegram for Chamberlain noting that the 'great mass of public opinion seems to be hardening in sense of feeling that we have gone to the limit of concession'.[76] Chamberlain was careful to point out to Hitler during their talks at Godesberg that he needed to consult his colleagues before making any firm commitments, but ministers in London feared that the very act of holding talks would create a momentum that would force the Prime Minister to accept terms which would prove difficult to disown at a later stage.

Halifax's behaviour following Chamberlain's return from Godesberg suggests that his views were in flux throughout this period. Despite his earlier anxieties, on 24 September he seemed to support in Cabinet the Prime Minister's view that it would be 'a great tragedy if we lost the opportunity of reaching an understanding with Germany'.[77] Some ministers including Duff Cooper and Hore-Belisha were horrified at the prospect of submitting to Hitler's timetable for the transfer of population and territory to the Reich, and supported mobilisation, but Halifax was in the words of Cadogan entirely '*défeatiste-pacifiste*'.[78] Most senior officials at the Foreign Office were by this time deeply perturbed at the Prime Minister's readiness to make concessions to Berlin, and responded with anger to the views articulated in their telegrams by Phipps and Henderson, who both continued to counsel a conciliatory policy. Cadogan told Halifax on the evening of 24 September that he would rather be 'defeated than dishonoured', and scolded the Foreign Secretary for his stance in Cabinet earlier in the day.[79] His words had an effect. Halifax told his Permanent Secretary the following day that after 'a sleepless night' he had come to believe that his advice to reject the Godesberg terms was correct.[80] It may perhaps be too simplistic to refer to this as a 'Damascene conversion', but the Foreign Secretary's change of heart in the night of 24–25 September certainly marked a significant moment in the development of his views, both about the crisis in particular and the future of policy towards Germany in general.

Halifax frankly told the Cabinet that met on 25 September that he had changed his mind and now believed Hitler had 'given us nothing and [was] dictating terms'. He went on to note that although he had worked closely with Chamberlain in recent weeks, 'He was not quite sure that their minds were still altogether as one'.[81] The Prime Minister was appalled at Halifax's change of heart – a 'horrible blow' as he described it in a note he passed at Cabinet to the Foreign Secretary – but whilst the Foreign Secretary admitted that he felt a 'brute' he re-emphasised that he could not 'reach any other conclusion at this moment'.[82] Halifax's change of heart paved the way for an anguished debate among his colleagues about the best way forward. Some ministers, including Simon and Maugham (the Lord Chancellor), agreed with the Prime Minister that pressure should now be put on Czechoslovakia to accept the Godesberg terms. Others, such as Stanley, argued that although war might be horrible 'it would be equally horrible in six months', and called for a decision to stand by France if the country decided to honour its treaty with Czechoslovakia. Halifax's seeming turn-around played a significant role in crystallising the unease that had been expressed by a number of his ministerial colleagues over the previous ten days, confirming the doubts of men like Duff Cooper,[83] and encouraging others such as Malcolm MacDonald to articulate their concern more forcefully. There is a danger in exaggerating the scale of Cabinet divisions during these fraught days, but it seems clear that Chamberlain's instinctive desire to force the Godesberg terms on the Czechs was stymied by opposition led by a Foreign

Secretary who, perhaps alone, had the political authority to offer serious opposition to the Prime Minister.

Halifax continued to push for a tougher policy in the wake of the Cabinet meeting on 25 September, drafting a press communiqué noting that Great Britain and Russia would 'certainly stand by France' should Paris come to the assistance of Czechoslovakia.[84] Chamberlain was angered by his Foreign Secretary's failure to seek approval before publishing the communiqué, but Halifax stubbornly continued to hold to his new position, refusing to authorise the dispatch of a telegram to Prague urging the government there to allow German troops to advance into Sudeten areas. By the evening of 27 September, Chamberlain had been forced to accept that the Cabinet was not going to accept Hitler's terms.[85] The crisis atmosphere rapidly spread across the whole country, as the Cabinet agreed to mobilise the fleet, and the press reported that war was imminent. The Prime Minister's famous broadcast on 27 September lamenting the prospect of Britain being dragged into a war over 'a far-away country between people of whom we know nothing' heightened the mood of public tension, although he made it clear that he had still not given up hope, and was ready to 'pay even a third visit to Germany, if I thought it would do any good'. The final events leading up to Chamberlain's dramatic flight to Munich on 29 September are too familiar to need recounting at length here. Following a conference with French ministers, Horace Wilson had been dispatched to Germany with a note from Chamberlain proposing further talks between Prague and Berlin, but his two conversations with the Fuehrer achieved little of substance.[86] The Prime Minister was actually speaking in the House of Commons about the crisis on 28 September when he was passed a note from Hitler inviting him back to Germany for four-party talks with the French and Italians, in response to an earlier British Note sketching out a possible compromise agreement.[87] His announcement of the invitation led to an eruption of relief both on the floor of the House and across the country. Simon later recalled in his memoirs how 'I saw men, some of whom have since spoken slightingly of what Chamberlain was trying to do, cross the floor in tears and with unrestrained emotion grasp him by the hand'.[88] The euphoria was played out on the streets of the capital when the Prime Minister returned from Munich two days later, waving his celebrated agreement with Hitler proclaiming the dawn of 'peace in our time'. Chamberlain had in fact feared that public opinion would be hostile to the agreement. His uncharacteristic triumphalism on the balcony of Downing Street was perhaps a product of his relief at the welcome of the crowds. Halifax for his part was ready to accept the new terms, since they allowed for a more orderly transfer of the Sudeten Germans to the Reich than under the Godesberg proposals, but his defence of the agreement in the House of Lords was noticeably more downbeat than Chamberlain's speech in the Commons. The Prime Minister went to great lengths to argue (not altogether correctly) that the Munich agreement was close to the original Anglo-French proposal agreed in London two weeks earlier, and contained 'very valuable provisions' that had been excluded from Hitler's Godesberg terms. He also told MPs that the agreement he signed with Hitler committing both countries to improving relations was more than 'a pious expression of hope'.[89] The Foreign Secretary by contrast preferred to use his speech to remind listeners that the real lesson of the crisis was the need to build up Britain's military strength more rapidly.

The war scare of September 1938 inevitably raised deep anxieties across British society, but while ministers repeatedly referred to 'public opinion' in their deliberations, they were as ever referring primarily to the views articulated in Westminster and Fleet Street. The science of opinion polls was still in its infancy in the late 1930s, and there is little sign that their findings made much impression on ministers. Such evidence as exists indicates that public opinion was in any case uncertain and contradictory throughout the crisis. Samuel Hoare took the primary responsibility for liaising with the press throughout the days and weeks leading up to the Munich agreement, and he was reasonably successful in securing positive coverage of the government's handling of the crisis.[90] Halifax himself was close to Geoffrey Dawson of *The Times*,[91] helping to prompt suspicions that he knew in advance of the controversial article that appeared in the paper in early September, suggesting that the secession of the Sudeten Germans offered the best way of resolving the crisis in central Europe.[92] In reality, though, there is little evidence that the Foreign Secretary made a really sustained effort to mould press coverage of developments during September. The Foreign Office News Department had already been effectively marginalised by the summer of 1938, since Chamberlain felt it was too inclined to cultivate contacts with journalists opposed to his policies, and there is little evidence that Halifax himself tried hard to oppose such a development. The Prime Minister was also anxious that Parliament should not be allowed to derail the government's policy, fearing that a bad tempered and divisive debate there might complicate delicate international negotiations. Chamberlain and Halifax both provided Opposition leaders with confidential briefings throughout the crisis, but they sought to head off criticism by limiting the amount of detailed information made public. As a result, few people beyond the heart of government knew many details about the real depth of the divisions in Cabinet until Duff Cooper resigned in protest following the Prime Minister's return from Munich. He was alone in his decision. Oliver Stanley was persuaded to remain in the Cabinet by Chamberlain, whilst other ministers seem to have convinced themselves that the agreement negotiated with Hitler represented a sufficient advance over the Godesberg terms to allow them to stay in office. In the short term, at least, the Prime Minister was surprisingly successful at managing the domestic political 'fall-out' of the Munich crisis. In the longer term, though, both parliamentary and public opinion began to change rapidly as the full significance of developments in Europe began to seek into the consciousness of both politicians and public.

Oliver Harvey noted in his diary at the end of September that Halifax had 'lost all his delusions' about Nazism.[93] There has certainly been much debate among scholars in subsequent decades both about the development of the Foreign Secretary's views in the wake of the Munich crisis, as well as the changing character of his relationship with Neville Chamberlain. The events of September 1938 undoubtedly encouraged the Foreign Secretary to think more carefully about the problems inherent in a policy based on the assumption that Hitler would respond to concessions by moderating his own demands. In the weeks following the Munich agreement, which he frankly acknowledged as no more than 'the lesser of two evils', he campaigned for increased rearmament in order to ensure that Britain never again had to negotiate from such a position of weakness.[94] The Foreign Secretary also favoured the establishment of a broader-based government, telling Chamberlain in early October that 'this is the psychological moment for endeavouring to get national unity', and he repeatedly showed himself willing to make overtures to the Conservative critics of the government.[95] The Prime Minister was unwilling to respond to such pressure, though, and was particularly opposed to any suggestion of taking Eden back into the fold since he was 'really dead against making terms with the dictators'.[96] Such comments suggest that the Prime Minister had not altogether given up hope of establishing some kind of *modus vivendi* with Nazi Germany in the wake of the September crisis. A good deal has of course been written about Chamberlain's views on foreign policy in the months between Munich and the German occupation of Prague in March 1939, which were not in truth always consistent, although the Prime Minister remained at least partly committed to the principles that had informed his policy in the eighteen months or so since he arrived at Number 10. Although he was ready to contemplate the possibility of war when secret intelligence was received early in 1939 suggesting an impending German attack on Holland,[97] he remained hopeful that diplomacy could still avert such a cataclysm. Halifax, by contrast, increasingly took the view that there was little chance of improving relations with Rome and Berlin. In January and February 1939, the Foreign Secretary pushed for a more definite commitment to France in response to rumours of a possible German strike into western Europe, supporting the introduction of National Service to underpin such a policy.[98] Halifax was also more cautious than the Prime Minister about the visit to Rome made by the two men early in 1939, making it clear that he was only prepared to make any concessions to Mussolini as part of a definite *quid pro quo*.[99] The Foreign Secretary seemed more ready than the Prime Minister to accept that Britain was likely to face a major war in the near future, and supported big increases in defence expenditure, a position that inevitably brought him into conflict with Simon at the Treasury. He also continued his campaign to use British resources to strengthen the economies of south-eastern Europe in an effort to reduce the risk of them falling under German influence.[100] In the words of Halifax's biographer, 'Events were moving against appeasement and among the Westminster and Whitehall cognoscenti it was known to be he who was leading the move inside the Government'.[101]

Halifax seems to have remained scrupulously loyal to Chamberlain throughout the six months after Munich, despite the growing tension between the two men, although it is not clear whether the Prime Minister always responded in kind. Oliver Harvey was convinced that the Prime Minister kept his Foreign Secretary in the dark on a number of occasions, most notably over the visit by Montagu Norman of the Bank of England to Germany in January 1939. Although Halifax may occasionally have contemplated resignation,[102] there is little evidence that he was ready to use such a threat as a tactic to get his own way in Cabinet, even though his departure from the government would probably have precipitated its collapse. He was critical of Duff Cooper's departure from office, in the wake of the Munich agreement, precisely because he believed that ministers had a moral responsibility to remain in office and devote their energies to dealing with the national crisis. The Foreign Secretary did, however, continue to develop his links with Conservative critics of appeasement, including Eden and Churchill, in an effort to prevent the growing political isolation of the government. Halifax's recognition that both public and political opinion were moving towards support for a harder line towards the dictators certainly helped to confirm his determination to pursue a tougher foreign policy. The primary impetus behind the Foreign Secretary's move away from appeasement was, though, his belief that concessions were likely to be treated as a sign of weakness in Rome and Berlin. Most senior members of the Foreign Office supported his position, and by the first few weeks of 1939 Halifax increasingly drew upon the advice of his officials in London, rather than the more cautionary counsels that continued to emanate from ambassadors like Henderson and Phipps. It would be a mistake to characterise the tension between the Foreign Secretary and the Prime Minister after Munich as a straightforward struggle between 'resister' and 'appeaser', given that such labels can never capture the fluid nuances of historical reality, but Halifax was certainly more inclined than Chamberlain to abandon the assumptions that had informed their policy before September 1938.

Halifax, the Polish guarantee and the Soviet negotiations

Hitler's destruction of the rump Czechoslovak state in March 1939 challenged any lingering belief that the German dictator's main objective was simply the creation of an ethnically homogeneous Reich, and led to a sharp change in coverage of international events in newspapers such as *The Times*, which rapidly began to change its previous position on policy towards Berlin. Chamberlain subsequently noted that he found the days leading up to the British guarantee to Poland on 31 March a time of 'nightmares and momentous decisions', although Halifax assured him that 'it was all child's play compared to last September'.[103] The Foreign Secretary had long since accepted that the German occupation of Prague was almost inevitable, but it seems to have come as far more of a blow to the Prime Minister, reflecting the two men's differing perspectives in the months following Munich. Chamberlain's initial speech to the House of Commons on 15 March was very cautious in tone, but two days later, apparently in response to representations from Halifax, he made a far tougher speech in Birmingham in which he stressed that Britain was not 'disinterested in what goes on in South-Eastern Europe'.[104] Following consultation with a handful of ministers, Halifax and Chamberlain proposed to Cabinet on 20 March that Britain should seek an agreement with France, Poland and the USSR, under which the four powers would agree to 'consult' in the case of any future threat to European peace. Such an agreement was in reality rather different from the one discussed two days earlier in Cabinet, which had envisaged a broader peace front, but Halifax suggested to ministers that the new proposal would have the necessary 'steadying effect' on Europe.[105] In the event, though, the proposal came to nothing, despite provisional approval by the French and Soviet governments,[106] since the Polish government was unwilling to accept close links with the communist regime in Moscow. Poland nevertheless continued to play a vital part in the Foreign Secretary's calculations about the future of central and south-eastern Europe. On 21 March, he told the Polish ambassador in London that the fate of Danzig was a matter 'of concern to all', a strong hint that he was considering the possibility of some kind of formal guarantee of the country's integrity. Four days later, Halifax argued in a meeting at the Foreign Office that Poland was critical to 'any effective scheme to hold up Germany in the event of aggression', suggesting that he was now focused as much on what would happen in the event of war as he was on preventing conflict from breaking out.[107] The Foreign Secretary seemed to confirm this position on 27 March when he told a meeting of the Foreign Policy Committee that he believed that Britain should go to war rather than accept a German occupation of Poland and Rumania.[108]

Halifax and Chamberlain worked closely together throughout the period leading up to the Polish guarantee, but the Foreign Secretary more often than not took the lead in responding to events.[109] Although the two men kept other ministers reasonably well informed about developments, there were occasions when they ignored the advice of their colleagues, perhaps most obviously at Foreign Policy Committee on 27 March when the reservations of Hoare and Stanley about excluding Russia from an agreement in the light of Polish objections were firmly discounted.[110] There were, however, some important differences between the Prime Minister and the Foreign Secretary in the last two weeks of March.[111] Halifax had not entirely given up on the hope that a firm diplomatic stance might deter Germany from aggression, but he was less optimistic than the Prime Minister about securing a peaceful outcome to the problems facing the continent. Chamberlain was by contrast still ready at least to consider territorial adjustments in central Europe to meet German demands. The Cabinet that met on

29 March discussed the establishment of a reciprocal security guarantee with Poland, under which each country would agree to come to the aid of the other in case of attack,[112] but their deliberations were overtaken by the events that took place later that day when Ian Colvin of the *News Chronicle* visited the Foreign Office with news that a German attack on Poland was imminent. Cadogan was sceptical of the information – many of the rumours that had reached London over the previous few months had proved false – but Halifax placed more credence on the reports and took the young journalist to meet Chamberlain. The Prime Minister too was struck by the urgency of Colvin's warning. The Cabinet that met on 30 March was therefore urged by the Foreign Secretary and the Prime Minister to approve some kind of guarantee to Poland, the first draft of which had been composed by Halifax (along with Cadogan and Butler) in the small hours of the morning.[113] Ministers approved the final draft the following day and, on the afternoon of 31 March, a weary-looking Chamberlain told the House of Commons that in the case of any threat to Polish independence 'His Majesty's Government would feel themselves bound at once to send the Polish Government all support in their power'.[114] Following the Italian attack on Albania a few days later, Britain responded by offering similar guarantees to Rumania and Greece. In an unpublished note written many years later, Halifax denied that the Chamberlain government was rushed into 'an indiscriminate distribution of guarantees' following the events of March 1938.[115] He was in a sense right, although there is little doubt that the key decisions were made against a very fraught and uncertain background. The Polish Guarantee was a logical outcome of the views that the Foreign Secretary had been developing since Munich, but it represented a more striking change of heart on the part of Chamberlain.

Labour MPs in the House of Commons were angered by the government's apparent refusal to consider a security pact that included the USSR, a sentiment echoed by anti-appeasers on the Conservative Party backbenches, who were ready to put aside their ideological antipathies for the Soviet regime in order to obtain a vital ally in the struggle against Nazism. A number of ministers, most notably Hoare and Stanley, also fretted about the danger of excluding Russia. Halifax and Chamberlain both had deep reservations about the prospect of any kind of agreement with Moscow, though, despite the fact that informal discussions reviewing relations between the two governments had taken place with the Soviet ambassador in London early in March, prior to a trip to Russia by the Overseas Trade Minister Robert Hudson. The Prime Minister freely confessed to being 'deeply suspicious' of the USSR.[116] He also recognised that the establishment of a formal alliance with Russia would effectively confirm that the main role of British diplomacy was now preparation for war rather than a search for peace. Halifax shared the Prime Minister's emotional dislike of the communist regime in Moscow, but it was not the only reason that he responded so cautiously to the prospect of closer ties with Moscow throughout April and early May.

Churchill's repeated support for a Grand Alliance had after all shown that even the most zealous critic of Soviet communism could reconsider their attitude when confronted with the hard logic of *realpolitik*. Halifax's reluctance to contemplate an alliance with Moscow before the middle of May was instead largely conditioned by his fear of alienating the Polish and Rumanian governments, which he believed would weaken rather than strengthen international resistance to Berlin.[117] Many years later he noted that 'An intelligent rabbit would hardly be expected to welcome the protection of an animal ten times its own size, whom it credited with the habits of a boa constrictor'.[118] There was as a result something decidedly lukewarm about the proposal made to Moscow by the British government in mid-April that the government there 'should make a public declaration stating that in the event of any act of aggression against a neighbour of the Soviet Union ... the assistance of the Soviet Union would be available if desired'.[119] The Soviet government predictably rejected this suggestion, proposing in return a comprehensive military pact between France, Britain and the USSR. Halifax and Chamberlain were both reluctant to go down such a road.

Christopher Hill has convincingly shown that the Cabinet played an important role in pushing the Prime Minister and the Foreign Secretary towards support for a Russian alliance in the second half of May, reflecting the fact that Cabinet government was as at least on this occasion a political reality rather than a constitutional myth. Nor, of course, can the process of discussion within the core executive be divorced from the wider climate of opinion in the Conservative Party, which was increasingly responsive to the strictures of Eden and Churchill. The warning against excluding Russia from international agreements sounded by Hoare and Stanley in March gradually came to convince a growing number of their Cabinet colleagues. Halifax still took a cautious line on the subject in the middle of May, opposing Stanley's call for agreement with Moscow,[120] but his attitude evolved rapidly over the next few days. The reasons for his change of heart are not altogether clear, particularly as there was still some difference of opinion within the Foreign Office. It seems likely that Halifax simply responded to the growing political and diplomatic logic for some kind of alliance. The Soviet government's manifest reluctance to consider anything less than a full-blown military agreement was also doubtless a factor in his decision. So too was his recognition that a majority of the Cabinet now favoured such a move. The Foreign Secretary's views were also influenced by a brief visit he made to Geneva at this time, in the course of which it became clear that the French favoured a tripartite alliance of some description. Halifax was an experienced enough politician to understand that he could not ignore the growing pressure for an alliance with the USSR, and he therefore recommended the idea to Cabinet on 24 May, just a few days after he had rejected it at Foreign Policy Committee. The Prime Minister for his part remained deeply sceptical about the prospect,[121] complaining privately at the change in heart displayed by his Cabinet colleagues,[122] but he was shrewd enough to realise that his only real supporter was the politically insignificant Rab Butler. Chamberlain therefore sought to make the best of the situation by proposing that any agreement should be linked to the League of Nations Covenant, on the Machiavellian grounds that amendment of the relevant articles would 'give us the opportunity of severing our relations with the Soviet if we want to'.[123] The decision to start serious negotiations with Moscow nevertheless shows the real boundaries to 'Prime Ministerial power'. Once Halifax had accepted the logic of seeking an agreement with the Soviet government, Chamberlain lacked the political strength to oppose such a move, even though he was aware that it was likely to destroy once and for all his (admittedly fast-fading) hopes of dealing with Germany through a process of negotiation.

The endless complexities of the negotiations for a tripartite alliance, which eventually failed in dramatic style with the signing of the Molotov–Ribbentrop Pact on 23 August, have been expertly dealt with elsewhere and need not be recounted in detail.[124] Although Halifax was deeply frustrated by the slow progress of the talks that took place in Moscow, he continued to argue throughout June that they represented 'the most important factor in the situation', and that it would be 'folly' not to push ahead with them given Britain's commitments in central Europe.[125] His refusal to visit Moscow in person to conduct the talks did not, as his biographer points out, reflect any lack of commitment to their success. It was instead inspired by a shrewd recognition that such a high-level visit would be interpreted as a sign of weakness by the Soviet government.[126] Despite his well-documented dislike of the Soviet regime, there is little substance to the charge that Halifax was reluctant to pursue an agreement with Moscow because of his revulsion at the atheistic character of the Bolshevik regime. Mutual suspicion certainly played a part in complicating the negotiations, but the Foreign Office documents on the talks, along with Cabinet reviews of their progress, show how difficult it was to overcome the very real obstacles to an agreement. The same is true of the account left by William Strang, who was sent to Moscow to help the British ambassador Sir William Seeds conduct the talks.[127] The Soviet Union was reluctant to be drawn into any firm commitment to fight as a result of German aggression in the west, and the British government was anxious to avoid concessions that might allow the USSR to move against the vulnerable Baltic states, which had been created in the wake of the Paris Peace settlement. Even Halifax's patience was wearing thin by the end of July, although he continued to search for an agreement in the weeks that followed. Chamberlain wrote to his sister in the middle of that month that he had always favoured taking a tougher line in the talks, but 'I could not have carried my colleagues with me'.[128] The Cabinet in general, and the Foreign Policy Committee in particular, played a significant role both in monitoring the progress of the talks and reviewing instructions sent to British representatives in Moscow. Chamberlain's critics were correct in believing that the Prime Minister was deeply sceptical about the value of an alliance with the Soviet Union, but the records show that his ministerial colleagues were able to push ahead with the policy despite his reservations. The ultimate failure of the talks owed more to Stalin's duplicity, along with the sheer problem of reconciling the positions of the two sides, than it did to any deliberate attempt by certain ministers in London to sabotage the talks.[129]

Conclusion

The actual announcement of the Molotov–Ribbentrop agreement on 23 August 1939 came as a 'complete shock' to the British government,[130] although the prospect of some kind of deal between Moscow and Berlin had of course long been feared in the western capitals. When Halifax signed the Anglo-Polish treaty two days later, on 25 August, following a series of complex and at times bad-tempered negotiations between London and Warsaw, he was firmly committed to the principle that Britain should stand by Poland in case of an invasion. Oliver Harvey noted in his diary on 27 August that he was terrified that the government would make 'another attempt at a Munich', and fretted that Horace Wilson and Rab Butler were already seeking ways of ensuring that a German seizure of Danzig should not lead to war.[131] Halifax's biographer has suggested that the Foreign Secretary never sought to resolve the Polish crisis by making concessions to Germany,[132] but his uncertain behaviour between the invasion of Poland on 1 September and the British declaration of war two days later has inevitably provided ammunition for those who wish to class him firmly among the appeasers. Halifax's readiness to support Chamberlain in postponing a declaration of war was in reality governed by his hope that Mussolini would put pressure on Berlin to agree to a peaceful solution, as well as by his determination to ensure that the British and French acted in tandem over the crisis, but there is little doubt that the Foreign Secretary's astute political judgement had for once deserted him. He failed to realise that any delay at such a critical juncture was likely to be seen as proof that the government was once again seeking to extract itself from its commitments. The Cabinet agreed in principle on the afternoon of 2 September that a midnight ultimatum should be sent to Germany, but it was willing to leave the exact details to Halifax and Chamberlain.[133] Ministers were subsequently perturbed by the Prime Minister's performance later that day in the House of Commons, when he failed to make it clear that Britain would declare war unless Germany agreed to an immediate withdrawal of its forces. The angry reaction from MPs on the floor of the House showed clearly that the mood of the Commons was in favour of war, and ministers subsequently demanded that Chamberlain should hold another Cabinet later that evening, at which a large majority opposed any further delay.[134] Despite the reservations of the Prime Minister and the Foreign Secretary, it was agreed that the ultimatum to Germany should be presented at nine o'clock the next morning. When no answer was received by 11.00 o'clock on 3 September, Chamberlain went on air to make his historic broadcast announcing to his fellow countrymen that Britain was 'now at war with Germany'.

Halifax's poor judgement in supporting Chamberlain's attempt to delay the declaration of war damaged his reputation both at the time and for posterity. The Foreign Secretary had long come to accept that a tougher line was needed to restrain German expansion in central Europe, but he had perhaps convinced himself that Hitler would never be so rash as to pursue a course of action that was bound to lead to war. When it became clear on 1 September that deterrence had failed, Halifax does for a time seem to have desperately cast around for some way of averting the ultimate catastrophe of a European war. To give too much attention to those fatal hours in early September is, though, to ignore just how much the Foreign Secretary's attitude towards the dictators had changed during the course of the previous year. Although it may be too simplistic to treat the Munich crisis as an unambiguous turning point in the evolution of Halifax's position – given that he supported economic measures to contain the dictator states before Munich, and was ready to agree to such 'appeasing' measures as the ratification of the Anglo-Italian agreement in its wake – the events of September 1938 marked a watershed in his view of international politics.

In a speech on 'British Foreign Policy: its Past, Present and Future', which Halifax gave in the last week of February 1939, the Foreign Secretary spelt out in some detail his foreign policy *credo*. In his customary thoughtful talk he questioned whether Britain could ever pursue a policy of splendid isolation, given the country's interest in developments on the continent, but he also warned that British governments should never 'encourage the weak by giving expectation of aid to resist the strong'. The Foreign Secretary went on to echo Salisbury's celebrated dictum that governments should never take any action that would not command public support, although he also cautioned his audience about the danger of allowing policy to be swayed by popular emotions. The most interesting part of Halifax's speech, however, focused on his attempt to determine how governments should relate their conduct of foreign policy to the world of ethics. He emphasised that 'I am not a believer in the divorce of politics from ethics', and approvingly quoted Pascal's maxim that 'Justice without power is unavailing, power without justice is tyrannical'. At the same time, though, he argued that Britain could not act as 'the world's conscience', and stressed that 'we must found our policy on concrete realities and vital interests'. Halifax made little sustained effort to relate his words directly to contemporary developments, but they were surely present in his mind at such a critical juncture in European politics, and the position he sketched out was broad enough to accommodate the changes that took place in his own policy prescriptions during his first eighteen months as Foreign Secretary.

It is no easy matter to divorce discussions of British foreign policy during the second half of the 1930s from broader ethical judgements about the morality of the decisions that were actually taken. Some of those who favoured a cautious policy overestimated the military strength of the dictator states, particularly in Europe, and tended to discount information suggesting that the forces available to the German and Italian governments were not so formidable as to preclude a firmer policy of opposition. It is nevertheless always important to remember that the best-known 'appeasers' were far from being pacifists in the face of the challenge from the dictator states, instead favouring a pragmatic policy of diplomatic negotiation and accommodation, designed to preserve peace until Britain's defence build-up had reached the point where the country could deal with the world from a position of strength. Lord Halifax never hid from himself or those around him that appeasement of the dictators in the period before the Munich crisis was an unpleasant business. He was, though, genuinely convinced that the military and strategic situation made it impossible for Britain to adopt a more robust policy in the Far East and central Europe. Halifax may have been incorrect in his assessment of the situation. It may also be that he was, like many of his generation, so appalled at the prospect of a future conflict that he was automatically inclined to oppose any course of action that could be interpreted as making war more likely. His behaviour in the year following the Munich crisis showed, though, that Halifax was a pragmatist who was able and willing to change his views. He became increasingly determined that Britain should play an active role in promoting the containment of Nazi Germany, once it became clear to him that such a policy represented the best way of responding to 'concrete realities', and that public opinion was increasingly set on such a course of action. Whilst Halifax was never in a position to impose his views on those around him, he used his immense experience and his natural political acumen to play a critical role in shaping the development of British foreign policy in the period leading up to the Second World War.

10 Conclusion

A vast amount has been written on the character of the political and administrative processes conventionally subsumed under the rubric of 'Cabinet Government'. Walter Bagehot observed in his classic book on the subject that the constant evolution of constitutional practice made it almost impossible to set down in definitive terms the way in which the British constitution operated at any given moment in time.[1] Ivor Jennings similarly acknowledged in the original version of his book on *Cabinet Government*, first published three-quarters of a century later in 1936, that 'The British Constitution is changing so rapidly that it is difficult to keep pace with it'.[2] Jennings was, however, still convinced that 'The Cabinet is the core of the British constitutional system ... It integrates what would otherwise be a heterogeneous collection of authorities exercising a vast array of functions. It provides unity to the British system of government'.[3] Thirty years later, by contrast, observers of the British political scene such as Richard Crossman increasingly took the view that Cabinet government had given way to Prime Ministerial government.[4] Great attention was also paid by leading students of post-war politics to the changing role of officials in the policy-making process. It became widely accepted that there was something unreal about the formal position laid down by Sir Warren Fisher in 1929, when he told a Royal Commission that 'Determination of policy is the function of ministers, and once a policy is determined it is the unquestioned and unquestionable business of the civil servant to strive to carry out the policy with precisely the same good will whether he agrees with it or not'.[5] Scholarly debates about Prime Ministerial power and minister–civil servant relations continue to this day, of course, but over the past fifteen years or so new attempts have been made to reframe the discussion by focusing on the concept of the 'core executive', identified in the introductory chapter as 'all those organisations and procedures which co-ordinate central government policies, and act as final arbiters between different parts of the government machine'.[6] Although such a definition creates its own problems when used as a tool to analyse the political-administrative process, it does at least have the virtue of facilitating recognition of the lack of clear boundaries and procedures that characterise the modern political system. Any serious attempt to understand the policy-making process must always be sensitive to its inherent 'messiness' and complexity.

The scholarly interest devoted since 1945 to the disintegration of British 'Cabinet Government' has in part been a response to changes in the policy-making process that have taken place since the Second World War. In reality, though, any sustained survey of British politics during the inter-war years (and indeed before) will show that developments such as the growth of Prime Ministerial power and the erosion of bureaucratic neutrality are part of a much longer pattern of development.[7] The fluid nature of the British constitution, governed as it is by a series of conventions that are themselves contestable and open to interpretation, means that a proper understanding of the policy-making process at any given moment must necessarily be rooted in the study of actual historical practice. The administrative context of decision-making in contemporary Britain is certainly far more complex than was the case between 1919 and 1939, given both the massive increase in the size of the bureaucracy and the greater scope of public policy. This should not, however, conceal the fact that policy-making between the two world wars was itself a complicated process. The influence of individuals and departments shifted according to innumerable factors, ranging from the personalities involved through to the political sensitivity of the particular issue under review. The inter-war foreign policy-making process was no exception to this general pattern.

It was seen in the introductory chapter that the formal constitutional sources of power of the British Foreign Secretary are strictly limited. Ernest Satow suggested in the original version of his classic *Guide to Diplomatic Practice* that the position of Ministers of Foreign Affairs in all countries was largely determined by domestic legislation and tradition (albeit that their role in inter-governmental communications was governed by certain international assumptions and expectations).[8] In the context of Britain, of course, this meant that the role and authority of the inter-war Foreign Secretary was not subject to any precise constitutional definition. Nor is it really possible to suggest that the nebulous constitutional conventions traditionally assigned a critical role in the British constitution laid down any binding rules about the position of a Foreign Secretary. The role of inter-war British foreign secretaries, including their ability to influence the outcome of the foreign policy-making process, was in practice determined by the way in which they operated within the complex web of domestic and international relationships in which they found themselves embedded. The men who served as foreign secretary between the two wars came to the job with a wide variety of expectations about what their role in government should be. Lord Curzon was convinced that he should take the lead in setting the course of British foreign policy, which helps to explain why he spent so much of his time at the Foreign Office railing against ministerial colleagues who sought to assert their own views on international affairs. John Simon, by contrast, was inclined to seek the guidance of his ministerial colleagues to the point where many of them accused him of being unwilling to take responsibility for difficult decisions. Austen Chamberlain fell somewhere between these two extremes, and was comfortable taking important policy initiatives, whilst simultaneously accepting the right of his ministerial colleagues to involve themselves in the foreign policy-making process. In strict constitutional terms, of course, the nature of British Cabinet government meant that decisions on foreign policy were deemed to be a matter of collective responsibility. More importantly, perhaps, in the years after 1918 a wide range of departments (and ministers) increasingly took the view that they needed to concern themselves with Britain's relations with the wider world in order to carry out their own core functions effectively. Constitutional, political and administrative realities combined to ensure that no inter-war Foreign Secretary could ever aspire to the degree of independence that Sir Edward Grey enjoyed when setting the course of British foreign policy before the First World War (although it should perhaps be remembered that Grey's freedom of manoeuvre was itself exceptional when looked at in a longer historical perspective).[9] The previous chapters have nevertheless shown that various strategies were open to a foreign secretary seeking to enhance their own role in the policy-making process.

It was noted in the introductory chapter that there are formidable obstacles facing any attempt to assess the role and influence of inter-war foreign secretaries, not least of which concerns the problem of determining where authoritative decisions about foreign policy were actually made. Although a scrutiny of the Cabinet minutes can tell us a good deal about the nature and extent of collective control of foreign policy during the years between 1919 and 1939, it would be far too simplistic to assume that the full Cabinet always provided the actual as opposed to the constitutional location for the most important decisions. Whilst the examples discussed in the previous chapters have shown that the full Cabinet was often the setting for genuine debate and decision-making on foreign policy – perhaps to an extent that might surprise those who assume that 'Cabinet Government' has always represented something of a constitutional myth – the exact situation fluctuated from government to government and policy to policy. Important decisions were often made in Cabinet Committee or through informal discussions among a small group of ministers. Other decisions were made within the Foreign Office or via the process of inter-departmental consultation. The inherent fluidity of the decision-making process makes it difficult to reach a clear verdict about the extent to which each of the men who served as foreign secretary between the wars was able to exert their influence on policy. Although a number of them arrived at the Foreign Office with definite ideas about the objectives they wanted to pursue whilst there, each of them had imbibed to a greater or lesser degree the culture of British political pragmatism that militated against too programmatic a view of their role. MacDonald and Henderson both believed that a Labour government should place its own distinctive stamp on British foreign policy, but neither man had any real intention of pursuing a distinctly 'socialist' foreign policy. Eden was genuinely committed to the League of Nations, at least in the first half of the 1930s, but when the events of 1935–36 showed the limitations of the Geneva system he was ready to interpret collective security in a more flexible and conventional manner. Austen Chamberlain was a confirmed 'francophile' on coming to office, but was prescient enough to understand that European security required at least the partial rehabilitation of Germany into the security architecture of the continent, despite the reservations of Paris. Even Curzon had no clear blueprint of what he hoped to achieve at the Foreign Office when he first arrived there, and the passion of his subsequent battles with other ministers was provoked as much by a desire to defend his authority as it was by disagreements over actual policy. The dynamism of the international environment in any case meant that a 'change of heart' was often no more than a logical response to changing circumstances. Most of the men who headed the Foreign Office during the inter-war years would have had little problem endorsing the celebrated dictum of Lord Keynes that 'when the facts change I change my mind. What do you do?'

Foreign Secretaries and the Foreign Office

Warren Fisher's description of civil servants as executors of decisions made by ministers was, as already noted, far too simplistic (a fact that was amply demonstrated by his own career at the Treasury). The notion of bureaucratic neutrality in the British constitutional system has always been something of a constitutional myth, a necessary fiction helping to define the uncertain boundaries of ministerial and collective responsibility, with the result that the actual relationship between ministers and their official advisers has always been subject to enormous variety. During the last ten years or so before the outbreak of war, in 1914, the Foreign Office in London witnessed important organisational and cultural changes that gave senior staff there greater opportunity to offer authoritative advice on questions of foreign policy. The weakening of Foreign Office influence on policy during the First World War and its aftermath was therefore particularly resented by a cohort of officials who were desperate to avoid a return to the situation that prevailed before the Hardinge–Crowe reforms of 1903–06, when even senior members of the Foreign Office could find themselves acting as little more than glorified clerks executing decisions made elsewhere. One of the reasons that Lord Curzon was so resented by his officials when he came to the Foreign Office in 1919 was precisely that they believed he placed little value on their expertise.

It is no easy matter to identify the shifting mechanisms through which debates about foreign policy took place within the Foreign Office between the wars, given both the complex flows of information and the fluidity inherent in its organisational culture. Junior officials working in one of the geographical departments clearly had less potential influence on policy than a senior Assistant Under-Secretary, but even the most cursory glance at minutes and memoranda shows that many of them still tried hard to influence opinion further up the bureaucratic hierarchy by arguing for a particular course of action. Senior officials, most notably those from Head of Department level upwards, were far more likely to be involved in detailed discussions about important questions of policy, but a great deal still depended on the personality of those involved and the context in which they operated. When Ralph Wigram and William Strang headed the Central Department in the 1930s, their position was enhanced both by the critical importance of the issues that came within their remit, as well as by their determination to articulate their own views on British policy towards western Europe. Laurence Collier's long tenure as head of the Northern Department similarly gave him considerable authority when policy towards the USSR was under review. The six men who served as Permanent Secretary between the wars were naturally best placed to act as a channel of authoritative advice to the head of the Foreign Office, although different foreign secretaries varied in the way in which they interacted with their senior advisers. Samuel Hoare relied heavily on Vansittart for advice during his six months at the Foreign Office, perhaps to the point of ignoring voices that might have encouraged him to take a more cautious line in his fateful talks with Pierre Laval in December 1935, whilst Anthony Eden was by contrast far more inclined to listen to the views of a range of officials. Austen Chamberlain had a high opinion of the three men who served as Permanent Secretary during his time at the Foreign Office – Eyre Crowe, William Tyrrell and Ronald Lindsay – but he too never allowed them to become the sole channel of 'official' advice. Arthur Henderson placed little faith in the opinions of Ronald Lindsay, prior to the latter's departure for the Washington Embassy, but he was more willing to pay heed to his successor (Vansittart). Halifax's relationship with Alexander Cadogan was also characterised by a considerable degree of openness and frankness, symbolised most dramatically by the role played by Cadogan in encouraging his chief to take a tougher line towards Germany during the Czechoslovak crisis of 1938.

A foreign secretary who was able to master the mass of material that came across his desk was of course better placed to evaluate the different views among his officials than one who did not. The growth in Foreign Office business after 1918 meant, though, that it was difficult for even the most hard-working minister to master more than a fraction of the paperwork generated by his department. When Curzon served as Foreign Secretary he was still just about able to scrutinize all the most important documents emanating both from overseas missions and within the Foreign Office itself. The same was not true of his successors. The flow of dispatches and telegrams into London more than trebled between the wars, and the increased bureaucratic load on ministers inevitably tended to allow officials greater *de facto* influence over questions of policy, although the exact situation depended as ever on the sensitivity of the issue under review. Every foreign secretary naturally took most interest when dealing with issues that were of particular domestic import or international sensitivity (not least because these were the topics that were most likely to become before the Cabinet and its committees for discussion). It is for example striking that during the Munich crisis of 1938, officials at the Foreign Office in London, with the exception of Cadogan and Vansittart, seem to have had little opportunity to exercise much influence on the decisions made either by the full Cabinet or the smaller group of ministers that steered day-to-day policy. The same was true in May 1927 when the decision was taken to break diplomatic relations with Moscow. The proper role of the inter-war Foreign Office was always subject to a process of debate and argument. The officials who worked there had for the most part imbibed the ethos that became the hallmark of the organisation in the years before 1914, seeing themselves as 'professionals' who had a profound understanding of the intricacies of diplomacy, as well as the depth of experience to advise on questions of international policy.[10] Ministers and senior bureaucrats in some other departments were, by contrast, inclined to challenge this self-image on the grounds that responding effectively to the increasingly complex international environment required a far broader expertise than could be found in the Foreign Office alone. Whilst they were ready to accept that the Foreign Secretary and his officials were bound to play a central role in the process of maintaining formal communications between Britain and other countries, they were less ready to accept that members of the diplomatic establishment alone possessed the skills and knowledge required to mould British policy.

The relationship between foreign secretaries and their junior ministers could also have a considerable impact on the way in which the former carried out their work. The two men who served as junior minister under Curzon had little influence either on policy or the day-to-day running of the Foreign Office, although Ronald McNeill may have played a part in encouraging a 'die-hard' line on issues such as Russia and the Near East.[11] Arthur Ponsonby was a more influential figure when he served under MacDonald in 1924, despite his frequent laments to the contrary, and he played a significant part in guiding the negotiations with Soviet representatives that took place in London during the summer. Hugh Dalton played a prominent role under Henderson in the second Labour Government, whilst Anthony Eden became the international face of British foreign policy when he served as Junior Minister under Simon (although the scale of his influence on important foreign policy decisions in London is perhaps open to question). Eden himself gave considerable weight to the opinions of Lord Cranborne when the two men served together at the Foreign Office. Rab Butler, by contrast, was a surprisingly peripheral figure in the Halifax Foreign Office. The role of junior Foreign Office ministers was in general a thankless one given their uncertain status and position. Ponsonby and Dalton were heartily disliked by the permanent staff at the Foreign Office, who made little effort to engage them in its day-to-day work, whilst McNeill, Locker-Lampson and Butler all struggled to define their role and responsibilities. A Foreign Secretary who developed a close working relationship with his junior minister could undoubtedly reap certain benefits, not least because it provided him with a 'sounding board', as well as helping him to remain in contact with wider currents of political opinion in Westminster and beyond. Conversely, though, a junior minister who proved ineffectual or unpopular with the permanent Foreign Office staff could easily become something of a liability.

The relationship between inter-war foreign secretaries and senior diplomats posted abroad also fluctuated according to the dictates of personality and circumstance. Some heads of mission were content to see themselves as a conduit between their own government and the one to which they were accredited. Others went to great lengths to influence policy. The precise boundaries of ambassadorial autonomy were as ever somewhat uncertain, but a number of inter-war ambassadors undoubtedly engaged in actions that were unauthorised and even opposed by their own government. Curzon was often frustrated by Lord D'Abernon's readiness to exploit his contacts with political and financial circles in London in order to push for his chosen policy towards Germany in the first half of the 1920s. Anthony Eden bitterly resented Eric Drummond's repeated attempts to use his influence to push for a closer relationship between Britain and Rome in the second half of the 1930s. Although much has been made of the decline in ambassadorial independence in the wake of the communications revolution that took place in the late nineteenth and early twentieth centuries, the evidence of the inter-war years suggests that a determined head of mission could still influence discussions about foreign policy back in Britain. Embassies abroad and the geographical departments at home between them possessed a range and depth of knowledge that could not be rivalled by any other government department, with the result that successive foreign secretaries enjoyed access to sources of detailed information that were not easily available to his ministerial colleagues. Nevertheless, whilst access to such a wide range of material could strengthen the hand of a Foreign Secretary in discussions over foreign policy in the Cabinet and its committees, the inter-war Foreign Office had no monopoly on information relevant to the conduct of Britain's external relations. Other departments such as the Treasury, the Colonial Office and the War Office possessed their own sources of expertise, which they were able to use to bolster their position in debates about policy. Nor, of course, was the Foreign Office's access to a huge range of material of much value if other critical actors simply refused to accept its recommendations. Successive foreign secretaries certainly enjoyed unrivalled access to expert advice on foreign affairs, but this did not automatically allow them to translate their privileged position into definite influence on policy.

Foreign Secretaries, Prime Ministers and the Cabinet

Five men served as British Prime Minister between 1919 and 1939: David Lloyd George, Andrew Bonar Law, Stanley Baldwin, Ramsay MacDonald and Neville Chamberlain. Bonar Law's tenure of power was too short to draw much in the way of firm conclusions about his handling of government business, including foreign affairs, but the other four men all developed their own distinctive Prime Ministerial 'style'. Lloyd George, MacDonald and Chamberlain instinctively viewed themselves as policy initiators, and sought to use their formidable powers to carve out a critical role for themselves across the whole field of government. Baldwin's style was notably different, since he was less inclined to intervene in areas that were the clear responsibility of one of his ministers. The correct Prime Ministerial role in the conduct of inter-war domestic and foreign affairs was, like everything else in British government, subject to uncertainty and flux. Despite its somewhat misleading name, the Cabinet Secretariat established under Maurice Hankey in 1916 was in essence accountable to the Prime Minister alone, and served to increase the 'reach' of the occupant of Number 10 across the whole spectrum of public policy. Many ministers assumed that the end of hostilities in 1918 would signal a decline in Lloyd George's domination of the coalition government, along with the institutional mechanisms that had made it possible, but such expectations quickly proved illusory. The growing role of the Prime Minister and the Cabinet Secretariat as a 'hub' of policy-making during the inter-war years was in reality bound up with broader changes in the political and administrative environment. The management of Britain's external relations was not immune to these pressures. The cataclysm of the First World War had undermined the authority of the 'old diplomacy', and created a widespread popular desire to avoid the horrors of war in the future, with the result that successive governments could not ignore altogether public opinion on issues such as collective security and rearmament. At the same time, the increasing complexity of the international environment meant that the boundaries between diplomacy, economic affairs and military matters became more uncertain than ever. The role played by inter-war prime ministers in foreign affairs was therefore governed to some degree by the fact that the effective conduct of foreign policy required co-ordination between many different government departments, which the traditional mechanisms of Cabinet government alone were not always able to provide.

Lloyd George's negative attitude towards the British diplomatic establishment was a significant factor in the decline of Foreign Office influence during his time at Number 10. The Prime Minister was determined to play a major international role following the end of the First World War, helping to shape the settlement reached at Paris, as well as attending such set-piece conferences as the one held at Genoa in 1922. Although Lloyd George faced a difficult political situation as head of a coalition government racked by personal and political tensions, the administrative 'revolution' that took place during his time at Number 10 helped him to assert himself in the face of the simmering dislike of many of his fellow ministers. It is therefore hardly surprising that he clashed so frequently with Curzon during the years between 1919 and 1922, when the Prime Minister was finally forced from office in the wake of the Chanak affair. Curzon for his part arrived at the Foreign Office seemingly unable to understand that his influence on foreign policy would ultimately depend on the extent to which he was able to win his fellow ministers round to his views. He bitterly resented attempts by ministers such as Churchill and Montagu to claim that their own departmental responsibilities gave them a right to help shape the pattern of Britain's foreign policy. Curzon was enraged above all, though, by what he viewed as Lloyd George's systematic efforts to undermine his position. It is hard even from this distance in time to offer any verdict about the rights and wrongs of the disagreements that festered between the Prime Minister and his Foreign Secretary. Lloyd George certainly failed on occasion to keep the Foreign Office informed about his talks with foreign politicians and diplomatic representatives, which represented a clear breach of protocol, as well as a threat to the orderly conduct of foreign affairs. On the other hand, though, much of Curzon's irritation with the Prime Minister stemmed from his own unrealistic hopes of establishing himself as the principal actor in the foreign policy-making process, which helps to explain why he also found himself at odds with Bonar Law and Baldwin when they in turn occupied Number 10. Curzon's self-regard alienated both his officials and his fellow ministers, with the ironic consequence of making it harder for him to obtain the influence that he believed should be his of right.

Lloyd George was in the awkward position of being a Liberal in a Cabinet dominated by Conservative ministers. His successor faced the difficult situation of heading a minority government that only commanded the support of around a third of MPs in the House of Commons. Ramsay MacDonald's decision to hold the offices of both Prime Minister and Foreign Secretary in the first Labour government nevertheless gave him a degree of control over the foreign policy-making process that had eluded Curzon. Whilst he could not ignore altogether the views of senior ministerial colleagues such as Philip Snowden and Arthur Henderson, who each had their own ideas about such vexed questions as Anglo-French relations and the League of Nations, he was far from scrupulous in keeping the Cabinet informed about important developments including progress at the London Conference on reparations and the negotiations for an Anglo-Soviet treaty. As a result, MacDonald not only made little real effort to promote greater popular control of foreign policy – something that he had supported so fervently at a previous stage in his career – but was if anything inclined to marginalise even the formal mechanisms of collective Cabinet scrutiny. The situation was somewhat more complex during the second Labour Government of 1929–31, when Arthur Henderson took charge at the Foreign Office. Mac-

Donald made no secret that he would continue to take a keen interest in foreign policy, particularly as regards the United States, whilst the long history of tension between the Prime Minister and Foreign Secretary in any case virtually guaranteed that they were never likely to co-operate easily with one another. Although Henderson's high standing in the Labour movement gave him considerable status within the two inter-war Labour Governments, which meant that he could not easily be eclipsed, the tension with MacDonald greatly complicated his time at the Foreign Office in dealing with issues ranging from Egypt through to naval disarmament.

Stanley Baldwin, as noted earlier, stood out from other inter-war prime ministers by his general lack of interest in foreign affairs, but his willingness to allow ministers some latitude in the formulation of policy could on occasion make life more difficult for the four men who served him as Foreign Secretary. Curzon complained bitterly at the lack of support he received from the Prime Minister during the Ruhr crisis of 1923. Chamberlain's failure to prevent the break with Russia in May 1927 came about in part because Baldwin was unwilling to back him against other 'die-hard' ministers such as Churchill and Birkenhead. Samuel Hoare told Neville Chamberlain in the summer of 1935 that the Prime Minister's reluctance to address the burgeoning crisis over Abyssinia was making it impossible to formulate an effective policy, whilst Eden's comments in the years that followed were still less complimentary. Baldwin's detachment from foreign affairs has, however, sometimes been exaggerated, particularly in the 1930s, when he was quick to realise that public unease about foreign and defence policy could have important domestic political implications. The complaints of his foreign secretaries seem to have been directed above all towards the Prime Minister's reluctance to engage in a *sustained* dialogue with them outside the formal confines of the Cabinet Room, which made it difficult for them to gauge whether they had his support when proposing a particular course of action. Baldwin's sphinx-like *persona* could be unnerving for all his ministers at times of crisis and difficulty.

Neville Chamberlain's determination to play a major role in the foreign policy-making process when he became Prime Minister contrasted sharply with the approach of his predecessor. Chamberlain's long years at the Treasury had given him an opportunity to immerse himself in the complexities of international politics, and he arrived at Number 10 determined to make a major effort to improve Britain's relations with Italy and Germany. The disintegration of his relationship with Anthony Eden, which ended with the latter's dramatic resignation in February 1938, was partly the result of differences over policy towards the dictator states. It was also, though, the consequence of a more deep-seated suspicion that developed in the second half of 1937 between the Foreign Office and Number 10. Eden's long years at the Foreign Office had led him to believe that the complexities of international affairs were best dealt with by those who had the expert knowledge and experience to deal with them (a position naturally endorsed by his officials). Chamberlain was by contrast inclined to view the diplomatic establishment as an obstacle to the development of new and imaginative approaches to foreign affairs. Some of Chamberlain's activities in the field of international affairs, perhaps most notably his cultivation of the 'secret channel' with Italy, were contrary to the protocol that required a prime minister to keep his ministers informed of any foray into areas that they might normally regard as their own preserve. There was also something questionable about his insistence on maintaining close relations with 'ambassadors of appeasement', such as Sir Nevile Henderson, given the potential consequences for the coherence and hierarchy of relations within the diplomatic establishment itself. Eden himself was nevertheless ready to acknowledge just a few weeks before resigning that every prime minister had a right to take a close personal interest in international affairs, and the months prior to his departure starkly revealed the difficulties inherent in trying to define 'correct' relations between a Prime Minister and his Foreign Secretary. The relationship that subsequently developed between Chamberlain and Halifax during 1938–39 was also marked on occasion by tension and disagreement, but they were for the most part successful in agreeing on the 'ground rules' governing their respective roles. Halifax was more politically experienced than Eden, and he commanded the Prime Minister's confidence to a far greater extent than his predecessor, which helped the two men to co-operate even when they disagreed about the best way of responding to the challenges faced by the British government on the eve of the Second World War. The elusive texture of 'personal chemistry' was able to compensate for the tensions caused by differences over policy.

The collective responsibility of ministers for policy meant, of course, that the whole Cabinet was bound to take at least some interest in decisions for which they were constitutionally accountable (which helps to explain why the Hoare–Laval pact became a source of such domestic political tension at the end of 1935). Many ministers could also legitimately claim that their departmental portfolio gave them a right to be involved in discussions about foreign affairs. As a result, one of the hardest tasks faced by inter-war foreign secretaries was defining an area of competence for themselves, whilst remaining sensitive to the fact that they could only carry out their job effectively by co-operating with their ministerial colleagues. Successive Chancellors of the Exchequer played an important role in the foreign policy-making process between 1919 and 1939, particularly in comparison with the situation before 1914, reflecting the growing importance of economic and financial questions on the international agenda between the two world wars. The Treasury was closely involved in preparations for such meetings as the London Conference on reparations in 1924 and the Ottawa Conference on imperial preference in 1932. Although members of the British diplomatic establishment became more financially literate during the inter-war years, the Treasury – along with the Board of Trade and the Bank of England –

provided much of the necessary expertise at negotiations dealing with questions such as reparations and trade. The views of successive Chancellors on international politics both influenced and were influenced by their views on financial and economic questions. The francophobic views articulated by Philip Snowden at the 1924 London Conference reflected his anger at the reluctance of the French government to face up to the consequences of the financial settlement reached at Versailles. Neville Chamberlain's support for closer relations with Japan in 1933–34 reflected his hope that such a move would allow for a reduction in defence spending at a time of domestic financial stringency. John Simon's support for 'appeasement' when at the Treasury in the late 1930s was similarly governed by his hope that the policy would forestall the need for still higher defence spending. The control of the purse strings gave all Chancellors considerable potential influence in discussions about Britain's relations with the rest of the world. The Treasury fought hard to increase its direct control over the size and composition of the inter-war diplomatic establishment, perhaps most notably during the reforms of 1919–20, whilst Sir Warren Fisher subsequently tried on a number of occasions to exert influence over senior Foreign Office appointments. Perhaps more importantly, though, by exercising a decisive influence on the scale and configuration of British defence spending, successive Chancellors helped to shape one of the most important parameters constraining the foreign policy options available to the British government. The Ten Year Rule continued to cast its shadow long after it had finally been abandoned in 1932. Although there is a danger in assuming that the relationship between a Foreign Secretary and Chancellor of the Exchequer was necessarily adversarial, there was always potential for conflict between the holders of the two offices, given their contrasting responsibilities and perspectives.

The ministers who headed the service departments also had an obvious interest in decisions about foreign policy, and even the briefest glance at inter-war Cabinet papers and Foreign Office records shows how the War Office, the Admiralty and the Air Ministry took a sustained interest in diplomatic questions. Senior figures within the British military establishment felt themselves to be in a difficult situation between the wars. The Chiefs of Staff Committee produced many pessimistic reports about the state of British forces, reflecting concern about the growing mismatch between Britain's international commitments and the military resources available to meet them. There were of course well-established mechanisms for seeking to reconcile Britain's diplomatic and military strategies, a process in which the Committee of Imperial Defence and its various committees played a crucial role, but the whole question remained one of considerable confusion and uncertainty throughout the inter-war period. Nor did the creation of the Foreign Policy Committee in the mid-1930s do much to improve the situation, since the service ministers were not routinely present at its meetings, a curious practice given the difficulties inherent in setting the boundaries between departments with a clear interest in Britain's external relations. It is therefore hardly surprising that there were often tensions between the service ministers and the Foreign Office. When Churchill was Minister of War in Lloyd George's government, he stridently opposed Curzon's policies in south Russia and the Middle East, on the grounds that the Foreign Office had given too little attention to the military consequences of its recommendations about policy towards the region. During the time Lord Londonderry headed the Air Ministry, in the early 1930s, he railed against the position on disarmament put forward by Simon, arguing that too little attention was being given by the diplomatic establishment to military matters when formulating proposals for the Disarmament Conference in Geneva. Eyres-Monsell used his position at the Admiralty to oppose any harsh policy towards Italy during the Abyssinian crisis of 1935, including the imposition of sanctions, on the grounds that Britain's naval weakness in the Mediterranean would make it difficult to defeat Mussolini without running the risk of serious military losses. Successive foreign secretaries varied in the way in which they responded to the views of service ministers and their advisers, but the military lobby nevertheless always had great potential 'clout' when international affairs were under discussion. The cautious response of the British government to such 'landmark' developments of the 1930s as Japan's aggression in Manchuria and Italy's incursion into east Africa was in large part conditioned by a desire to avoid engagements that might reveal the country's lack of military preparedness.

The boundaries between the responsibility of the Foreign Office and other major departments of state such as the Colonial Office were also uncertain, with inevitable consequences for the relationship between the individuals who headed them. The establishment of the Middle East department within the Colonial Office at the start of 1921, for example, represented a clear defeat for Curzon at the hands of Churchill, and threatened to undermine his position as the principal architect of British policy in the region. Nor was this an isolated incident. When Amery served as Colonial Secretary, during Baldwin's second administration, he often came into conflict with Austen Chamberlain over policy towards China. The Dominions Office was also frequently involved in discussion about foreign policy in the 1920s and 1930s, including the vexed question of Britain's role in Europe, which was a particularly sensitive issue given the reluctance of most of the dominion governments to be dragged into conflict there. Although it is possible to exaggerate the impact of the dominions on the evolution of 'appeasement', ministers and officials in London were genuinely anxious to gauge dominion opinion in order to avoid major divisions within the Empire. The India Office, too, was frequently involved in discussion about foreign policy – above all as it concerned the Middle East and Asia. Edwin Montagu's reluctance to support any action that might lead to conflict between Britain and Turkey in 1919–20 was based on his concern about its possible impact on Indian Muslims, whilst Birkenhead's angry demands for a tougher policy towards the USSR during 1925–27 was in part predicated on his concern about the impact of Soviet propaganda on the sub-continent. The involvement of such assertive ministers as Birkenhead and Amery in the foreign policy-making process represented a 'check' on the Foreign Secretary, since the collective nature of Cabinet decision-making, along with the process of inter-departmental consultation, provided them with repeated opportunities to mobilise support for their own favoured policies. Clashes of personality and opinion easily became bound up with broader conflicts of institutional perspective to create a series of tensions that exercised a profound impact on the decision-making process at a wide variety of levels.

The world beyond Whitehall

The previous chapters have suggested that the sensitivity of international affairs between 1919 and 1939 meant that decisions on policy were inevitably shaped to some extent by 'public opinion', albeit that inter-war foreign secretaries were generally uncertain about how to identify popular attitudes on the key problems facing them. The Foreign Office News Department provided a mechanism for shaping debate on a whole range of international issues, but its *modus operandi* was always rudimentary (although under the energetic leadership of Rex Leeper in the 1930s it did become more effective at building links with senior journalists prior to its eclipse by the Number Ten Press Office). Whilst inter-war foreign secretaries varied in the skill with which they managed the press, none of them was particularly adept at mobilising popular support in a way that might have enhanced their own position within government. Curzon made little effort to cultivate leading journalists or proprietors, despite fuming against press coverage of his activities. Simon proved spectacularly ineffective at finding ways of countering the newspaper campaigns that were mounted against him during his time as Foreign Secretary. Austen Chamberlain also railed against the press when at the Foreign Office, but he failed to counter the activities of fellow ministers like Churchill and Birkenhead, who were both far more skilful at cultivating links with Fleet Street in order to increase their own authority and profile. Anthony Eden enjoyed more positive press coverage than any other inter-war foreign secretary, consciously or unconsciously trading on his reputation as the most glamorous politician of his generation, but even he found it difficult to use his nebulous popularity to promote his position within government. Nor did Sam Hoare's close links with the Beaverbrook press do much to calm the storm that erupted around him at the end of 1935 following his agreement with Laval. Senior Foreign Office staff such as Vansittart and Tyrrell did of course establish their own contacts with the press, but these did not necessarily operate in a way that strengthened the hand of their political master. The sensitivity and confidentiality of international affairs in any case meant that there were always limits to the freedom with which senior members of the Foreign Office could legitimately seek to bolster their position by arguing their case beyond the confines of Whitehall.

Although inter-war foreign secretaries could not afford to ignore the press, even if they were uncertain how to handle it, they were more confident when dealing (or in most cases not dealing) with the plethora of 'lobby groups' that emerged between the wars. The Foreign Office and other government departments generally ignored the various pacifist organisations that mushroomed during the period, ranging from the confessional groups like the Anglican Pacifist Fellowship through to broader organisations such as the Peace Pledge Union. The same was true of organisations that were formed to influence policy on particular issues such as the Chanak and Abyssinian crises. The 'Hands-Off Russia' campaign of the early 1920s seemed for a short time to presage a greater effort by organised labour to exert a decisive impact on British foreign policy, but in the years that followed left-wing agitation was seldom successful at influencing government policy, even on such controversial issues as the Spanish Civil War. Most inter-war foreign secretaries were in any case inclined to resent the activities of organisations that they believed lacked both the expertise and the constitutional right to influence the conduct of foreign affairs. Successive foreign secretaries did of course deal extensively with a wide variety of British businessmen and financiers in the course of their work, but such contacts normally took the form of private discussions rather than more formal 'lobbying' activity. The organisation that most engaged the attention of the Foreign Office between the wars was naturally the League of Nations Union. Although most inter-war foreign secretaries looked upon the LNU with considerable suspicion, they were seldom able to ignore it altogether, given the potential clout it derived from its distinctive combination of a mass membership and an 'establishment' leadership. It nevertheless remains difficult to identify many cases where the LNU exercised a decisive impact either on individual foreign secretaries or on the development of British foreign policy more generally.

The critics of the old diplomacy had often called for greater scrutiny of foreign affairs by the House of Commons in the years before 1918. The domestic political sensitivity of international questions meant that there was often passionate debate there during the inter-war years, but it is seldom easy to gauge the extent to which this directly impinged on the various recommendations on policy put forward by the Foreign Office. Every foreign secretary was naturally concerned to present their policies in the best possible light, and took considerable care to plan their strategy before a particularly important or sensitive debate. Curzon, Halifax and Reading all sat in the House of Lords during their time at the Foreign Office, which protected them from the robust criticism that was a feature of debate and questions in the House of Commons, but their absence from the lower House also made it harder for them to mobilise support among MPs. Simon did of course sit in the House of Commons, but as a Liberal National he was unable to rely on a strong Parliamentary following, whilst MacDonald and Henderson both found themselves in the awkward position of having responsibility for foreign affairs in a minority government. Austen Chamberlain commanded the respect of MPs, but little real popularity, and although his sincerity was unquestioned by his listeners he lacked the presence to mobilise real enthusiasm. Eden commanded a loyal following among a younger group of Conservative MPs when he was in charge at the Foreign Office, but the events surrounding his resignation in 1938 showed how difficult it was to convert such support into real influence within government. The impact of Parliament was undoubtedly greatest at times of international or domestic crisis. The decision by Baldwin's Cabinet to distance themselves from Samuel Hoare in the wake of the Hoare–Laval pact, for example, was in large part due to ministers' concerns about the unease on the government backbenches. For the most part, though, the influence of Parliament on the foreign policy-making process expressed itself less via the formal scrutiny of government decisions and more by its potential for acting as a public arena for damaging disclosures and debate. Every foreign secretary had to remain mindful of the threat that criticism in the Commons or the Lords would be reported in the press, and might serve to agitate a public opinion that remained perturbed and perplexed about the perils facing Britain in an increasingly uncertain world. 'Public opinion' itself remained something of an abstraction to those responsible for making foreign policy between the wars. When the phrase cropped up in Cabinet discussions or during meetings at the Foreign Office, it was more often than not a kind of short-hand, used to refer to the coterie of newspaper editors and other 'establishment' figures who took an interest in Britain's relations with the wider world. Every foreign secretary nevertheless had to remain sensitive to the fact that the foreign policy-making process could not be entirely insulated from the wider climate of opinion. Even Lord Curzon acknowledged that public reluctance to support any kind of adventurist foreign policy placed constraints on the options that were available to the British government.

Although the previous few pages have focused on the way in which political and bureaucratic factors shaped the role of individual foreign secretaries between the wars, it should of course never be forgotten that the policy-making process was indelibly shaped by personal relations between those involved in making decisions. The difficult relationship between Lloyd George and Curzon cannot be understood simply in terms of 'competing perspectives' and 'differences of policy'. The two men frankly disliked one another. The same was true of Henderson and MacDonald. Nor were such tensions simply a consequence of clashing egos between politicians determined to assert themselves within Cabinet. The texture of personal relations could also prove a decisive factor in determining how ministers dealt with their officials. Hoare's reliance on Vansittart during his short time at the Foreign Office in 1935 was in part a result of the fact that the two men got on well together. Anthony Eden, by contrast, found Vansittart's assertive personality difficult to deal with when he replaced Hoare as

Foreign Secretary. A high degree of personal animosity need not of course make it impossible for the individuals concerned to develop an effective working relationship. If it were then government in twentieth-century Britain would often have faced gridlock! Curzon and Hardinge seem to have worked reasonably well together during the period 1919–20, when the former was Foreign Secretary and the latter Permanent Secretary, since the marked personal antipathy between the two men was counteracted by a certain mutual professional respect. Nor can questions of personal relations be entirely divorced from broader questions of agreement and disagreement about policy. The difficult personal relationship between Eden and Neville Chamberlain was in large part a *consequence* rather than a *cause* of their conflict over how best to respond to the international challenges facing Britain in the late 1930s. Simon's poor personal relations with his colleagues, by contrast, seem to have developed independently of differences over policy. And, ironically, the appalling relationship between Curzon and Lloyd George came about despite a fair degree of symmetry between the two men's views over most important international questions other than policy towards the Near East.

It remains very difficult to categorise with any precision how something so elusive as 'personality' actually impacts on the workings of the core executive, although the previous chapters have provided at least some insight into the process. Each inter-war foreign minister had certain strengths that they brought to their job. Austen Chamberlain had a deserved reputation for probity that meant that he was generally trusted and respected both by his officials and his ministerial colleagues. The same was true of Halifax. Curzon could point to his enormous experience as evidence that he had the skills and knowledge to perform effectively as Foreign Secretary. Simon was well respected for his intellectual ability when he was appointed to the Foreign Office, whilst Eden was renowned for his 'flair' and ability to win over opponents both at home and abroad. Henderson had a reputation for good-natured 'plain-speaking'. It was, however, only too easy for virtues to turn into vices. Austen Chamberlain's earnest approach to all his ministerial portfolios, including the Foreign Office, led some of his colleagues to dismiss him as a grey man who 'always played the game and always lost it'. Curzon's self-confidence was quickly seen by those around him as evidence of his overbearing arrogance. Simon's intellectual scrupulousness soon came across to many ministers and Foreign Office staff as a simple reluctance to make up his mind. Henderson's 'plain-speaking' on occasion appeared downright rude. And, to make the whole situation more complex, different personal qualities proved to be more or less advantageous according to the setting in which they were exercised. Eden was adept at using his charm to win the loyalty of many of those who served him at the Foreign Office, particularly among a younger cohort of officials, but he failed to exert the same kind of influence on his Cabinet colleagues. Hoare was by contrast generally better at building relations with his Cabinet colleagues than with his Foreign

Office staff (at least until the fatal days of the Hoare–Laval pact). Simon and Curzon struggled to win the trust of both officials and ministers. Halifax was perhaps more effective than any other inter-war foreign secretary at winning the respect both of his ministerial colleagues and his official advisers – something of an historical irony given that he served as Foreign Secretary during the most critical days of all. Nevertheless, none of the eight men whose careers are reviewed in this book possessed the personal 'presence' to dominate the policy-making process in all its various settings and guises. Even the most personable and politically astute figure could not possibly have 'smoothed away' all the political and bureaucratic tensions that were inherent in the inter-war foreign policy-making process.

The previous chapters have shown how difficult it is to compare systematically the role and *modus operandi* of the men who headed the Foreign Office between the wars. The international environment that confronted Lord Curzon in the early 1920s was very different from the one facing Lord Halifax in the late 1930s. The basic challenge facing British foreign policy-makers during the inter-war period was, though, always the same: namely, the fundamental mismatch between the scale of their country's global interests and the level of resources available to protect them. The old maxim that every political career ends in failure probably applied with particular force to inter-war foreign secretaries, who were charged with the impossible task of seeking to maintain the broad international *status quo* in the face of massive challenges both in Europe and beyond. There were nevertheless marked differences in the way in which the men who headed the Foreign Office between the two world wars approached their job. Each of them had to master two distinct environments: an international environment that required them to react to an ever-changing and intractable series of challenges, and a domestic environment that set boundaries to the nature and range of policies that could be adopted in response to them. Performing such a difficult and delicate task required a wide range of skills. It should hardly be a matter for surprise that none of the foreign secretaries whose careers have been examined in this book managed to master them all.

Notes

1 Introduction

1 A useful – and implicitly comparative – account of the men who served as foreign secretary in the decades before the First World War can be found in Keith Wilson (ed.), *British Foreign Secretaries and Foreign Policy: From Crimean War to First World War* (London, 1987). On a more recent period, see the excellent series of essays in Kevin Theakston (ed.) *British Foreign Secretaries since 1974* (London, 2004).

2 The best book length treatment of the nineteenth-century Foreign Office can be found in Ray L. Jones, *The Nineteenth Century Foreign Office: An Administrative History* (London, 1971).

3 For personal accounts emphasising the routine nature of the work carried out by most Foreign Office clerks, see Sir James Rennell Rodd, *Social and Diplomatic Memoirs*, Vol. 1 (London, 1922), p. 40; H.J. Bruce, *Silken Dalliance* (London, 1946), p. 81.

4 For contrasting treatments of the Foreign Office reforms, see Sibyl Crowe and Edward Corp, *Our Ablest Public Servant: Sir Eyre Crowe* (Braunton, 1993), pp. 88–109; Jones, *Nineteenth Century Foreign Office*, pp. 111–35; Zara Steiner, 'The Last Years of the Old Foreign Office, 1898–1905', *Historical Journal*, 6, 1 (1963), pp. 59–90.

5 Valerie Cromwell and Zara Steiner, 'The Foreign Office before 1914: A Study in Resistance', in Gillian Sutherland (ed.), *Studies in the Growth of Nineteenth Century Government* (London, 1972), pp. 167–94.

6 For a summary of this development, see Michael Hughes, *Diplomacy Before the Russian Revolution* (London, 2000), pp. 28–9.

7 For a somewhat different view, see J.A.S. Grenville, *Lord Salisbury and Foreign Policy at the Close of the Nineteenth Century* (London, 1964), pp. 3–23.

8 Hughes, *Diplomacy before the Russian Revolution*, p. 33.

9 On Hardinge, see Hardinge of Penshurst, *Old Diplomacy* (London, 1947); Briton Cooper Busch, *Hardinge of Penshurst: A Study in the Old Diplomacy* (Hamden, Ct., 1980).

10 Quoted in Catherine Ann Cline, 'E.D. Morel and the Crusade against the Foreign Office', *Journal of Modern History*, 39, 2 (1967), p. 131.

11 See, for example, E.D. Morel, *Morocco in Diplomacy* (London, 1912), pp. 72–3.

12 On the Union of Democratic Control, see H.M. Swanick, *Builders of Peace* (London, 1924).

13 For an excellent discussion of radical attitudes towards the war in several countries, see Arno Mayer, *Political Origins of the New Diplomacy, 1917–1918* (New Haven, 1959).

14 Useful discussion of this theme can be found in Gordon A. Craig, 'The British Foreign Office from Grey to Austen Chamberlain', in Gordon A. Craig and Felix Gilbert (eds), *The Diplomats: 1919–1939* (Princeton, 1981), pp. 15–48.

15 *War Memoirs of David Lloyd George*, Vol. 1 (London, 1938), pp. 56–7, 59.

16 For further details, see Chapter 2. Also see Craig, 'The British Foreign Office', pp. 18–19.

17 Cecil's own description of the development of his thinking about international relations can be traced in his two books *All the Way* (London, 1949) and *A Great Experiment* (London, 1941).

18 For a useful discussion of proceedings at the Versailles Conference, see Alan Sharp, *The Versailles Settlement: Peacemaking in Paris – 1919* (Basingstoke, 1991); Margaret MacMillan, *Peacemakers: the Paris Conference of 1919 and its Attempt to End War* (London, 2001).

19 For useful material about the origins of the League of Nations, see Elmer Bendiner, *A Time for Angels* (London, 1975); F.S. Northedge, *The League of Nations: its Life and Times* (Leicester, 1986).

20 This definition is the one used in the introduction to R.A.W. Rhodes and Patrick Dunleavy (eds), *Prime Minister, Cabinet and Core Executive* (Basingstoke, 1995), p. 12.

21 Ephraim Maisel, *The Foreign Office and Foreign Policy, 1919–1926* (Brighton, 1994), p. 61.

22 See for example the approach taken in the series of essays found in T.G. Otte and Constantine A. Pagedas (eds), *Personalities, War and Diplomacy: Essays in International History* (London, 1997). I have made particular use of the introduction by Otte in the following paragraph. For a useful defence of the value of biography as a tool in administrative history, see the essay by Kevin Theakston on 'The Biographical Approach to Public Administration: Potential, Purpose and Problems' in Kevin Theakston (ed.), *Bureaucrats and Leadership* (New York, 1999), pp. 1–16.

23 Quoted in Otte and Pagedas, *Personalities, War and Diplomacy*, p. 1.

24 On this topic, see Zara Steiner, 'On Writing International History: Chaps, Maps and Much More', *International Affairs*, 73, 3 (1997), pp. 531–46.

25 For some useful reflections on the role of foreign ministers in different countries during the early years of the twentieth century, see Ernest Satow, *A Guide to Diplomatic Practice* (London, 1917), pp. 9–12.

26 Weber's views on the vexed question of charismatic authority can most conveniently be studied in the chapter on 'The Sociology of Charismatic Authority' in H.H. Gerth and C. Wright Mills, *From Max Weber: Essays in Sociology* (London, 1957), pp. 245–52.

27 For further details on the role of Cliveden in British politics, see Norman Rose, *The Cliveden Set: Portrait of an Exclusive Fraternity* (London, 2000).

28 For a valuable discussion of the concept of 'balance of power' in Foreign Office thinking between the wars, see Brian McKercher and M.L. Roi, 'Ideal and Punch-Bag: Conflicting Views of the Balance of Power and their Influence on Inter-war British Foreign Policy', *Diplomacy and Statecraft*, 12, 2 (2001), pp. 47–78.

2 Lord Curzon at the Foreign Office (1919–24)

1 For a valuable discussion of the significance of 'splendid isolation' in British foreign policy, see John Charmley, *Splendid Isolation: Britain, the Balance of Power and the Origins of the First World War* (London, 1999).

2 David Gilmour, 'Empire and the East: the Orientalism of Lord Curzon', *Asian Affairs*, 26, 3 (1995), p. 270.

3   For details, see Peter King, *The Viceroy's Fall: How Kitchener destroyed Curzon* (London, 1986).

4   John Fisher, *Curzon and British Imperialism in the Middle East, 1916–19* (London, 1988), p. 9.

5   For a fascinating discussion of Curzon's career, effectively focusing on the eventual failure of his hopes of becoming Prime Minister, see D.R. Thorpe, *The Uncrowned Prime Ministers* (London, 1980), pp. 92–163.

6   *Lord Riddell's Intimate Diary of the Peace Conference and After* (London, 1933), p. 410.

7   George Nathaniel Curzon, *Persia and the Persian Question* (London, 1892).

8   For some useful comments on the character of Curzon's imperialism, see Harold Nicolson, *Curzon: the Last Phase* (London, 1934), p. 12ff.

9   Curzon Papers, Mss Eur. F 112/307, Statement by Curzon to the 1921 Imperial Conference; Statement by Curzon to the 1923 Imperial Conference.

10 G.H. Bennett, *British Foreign Policy during the Curzon Period, 1919–24* (Basingstoke, 1995), p. 10.

11 J.D. Gregory, *On the Edge of Diplomacy* (London, 1928), p. 245.

12 For Hardinge's acerbic comments on Curzon, see his *Old Diplomacy*, pp. 243–4. Also see Busch, *Hardinge of Penshurst*, pp. 295–6.

13 Hardinge Papers, 45, Hardinge to Curzon, 10 May 1922.

14 Curzon Papers, MSS Eur. F 112/199, Hardinge to Curzon, 22 March, 1920.

15 Crowe and Corp, *Our Ablest Public Servant*, pp. 398–9

16 Quoted in John Vincent (ed.), *The Crawford Papers* (Manchester, 1984), p. 422.

17 For Nicolson's somewhat controversial treatment of Curzon, see Nicolson, *Curzon*. Eric Phipps, who subsequently served as British ambassador in Berlin and Paris, also praised Curzon as 'consistently kind'; Phipps Papers, PHPP 9/1, 'Diplomatic Light and Shade in Paris and Elsewhere', p. 84.

18 For useful material on these changes, see Christina Larner, 'The Amalgamation of the Diplomatic Service with the Foreign Office', *Journal of Contemporary History*, 7, 1–2 (1972), pp. 107–26; Z.S. Steiner and M.L Dockrill, 'The Foreign Office Reforms, 1919–1921', *Historical Journal*, 17, 1 (1974), pp. 131–56; Maisel, *Foreign Office and Foreign Policy, passim*.

19 See, for example, Crowe Papers, MS Eng.d.2906, Crowe to wife, 18 January 1923, in which Crowe (in Lausanne) complains that Curzon does nothing but discuss issues of policy with him.

20 Assistant Under-Secretaries were given direct access to the Foreign Secretary in the Curzon Foreign Office. Crowe and Corp, *Our Ablest Public Servant*, p. 399.

21 Thorpe, *Uncrowned Prime Ministers*, p. 93. For a useful overview of Anglo-French relations during Curzon's time at the Foreign Office, see Alan Sharp, 'Anglo-French Relations from Versailles to Locarno', in Alan Sharp and Glyn Stone (eds), *Anglo-French Relations in the Twentieth Century: Rivalry and Cooperation* (London, 2000), pp. 120–38. The Anglo-French relationship is well located in the broader question of European security in Anne Orde, *Great Britain and International Security, 1920–1926* (London, 1978). The role of the League of Nations in Anglo-French relations is explored in Ruth Henig, 'Britain, France and the League of Nations in the 1920s', in Sharp and Stone, *Anglo-French Relations*, pp. 139–57.

22 For further discussion of this plot against Curzon, see K.M. Wilson, 'A Venture in the "Caverns of Intrigue": the Conspiracy against Lord Curzon and his Foreign Policy, 1922–3', *Historical Research*, 70, 173 (1997), pp. 312–36. Gwynne's views on Curzon are graphically spelt out in his letter to Stanley Baldwin, in Baldwin Papers, 114, Gwynne to Baldwin, 13 June 1923.

23 The details in the following paragraph are drawn from Viscount D'Abernon, *An Ambassador of Peace*, 3 vols (London, 1929–30); G.L. Johnson, *The Berlin*

Embassy of Lord D'Abernon; Alan Sharp, 'Lord Curzon and British Policy towards the Franco-Belgian Occupation of the Ruhr in 1923', *Diplomacy and Statecraft*, 8, 2 (1997), pp. 82–96.

24 See, for example, the numerous examples contained in Derby Papers, 920 Der (17), 28/3.

25 Derby Papers, 920 Der (17), 28/1/6, Derby diary entry 23 May 1920.

26 Derby Papers, 920 Der (17), 28/2/2, Curzon to Derby, 25 November 1919.

27 See, for example, Derby Papers, 920 Der (17), 28/3, Derby to Churchill, 17 April 1920, complaining that the military attaché in Paris was being bypassed by the War Office.

28 See, for example, the letters from Hardinge, contained in Curzon Papers, MSS Eur. F112/199.

29 Hardinge Papers, 45, Hardinge to Curzon, 12 September 1922.

30 Crewe Papers, C/12, Curzon to Crewe, 20 October 1922 (asking Crewe to take the Paris Embassy).

31 Curzon Papers, Mss Eur. F 112/215, Churchill to Curzon, 20 May 1920.

32 CAB 2/3, Minutes of the 132nd meeting of the Committee on Imperial Defence, 29 June 1920.

33 Maisel, *Foreign Office and Foreign Policy*, p. 63.

34 The best general discussion of the Lloyd George government remains K.O. Morgan, *Consensus and Disunity: The Lloyd George Coalition Government, 1918–1922* (Oxford, 1979).

35 Curzon Papers, MSS Eur. F 112/319, Curzon's notes on the Fall of the Lloyd George Government, 30 November 1922.

36 *Lord Riddel's Intimate Diary of the Peace Conference*, p. 312.

37 Alan Sharp's assertion that Curzon's loss of power and influence was an integral part of the 'eclipse' of the Foreign Office has in recent years come under attack for failing to realise that the relationship between the Foreign Secretary and his fellow ministers, most notably Lloyd George, was less adversarial than sometimes imagined. Alan J. Sharp, 'The Foreign Office in Eclipse, 1919–22', *History*, 61, 202 (1976), pp. 198–218; Gaynor Johnson, 'Curzon, Lloyd George and the Control of British Foreign Policy: A Reassessment', *Diplomacy and Statecraft*, 11, 3 (2000), pp. 49–71; G.H. Bennett, 'Lloyd George, Curzon and the Control of British Foreign Policy', *Australian Journal of Politics and History*, 45, 4 (1999), pp. 467–82.

38 On the complex build-up to the Cannes negotiations, see Bennett, *British Foreign Policy during the Curzon Period*, pp. 22–5.

39 Among the vast literature on the impact of reparations on the international politics of the 1920s, see in particular Bruce Kent, *The Spoils of War: the Economics, Politics and Diplomacy of Reparations, 1918–1932* (Oxford, 1989).

40 For a general discussion of British policy towards the USSR during these years, see Richard Ullman, *Anglo-Soviet Relations, 1917–1921*, 3 vols (Princeton, 1961–72); Stephen White, *Britain and the Bolshevik Revolution* (London, 1979). Useful material on debate about Russian affairs at the Peace Conference can be found in John M. Thompson, *Russia, Bolshevism and the Versailles Peace* (Princeton, 1966).

41 For further details of the negotiations, see M.V. Glenny, 'The Anglo-Soviet Trade Agreement: March 1921', *Journal of Contemporary History*, 5, 2 (1970), pp. 63–82.

42 Curzon Papers, Mss Eur. F 112/236, Copy of Cabinet Paper 1350 (20), 'Negotiations with M. Krassin. Note by Lord Curzon', 27 May 1920.

43 Curzon Papers, Mss Eur. F 112/236, 'Kameneff and Krassin', Note by Curzon dated 2 September 1920.

44 Curzon Papers, Mss Eur. F. 112/236, 'Kameneff and Krassin'.

45 Curzon Papers, Mss Eur. F. 112/217A, Hankey to Curzon, 12 November 1920.

46 The relevant extract from the Cabinet minutes for 18 November 1920 can be found in Gilbert, *Churchill*, Vol. 4 Companion, Part 2, pp. 1242–6.

47 On the British Commercial Mission, see Michael Hughes, *Inside the Enigma: British Officials in Russia, 1900–1939* (London, 1997) p. 185 ff.

48 For useful background on this whole question, see Erik Goldstein, 'Great Britain and Greater Greece, 1917–1920', *Historical Journal*, 32, 2 (1989), pp. 339–56.

49 For a review of Curzon's negotiations with representatives of the French government in Paris on 20–21 September 1922, see CAB 24/139, CP 4201 (22), CP 4202 (22), CP 4203 (22).

50 CAB 23/31, Minutes of a Conference of Ministers, 29 September 1922.

51 A useful discussion of attitudes within the Conservative Party towards the Chanak crisis can be found in Inbal Rose, *Conservatism and Foreign Policy during the Lloyd George Coalition, 1918–1922* (London, 1999), pp. 228–47.

52 On the events surrounding Lloyd George's departure from Number 10, and the collapse of the coalition (particularly as it impacted on the Foreign Secretary), see Gilmour, *Curzon*, pp. 549–55. For a more general discussion, see Morgan, *Consensus and Disunity*, pp. 280–356.

53 Earl of Ronaldshay, *Curzon* (London, 1928),Vol.3, p. 314. Curzon's confidential memorandum on the fall of the Lloyd George government, written for posterity, can be found in Curzon Papers Eur. F 112/319.

54 Ronaldshay, *Curzon*, pp. 316–17.

55 John P. Mackintosh, *The British Cabinet* (London, 1962), p. 359.

56 This idea, which has been suggested by a number of recent historians, was in fact put forward many years ago by Harold Nicolson. See Nicolson, *Curzon*, p. 59.

57 A useful discussion of these issues can be found in Mackintosh, *The British Cabinet*, pp. 355–56.

58 Morgan, *Consensus and Disunity*, p. 112.

59 Quoted in Thorpe, *Uncrowned Prime Ministers* p. 136.

60 On Hankey's career, see the magisterial three-volume study by Stephen Roskill, *Hankey: Man of Secrets* (London, 1970–74); on Hankey's role in developing the Cabinet Secretariat, see John F. Naylor, *A Man and an Institution* (Cambridge, 1984).

61 Hankey Papers, HNKY 1/5, Hankey diary, 14 March 1920.

62 Curzon Papers, Mss Eur. F 112/212A, Hankey to Curzon, 25 October 1919.

63 Naylor, *A Man and an Institution*, p. 76. An interesting insight into Hankey's views can be found in his book, Maurice Hankey, *Diplomacy By Conference: Studies in Public Affairs, 1920–1946* (London, 1946). On British diplomatic planning for the Washington Conference, including useful information on the role of both Hankey and Curzon, see Erik Goldstein, 'The Evolution of British Diplomatic Strategy for the Washington Conference', in Erik Goldstein and John Maurer (eds), *The Washington Conference, 1921–22* (London, 1994), pp. 4–34

64 Curzon Papers, Mss Eur. F 112/212A, Hankey to Curzon, 25 October 1919.

65 Hankey Papers, HNKY 1/5, Hankey diary, 8 November 1922.

66 Baldwin Papers, 114, Curzon to Baldwin, 14 June 1923.

67 Further details can be found in Hankey's diary in Hankey Papers, HNKY 1/5.

68 Erik Goldstein, 'The British Official Mind and the Lausanne Conference, 1922–23', *Diplomacy and Statecraft*, 14, 2 (2003), pp. 185–206.

69 The most detailed biography of Baldwin is still Keith Middlemas and John Barnes, *Baldwin: A Biography* (London, 1969). For a more recent interpretative

account, see Philip Williamson, *Stanley Baldwin: Conservative Leadership and National Values* (Cambridge, 1999). On Bonar Law, see R.J.Q. Adams, *Bonar Law* (London, 1999).

70 Bennett, *British Foreign Policy during the Curzon Period*, pp. 180–1.

71 Crewe Papers, C/12, Curzon to Crewe, 5 January 1923.

72 On British policy during the Ruhr crisis, see Elspeth Y. O'Riordan, *Britain and the Ruhr Crisis* (London, 2001). For a more general discussion, see Conan Fischer, *The Ruhr Crisis, 1923–1924* (Oxford, 2003). For the pressure on Baldwin to marginalise Curzon in handling the crisis, see Baldwin Papers, 114, Gwynne to Baldwin, 13 June 1923.

73 For further details of Curzon's role in the Ruhr crisis, see Sharp, 'Lord Curzon and British Policy towards the Franco-Belgian Occupation of the Ruhr'; Bennet, *British Foreign Policy during the Curzon Period*, p. 31 ff. For Curzon's deep loathing of Poincaré, see Crewe Papers, C/12, Curzon to Crewe, 20 February 1923; Curzon to Crewe, 12 November 1923.

74 On the struggle to replace Bonar Law, see Middlemas and Barnes, *Baldwin*, pp. 158–77; Gilmour, *Curzon*, pp. 579–86; Thorpe, *The Uncrowned Prime Ministers*, pp. 142–57.

75 Gilmour, *Curzon*, p. 583.

76 Quoted in Wilson, 'Caverns of Intrigue', p. 327.

77 Quoted in Wilson, 'Caverns of Intrigue', p. 330.

78 Leo Amery, *My Political Life* (London, 1953–55), Vol. 2, p. 259.

79 J.C.C. Davidson, *Memoirs of a Conservative* (London, 1969), p. 147.

80 Randolph S. Churchill, *Lord Derby: King of Lancashire* (London, 1959), p. 427.

81 Baldwin Papers, 111, Derby to Baldwin, 2 July 1923.

82 Chartwell Papers, CHAR 2/118, Montagu to Churchill, 27 December 1921.

83 Bennett, *British Foreign Policy in the Curzon Period*, p. 84.

84 For details, see Steiner and Dockrill, 'Foreign Office Reforms'.

85 Eunan O'Halpin, *Head of the Civil Service* (London, 1989), p. 82.

86 CAB 23/21, Cabinet 29, 19 May 1920. See, too, Crewe Papers, C/12, Curzon to Crewe, 5 January 1923.

87 On Curzon's lack of interest in financial and economic questions, see Nicolson, *Curzon*, p. 235.

88 Gilbert, *Churchill*, Vol. 4, p. 264; Curzon Papers, Mss Eur. F 112/275, Meeting of the Inter-Departmental Conference on Middle Eastern Affairs, 6 March 1919 (comments by Curzon).

89 Curzon Papers, Mss Eur. F 112/275, Meeting of the Inter-Departmental Conference on Middle Eastern Affairs, 6 March 1919 (comments by Churchill); Mss Eur. F 112/209, Churchill to Curzon, 10 September 1919. For a recent treatment of Churchill's attitude towards the USSR throughout his long career, see David Carlton, *Churchill and the Soviet Union* (Manchester, 2000).

90 A somewhat more negative analysis of Curzon's ability to defend his chosen policy towards the Caucasus can be found in John Fisher, 'On the Glacis of India: Lord Curzon and British Foreign Policy in the Caucasus, 1919', *Diplomacy and Statecraft*, 8, 2 (1997), pp. 50–82.

91 CAB 24/95, CP 594 (20), Curzon Memorandum on 'The Evacuation of Batoum', 9 February 1920.

92 CAB 23/21, Cabinet 33, 7 June 1920; Cabinet 35, 11 June 1920.

93 Curzon Papers, Mss Eur. F 112/215, Churchill to Curzon, 20 May 1920.

94 Curzon to Churchill, 13 June 1921, in Gilbert, *Churchill*, Vol. 4, Companion, Part 3, pp. 1503–4.

95 Curzon Papers, Mss Eur. F 112/281, Copy of Cabinet Paper 1320 (20), 'Papers relating to transfer of Middle Eastern Affairs to the Colonial Office and creation of a new Department there' (by Churchill, dated 1 May 1920).

96 Curzon Papers, Mss Eur. F 112/281, Copy of Cabinet Paper 1434 (20), 'Future Administration of the Middle East' (by Curzon, dated 8 June 1920).

97 See, for example, Curzon Papers, Mss Eur. F 112/281, Copy of Cabinet Paper 1402 (20), 'Mesopotamia and the Middle East: Question of Future Control' (by Montagu, dated 1 June 1920).

98 CAB 23/23, Cabinet 82, 31 December 1920. For a review of all these developments, see H. Mejcher, 'British Middle East Policy, 1917–21: The Inter-Departmental Level', *Journal of Contemporary History*, 8, 4 (1973), pp. 81–101; also Gilbert, *Churchill*, Vol. 4, pp. 507–30. A somewhat different view over the struggle to control policy in the Middle East can be found in Johnson, 'Curzon, Lloyd George and British Foreign Policy', p. 62.

99 Churchill to Lloyd George, 14 January 1921, in Gilbert, *Churchill*, Vol. 4, Companion, Part 2, p. 1310.

100 Curzon to Lady Curzon, 14 February 1921, in Gilbert, *Churchill*, Vol. 4, Companion, Part 2, p. 1349.

101 Curzon Papers, Mss Eur. F 112/307, Statement by Curzon to the 1923 Imperial Conference.

102 For a useful overview of the development of the press, see the relevant chapters of Stephen Koss, *The Rise and Fall of the Political Press in Britain* (London, 1990).

103 *The Times*, 27 March 1920.

104 *The Times*, 2 November 1920.

105 *The Times*, 13 July 1921.

106 *The History of the Times*, Vol. 4, 1912–1948, Part 2, p. 733.

107 *History of the Times*, Vol. 4, 1912–1948, Part 2, p. 606; Henry Wickham Steed, *Through Thirty Years* (London, 1924), Vol. 2, p. 365.

108 For a brief review of Beaverbrook's later assault on the memory of Curzon, see Gilmour, Curzon, xii–xiii. Beaverbrook's own account of the Lloyd George government, written many decades later, can be found in Max Aitken (Beaverbrook), *The Decline and Fall of Lloyd George, and Great was the Fall Thereof* (London, 1963).

109 Beaverbrook was, for example, present at meetings where the possibility of replacing Curzon was openly canvassed. Anne Chisholm and Michael Davies, *Beaverbrook: A Life* (London, 1992), p. 184. Also see a typical account of Beaverbrook's attempts to exert his personal influence over the development of British politics, in Derby Papers, 920 Der (17), 28/1/6, Derby diary, 2 February 1920.

110 *Parliamentary Debates (Lords) 1920*, Vol. 42, Cols.277–8, 16 November 1920.

111 See, for example, the letter by W. Ormsby-Gore *et al.* on policy towards the Balkans in *The Times*, 17 February 1920.

112 On the LNU, see Donald S. Birn, *The League of Nations Union, 1918–1945* (Oxford, 1981).

113 For Curzon's views about the new diplomacy, see Ronaldshay, Curzon, Vol. 3, pp. 225–5.

114 *The Times*, 31 December 1920.

115 On the Primrose League, see Janet Henderson Robb, *The Primrose League, 1883–1906* (New York, 1942), p. 218.

116 *The Times*, 23 February 1920.

117 *The Times*, 7 August 1920.

118 *The Times*, 14 August 1920.

119 *The Times*, 17 August 1920.

120 Curzon Papers, MSS Eur. F 112/307, Curzon statement to 1921 Imperial Conference, 22 June 1921.

121 Nicolson, *Curzon*, pp. 60–1.

122 Ronaldshay, *Curzon*, Vol. 3, p. 254.

3 Ramsay MacDonald at the Foreign Office (1924)

1 *English Review*, January 1924, pp. 3–4.
2 *The Times*, 9 January 1924 (letter by George Tyrrell).
3 Philip Snowden, *An Autobiography* (London, 1934), Vol. 2, pp. 607–8.
4 J.R. Clynes, *Memoirs* (London, 1937), Vol. 2, p. 20.
5 On MacDonald's role in the Union of Democratic Control, see H. Hanak, 'The Union of Democratic Control during the First World War', *Bulletin of the Institute of Historical Research*, 36, 94 (1963), pp. 168–80.
6 Public Record Office, MacDonald Papers, PRO 30/69/1044 (extract from *Labour Leader*). See too such UDC pamphlets as J. Ramsay MacDonald, *War and the Workers* (London, 1915), in which the author attacked the 'stiff correctness' of diplomats who treated public opinion 'with supreme contempt'.
7 J. Ramsay MacDonald, *The Foreign Policy of the Labour Party* (London, 1923), p. 8.
8 For a helpful biography of Ponsonby, see Raymond A. Jones, *Arthur Ponsonby: The Politics of Life* (Bromley, 1989).
9 Ponsonby's own ideas about the various questions under review by the Commission can be found in *British Parliamentary Papers, 1914–1916*, 11 (cd 7749), Royal Commission on the Civil Service (evidence submitted by witnesses).
10 Arthur Ponsonby, *Parliament and Foreign Policy* (London, 1914), p. 2.
11 For details about the implementation of the reforms, see Zara Steiner and M.L. Dockrill, 'The Foreign Office Reforms, 1919–1921', *Historical Journal*, 17, 1 (1974), pp. 131–56; Christina Larner, 'The Amalgamation of the Diplomatic Service with the Foreign Office', *Journal of Contemporary History*, 7, 1–2 (1972), pp. 107–26.
12 David Marquand, *Ramsay MacDonald* (London, 1977), p. 330.
13 MacDonald, *Foreign Policy of the Labour Party*, p. 43.
14 *Parliamentary Debates (Commons) 1924*, Vol. 169, Col.767, 12 February 1924.
15 Snowden, *Autobiography*, Vol. 2, p. 595. On MacDonald's approach to Cabinet-making generally, see Richard W. Lyman, *The First Labour Government* (London, 1957), pp. 99–105; Sidney Webb, 'The First Labour Government', *Political Quarterly*, 32 (1961), pp. 6–44.
16 Marquand, *MacDonald*, pp. 299–300; Jones, *Ponsonby*, p. 141; Chris Wrigley, *Arthur Henderson* (Cardiff, 1990), pp. 150–51.
17 Wrigley, *Henderson*, p. 151.
18 Oxford Dictionary of National Biography (entry on MacDonald).
19 Jones, *Ponsonby*, p. 141.
20 *Parliamentary Debates 1924 (Commons)*, Vol. 169, Col.771, 12 February 1924. MacDonald continued to articulate the same line throughout his time at the Foreign Office. See, for example, PRO 30/69/183, MacDonald to Hulme-Williams, 11 August 1924.
21 MacDonald, *War and the Workers*, p. 13.
22 FO 800/219, MacDonald to Chicherin, 1 February 1924.
23 FO 800/218, MacDonald to Poincaré, 26 January 1924.
24 D'Abernon, *Ambassador of Peace*, Vol. 3, p. 98.
25 Lord Parmoor, *A Retrospect: Looking Back over a Life of more than Eighty Years* (London, 1936), p. 188.
26 See, for example, the evidence given to the Royal Commission on Reform of the Civil Service in 1914 by Maurice De Bunsen (ambassador in Madrid), in *British Parliamentary Papers, 1914–1916*, 11 (cd 7749), Royal Commission on the Civil Service (evidence submitted by witnesses).
27 Stephen Roskill, *Hankey*, Vol. 2, p. 367.
28 Thomas Jones, *Whitehall Diary* (London, 1969–71), Vol. 1, p. 276 (Diary entry for 9 April 1924).

29 See, for example, David Lloyd George, *War Memoirs*, Vol. 1, pp. 29–31; Richard Burdon Haldane, *An Autobiography* (London, 1929), p. 217.

30 Margaret Cole (ed.), *Beatrice Webb's Diaries, 1924–1932* (London, 1956), pp. 13–14 (Diary entry for 6 March 1924).

31 For a useful account of the 'perfect' way in which MacDonald ran the Cabinet, see Webb, 'First Labour Government'. Webb confirmed that the Prime Minister 'seldom troubled' his ministers with foreign affairs.

32 CAB 23/48, Cabinet 26, 10 April 1924.

33 CAB 23/48, Cabinet 35, 30 May 1924. The formal Note rejecting the Draft Treaty was not dispatched until July.

34 CAB 23/48, Cabinet 38, 18 June 1924.

35 CAB 23/48, Cabinet 47, 5 August 1924.

36 Ministers were allowed to see the minutes of the meetings of the British Empire Delegation, but not those pertaining to the actual negotiations. For details, see CAB 23/48, Cabinet 43, 22 July 1924.

37 The minutes of the full CID for 1924 can be found in CAB 2/4. On the relationship between Hankey and MacDonald over the CID, see Roskill, *Hankey*, Vol. 2, p. 358 ff.

38 A somewhat more negative appraisal of Hankey's role can be found in Webb, 'First Labour Government', p. 18

39 Roskill, *Hankey*, Vol. 2, p. 369 (Diary entry for 11 October 1924).

40 A useful discussion of the Anglo-French relationship in 1924, including material on the divisions within the Labour movement, can be found in Alan Cassels, 'Repairing the Entente Cordiale and the New Diplomacy', *Historical Journal*, 23, 1 (1980), pp. 133–53. It is, though, hard to accept Cassels' conclusion that MacDonald's actions in 1924 were primarily rooted in his earlier commitment to establishing a 'new diplomacy'.

41 Henderson had lost his seat at the 1923 General Election, but returned two months later after the Burnley by-election, serving as Home Secretary in the new government. There was of course a long history of tension between MacDonald and Henderson on international affairs dating back to 1914. For details, see Christopher Howard, 'MacDonald, Henderson and the Outbreak of War, 1914', *Historical Journal*, 20, 4 (1977), pp. 871–91.

42 *Parliamentary Debates (Commons) 1924*, Vol. 170, Col. 46, 25 February 1925; Cols 605–8, 27 February 1924.

43 For a useful summary of Henderson's views on international relations in the middle of the 1920s, see Henry R. Winkler, in Craig and Gilbert, *The Diplomats, 1919–1939*, esp. pp. 312–19.

44 CAB 23/48, Cabinet 51 (24), 29 September 1924. For Parmoor's response, insisting that he had remained faithful to his instructions, see PRO 30/69/200, Parmoor to MacDonald, 1 October 1924.

45 *The Times*, 13 October 1924 (reporting speech by Henderson at Burnley).

46 Records relating to the London Conference of 1924 can be found in CAB 29/103–6.

47 Snowden, *Autobiography*, Vol. 2, p. 675.

48 Quoted in Marquand, *MacDonald*, p. 347.

49 CAB 24/168, CP 415 (24), 'Memorandum by the Chancellor of the Exchequer', 28 July 1924.

50 Eyre Crowe also predictably opposed the loan. See FO 371/10519/N7714, Minute by Crowe dated 28 July 1924.

51 J. Ramsay MacDonald, *War and the Workers*, p. 14.

52 Biographical details derived from the *Foreign Office List, 1924, Who's Who*, and *The Dictionary of National Biography*.

53 Maisel, *Foreign Office*, p. 132.

54 Maisel, *Foreign Office*, pp. 132–4.
55 Maisel, *Foreign Office*, p. 130. For another positive review by a Foreign Office official of MacDonald's attitude towards his staff, see the comments reported by Herbert Asquith in his *Memoirs and Reflections* (London, 1928), Vol. 2, p. 191. See too, Haldane's view, quoted in Sir Frederick Maurice, *Haldane, 1915–1928: The Life of Viscount Haldane of Cloan* (London, 1937–39), Vol. 2, p. 152.
56 PRO 30/69/200, MacDonald to Parmoor, 13 August 1924.
57 Crowe and Corp, *Our Ablest Public Servant*, p. 448. The question of Crowe's status as a delegate at the London Conference, desired by MacDonald, was discussed at length in Cabinet. See CAB 23/48, Cabinet 41, 15 July 1924.
58 See FO 800/218 (contains correspondence with Crewe) and FO 800/219 (contains correspondence with D'Abernon).
59 Parmoor, *Retrospect*, p. 196.
60 PRO 30/69/200, Parmoor to MacDonald, 12 August 1924.
61 Jones, *Ponsonby*, p. 141.
62 Jones, *Ponsonby*, p. 146.
63 *Parliamentary Debates (Commons) 1924*, Vol. 171, Cols.2001–3. The move was predictably welcomed by organisations such as the UDC. See PRO 30/69/232, Hobson to MacDonald, 22 May 1924.
64 *Beatrice Webb's Diary*, p. 4 (Diary entry for 8 February).
65 Crowe and Corp, *Our Ablest Public Servant*, p. 457.
66 See, for example, the various documents that cast light on the Foreign Office's role in preparing for the Conference contained in FO 371/10503, or the memorandum by Maxe on 'The Policy to be adopted at the forthcoming negotiations with Soviet representatives', dated 22 March 1924, in FO 371/10511/N2562. A particularly important role was played by Sir Sydney Chapman, Permanent Secretary at the Board of Trade.
67 FO 371/10511/N2554, Gregory to Chapman (Board of Trade), 21 March 1924.
68 Crowe and Corp, *Our Ablest Public Servant*, p. 457.
69 Lyman, *First Labour Government*, p. 193
70 A.A. Purcell and E.D. Morel, *The Workers and the Anglo-Russian Treaty* (London, 1924).
71 *Parliamentary Debates (Commons) 1924*, Vol. 176, Col.3021, 6 August 1924 (statement by McNeil).
72 Lyman, *First Labour Government*, p. 157.
73 For further details on the Labour Party's role in this episode, see Ullman, *The Anglo-Soviet Accord*, pp. 49–52; for a longer discussion, see White, *Britain and the Bolshevik Revolution*, pp. 27–54.
74 A. Fenner Brockway, *Inside the Left* (London, 1942), p. 10.
75 *The Times*, 29 August 1924.
76 See, for example, PRO 30/69/200, MacDonald to Parmoor, 11 August 1924.
77 PRO 30/69/2, Morel to MacDonald, 24 January 1924.
78 PRO 30/69/192, Hobson to MacDonald, 22 May 1924; MacDonald to Hobson, 27 May 1924.
79 FO 800/218, Brailsford to MacDonald, 3 February 1924; F.O. draft tel. to Paris Embassy, 14 February 1924.
80 PRO 30/69/2, Gower to Mills, 16 February 1924.
81 For a useful discussion of Liberal attitudes on international politics between the two world wars, see Richard Grayson, *Liberals, International Relations and Appeasement: The Liberal Party, 1919–1939* (London, 2001).
82 For a persuasive article along these lines, see Duncan Tanner, 'The Development of British Socialism, 1900–1918', *Parliamentary History*, 16, 1 (1997), pp. 48–66.
83 CAB 24/167, CP 309 (24), MacDonald, 'Draft Letter to the Secretary General of the League of Nations', 21 May 1924.

84　PRO 30/69/183, MacDonald to Hulme-Williams, 11 August 1924.

85　The most useful source among the vast (and often unsound) literature on the Zinov'ev Letter, making use of material not available to most historians, can be found in Gill Bennett, *A Most Extraordinary and Mysterious Business: the Zinov'ev Letter of 1924* (London, 1999).

86　*Diary of Beatrice Webb*, p. 42 (Diary entry for 2 September 1924). See, also, PRO 30/69/200, MacDonald to Parmoor, 13 August 1924, in which MacDonald notes that he seldom consulted officials on League affairs 'since I know the position myself'.

87　For a useful review of Hankey's role in this respect, see Roskill, *Hankey*, Vol. 2, Chapter 13.

4　Austen Chamberlain at the Foreign Office (1924–29)

1　*The Times*, 18 March 1937.

2　David Dutton, *Austen Chamberlain: Gentleman in Politics* (Bolton, 1985), p. 2; B.J.C. McKercher, 'Austen Chamberlain's Control of Foreign Policy', *International History Review*, 6, 4 (1984), p. 570; Richard S. Grayson, *Austen Chamberlain and the Commitment to Europe* (London, 1997), p. 2.

3　Dutton, *Austen Chamberlain*, p. 2.

4　*The Times*, 17 March 1937.

5　Chamberlain continued to defend Locarno to his final years. See the essay on 'The Treaty of Locarno – Britain's Guarantee', in Sir Austen Chamberlain, *Down the Years* (London, 1935), pp. 151–71.

6　For some interesting comments on Austen Chamberlain's attempt to model himself on his father in public life, see Leo Amery, *My Political Life* (London, 1953–55), Vol. 2, p. 303.

7　Sir Charles Petrie, *The Life and Letters of the Right Hon. Sir Austen Chamberlain* (London, 1939), Vol. 2, p. 251.

8　For details of Chamberlain's time in France and Germany, see Chamberlain, *Down the Years*, pp. 13–47.

9　CAB 24/172, CP 122 (25), Austen Chamberlain, 'British Foreign Policy and the Problem of Security', 26 February 1925.

10　See, for example, Orde, *Great Britain and International Security*, p. 210; Paul Kennedy, *The Realities behind Diplomacy* (London, 1981), p. 269. For a somewhat different view, arguing that Locarno was always intended to presage sustained British involvement in the struggle to 'keep the peace' between France and Germany, see S. Eyre Crowe, 'Sir Eyre Crowe and the Locarno Pact', *English Historical Review*, 87, 342 (1972), pp. 49–74; Frank Magee, 'Limited Liability? Britain and the Treaty of Locarno', *Twentieth-Century British History*, 6, 1 (1995), pp. 1–22. A valuable discussion that touches on Locarno, within the context of thinking about the 'balance of power', can be found in McKercher and Roi, 'Ideal and Punchbag', 12, 2 (2001), pp. 60–1.

11　Petrie, *Life and Letters of Chamberlain*, Vol. 2, p. 269.

12　Austen Chamberlain, *The League of Nations* (Glasgow, 1926), pp. 28–9.

13　Petrie, *Life and Letters of Chamberlain*, Vol. 2, p. 246.

14　McKercher, 'Chamberlain's Control of British Foreign Policy', p. 573.

15　Dutton, *Austen Chamberlain*, p. 2.

16　Austen Chamberlain Papers, AC 53/130, Austen Chamberlain to Churchill, 2 February 1926.

17　Austen Chamberlain Papers, AC 54/25, Austen Chamberlain to Sir John Anderson, 24 January 1927. A useful description of the 'diplomatic machine' in the second half of the 1920s can be found in Grayson, *Austen Chamberlain and the Commitment to Europe*, pp. 14–30.

18 See, for example, the comments by Chamberlain on Crowe in Austen Chamberlain Papers, AC5/1/352, Austen Chamberlain to Hilda Chamberlain, 25 April 1925.

19 See, for example, his letter to Tyrrell, reproduced in Petrie, *Chamberlain*, Vol. 2, pp. 247–8.

20 For some useful comments on Chamberlain's relationship with his officials, see B.J.C. McKercher, 'A Sane and Sensible Diplomacy: Austen Chamberlain, Japan, and the Naval Balance of Power in the Pacific Ocean', *Canadian Journal of History*, 21, 2 (1986), pp. 187–213.

21 For one of Chamberlain's many complaints about his workload, see Robert C. Self (ed), *The Austen Chamberlain Diary Letters* (Cambridge, 1995), p. 273, Chamberlain to Ida Chamberlain, 28 December 1924.

22 Erik Goldstein, 'The Evolution of British Diplomatic Strategy for the Locarno Pact, 1924–1925', in Michael Dockrill and Brian McKercher (eds), *Diplomacy and World Power* (Cambridge, 1996), p. 128.

23 *Austen Chamberlain Diary Letters*, p. 265.

24 On the relationship between Crowe and Chamberlain, see Goldstein, 'Evolution of British Diplomatic Strategy', pp. 127–9. Goldstein usefully places discussions in the Foreign Office within the broader debate about the balance of power.

25 For a valuable discussion of D'Abernon's role in the whole Locarno process, emphasising the difference between the views of the Foreign Secretary and ambassador on European security, see Gaynor Johnson, 'Lord D'Abernon, Austen Chamberlain and the Origins of the Treaty of Locarno', *Electronic Journal of International History*, Article 2 (2000).

26 CAB 24/172, CP 122 (24), Austen Chamberlain, 'British Foreign Policy and the Problem of Security', 26 February 1925.

27 Austen Chamberlain Papers, AC 53/54, Baldwin to Austen Chamberlain, 21 December 1926.

28 Austen Chamberlain Papers, AC 53/122, letter by Austen Chamberlain dated 15 June 1926.

29 For a useful treatment of Baldwin's management style, see Middlemas and Barnes, *Baldwin*, pp. 479–506. Further discussion of this subject can be found in Williamson, *Stanley Baldwin*, esp. pp. 27–60.

30 McKercher, 'Sane and Sensible Diplomacy', pp. 193–4.

31 David Carlton, 'Great Britain and the League Crisis of 1926', *Historical Journal*, 11, 2 (1968), pp. 354–64.

32 For a discussion of one such case, see Austen Chamberlain Papers, AC 52/59, Amery to Austen Chamberlain, 8 October 1925.

33 *Documents on British Foreign Policy*, Ser. 1, Vol. 27 (Doc. 180), Minute by Secretary of State, 4 January 1925.

34 Chamberlain, *League of Nations*, p. 22.

35 Among the large literature on Locarno and its aftermath, one of the best overviews remains Jon Jacobson, *Germany and the West: Locarno Diplomacy, 1925–1929* (Princeton, 1972).

36 DBFP, Ser. 1, Vol. 27 (Doc. 185), 'Notes on the Advantages and Disadvantages of an Anglo-French Pact', Foreign Office memorandum, 15 January 1925.

37 DBFP, Ser. 1, Vol. 27 (Doc. 191), Hankey to Lampson, 26 January 1925.

38 Crowe and Corp, *Our Ablest Public Servant*, p. 474.

39 DBFP, Ser. 1, Vol. 27 (Doc 186), Minute by Headlam-Morley on 'Notes by McNeill on Substitute for Geneva Protocol', 16 January 1925. For further details of Headlam-Morley's views, see Goldstein, 'Evolution of British Diplomatic Strategy'.

40 DBFP, Ser. 1, Vol. 27 (Doc. 205), 'Memorandum by Nicolson on British

Policy'; Crowe and Corp, *Our Ablest Public Servant*, p. 475. Nicolson had written a report the previous month summarising the result of an internal Foreign Office conference at which it was agreed to recommend a pact with France. For details, see Grayson, *Austen Chamberlain and the Commitment to Europe*, p. 38.

41 *DBFP*, Ser. 1, Vol. 27 (Doc. 189), D'Abernon to Austen Chamberlain, 20 January 1925. For a discussion on the difference between the views of the Foreign Secretary and ambassador to Berlin on European security, see Johnson, 'Lord D'Abernon, Austen Chamberlain and the Origins of the Treaty of Locarno'.

42 F.G. Stambrook, 'Das Kind: Lord D'Abernon and the Origins of the Locarno Pact', *Central European History*, 1, 3 (1968), pp. 233–63. For a somewhat different view, see Gaynor Johnson, 'Das Kind Revisited: Lord D'Abernon and German Security Policy, 1922–1925', *Contemporary European History*, 9, 2 (2000), pp. 209–24.

43 For Chamberlain's initial sceptical reaction, and subsequent change of heart, see Crewe Papers, C8, Chamberlain to Crewe, 3 February 1925.

44 *DBFP*, Ser. 1, Vol. 27 (Doc. 200), Austen Chamberlain to Crewe, 16 February 1925.

45 Grayson, *Austen Chamberlain and the Commitment to Europe*, pp. 44–57 provides an eloquent statement of his own views and a helpful review of the ideas put forward by other historians.

46 *DBFP*, Ser. 1, Vol. 25 (Doc. 200), Austen Chamberlain to Crewe, 16 February 1925; Crewe Papers, C8, Chamberlain to Crewe, 20 February 1925.

47 CAB 2/4, Minutes of the 195th Meeting of the CID, 13 February 1925.

48 CAB 24/172, CP 113 (25), Memorandum by Secretary of State for War (Worthington-Evans), 26 February 1925; CP 121 (25), Memorandum by Hoare on 'Reduction of Armaments', 27 February 1925.

49 Austen Chamberlain Papers, AC 52/156, notes encld. with Churchill to Austen Chamberlain, 23 February 1925.

50 CAB 24/172, CP 118 (25), Memorandum by Chancellor of the Exchequer (Churchill) on 'French and Belgian Security', 24 February 1925.

51 CAB 23/49, Cabinet 12, 2 March 1925.

52 Middlemas and Barnes, *Baldwin*, p. 351; Roskill, *Hankey*, Vol. 2, pp. 396–7.

53 CAB 23/49, Cabinet 13, 4 March 1925.

54 Middlemas and Barnes, *Baldwin*, pp. 352–56; Grayson, *Austen Chamberlain and the Commitment to Europe*, pp. 50–7.

55 It is certainly true that the documents sent back by Chamberlain to London at this time were marked by his concern to prevent a break with France, but he does not seem to have reintroduced the idea of a separate Anglo-French Pact. See, for example, *DBFP*, Ser. 1, Vol. 27 (Doc. 227), Chamberlain to Crewe, 8 March 1925.

56 Austen Chamberlain Papers, AC 52/240, Crowe to Austen Chamberlain, 12 March 1925.

57 Quoted in Middlemas and Barnes, *Baldwin*, p. 355.

58 Middlemas and Barnes, *Baldwin*, p. 356.

59 Austen Chamberlain Papers, AC 6/1/603, Austen Chamberlain to Ivy Chamberlain, 15 March 1925.

60 CAB 23/49, Cabinet 17, 20 March 1925.

61 See, for example, the comments by Amery on 26 May 1925, contained in *DBFP*, Ser. 1, Vol. 27, (Doc. 343) 'Notes on Meeting of Committee of the Cabinet', 26 May 1925.

62 See, for example, *DBFP*, Ser. 1, Vol. 27, (Doc. 321), 'Memorandum by Mr Chamberlain for the Cabinet, 14 May 1925, in which the Foreign Secretary asked for comments on the French response to the original German proposals for a security pact.

63 See, for example, CAB 23/50, Cabinet 27, 28 May 1925, at which it was agreed to set up a cabinet committee to determine how to reply to the French response to the original German proposals for some kind of security pact. The conclusions of the two meetings of the Committee on Security can be found in CAB 27/275.

64 See, for example, AC 52/51, Austen Chamberlain to Amery, 6 August 1925.

65 FO 800/257, Austen Chamberlain to Crewe, 2 April 1925.

66 *DBFP*, Ser. 1, Vol. 27 (Doc. 203), Sargent to Lampson, 18 February 1925 (commenting on enclosed memorandum by Heywood).

67 See, for example, the comments of the left-wing MP Thurtle in *Parliamentary Debates (Commons) 1925*, Vol. 188, Col.500, 18 November 1925.

68 *Parliamentary Debates (Commons) 1924–25*, Vol. 181, 5 March 1925, Col.701.

69 *Parliamentary Debates (Commons) 1924–25*, Vol. 181, 5 March 1925, Col.707.

70 *Parliamentary Debates (Commons) 1924–25*, Vol. 185, 24 June 1925, Col.1561.

71 *Parliamentary Debates (Commons) 1924–25*, Vol. 185, 24 June 1925, Col.1555.

72 *Parliamentary Debates (Commons) 1924–25*, Vol. 188, 18 November 1925, Col.500.

73 *Parliamentary Debates (Commons) 1924–25*, Vol. 181, 5 March 1925, Col.715.

74 *History of the Times*, Vol. 4, 1912–1928, Pt.2, p. 801.

75 *The Times*, 2 June 1925.

76 *The Times*, 19 June 1925.

77 *The Times*, 15 March 1925, 11 June 1925.

78 Grayson, *Austen Chamberlain and the Commitment to Europe*, p. 50.

79 Quoted in Grayson, *Austen Chamberlain and the Commitment to Europe*, p. 61.

80 A.J.P. Taylor, *The Origins of the Second World War* (London, 1963), p. 82.

81 *DBFP*, Ser. 1, Vol. 25 (Doc. 267), Chamberlain to Rakovskii, 21 November 1924.

82 Gilbert, *Churchill*, Companion, Vol. 5, Part 1, p. 245 (Churchill to Chamberlain, 14 November 1924).

83 *Parliamentary Debates (Commons) 1926*, Vol. 197, 25 June 1926, Col.772.

84 *DBFP*, Ser. 1, Vol. 25 (Doc. 264), Minute by Austen Chamberlain and encls, 11 November 1924.

85 For a general discussion of Churchill's views on Russia, see Carlton, *Churchill and the Soviet Union*.

86 See, for example, *The Speeches of Lord Birkenhead* (London, 1929), p. 208.

87 See, for example, *DBFP*, Ser. 1, Vol. 25 (Doc. 300), Chamberlain to Loraine (Tehran), 22 January 1925; *DBFP*, Ser. 1, Vol. 25 (Doc. 303), Humphrys (Kabul) to Austen Chamberlain, 4 February 1925.

88 FO 800/258, Austen Chamberlain to Prime Minister, 24 July 1925.

89 FO 800/258, Austen Chamberlain to Baldwin, 24 July 1925.

90 Earl of Birkenhead, *Frederick Edwin: Earl of Birkenhead* (London, 1933), Vol. 2, p. 271.

91 Gilbert, *Winston S. Churchill*, Companion, Vol. 5, Part 1, p. 706 (draft of article for British Gazette).

92 *Daily Mail*, 8 June 1926, 15 June 1926.

93 *Daily Mail*, 10 June 1926.

94 *Parliamentary Debates (Commons) 1926*, Vol. 197, 25 June 1926, Col.699.

95 CAB 23/53, Cabinet 40, 16 June 1926.

96 *Austen Chamberlain Diary Letters*, Chamberlain to Ida Chamberlain, 19 June 1926.

97 John Robert Ferris, *The Evolution of British Strategic Policy, 1919–1926* (Basingstoke, 1989), p. 1.

98 CAB 4/14. No.655, General Staff Memorandum on 'The Extension of Soviet Influence in Asia', 15 December 1925.

99 CAB 6/5, No142D, 'Afghanistan' (Paper by Birkenhead, June 1926).
100 CAB 6/5 No.149D, 'Dispatch from the Government of India to the Secretary of State for India', 7 October 1926.
101 See, for example, the attack by Milne on the military advisers to the Indian government in CAB 6/5, No.149D appendix, 'Memorandum by the CIGS on Integrity of Afghanistan' (undated).
102 CAB 2/4, Minutes of the 215th meeting of the Committee on Imperial Defence, 22 July 1926.
103 Austen Chamberlain Papers, AC 53/569, Austen Chamberlain to Tyrrell, 9 December 1926.
104 Irwin Papers, Mss Eur., C 152/3, Birkenhead to Irwin, 22 January 1927.
105 FO 371/12589/N229 (minutes from Cabinet meeting on 17 January 1927).
106 Austen Chamberlain Papers, AC 54/35, Austen Chamberlain to Balfour, 22 January 1927.
107 Austen Chamberlain Papers, AC 54/335, Austen Chamberlain to Lindsay, 1 March 1927. For further material offering an insight into Chamberlain's views on Russia around this time, see Austen Chamberlain Papers, AC 54/35, Austen Chamberlain to Balfour, 22 January 1927.
108 CAB 23/54, Cabinet 12, 18 February 1927.
109 For a useful review of the intelligence dimension of the Arcos raid, see Christopher Andrew, 'British Intelligence and the Breach with Russia in 1927', *Historical Journal*, 25, 4 (1982), pp. 957–64.
110 FO 371/12602/N2289, 'Report on the Documentary Evidence Implicating Officials of the Russian Trade Delegation and Arcos in Revolutionary Propaganda and Espionage'.
111 FO 371/12602/N2289, Note by Palareit on the situation following the Arcos raid.
112 For Chamberlain's views, see CAB 23/55, Cabinet 33, 23 May 1927.
113 For a general review of British policy towards China during this period, see the relevant portions of William Roger Louis, *British Strategy in the Far East, 1919–1939* (Oxford, 1971). A more succinct but very helpful account can be found in McKercher, 'A Sane and Sensible Diplomacy', which is particularly valuable for placing the British reaction to developments in China in a broader strategic context.
114 On Chamberlain's support for a strong navy, see Davidson, *Memoirs of a Conservative*, p. 213. Chamberlain confessed that he felt 'ignorant' about east Asia which doubtless explains why he was so ready to follow his officials' advice. See Ferris, *Evolution of British Strategic Policy*, p. 144.
115 Baldwin Papers, 115, Amery to Baldwin, 18 September 1926.
116 CAB 24/182, CP 399, 'British Policy on China' (by Wellesley), 23 November 1926.
117 CAB 27/337, Committee on China, 1926–27, Minutes of the Meeting on 30 November 1926.
118 Austen Chamberlain papers, AC 54/313, Lampson to Austen Chamberlain, 9 March 1927.
119 Austen Chamberlain papers, AC 54/298, Jix to Austen Chamberlain, 7 January 1927.
120 *The Leo Amery Diaries*, Vol. 1, p. 493 (Diary entry for 19 January 1927).
121 The following paragraph relies heavily on B.J.C. McKercher, 'Belligerent Rights in 1927–1929: Foreign Policy versus Naval Policy in the Second Baldwin Government', *Historical Journal*, 29, 4 (1986), pp. 963–74.
122 On the 1927 Naval Conference, see David Carlton, 'Great Britain and the Coolidge Naval Conference of 1927', *Political Science Quarterly*, 83, 4 (1968), pp. 573–98.

123 McKercher, 'Belligerent Rights', p. 971.
124 McKercher, 'Belligerent Rights', p. 972; Cab 23/59, Cabinet 55, 7 December 1928.
125 McKercher, 'Chamberlain's Control of Foreign Policy'.

5 Arthur Henderson at the Foreign Office (1929–31)

1 Clynes, *Memoirs*, Vol. 2, p. 112. Further information can be found in MacDonald's own diary, PRO 30/69/1753/1, Diary entry 4 June 1929.
2 Snowden, *Autobiography*, Vol. 2, p. 760.
3 Quoted in John Connell, *The Office: A Study of British Foreign Policy and its Makers, 1919–1951* (London, 1958), p. 94.
4 Arthur Henderson, *The League of Nations and Labour* (London, 1918); Arthur Henderson, *Labour and Foreign Affairs* (London, 1922).
5 *Minutes of the Annual Conference of the Wesleyan Methodist Church, 1917*. For a discussion of Methodist attitudes towards international politics in the first half of the twentieth century, see Michael Hughes, 'The Development of Methodist Pacifism 1899–1939', *Proceedings of the Wesley Historical Society*, 53, 6 (2002), pp. 203–15.
6 Three useful if contrasting accounts of the 1929–31 Labour government can be found in Neil Riddell, *Labour in Crisis: The Second Labour Government, 1929–1931* (Manchester, 1999); Philip Williamson, *National Crisis and National Government: British Politics, the Economy and Empire, 1926–1932* (Cambridge, 1992); Robert Skidelsky, *Politicians and the Slump: The Labour Government of 1929–1931* (London, 1967).
7 Connell, *The Office*, p. 95. Henderson had already been briefed by Chamberlain about the 'v[ery] good staff' at the Foreign Office. See FO 800/280, Chamberlain to Henderson, 7 June 1929.
8 Hugh Dalton, 'British Foreign Policy, 1929–31', *The Political Quarterly*, 2, 4 (1931), pp. 485–505.
9 Cited in Mary Agnes Hamilton, *Arthur Henderson: A Biography* (London, 1938), pp. 285–6.
10 FO 800/272, Sargent to Phipps, 20 December 1929.
11 Hugh Dalton, *Political Diary of Hugh Dalton, 1918–1940, 1945–1960* (London, 1986), p. 103 (Diary entry for 14 April 1930).
12 Gordon Waterfield, *Professional Diplomat: Sir Percy Loraine* (London, 1973), pp. 177–8.
13 Dalton, *Diary*, p. 64 (Diary entry for 23 August 1929).
14 Lord Vansittart, *The Mist Procession* (London, 1958), p. 397.
15 For a useful analysis of the role of the balance of power in British thinking about foreign policy between the wars, see McKercher and Roi, 'Ideal and Punchbag'.
16 For a pithy statement of Vansittart's views shortly after becoming Permanent Secretary, see CAB 4/21, CID 1056B, Foreign Office Memorandum on 'The Basis of the Service Estimates'.
17 Earl of Avon, *Facing the Dictators* (London, 1962), p. 242.
18 See, for example, FO 800/280, Howard to Henderson, 13 June 1929.
19 FO 800/283, Rumbold to Henderson, 6 March 1931.
20 For a useful discussion of Henderson's *modus operandi* whilst at the Foreign Office, see Henry R. Winkler, 'Arthur Henderson', in Craig and Gilbert (eds), *The Diplomats, 1919–1939*, pp. 320–1.
21 Dalton, *Diary*, p. 65 (Diary entry for 1–25 September, 1929).
22 Dalton, *Diary*, p. 72, (Diary entry for 8 November 1929).
23 Dalton, *Diary*, p. 99 (Diary entry for 21 March 1930).
24 Cecil, *All the Way*, p. 194.

25 For the contrasting attitudes of the two men on the outbreak of war in 1914, see Christopher Howard, 'MacDonald, Henderson and the Outbreak of War, 1914', in *Historical Journal*, 20, 4 (1977), pp. 871–91.
26 For Henderson's views on the Optional Clause, see CAB 24/204, Henderson covering note to CP 192 (29), Foreign Office memorandum on 'The Optional Clause and Possible Reservations'. A useful general discussion of the attitude of the second Labour Government towards the Optional Clause in general, and the League in particular, can be found in Winkler, 'Arthur Henderson', pp. 327–34.
27 Henderson did, however, also face pressure from some ministers to reduce the number of 'reservations'. See FO 800/280, Parmoor to Henderson, 15 July 1929.
28 Emanuel Shinwell, *The Labour Story* (London, 1963), pp. 135–6.
29 Dalton, *Diary*, p. 68 (Diary entry for 22 October 1929).
30 David Carlton, *MacDonald versus Henderson: The Foreign Policy of the Second Labour Government* (London, 1970), p. 23.
31 Dalton, *Diary*, p. 134 (Diary entry for 12 December 1930).
32 On the press during the time of the Labour Government of 1929–31 (including agitation on the whole question of imperial preference), see the relevant sections of Koss, *Rise and Fall of the Political Press*. On Beaverbrook's imperial crusade in 1930–31, see A.J.P. Taylor, *Beaverbrook* (London, 1972), pp. 359–403.
33 There was in fact some division within the LNU during this period between the supporters of an international police force, such as David Davies, and those who looked on such a development with concern. For details, see Birn, *League of Nations Union*, pp. 87–8. See, too, Michael Pugh, 'An International Police Force: Lord Davies and the British Debate in the 1930s', *International Relations*, 9, 4 (1988), pp. 335–51.
34 A useful discussion of the attitude of the Labour Party towards Russia, including the period 1929–31, can be found in the relevant section of Andrew Williams, *The Attitude of the Labour Party towards the USSR, 1924–1934* (Manchester, 1989). On the developments leading up to the restoration of diplomatic relations, see Donald Lammers, 'The Second Labour Government and the Restoration of Relations with Soviet Russia (1929)', *Bulletin of the Institute of Historical Research*, 37, 95 (1964), pp. 60–72.
35 The complex inter-departmental aspect of the negotiations to restore diplomatic relations with Moscow are usefully revealed in the various documents contained in FO 371/14032–3.
36 The following section draws heavily on John Charmley, *Lord Lloyd and the Decline of the British Empire* (London, 1987), pp. 150–69. For a very different view of the events surrounding Lloyd's dismissal, see Hamilton, *Arthur Henderson*, pp. 298–304.
37 William Tyrrell, quoted in Charmley, *Lord Lloyd*, p. 145.
38 Henderson's review of his relations with Lloyd can be found in Sir Nevile Henderson, *Water Under the Bridges* (London, 1945), pp. 150–2.
39 Austen Chamberlain papers, AC 5/1/435, Austen Chamberlain to Hilda Chamberlain, 22 October 1927.
40 Vansittart, *Mist Procession*, p. 372.
41 Charmley, *Lord Lloyd*, p. 158.
42 Charmley, *Lord Lloyd*, p. 160.
43 Charmley, *Lord Lloyd*, p. 164.
44 Dalton, *Diary*, pp. 102–3 (Diary entry for 14 April 1930); p. 105, (Diary entry for 7 May 1930). A useful discussion focusing on the attitude of Sir Percy Loraine can be found in Waterfield, *Professional Diplomat*, pp. 157–83.
45 PRO 30/69/1753/1, MacDonald diary entries, 24 July 1929; 8 May 1930.

46 Hugh Dalton, *Call Back Yesterday* (London, 1953), p. 227. It is perhaps striking that Dalton said nothing of this threat in his diary, perhaps raising questions about the accuracy of his later account.
47 See, for example, minutes of the Cabinet Committee on Egypt in CAB 27/387.
48 CAB 24/205, CP 203 (29), Snowden Memorandum on 'German Reparations: Policy to be Adopted towards the Young Report', 15 July 1929.
49 CAB 23/61, Cabinet 29, 17 July 1929.
50 Snowden, *Autobiography*, Vol. 2, p. 791.
51 Dalton, *Diary*, p. 63 (Diary entry for 10–19 August 1929).
52 PRO 30/69/1753/1, MacDonald diary entry, 27 August 1929 (reflecting on the events of the previous few weeks).
53 The proceedings of the Political Commission, which cast light on Henderson's role, can be found in CAB 29/115. Henderson's discussion of the negotiations is contained in his dispatch to Lindsay on 30 August, 1929, contained in CAB 24/206, CP 263 (29), 'The Hague Conference: the Political Discussions'. A copy of the Report of the Political Commission can be found in CAB 29/107.
54 PRO 30/69/1753/1, MacDonald diary entry, 20 November 1929.
55 For two contrasting accounts about the circumstances surrounding Vansittart's appointment as Permanent Secretary, see Carlton, *MacDonald versus Henderson*, p. 23; O'Halpin, *Head of the Civil Service*, p. 184.
56 O'Halpin, *Head of the Civil Service*, pp. 184–6. See, too, Donald Graeme Boadle, 'The Formation of the Foreign Office Economic Relations Section, 1930–1937', *Historical Journal*, 20, 4 (1977), pp. 919–36.
57 Cab 23/67, Cabinet 37, 3 July 1931.
58 Cab 23/67, Cabinet 36, 1 July 1931.
59 The following section, whilst based on a study of the relevant documents, draws heavily on the interpretation provided in Carlton, *MacDonald versus Henderson*, pp. 197–217.
60 FO 408/58, 'Notes of a Conference on 15 July 1931.
61 *DBFP*, Ser. 2, Vol. 2 (Doc. 194), Henderson to MacDonald in Tyrrell to Vansittart, 15 July 1931. CAB 24/222, CP 182 (32), 'Memorandum by Henderson on a Visit to Paris, 15–19 July 1931'.
62 FO 408/58, MacDonald to Henderson, in Vansittart to Tyrrell, 16 July 1931.
63 FO 408/58, Snowden to Henderson in Vansittart to Tyrrell, 17 July 1931.
64 A useful account of the various attempts to promote disarmament during the 1920s can be found in Dick Richardson, *The Evolution of British Disarmament Policy in the 1920s* (London, 1989).
65 *DBFP*, Ser. 1A, Vol. 6 (Doc. 379), Memorandum by Cadogan dated 13 March 1929 (with minute by Lindsay).
66 Orest M. Babij, 'The Second Labour Government and Maritime Security', *Diplomacy and Statecraft*, 6, 3 (1995), p. 647.
67 Babij, 'The Second Labour Government and Maritime Security', p. 649.
68 PRO 30/69/1753/1, MacDonald diary entry, 3 November 1929. See too MacDonald's report to the Cabinet in CAB 23/62, Cabinet 44, 1 November 1929.
69 Carlton, *MacDonald versus Henderson*, p. 117.
70 For the full records, see CAB 29/117, Minutes of the Cabinet Committee on the London Naval Conference.
71 See for example CAB 23/63, Cabinet 30, 14 July 1930.
72 CAB 29/117, Meeting of members of Cabinet Committee on the London Naval Conference, 9 January 1930.
73 For details, see Dalton, *Diary*, pp. 88–9 (Diary entry for 20 January 1930). Agreement on the battleship issue had been reached on 14 January in Cabinet. See CAB 23/63, Cabinet 1, 14 January 1930.
74 For the Treasury's view in advance of the London Naval Conference, see CAB

24/209, Treasury Memorandum on 'The Financial Aspects of the Naval Conference', 16 December 1929.

75 CAB 29/128, Meeting of members of the British delegation to the London Naval Conference, 16 February 1930. MacDonald's private views were spelled out in a letter to the Churchman Cosmo Lang, when he noted that the Conference showed that 'when you scratch below the European mind, you find very little change from what you would have found any time between 1906 and 1911'. PRO 30/69/676, MacDonald to Lang, 24 April 1930.

76 FO 800/281, Henderson to MacDonald, 3 April 1930.

77 Gregory C. Kennedy, 'Britain's Policy-Making Elite, the Disarmament Policy, and Public Opinion, 1927–1932', *Albion*, 26, 4 (1994), p. 639.

78 Babij, 'The Second Labour Government and Maritime Security', p. 655.

79 A useful discussion of Henderson's role in the crisis of August 1931 can be found in Andrew Thorpe, 'Arthur Henderson and the British Political Crisis of 1931', *Historical Journal*, 31, 1 (1988), pp. 117–39.

80 Winkler, 'Arthur Henderson'.

6 Sir John Simon at the Foreign Office (1931–35)

1 David Dutton, *Simon: A Political Biography of Sir John Simon* (London, 1992), pp. 121–2.

2 Cato, *Guilty Men* (London, 1940).

3 For a useful recent discussion of the importance of the withdrawal of the Samuelites in 1932, see David Dutton, '1932: A Neglected Date in the History of the Decline of the Liberal Party', *Twentieth-Century British History*, 14, 1 (2003), pp. 43–60.

4 For a useful discussion of the various strands of Liberal thinking on international politics in the inter-war years, see Grayson, *Liberals, International Relations and Appeasement*.

5 PRO 30/69/678 Part 2, Simon to MacDonald, 30 December 1932.

6 Avon Papers, AP 20/1/13, Eden diary entry, 13 January 1933.

7 *The Austen Chamberlain Diary Letters*, p. 458, Austen Chamberlain to Hilda Chamberlain, 10 February 1934.

8 Viscount Simon, *Retrospect: The Memoirs of the Rt Hon. Viscount Simon* (London, 1952), p. 177.

9 Vansittart, *Mist Procession*, pp. 427–8.

10 See, for example, Simon Papers, 70, Vansittart to Simon, 23 December 1931.

11 For a useful insight into Wigram's *modus operandi*, see Hankey Papers, HNKY 4/24, Wigram to Hankey, 16 July 1932; 25 July 1932.

12 *Austen Chamberlain Diary Letters*, p. 447, Austen Chamberlain to Hilda Chamberlain, 13 August 1933.

13 On Tyrrell's attitude towards Simon, see PRO 30/69/1753/1, MacDonald diary entry, 11 December 1933.

14 *Austen Chamberlain Diary Letters*, p. 458, Austen Chamberlain to Ida Chamberlain, 3 February 1934; p. 459, to Hilda Chamberlain, 10 February 1934.

15 Avon Papers, AP 14/1/153, Cadogan to Eden, 14 January 1933.

16 See, for example, Avon, *Facing the Dictators*, pp. 28, 219–20.

17 For a useful discussion of this question, see David Dutton, 'Simon and Eden at the Foreign Office', *Review of International Studies*, 20, 1 (1994), pp. 35–52.

18 Avon Papers, AP 14/1/346, Gilbert Murray to Eden, 6 July 1934.

19 PRO 30/69/678 Part 2, MacDonald to Simon, 23 December 1932.

20 PRO 30/69/678 Part 2, Simon to MacDonald, 30 December 1932.

21 Baldwin Papers, 121, Ormsby-Gore to Baldwin, 1 October 1933.

22 MacDonald Papers, PRO 30/69/1753/1, MacDonald diary entry, 17 November 1933.
23 Neville Chamberlain Papers, NC 2/23A, Neville Chamberlain diary entry, January 1934.
24 Avon Papers, AP 20/1/14, Eden diary entry, 7 November 1934; Baldwin Papers, 121, Ormsby-Gore to Baldwin, 1 October 1933.
25 Dutton, *Simon*, p. 118. Some of Simon's contemporaries were also shrewd enough to realise that the scale of the problems faced by the Foreign Secretary were insurmountable. See, for example, Major-General A.C. Temperley, *The Whispering Gallery of Europe* (London, 1938), p. 217.
26 A useful discussion of the problems faced by the Liberal Nationals in the early 1930s can be found in Graham D. Goodlad, 'The Liberal Nationals, 1931–1940: The Problems of a Party in "Partnership Government"', *Historical Journal*, 38, 1 (1995), pp. 133–43.
27 Dutton, *Simon*, p. 124.
28 PRO 30/69/1753/1, MacDonald diary entry, 17 November 1933.
29 See, for example, PRO 30/69/677, MacDonald to Simon, 14 November 1931.
30 PRO 30/69/678 Part 2, Simon to MacDonald, 30 December 1932.
31 Middlemas and Barnes, *Baldwin*, pp. 745–7. For a challenge to the idea that Labour's victory in the Fulham by-election was in fact due to its candidate's opposition to rearmament, see Richard Heller, 'East Fulham Revisited', *Journal of Contemporary History*, 6, 3 (1971), pp. 172–96.
32 On the developments leading up to the Lausanne Conference, see Kent, *Spoils of War*, pp. 322–72.
33 Simon Papers, 70, Simon to Neville Chamberlain, 7 January 1932.
34 Dutton, *Simon*, p. 120.
35 For further details on the reaction of the air lobby to developments at the Disarmament Conference, see Philip S. Meilinger, 'Clipping the Bomber's Wings: The Geneva Disarmament Conference and the Royal Air Force, 1932–1934', *War in History*, 6, 3 (1999), pp. 306–30.
36 Avon Papers, 14/1/194, Londonderry to Eden, 11 July 1933.
37 PRO 30/69/679, MacDonald to Simon, 22 September 1933.
38 For a useful discussion of the press during the first National Government, see Koss, *Political Press*, p. 943.ff.
39 See, for example, Christopher Thorne, 'Viscount Cecil, the Government and the Far Eastern Crisis of 1931', *Historical Journal*, 14, 4 (1971), pp. 805–26.
40 Michael Hughes, 'The Foreign Secretary Goes to Court: Sir John Simon and his Critics', *Twentieth-Century British History*, 14, 4 (2003), pp. 339–59.
41 Simon Papers, 7, Simon diary entry, 22 November 1934.
42 See, for example, Christopher Thorne, *The Limits of Foreign Policy: the West, the League and the Far Eastern Crisis of 1931–1933* (London, 1972), p. 140ff; F.S. Northedge, *The Troubled Giant: Britain among the Great Powers, 1916–1939* (London, 1966), pp. 348–51.
43 For a useful discussion of British responses in the face of the Japanese threat to Shanghai, see Christopher Thorne, 'The Shanghai Crisis of 1932: The Basis of British Policy', *American Historical Review*, 75, 6 (1970), pp. 1616–49.
44 See also Lindley's revealing private letter to Simon in FO 800/282, 23 December 1931.
45 See, for example, *DBFP*, Ser. 2, Vol. 9 (Doc. 33), Lindley tel. 28 December 1931.
46 *DBFP*, Ser. 2, Vol. 9 (Doc. 21), Memorandum by Wellesley, 22 December 1931.
47 *DBFP*, Ser. 2, Vol. 9 (Doc. 239), Memorandum by Wellesley, 1 February 1932.

48 See, for example, *DBFP*, Ser. 2, Vol. 9 (Doc. 216), Memorandum by Pratt, January 1932; Doc. 535, Memorandum by Pratt, 21 February 1932.

49 *DBFP*, Ser. 2, Vol. 9 (Doc. 176), Minute by Leeper, 30 January 1932.

50 See, for example, the discussion in CAB 23/70, Cabinet 17, 9 March, 1932. The deliberations of the Far Eastern Committee are contained in CAB 27/482.

51 See, for example, the Chiefs of Staff memorandum on 'Economic Sanctions against Japan', CAB 24/228, CP 92 (32).

52 See, for example, the review of Simon's activities in CAB 23/70, Cabinet 12, 10 February 1932; Cab 14, 17 February 1932.

53 CAB 23/70, Cabinet 10, 29 January 1932.

54 CAB 23/70, Cabinet 9, 27 January 1932.

55 Henry Lewis Stimson, *The Far Eastern Crisis: Recollections and Observations* (London, 1936).

56 See, for example, Simon's letter to MacDonald, in *DBFP*, Ser. 2, Vol. 9 (Doc. 153), 29 January 1932.

57 Roskill, *Hankey*, Vol. 3, pp. 73–4 (Diary entry, 4 March 1933).

58 Philip Noel-Baker, *The First World Disarmament Conference and why it Failed* (Oxford, 1979).

59 N.H. Gibbs, *Rearmament Policy* (London, 1976), pp. 82–3.

60 See, for example, CAB 53/23, CoS 271 (31), Chiefs of Staff Sixth Annual Review of Defence Policy; CoS 295 (32), Annual Review of Defence Policy for 1932.

61 CAB 24/229, CP 105 (32), 'Note by the Treasury on the Annual Review for 1932'.

62 A valuable recent discussion of British policy at the Disarmament Conference can be found in Carolyn J. Kitching, *Britain and the Geneva Disarmament Conference* (London, 1998).

63 On the whole question of British air policy, see the relevant sections of Uwe Bialer, *The Shadow of the Bomber* (London, 1980); Malcolm Smith, *British Air Strategy between the Wars* (Oxford, 1984); Meilinger, 'Clipping the Bomber's Wings'.

64 Dutton, *Simon*, p. 154.

65 FO 800/287, Simon to Tyrrell, 9 June 1932.

66 For an interesting insight into the views of some British officials about the futility of the Disarmament Conference, see Andrew Webster, 'The Disenchantment Conference: Frustration and Humour at the World Disarmament Conference, 1932', *Diplomacy and Statecraft*, 11, 3 (2000), pp. 72–80.

67 Avon, *Facing the Dictators*, p. 47.

68 CAB 23/71, Cabinet 38 (32), 24 June 1932.

69 For Baldwin's support for the abolition of military aircraft, see CAB 23/71, Cabinet 26, 4 May 1932; Cabinet 27, 11 May 1932. For Londonderry's opposition, see, for example, CAB 24/228, CP 82 (32), Londonderry, 'Air Disarmament and the Abolition of Bombing Aircraft'. Further information can also be found in Meilinger, 'Clipping the Bomber's Wings'.

70 Avon Papers, AP 20/1/12, Eden diary entry, 26 July 1932.

71 PRO 30/69/1753/1, MacDonald diary entry, 22 September 1932.

72 Roskill, *Hankey*, Vol. 3, p. 61 (Diary entry, 23 October 1932).

73 Neville Chamberlain papers, NC 7/11/25/39, Neville Chamberlain to Simon, 28 October 1932.

74 Dutton, *Simon*, p. 164.

75 Temperley, *Whispering Gallery of Europe*, p. 218.

76 Baldwin Papers, 129, Eden to Baldwin, 22 February 1933.

77 Avon, *Facing the Dictators*, p. 31.

78 David Marquand, *MacDonald*, pp. 753–4. For further details on the visit to Rome, see Aage Trommer, 'MacDonald in Geneva in March 1933. A Study in Britain's European Policy', *Scandinavian Journal of History*, 1, 3–4 (1976), pp. 293–312.

79 For details, see the relevant section of Kitching, *Britain and the Geneva Conference*.

80 CAB 24/244, CP 255 (33), 'Disarmament: Draft Plan', 1 November 1933.

81 *The Times*, 15 November 1933.

82 CAB 23/77, Cabinet 60, 6 November 1933; Cabinet 61, 8 November 1933.

83 PRO 30/69/1753/1, MacDonald diary entry, 17 November 1933.

84 Dutton, *Simon*, p. 178.

85 See for example CAB 23/77, Cabinet 54, 23 October 1933.

86 CAB 53/23, CoS 310 (33), Chiefs of Staff Annual Review of Defence Policy, 12 October 1933.

87 CAB 23/77, Cabinet 57, 26 October 1933. A useful discussion of the tension between the Foreign Office and the Treasury over Japan, emphasising the important differences in the two departments' institutional perspectives, can be found in Gill Bennett, 'British Policy in the Far East, 1933–1936: Treasury and Foreign Office', *Modern Asian Studies*, 26, 3 (1992), pp. 545–68. A more general discussion of Chamberlain's approach to international politics in 1933–34 can be found in Peter Bell, *Chamberlain, Germany and Japan, 1933–34* (Basingstoke, 1996).

88 A useful review of Fisher's views on rearmament in the 1930s can be found in G.C. Peden, 'Sir Warren Fisher and British Rearmament against Germany', *English Historical Review*, 94, 370 (1979), pp. 29–47. For Hankey's work on the DRC, see Roskill, *Hankey*, Vol. 3, p. 87ff. For Vansittart's role on the DRC, see Charles Morrissey and M.A. Ramsay, 'Giving a Lead in the Right Direction: Sir Robert Vansittart and the Defence Requirements Sub-Committee', *Diplomacy and Statecraft*, 6, 1 (1995), pp. 39–60. For a valuable article arguing the case that civilian officials took the lead in the move towards rearmament in the mid-1930s, see B.J.C. McKercher, 'From Disarmament to Rearmament: British Civil-Military Relations and Rearmament, 1933–1936', *Defence Studies*, 1, 1 (2001), pp. 21–48. For the papers and minutes of the DRC, see CAB 16/109. Among the vast literature on British rearmament in the 1930s, see for example Robert J. Shay, *British Rearmament in the 1930s: Politics and Profits* (Princeton, 1977).

89 The views of senior Foreign Office officials in late 1933 and early 1934 can be traced in CAB 24/248, CP 77 (34) 'Situation in the Far East, 1933–34'. A fuller discussion of views within the Foreign Office towards Japan at this time can be found in Bell, *Chamberlain, Germany and Japan*, pp. 53–8.

90 Simon Bourette-Knowles, 'The Global Micawber: Sir Robert Vansittart, the Treasury and the Global Balance of Power, 1933–35', *Diplomacy and Statecraft* 6, 1 (1995), pp. 91–121.

91 On the Metro-Vickers affair, see Gordon W. Morrell, *Britain Confronts the Stalin Revolution: Anglo-Soviet Relations and the Metro-Vickers Crisis* (Waterloo, Ont., 1995).

92 For a useful discussion of this topic, see Michael Roi, *Alternative to Appeasement: Sir Robert Vansittart and Alliance Diplomacy, 1934–37* (Westport, Ct., 1997), pp. 41–5. Useful material can also be found in Robert Manne, 'The Foreign Office and the Failure of Anglo-Soviet Rapprochement', *Journal of Contemporary History*, 16, 4 (1981), pp. 725–55. A helpful analysis of the role of anti-Communist sentiment in undermining any rapprochement can be found in Michael Jabara Carley, 'A Fearful Concatenation of Circumstances: the Anglo-Soviet Rapprochement, 1934–36', *Contemporary European History*, 5, 1 (1996), pp. 29–69.

93 CAB 23/78, Cabinet 9, 14 March 1934.

94 CAB 23/78, Cabinet 10, 19 March 1934; CAB 24/248, CP 80 (34), Simon paper on 'Imperial Defence Policy', 16 March 1934. A somewhat different view can be found in Bennett, 'British Policy and the Far East', p. 550.

95 A useful detailed account of debates within the British government over policy towards Japan during this period can be found in Bell, *Chamberlain, Germany and Japan*.

96 For evidence that some elements in the Japanese government had been interested improved relations since the end of 1933, see FO 371/18184/F591, Snow to Orde, 22 December 1933.

97 FO 371/18169/F4270, Minute by Simon, dated 4 August 1934.

98 Simon Papers, 79, Simon to Neville Chamberlain, 7 September 1934.

99 Neville Chamberlain Papers, NC 2 23/A, Neville Chamberlain diary entry, 9 October 1934.

100 A valuable discussion of the strategic and diplomatic issues surrounding the October naval discussions can be found in Meredith W. Berg, 'Protecting National Interests by Treaty: The Second London Naval Conference, 1934–1936', in B.J.C. McKercher (ed.), *Arms Limitation and Disarmament, 1899–1939* (Westport, Ct, 1992), pp. 203–27.

101 Among the massive literature looking at the impact of the Treasury on rearmament in the 1930s, particularly in the context of the impact of financial constraint on appeasement, see Peden, *British Rearmament and the Treasury*; John Ruggiero, *Neville Chamberlain and British Rearmament* (Westport, Ct., 1999).

102 CAB 23/78, Cabinet 10, 19 March 1934.

103 CAB 24/248, CP 68 (34), John Simon, 'Consequences of a Breakdown of the Disarmament Conference', 9 March 1934.

104 Quoted in Dutton, *Simon*, p. 185.

105 *DBFP*, Ser. 2, Vol. 6 (Doc. 212), Simon letter to Phipps, 26 January 1934.

106 For a general discussion about the Cabinet's discussion over the implementation of the DRC proposals in 1934, see Bell, *Chamberlain, Germany and Japan*, 105–44; Ruggiero, *Neville Chamberlain and Rearmament*, pp. 26–32. A very useful recent discussion, taking a broadly negative stance towards Chamberlain's activities, can be found in Keith Neilson, 'The Defence Requirements Committee, British Strategic Foreign Policy, Neville Chamberlain and the Path to Appeasement', *English Historical Review*, 118, 477 (2003), pp. 651–84. Bell, *Chamberlain, Germany and Japan* takes a more positive line.

107 See, for example, DBFP, Ser. 2, Vol. 6 (Docs.313, 363).

108 For further details, see Hughes, 'The Foreign Secretary Goes to Court'.

109 See CAB 27/506, Discussions of the Ministerial Disarmament Committee from March to May 1934.

110 CAB 23/80, Cabinet 41, 21 November 1934.

111 Neville Chamberlain papers, NC 18/1/898, Neville Chamberlain to Ida and Hilda Chamberlain, 9 December 1934.

112 CAB 24/253, CP 6 (35), John Simon, 'Material for Impending Discussions with French Ministers', 9 January 1935; CAB 23/81, Cabinet 2, 9 January 1935.

113 CAB 24/253, CP 33 (35), 'Scheme by the French Delegation for an International Air Agreement'.

114 CAB 23/81, Cabinet 11, 25 February 1935.

115 CAB 24/254, CP 63 (35), John Simon, 'Proposed Reply to German Announcement on Rearmament', 17 March 1935.

116 CAB 23/81, Cabinet 16, 20 March 1935. MacDonald noted in his diary that Simon was not in fact keen on going to Berlin, although this suggestion does not appear in keeping with the rest of the evidence. PRO 30/69/1753/1, MacDonald diary entry, 24 March 1935.

117 Baldwin Papers 123, Ormsby-Gore to Baldwin, March 1935.
118 CAB 24/254 CP 69 (35), 'Notes of Anglo-German Conversations', March 1935.
119 CAB 23/81, Cabinets 20–21, 8 April 1935.
120 For the concerns of Anthony Eden on this subject, by contrast, see Baldwin Papers, 123, Eden to Simon, 21 May 1935.
121 PRO 30/69/1753/1, MacDonald diary entry, 2 April 1935.
122 For an interpretation of the Anglo-Naval German Treaty along these lines, see J.A. Maiolo, *The Royal Navy and Nazi Germany, 1933–39. A Study in Appeasement and the Origins of the Second World War* (New York, 1998), pp. 11–37.
123 Hines H. Hall, 'The Foreign Policy-Making Process in Britain, 1934–1935, and the Origins of the Anglo-German Naval Agreement', *Historical Journal*, 19, 2 (1976), pp. 477–99.
124 Michael L. Roi, *Alternative to Appeasement*, pp. 63–4.
125 Hankey Papers, HNKY 4/27, Vansittart to Hankey, 22 May 1935.
126 CAB 24/253, CP 43 (35), Hankey Memorandum on 'The Proposed Air Bombing Convention', 14 February 1935.
127 Roi, *Alternative to Appeasement*, p. 78.
128 Quoted in Dutton, *Simon*, p. 206.
129 Hankey Papers, HNKY 1/7, Hankey diary entry 3 October 1932.
130 Books presenting this general view include Peden, *British Rearmament and the Treasury*; Shay, *British Rearmament in the 1930s*; Brian Bond, *British Military Policy Between the Two World Wars* (Oxford, 1980).

7 Sir Samuel Hoare at the Foreign Office (1935)

1 Viscount Templewood, *Nine Troubled Years* (London, 1954), pp. 108, 137.
2 J.A. Cross, *Sir Samuel Hoare* (London, 1977), p. 181.
3 Avon, *Facing the Dictators*, p. 217.
4 Templewood, *Nine Troubled Years*, p. 108.
5 Templewood, *Nine Troubled Years*, p. 109.
6 Templewood, *Nine Troubled Years*, p. 110.
7 A useful general discussion of these developments can be found in Martin Ceadel, *Pacifism in Britain*, esp. pp. 122–92. See, too, Michael Pugh, 'Pacifism and Politics in Britain, 1931–1935', *Historical Journal*, 23, 3 (1980), pp. 641–56; J.A. Thompson, 'The Peace Ballot and the Public', *Albion*, 13, 4 (1981), pp. 380–92.
8 Material and correspondence relating to Hoare's research for his book can be found in Templewood Papers, 19, 5.
9 Among the vast literature on the subject, see in particular the full-length studies by Frank Hardie, *The Abyssinian Crisis* (London, 1974); George W. Baer, *The Coming of the Italian-Ethiopian War* (Cambridge, Mass., 1967); George Baer, *Test-Case: Italy, Ethiopia and the League of Nations* (Stanford, 1976).
10 Templewood, *Nine Troubled Years*, p. 137.
11 Quoted in Norman Rose, *Vansittart: Study of a Diplomat* (London, 1978), p. 164.
12 Robertson suggests that senior Foreign Office officials were determined to persuade the Foreign Secretary on coming to office to abandon a definite Cabinet policy to put pressure on Italy through the League, but the evidence does not support such a clear-cut interpretation. James C. Robertson, 'The Hoare–Laval Plan', *Journal of Contemporary History*, 10, 3 (1975), p. 441.
13 *DBFP*, Ser. 2, Vol. 15 (Docs 253, 254), Minutes by Scrivener and Oliphant.
14 *DBFP*, Ser. 2, Vol. 14 (Doc. 308), 'Note by Vansittart for Hoare', 16 June 1935.
15 CAB 23/82, Cabinet 33, 19 June 1935.

16 FO 800/295, Hoare to Drummond, 27 July 1935.
17 Templewood Papers, 8, 3, Drummond to Hoare, 31 July 1935.
18 FO 800/295, Hoare to Clerk, 24 August, 1935.
19 Templewood, *Nine Troubled Years*, p. 136.
20 Avon, *Facing the Dictators*, p. 218.
21 Quoted in Cross, *Hoare*, p. 186. Neville Chamberlain took a rather different view. See Neville Chamberlain Papers, NC 18/1/923, Neville Chamberlain to Hilda Chamberlain, 22 June 1935.
22 Avon, *Facing the Dictators*, p. 269.
23 See, for example, the correspondence in Avon Papers, AP 14/1 (various).
24 Avon Papers, AP 14/1/450J, Hoare to Eden, 14 October 1935.
25 David Carlton, *Anthony Eden: A Biography* (London, 1981), pp. 65–6.
26 Templewood, *Nine Troubled Years*, p. 155.
27 For Peterson's recollections of the Abyssinian crisis, see the relevant pages of Maurice Peterson, *Both Sides of the Curtain* (London, 1950).
28 Middlemass and Barnes, *Baldwin*, p. 834.
29 For Ormsby-Gore's views, see Baldwin Papers, 123, Ormsby-Gore to Baldwin, 8 September 1935.
30 FO 800/295, Hoare to Neville Chamberlain, 16 August 1935.
31 DBFP, Ser. 2, Vol. 14 (Doc. 426), Conclusions of a Meeting of Ministers held on 6 August 1935.
32 CAB 23/82, Conclusions of a Conference of Ministers, 21 August 1935; Cabinet 42, 22 August, 1935.
33 Neville Chamberlain Papers, NC 18/1/925, Neville Chamberlain to Hilda Chamberlain, 14 July 1935; NC 18/1/929, Neville Chamberlain to Ida Chamberlain, 25 August 1935.
34 Templewood Papers, 8, 1, Hoare to Neville Chamberlain, 17 September 1935.
35 Neville Chamberlain was apparently the only minister other than Baldwin to read Hoare's September speech in Geneva in advance. See Baldwin Papers, 123, Hoare to Baldwin, 5 September 1935.
36 See, for example, CAB 24/256, CP 176 (35), 'Summary of Recent Developments' (compiled by Hankey).
37 See, for example, CAB 53/25, CoS 392 (35), 'Memorandum on Italy–Abyssinia Dispute', 9 August 1935.
38 DBFP, Ser. 2, Vol. 14 (Doc. 431), Chatfield to Vansittart, 8 August 1935. Chatfield's tone of sarcasm reflected his instinctive scepticism about the League.
39 For a discussion of the impact of the international crisis on the election, see James C. Robertson, 'The British General Election of 1935', *Journal of Contemporary History*, 9, 1 (1974), pp. 149–64.
40 For useful comments on Hoare's caution about giving any impression that he was ready to take a soft line towards Italy during the period leading up to the election, see R.A.C. Parker, 'Great Britain, France and the Ethiopian Crisis, 1935–1936', *English Historical Review*, 89, 351 (1974), p. 311.
41 For details of Hoare's meetings with political leaders, see DBFP, Ser. 2, Vol. 14 (Docs 476, 477, 480, 481, 483, 484).
42 See, for example, Templewood Papers, 8, 1, Dawson to Hoare, 30 August 1935; Beaverbrook to Hoare, 10 September 1935; Hoare to Beaverbrook, 14 September 1935.
43 See, for example, CAB 23/82, Cabinet 42, 22 August 1935.
44 For a useful discussion of Labour attitudes during this period, see Paul Corthorn, 'The Labour Party and the League of Nations: The Socialist League's Role in the Sanctions Crisis of 1935', *Twentieth-Century British History*, 13, 1 (2002), pp. 62–85.
45 Avon, *Facing the Dictators*, p. 249. For a broader discussion of Anglo-French rela-

tions during the Abyssinian crisis, see Richard Davis, *Anglo-French Relations before the Second World War: Appeasement and Crisis* (Basingstoke, 2001), pp. 27–123; Nicholas Rostow, *Anglo-French Relations, 1934–36* (London, 1984), pp. 180–232; Parker, 'Great Britain, France and the Ethiopian Crisis'.

46 For a useful summary of developments in July and August, particularly relating to Abyssinia, see Davis, *Anglo-French Relations*, pp. 63–78.

47 On the October crisis, see Davis, *Anglo-French Relations*, pp. 80–3.

48 Templewood, *Nine Troubled Years*, p. 113.

49 FO 800/295, Hoare to Wigram, 14 September 1935.

50 For an argument along these lines, see Robertson, 'Hoare–Laval Pact'.

51 CAB 23/82, Conclusions of a Conference of Ministers, 21 August 1935.

52 CAB 23/82, Cabinet 43, 24 September 1935.

53 Stephen Roskill, *Hankey*, Vol. 3, pp. 186–9 (Diary entry for 25 November 1935).

54 *DBFP*, Ser. 2, Vol. 15 (Docs 253, 254), Telegrams from Clerk to Foreign Office, 25 November, 1935. Both Oliphant and Scrivener minuted that they were opposed to the terms.

55 CAB 23/82, Cabinet 50, 2 December, 1935.

56 Quoted in Middlemas and Barnes, *Baldwin*, p. 881.

57 Thomas Jones, *A Diary with Letters, 1931–1955* (Oxford, 1954), p. 159; Avon, *Facing the Dictators*, p. 298.

58 Avon, *Facing the Dictators*, p. 298; Neville Chamberlain Papers, NC 18/1/942, Neville Chamberlain to Hilda Chamberlain, 15 December 1935.

59 The full agreement signed by Hoare and Laval can be found in *DBFP*, Ser. 2, Vol. 15 (Doc. 336).

60 For Hoare's account of the negotiations and agreement, see Templewood, *Nine Troubled Years*, pp. 179–82.

61 PRO 30/69/1753/1, MacDonald diary entry, 9 December 1935.

62 Avon, *Facing the Dictators*, pp. 302–3.

63 CAB 23/82, Cabinet 52, 9 December 1935.

64 Quoted Dutton, *Simon*, p. 232.

65 The words on the convention of collective responsibility are those of Lord Salisbury, quoted in W. Ivor Jennings, *Cabinet Government* (Cambridge, 1936), p. 217.

66 CAB 23/82, Cabinet 54, 11 December 1935.

67 *DBFP*, Ser. 2, Vol. 15 (Doc. 353), Eden to Barton, 10 December 1935; Doc. 356, Eden to Drummond, 10 December 1935.

68 *Parliamentary Debates (Commons) 1935–6*, Vol. 307, 10th December 1935, Col. 856; also see Marguerite Potter, 'What Sealed Baldwin's Lips?', *Historian*, 27, 1 (1964), pp. 21–36.

69 *Parliamentary Debates (Commons) 1935–6*, Vol. 307, 10th December 1935, Col. 823.

70 Ian Colvin, *Vansittart in Office* (London, 1965), p. 81.

71 Neville Chamberlain Papers, NC 18/1/942, Neville Chamberlain to Hilda Chamberlain, 15 December 1935. Further useful information about Chamberlain's activities during these critical days can be found in the relevant pages of his diary in Neville Chamberlain Papers, NC 2/23A. Chamberlain himself was in fact Hoare's staunchest defender in Cabinet during the third week of December.

72 CAB 23/82, Cabinet 55, 17 December 1935.

73 PRO 30/69/1753/1, MacDonald diary entry, 15 December 1935.

74 CAB 23/90B, Cabinet 56, 18 December 1935 (Most secret summary of discussions).

75 All the following quotations are from the Commons debate on 19th December, transcribed in *Parliamentary Debates (Commons) 1935–6*, Vol. 307.

76 Templewood Papers, 8, 5a, Amery to Hoare, 19 December 1935.
77 Templewood Papers, 8, 5a, Leeper to Hoare, 19 December 1935.
78 Templewood Papers, 8, 5a, Muggeridge to Hoare, 19 December 1935; Gordon-Lennox to Hoare, 23 December 1935.
79 Templewood Papers, 8, 5a, Clive Wigram to Hoare, 19 December 1935.

8 Anthony Eden at the Foreign Office (1935–38)

1 Avon, *Facing the Dictators*, pp. 7–8.
2 *The Times*, 19 December 1935.
3 Avon, *Facing the Dictators*, pp. 19, 316.
4 For the views of Alexander Cadogan, for example, see Cadogan Papers, ACAD 1/6, Cadogan diary entries for 9 and 15 January 1937.
5 For a detailed description of Eden's wartime experiences, see Anthony Eden, *Another World, 1897–1917* (London, 1976).
6 Anthony Eden, *British Foreign Policy Speech to the East and West Fulham Conservative and Unionist Association* (London, 1935).
7 See Carlton, *Eden*, p. 57ff for a rather different view of Eden's attitude towards the League.
8 Eden, *British Foreign Policy*.
9 *Parliamentary Debates (Commons) 1936–1937*, Vol. 319, Cols. 92–107, 19 January 1937.
10 For a further discussion of this theme, see Peter Beck, 'Politicians versus Historians: Lord Avon's "Appeasement Battle" against 'Lamentably Appeasement-Minded Historians', *Twentieth Century British History* 9, 3 (1998), pp. 396–419; for a more specific example of Eden's sometimes difficult relationship with historians, see Strang Papers, STRN 2/12, correspondence between Eden and Northedge.
11 Avon, *Facing the Dictators*, p. 221ff.
12 Avon, *Facing the Dictators*, p. 319. On the relationship between Eden and Warren Fisher, see O'Halpin, *Head of the Civil Service*, p. 249ff.
13 Halifax Papers, A4 410.21.1, Eden to Halifax, 1 August 1937.
14 Avon Papers, AP 14/1/574, Cranborne to Eden, 16 June 1936.
15 Cadogan subsequently told Hoare that Eden was 'demented' on Spain. Templewood Papers, 19, 5 (Interview with Cadogan).
16 Avon, *Facing the Dictators*, pp. 241–2.
17 Avon Papers, AP 14/1/641B, Eden to Baldwin, 8 January 1937.
18 Neville Chamberlain Papers, NC 18/1/1031, Neville Chamberlain to Ida Chamberlain, 12 December 1937.
19 Phipps Papers, PHPP 1, 1/17, copy of Phipps tel. to Eden, 22 October 1936.
20 For a discussion of Phipps's career in Paris, see John Herman, *The Paris Embassy of Sir Eric Phipps* (Brighton, 1998).
21 Herman, *Paris Embassy of Sir Eric Phipps*, p. 69.
22 Donald Cameron Watt, 'Chamberlain's Ambassadors', in Dockrill and McKercher, *Diplomacy and World Power*, pp. 136–70.
23 On the circumstances surrounding Henderson's appointment, see Peter Neville, *Appeasing Hitler: The Diplomacy of Sir Nevile Henderson, 1937–1939* (Basingstoke, 2000), p. 20.ff.
24 Avon, *Facing the Dictators*, p. 504.
25 Nevile Henderson, *Failure of a Mission: Berlin, 1937–1939* (London, 1940), p. 18.
26 Henderson, *Failure of a Mission*, p. 16.
27 Halifax Papers, A4 410.3.2, various letters between Halifax and Henderson.
28 FO 800/268, Eden to Henderson, 22 June 1937.

29 Avon, *Facing the Dictators*, p. 318.
30 See, for example, Avon Papers, AP 14/1/557, Baldwin to Eden, 8 August 1936, in which the Prime Minister sought to ensure that he was 'in complete accord' with his Foreign Secretary prior to a meeting of Cabinet.
31 On the supposedly poor state of Britain's air defences, see CAB 53/27, 'The condition of our forces to meet a possible war with Germany' (Memorandum approved by the Chief of Staff sub-committee); on ministers' anxiety about public opinion, see CAB 23/83, Cabinet 18, 11 March 1936; Cabinet 21, 18 March 1936.
32 CAB 24/260, CP 73 (36), Anthony Eden, 'Germany and the Locarno Treaty', 8 March 1936.
33 CAB 23/83, Cabinet 18, 11 March 1936.
34 PREM 1/194, Simon to Baldwin, 25 March 1936.
35 CAB 23/83, Cabinet 11, 26 February 1936.
36 CAB 23/83, Cabinet 39, 27 May 1936.
37 CAB 23/83, Cabinet 40, 29 May 1936.
38 Neville Chamberlain Papers, NC 18/1/965, Neville Chamberlain to Hilda Chamberlain, 14 June 1936.
39 See, for example, Avon Papers, AP 14/1/599A, Eden to Roger Lumley, 13 June 1936, in which he describes Chamberlain's intervention as 'a most unfortunate business' but 'it can't now be helped'.
40 Phipps Papers, PHPP 1, 2/25, Wigram to Phipps, 28 May 1936.
41 Jones, *Diary with Letters*, pp. 222–4 (Diary entry, 16 June 1936).
42 CAB 27/622, First Meeting of the Foreign Policy Committee, 30 April 1936.
43 CAB 27/626, FP 8 (36), Eden memorandum on 'Reform of League of Nations', 20 August 1936.
44 Cadogan Papers, ACAD 1/6, Cadogan diary entry for 9 January 1937 (reporting comment by Cranborne).
45 CAB 23/87, Meeting of Ministers, 8 January 1937; on Churchill's views, see R.A.C. Parker, *Churchill and Appeasement* (Basingstoke, 2000), pp. 117–19.
46 Quoted in Carlton, *Eden*, p. 87.
47 CAB 24/267, CP 6 (37), Eden memorandum on 'Spain', 8 January 1937.
48 CAB 23/87, Meeting of Ministers, 8 January 1937.
49 Cadogan Papers, ACAD 1/6, Cadogan diary entry, 15 January 1937.
50 Avon Papers, AP 20/1/17, Eden diary entry, 6 March 1937.
51 On the role of the Treasury in the rearmament process during these years, see the relevant sections of Peden, *British Rearmament and the Treasury*; Ruggiero, *Neville Chamberlain and British Rearmament*. For a useful critique of the argument that the Treasury exercised undue influence on the foreign policy process *per se*, see Peter Neville, 'Lord Vansittart, Sir Walford Selby, and the Debate about Treasury Interference in the Conduct of British Foreign Policy in the 1930s', *Journal of Contemporary History*, 36, 4 (2001), pp. 623–33.
52 For a brief review of the contemporary debate on this issue, see Carlton, *Eden*, pp. 94–6.
53 CAB 27/622, Meeting of the Foreign Policy Committee, 18 March 1937. On the broader question of the role of colonies in Anglo-German relations in the 1930s, see Andrew J. Crozier, *Appeasement and Germany's Last Bid for Colonies* (Basingstoke, 1988).
54 Neville Chamberlain Papers, NC 18/1/929, Neville Chamberlain to Ida Chamberlain, 25 August 1935.
55 Neville Chamberlain Papers, NC 18/1/952, Neville Chamberlain to Hilda Chamberlain, 21 March 1936.
56 Neville Chamberlain Papers, NC 18/1/1014, Neville Chamberlain to Hilda Chamberlain, 1 August 1937.

57 For information on the Conservative critics of appeasement, see Neville Thompson, *The Anti-Appeasers: Conservative Opposition to Appeasement in the 1930s* (Oxford, 1971). A valuable recent analysis can be found in N.J. Crowson, *Facing Fascism: the Conservative Party and the European Dictators, 1935–1940* (London, 1997).

58 For further details of Chamberlain's management of the press in order to promote his appeasement policies, see Richard Cockett, *Twilight of Truth; Chamberlain, Appeasement and the Manipulation of the Press* (London, 1989).

59 Earl of Halifax, *Fulness of Days* (London, 1957), p. 231.

60 Neville Chamberlain Papers, NC 18/1/1014, Neville Chamberlain to Hilda Chamberlain, 1 August 1937; NC 18/1/1015, to Ida Chamberlain, 8 August, 1937.

61 Neville Chamberlain Papers, NC 18/1/1027, Neville Chamberlain to Hilda Chamberlain, 6 November 1937.

62 A great deal of new information on the 'secret channel' can be found in William C. Mills, 'Sir Joseph Ball, Adrian Dingli, and Neville Chamberlain's "Secret Channel" to Italy 1937–40', *International History Review*, 24, 2 (2002), pp. 278–317.

63 *DBFP*, Ser. 2, Vol. 19 (Doc. 65), Chamberlain to Mussolini, 27 July 1937.

64 Avon, *Facing the Dictators*, p. 453.

65 FO 371/21160/R4977, Lampson to Foreign Office, 20 July 1937 (minutes by Sargent and Vansittart).

66 FO 371/21161/R 6095 (minute by Eden, 28 August 1937).

67 FO 371/21163/R8106 (Memorandum by Ingram on 'Anglo-Italian Relations' along with comments by Eden).

68 Halifax Papers, A4 410. 21.1 Eden to Halifax, 1 August 1937. Halifax does not seem to have taken much notice of Eden's strictures; see Neville Chamberlain papers, NC 18/1/1015, Neville Chamberlain to Ida Chamberlain, 8 August 1937.

69 Neville Chamberlain Papers, NC 18/1/1018, Neville Chamberlain to Hilda Chamberlain, 29 August 1937.

70 Neville Chamberlain Papers, NC 18/1/1021, Neville Chamberlain to Ida Chamberlain, 19 September 1937; NC 18/1/1027, to Hilda Chamberlain, 6 November 1937.

71 For a useful discussion of British policy-making in the period leading up to Nyon, focusing on the struggle between the Prime Minister and the Foreign Secretary, see William C. Mills, 'The Nyon Conference: Neville Chamberlain, Anthony Eden and the Appeasement of Italy in 1937', *International History Review*, 15, 1 (1993), pp. 1–22.

72 See, for example, CAB 27/626, FP 27 (36), Eden to Phipps, 27 April 1937. For further information about the role of colonial questions in Anglo-German discussions, see Crozier, *Appeasement and Germany's Last Bid for Colonies*.

73 For documents relating to the origins of the visit, see Halifax Papers, A4 410.3.2.

74 *Diplomatic Diaries of Olivery Harvey, 1937–1940* (London, 1970), p. 57 (Diary entry for 7 November 1937).

75 Halifax's impressions of the trip can be found in Halifax, *Fulness of Days*, pp. 184–91; also various documents in Halifax Papers, A4 410. 3.3.

76 CAB 27/626, FP 41 (36), Eden, 'The Next Steps towards a General Settlement with Germany'.

77 *Diplomatic Diaries of Oliver Harvey*, p. 59 (Diary entry for 11 November 1937).

78 *Diplomatic Diaries of Oliver Harvey*, p. 56 (Diary entry for 3 November 1937).

79 The Foreign Office correspondence on the Roosevelt telegram (including minutes by Eden and senior officials) can be found in FO 371/21526/A2127.

80 Mills, 'Secret Channel', p. 292.
81 On British policy in the wake of the outbreak of the Sino-Japanese War, see Anthony Best, *Britain, Japan and Pearl Harbour: Avoiding War in East Asia, 1936–1941* (London, 1995), pp. 37–60.
82 Neville Chamberlain's diary, quoted in Carlton, *Eden*, p. 122.
83 Winston Churchill, *A History of the Second World War*, Vol. 1, *The Gathering Storm* (London, 1955), p. 201.
84 FO 371/22042/R930, Eden to Perth, 1 February 1938.
85 Avon Papers, AP 20/6/2, Eden to Neville Chamberlain, 1 January 1938.
86 Neville Chamberlain Papers, NC 2/24A, Neville Chamberlain Diary, entry for period 19–27 February 1938.
87 Avon Papers, AP 13/1/64K, Eden to Neville Chamberlain, 8 February 1938.
88 Avon Papers, AP 13/1/64L, Neville Chamberlain to Eden, 8 February 1938.
89 Mills, 'Secret Channel'. For further details, see Templewood Papers, 19, 5, Interview with Sir Joseph Ball; Strang Papers, STRN 2/12, Avon-Northedge correspondence (various letters).
90 Avon, *Facing the Dictators*, p. 575; Cockett, *Twilight of Truth*, pp. 49–50.
91 *Ciano's Diplomatic Papers* (London, 1948), p. 182–3.
92 Avon Papers, AP 20/1/18, Eden diary entry for period 17–24 February 1938.
93 Neville Chamberlain Papers, NC 18/1/1040, Neville Chamberlain to Hilda Chamberlain, 27 February 1938.
94 See, for example, Avon, *Dictators*, pp. 586–606; Templewood, *Nine Troubled Years*, pp. 276–84. Halifax's notes can be found in Templewood Papers, 10, 3, 'Record of events connected with Anthony Eden's resignation, February 19th–20th 1938'; Chamberlain's account can be found in Neville Chamberlain Papers, NC 2/24A, Neville Chamberlain diary entry for 19–27 February 1938; also see NC 18/1/1040, Chamberlain to Hilda Chamberlain, 27 February 1938.
95 CAB 23/91, Cabinet 6 (38), 19 February 1938.
96 CAB 23/91, Cabinet 7 (38), 20 February 1938.
97 Templewood Papers, 10, 3, Halifax, 'Record'.
98 *The Times*, 22 February 1938.
99 On the Conservative anti-appeasers, see Crowson, *Facing Fascism, passim*.
100 For Eden's statement and the subsequent debate, see *Parliamentary Debates (Commons), 1937–38*, Vol. 322, 21 February 1938.
101 Avon Papers, AP 8/2/33, Cadogan to Eden, 22 February 1938.
102 Avon Papers, AP 8/2/174, Oliphant to Eden, 21 February 1938.
103 Avon Papers, AP 8/2/128, Lampson (Cairo) to Eden, 24 February 1938. For letters from Campbell and Rumbold, see Avon, *Facing the Dictators*, pp. 602–3.
104 Avon Papers, AP 8/2/105, Harvey to Eden, 20 March 1938.
105 Avon Papers, AP 8/2/96, Halifax to Eden, 21 February 1938.
106 Avon Papers, AP 20/6/3, Neville Chamberlain to Eden, 2 January 1938.
107 Avon Papers, AP 20/6/5, Eden to Neville Chamberlain, 9 January 1938.
108 Templewood Papers, 10, 3, Halifax, 'Record'.
109 *Diplomatic Diaries of Oliver Harvey*, p. 150 (Diary entry for 15 October 1937).
110 Templewood Papers, 10, 3, Halifax, 'Record'.
111 Avon, *Facing the Dictators*, p. 587.
112 Avon Papers, AP 20/1/16, Eden Diary, 20 May 1936.
113 For Halifax's rejection of the comparison, see Halifax Papers, A2 278.107, Halifax to Strang, 7 January 1957.
114 Templewood Papers, 19, 5, Interview with Ball.
115 Avon, *Facing the Dictators*, p. 575.
116 Strang Papers, STRN 2/12, Avon to Northedge, 15, 18 August 1966; Cadogan to Strang, 8 February 1967; Avon to Strang, 29 September 1971.
117 Halifax Papers, A2 278.107, Halifax to Strang, 7 January 1957.

9 Lord Halifax at the Foreign Office (1938–39)

1 Churchill, *Gathering Storm*, p. 216.

2 On the second Viscount Halifax, see John Gilbert Lockhart, *Viscount Halifax* (London, 1935–36), 2 vols.

3 For a discussion of religion on the views of leading Conservatives towards the totalitarian regimes during the 1930s, see Philip Williamson, 'Christian Conservatives and the Totalitarian Challenge, 1933–1940', *English Historical Review*, 115, 462 (2000), pp. 607–42.

4 For some useful comments on this theme, see the relevant sections of Martin Ceadel, *Pacifism in Britain, 1914–1945: the Defining of a Faith* (Oxford, 1980).

5 Andrew Roberts, *The Holy Fox: A Biography of Lord Halifax* (London, 1991), p. 7.

6 H.E.E. Craster (ed.), *Speeches on Foreign Policy by Lord Halifax* (London, 1940), p. 37.

7 The development of Craigie's views is well covered in Best, *Britain, Japan, and Pearl Harbour*.

8 On the development of Phipps's views, see Herman, *Paris Embassy of Sir Eric Phipps*.

9 On Newton, see Peter Neville, 'Nevile Henderson and Basil Newton: Two British Envoys in the Czech Crisis, 1938', *Diplomacy and Statecraft*, 10, 2–3 (1999), pp. 258–75.

10 For a somewhat different view, which argues that this policy was if anything more typical of Chamberlain, see John Charmley, *Chamberlain and the Lost Peace* (London, 1989), pp. 74–5.

11 A valuable discussion on the views of the Foreign Office following Munich can be found in Donald Lammers, 'From Whitehall after Munich: The Foreign Office and the Future Course of British Foreign Policy', *Historical Journal*, 16, 4 (1973), pp. 831–56.

12 *The Diaries of Sir Alexander Cadogan*, David Dilks (ed.) (London, 1971), p. 163 (Diary entry for 26 March 1939).

13 *Diplomatic Diaries of Oliver Harvey*, p. 156 (Diary entry for 24 June 1938); Cadogan, *Diaries*, p. 71 (Diary entry for 25 April 1938).

14 For some useful comments on this theme, see the closing section of B.J.C. McKercher, 'Old Diplomacy and New: the Foreign Office and Foreign Policy, 1919–1939', in Dockrill and McKercher, *Diplomacy and World Power*, pp. 79–114.

15 Lord Butler, *Art of the Possible: The Memoirs of Lord Butler* (London, 1971), pp. 76–7.

16 Harold Nicolson, *Diaries and Letters, 1939–45* (London, 1966–68), Vol. 1, p. 40. For a useful discussion of Butler's later efforts to distance himself from appeasement, see Paul Stafford, 'Political Biography and the Art of the Possible: R.A. Butler at the Foreign Office, 1938–1939', *Historical Journal*, 28, 4 (1985), pp. 901–22.

17 Butler, *Art of the Possible*, p. 66. For a rather different view of Butler's role, see Patrick Cosgrave, *R.A. Butler: An English Life* (London, 1981), pp. 43–4.

18 Butler, *Art of the Possible*, p. 77.

19 Anthony Howard, *RAB: The Life of R.A. Butler* (London, 1987), p. 83.

20 Maurice Cowling, *The Impact of Hitler: British Politics and British Policy, 1933–1939* (Cambridge, 1975), pp. 272–3.

21 Keith Middlemas, *Diplomacy of Illusion: The British Government and Germany, 1937–1939* (London, 1972), p. 449. A rather similar view was offered to one of Halifax's biographers by William Strang. See Birkenhead, *Halifax*, p. 421.

22 For a discussion of divisions within the Conservative Party see the relevant sec-

tions of Crowson, *Facing Fascism*. Also see Thompson, *The Anti-Appeasers*. A great deal of useful material can also be found in Graham Stewart, *Burying Caesar: Churchill, Chamberlain and the Battle for the Tory Party* (London, 1999).

23 Cockett, *Twilight of Truth*, pp. 53–4.

24 Christopher Hill, *Cabinet Decisions on Foreign Policy: The British Experience, October 1938–June 1941* (Cambridge, 1991).

25 Halifax, *Fulness of Days*, p. 231; Halifax Papers, A 278. 107, Halifax to Strang, 7 January 1957.

26 Neville Chamberlain Papers, NC 7/11/32/111, Halifax to Neville Chamberlain, 10 March 1939; NC 7/11/32/112, Chamberlain to Halifax, 11 March 1939. For Foreign Office views of the event, see Cadogan, *Diaries*, p. 155 (Diary entry for 10 March 1939); *Diplomatic Diaries of Oliver Harvey*, p. 260 (Diary entry for 10 March 1939).

27 Neville Chamberlain Papers, NC 18/1/1069, Neville Chamberlain to Ida Chamberlain, 19 September 1938.

28 Templewood, *Nine Troubled Years*, p. 318.

29 Templewood, *Nine Troubled Years*, pp. 329–30.

30 For useful information on Fisher's declining influence in the late 1930s, see O'Halpin, *Head of the Civil Service*, p. 266 ff.

31 CAB 23/92, Cabinet 12, 12 March 1938.

32 FO 800/269, Cadogan to Henderson, 22 April 1938.

33 Charmley, *Lost Peace*, pp. 64–5.

34 FO 800/269, Halifax to Henderson, 19 March 1938.

35 CAB 23/92, Cabinet 13, 14 March 1938.

36 CAB 53/23, CoS 697 (38), 'Military Implications of German Aggression against Czechoslovakia', 28 March 1938 (but various drafts circulating ten days earlier).

37 CAB 27/623, Minutes of the 26th meeting of the Foreign Policy Committee, 18 March 1938.

38 CAB 23/93, Cabinet 15, 22 March 1938.

39 CAB 23/93, Cabinet 14, 16 March 1938.

40 CAB 23/93, Cabinet 15, 22 March 1938.

41 *Parliamentary Debates (Commons) 1937–38*, Vol. 333, Col. 1405, 24 March 1938.

42 CAB 23/93, Cabinet 22, 4 May 1938.

43 Neville Chamberlain Papers, NC 18/1/1042, Neville Chamberlain to Ida Chamberlain, 20 March 1938.

44 For Henderson's view of the May crisis, see Henderson, *Failure of a Mission*, pp. 134–40; also see Neville, *Appeasing Hitler*, pp. 71–7.

45 *DBFP*, Ser. 3, Vol. 1 (Doc. 250), Halifax to Henderson, 21 May 1938.

46 CAB 23/93, Cabinet 26, 25 May 1938.

47 Neville Chamberlain Papers, NC 18/1/1042, Neville Chamberlain to Ida Chamberlain, 20 March 1938.

48 FO 800/269, Halifax to Henderson, 19 March 1938.

49 FO 800/269, Halifax to Henderson, 22 April 1938.

50 FO 800/269, Cadogan to Henderson, 22 April 1938.

51 See, for example, FO 371/21719, C4528/1941/18, Minute by Speaight, 21 May 1938; Lord Strang, *Home and Abroad* (London, 1956), p. 129ff.

52 FO 371/21717/C3865, Memorandum by Hadow on 'Czechoslovakia'. For a discussion of Hadow's views, see Lindsay W. Michie, *Portrait of an Appeaser: Robert Hadow, First Secretary at the Foreign Office, 1933–1939* (Westport, Ct., 1996).

53 FO 371/2717/C3837, Sargent to Cadogan, 30 April 1938.

54 CAB 24/274, CP 50 (38), 'Anglo-Italian Conversations', 28 February 1938.

55 *Parliamentary Debates Commons (Commons) 1937–38*, Vol. 335, Col. 544, 2 May 1938.

56 CAB 27/623, 30th meeting of the Foreign Policy Committee, 1 June 1938.

57 CAB 23/94, Cabinet 31, 6 July 1938; Cabinet 32, 13 July 1938.

58 On the Runciman mission, see Paul Vysny, *The Runciman Mission to Czechoslovakia, 1938: Prelude to Munich* (Basingstoke, 2003).

59 CAB 23/94, Meeting of Ministers, 30 August 1938.

60 Cadogan, *Diaries*, p. 97 (Diary entry for 12 September 1938).

61 FO 800/371, Halifax to Henderson, 8 August 1938.

62 Neville, *Appeasing Hitler*, pp. 99–100.

63 See, for example, Henderson's comments in CAB 24/278, CP 196 (38), containing Henderson to Halifax, 8 September 1939.

64 Charmley, *Lost Peace*, p. 99.

65 A useful general discussion of British attitudes towards France during 1938 can be found in Michael Dockrill, *British Establishment Perceptions of France, 1936–1940* (Basingstoke, 1998), pp. 77–107.

66 *DBFP*, Ser. 3, Vol. 2 (Doc. 862), Neville Chamberlain to Hitler in Halifax to Henderson, 13 September 1938.

67 Neville Chamberlain Papers, NC 18/1/1066, Chamberlain to Ida Chamberlain, 3 September 1938.

68 CAB 23/95, Cabinet 38, 14 September 1939.

69 *DBFP*, Ser. 3, Vol. 2 (Doc. 895), Notes by Chamberlain on Conversation with Hitler, 15 September 1938.

70 Neville Chamberlain Papers, NC 18/1/1069, Neville Chamberlain to Ida Chamberlain, 19 September 1938.

71 For a fascinating account of the competing views between officials at the Berlin Embassy during Henderson's time there, see Bruce G. Strang, 'Two Unequal Tempers: Sir George Ogilvie-Forbes, Sir Nevile Henderson and British Foreign Policy, 1938–1939', *Diplomacy and Statecraft*, 5, 1 (1994), pp. 107–37.

72 Erik Goldstein, 'Neville Chamberlain, the British Official Mind and the Munich Crisis', *Diplomacy and Statecraft*, 10, 2–3 (1999), pp. 276–92.

73 CAB 23/95, Cabinet 39 (38), 17 September 1938.

74 *DBFP*, Ser. 3, Vol. 2 (Doc. 928), Records of Anglo-French Conversations, 18 September 1938; Doc. 937, Halifax to Newton, 19 September 1938.

75 For the relevant telegrams, including an exchange with Chamberlain over the issues, see *DBFP*, Ser. 3, Vol. 2 (Docs 1031, 1035, 1049).

76 *DBFP*, Ser. 3, Vol. 2 (Doc. 1058), Halifax to British delegation 23 September 1939. For some useful further hints on the differences between Chamberlain and his ministers, see Ivone Kirkpatrick, *Inner Circle: the Memoirs of Ivone Kirkpatrick* (London, 1959), p. 118.

77 CAB 23/95, Cabinet 42, 24 September 1938.

78 CAB 23/95, Cabinet 42, 24 September 1938; Cadogan, *Diaries*, p. 103 (Diary entry for 24 September 1938).

79 Cadogan, *Diaries*, p. 104 (Diary entry for 24 September 1938).

80 A useful discussion of the influence of Cadogan on Halifax at this vital time can be found in Peter Neville, 'Sir Alexander Cadogan and Lord Halifax's "Damascus Road" Conversion over the Godesberg Terms, 1938', *Diplomacy and Statecraft*, 11, 3 (2000), pp. 81–90. Neville is less inclined, though, to see the 'conversion' as a harbinger of a fundamental change of heart by Halifax towards 'appeasement'.

81 CAB 23/95, Cabinet 43, 25 September 1938.

82 Halifax Papers, A4 410.3.7.

83 Duff Cooper's own memories of this time can be found in Duff Cooper

(Viscount Norwich), *Old Men Forget: the Autobiography of Duff Cooper* (London, 1953), pp. 213–33. Also see John Charmley, *Duff Cooper: The Authorised Biography* (London, 1987), pp. 113–31.

84 *DBFP*, Ser. 3, Vol. 2 (Doc. 1111), Press communiqué, 26 September 1938.

85 CAB 23/95, Cabinet 46, 27 September 1938.

86 *DBFP*, Ser. 3, Vol. 2 (Doc. 1118), Conversation between Wilson and Hitler, 26 September 1938; Doc. 1129, Conversation between Wilson and Hitler, 27 September 1938.

87 *DBFP*, Ser. 3, Vol. 2 (Doc. 1174), Note by Cadogan, 28 September 1938.

88 Simon, *Retrospect*, p. 247.

89 *Parliamentary Debates (Commons) 1937–38*, Vol. 339, Cols 40–50, 3 October 1938.

90 On Hoare's recollections of his role during the Munich crisis, see Templewood, *Nine Troubled Years*, pp. 301–17.

91 Halifax's assessment of Dawson can be found in his Introduction to John Evelyn Wrench, *Geoffrey Dawson and Our Times* (London, 1955).

92 Butler, *Art of the Possible*, p. 69; for Halifax's recollection of the incident, see Halifax Papers, A2 278. 204, Halifax to Wrench, 29 April 1954.

93 *Diplomatic Diaries of Oliver Harvey*, p. 202 (Diary entry for 29 September 1938).

94 CAB 23/95, Cabinet 48, 3 October 1938.

95 Neville Chamberlain Papers, NC 7/11/31/124A, Halifax to Neville Chamberlain, 11 October 1938.

96 Neville Chamberlain Papers, NC 18/1/1072, Neville Chamberlain to Hilda Chamberlain, 15 October 1938.

97 CAB 27/624, 36th meeting of the Foreign Policy Committee, 26 January 1939.

98 Bruce G. Strang, 'Once More unto the Breach: Britain's Guarantee to Poland, March 1939', *Journal of Contemporary History*, 31, 4 (1996), p. 725.

99 CAB 23/96, Cabinet 60, 21 December 1938.

100 See, for example, CAB 27/624, 37th meeting of the Foreign Policy Committee, 8 February 1939.

101 Roberts, *Holy Fox*, p. 132.

102 Roberts, *Holy Fox*, p. 132.

103 Neville Chamberlain Papers, NC 18/1/1092, Neville Chamberlain to Hilda Chamberlain, 2 April 1939.

104 *Parliamentary Debates (Commons) 1938–39*, Vol. 345, Cols. 435–40, 15 March 1939; *The Times*, 18 March 1939.

105 Hill, *Cabinet Decisions*, pp. 24–7; CAB 23/98, Cabinet 13, 20 March 1939.

106 CAB 23/98, Cabinet 13, 20 March 1939. For Chamberlain's role in initiating and drafting the pact, see Neville Chamberlain Papers, NC 18/1/1090, Neville Chamberlain to Hilda Chamberlain, 19 March 1939; NC 18/1/1091, Neville Chamberlain to Ida Chamberlain, 26 March, 1939. For Cadogan's doubts about Chamberlain's firmness, see Cadogan, *Diaries*, p. 162 (Diary entry for 20 March 1939). Roberts, *Holy Fox*, pp. 145–8 offers a rather different view of the Chamberlain–Halifax relationship at this time.

107 *Diplomatic Diaries of Oliver Harvey*, p. 268 (Diary entry for 25 March 1939).

108 CAB 27/624, 38th meeting of the Foreign Policy Committee, 27 March 1939.

109 On the Polish guarantee and its place in Anglo-Polish relations, see Simon Newman, *March 1939. The British Guarantee to Poland: A study in the Continuity of British Foreign Policy* (Oxford, 1976). A useful summary of the literature can be found in Strang, 'Britain's Guarantee to Poland', pp. 723–5.

110 For a useful discussion of the role of Cabinet during the second half of March 1939, see Hill, *Cabinet Decisions*, pp. 18–47.

111 Charmley, *Lost Peace*, p. 169 ff.

112 CAB 23/98, Cabinet 15, 29 March 1939.
113 Cadogan, *Diary*, pp. 164–5, 29 March 1939.
114 *Parliamentary Debates (Commons) 1938–9*, Vol. 345, Col. 2415, 31 March 1939.
115 Halifax Papers, A4 410.12.1, Unpublished note by Halifax following publication of *British Documents on Foreign Policy*.
116 Neville Chamberlain Papers, NC 18/1/1096, Neville Chamberlain to Hilda Chamberlain, 29 April 1938.
117 See, for example, CAB 27/624, 43rd meeting of the Foreign Policy Committee, 19 April 1939.
118 Halifax Papers, A4 410.12.1, Unpublished note by Halifax following publication of *British Documents on Foreign Policy*.
119 Lord Strang, *Home and Abroad*, p. 163.
120 CAB 27/624, 47th meeting of the Foreign Policy Committee, 16 May 1939.
121 CAB 27/624, 48th meeting of the Foreign Policy Committee, 19 May 1939.
122 Neville Chamberlain Papers, NC 18/1/1100, 21 May 1939, Neville Chamberlain to Ida Chamberlain, 21 May 1939.
123 Neville Chamberlain Papers, NC 18/1/1101, Neville Chamberlain to Hilda Chamberlain, 28 May 1939.
124 The best discussion of Anglo-Soviet relations in 1939 can be found in Michael Jabara Carley, *1939: The Alliance that Never was and the Coming of World War II* (Chicago, 1999). A useful analysis of the 'complex and exasperatingly slow-moving talks' by one of the participants can be found in Lord Strang, *The Moscow Negotiations, 1939* (Leeds, 1938).
125 FO 800/270, Halifax to Henderson, 14 June 1939; 30 June 1939.
126 Roberts, *Holy Fox*, p. 159. For a somewhat different view, see Birkenhead, *Halifax*, p. 440.
127 Strang, *The Moscow Negotiations*.
128 Neville Chamberlain Papers, NC 18/1/1107, Neville Chamberlain to Hilda Chamberlain, 15 July 1939.
129 For a discussion of the way in which the British government actually renewed its search for an agreement with Moscow after the outbreak of war, despite the *débâcle* of the Nazi-Soviet Pact, see Michael Jabara Carley, 'A Situation of Delicacy and Danger: Anglo-Soviet Relations, August 1939–March 1940', *Contemporary European History*, 8, 2 (1999), pp. 175–208.
130 *Diplomatic Diaries of Oliver Harvey*, p. 303 (Diary entry for 23 August 1939).
131 *Diplomatic Diaries of Oliver Harvey*, pp. 307–8 (Diary entry for 27th August 1939).
132 Roberts, *Holy Fox*, p. 168.
133 CAB 23/101, Cabinet 48, 2 September 1939.
134 CAB 23/101, Cabinet 49, 2 September 1939.

10 Conclusion

1 Walter Bagehot, *The English Consitution* (London, 1993).
2 Jennings, *Cabinet Government* (Cambridge, 1936), p. xii.
3 Jennings, *Cabinet Government*, p. 1.
4 Richard Crossman, *The Diaries of a Cabinet Minister*, 3 vols (London, 1975–77).
5 Quoted in Jennings, *Cabinet Government*, pp. 98–9.
6 This definition is the one used in the introduction to Rhodes and Dunleavy (eds), *Cabinet and Core Executive*, p. 12.
7 For some comments on this theme, see Mackintosh, *British Cabinet*, p. 381.
8 For Satow's discussion of the role and function of foreign ministers, see Satow, *Guide to Diplomatic Practice*, Vol. 1, pp. 8–12.
9 For a useful series of essays that cast light on the operation of the Grey Foreign

Office, see F.H. Hinsley (ed.), *British Foreign Policy under Sir Edward Grey* (Cambridge, 1977). A seminal discussion of the Foreign Office on the eve of 1914 can be found in Zara Steiner, *The Foreign Office and Foreign Policy, 1898–1914* (Cambridge, 1969). A longer perspective on the role of the British diplomatic establishment can be found in Jones, *Nineteenth-Century Foreign Office*. Also see Raymond A. Jones, *The British Diplomatic Service, 1815–1914* (Gerrards Cross, 1983). The work of Jones, in particular, shows that the independence enjoyed by Grey was in fact exceptional rather than normal for foreign secretaries in the hundred years before 1914.

10 For some comments on this theme, see Michael Hughes, 'The Peripatetic Career Structure of the British Diplomatic Establishment', *Diplomacy and Statecraft*, 14, 1 (2003), pp. 29–48.

11 Bennett, *British Foreign Policy during the Curzon Period*, pp. 17–20.

Bibliography

A complete list of the archival and published material used in the preparation of this volume would be enormous. The material listed below therefore refers only to publications and archival material mentioned in the footnotes. The date and place of publication given is the date of the edition used and not necessarily the first date of publication. In cases where publication took place simultaneously in the United Kingdom and abroad, only the place of publication in the United Kingdom is listed

Public Record Office (Kew)

CAB 2 (Committee of Imperial Defence Minutes)
CAB 4 (Committee of Imperial Defence Papers, Series B)
CAB 6 (Committee of Imperial Defence Papers, Series D)
CAB 23 (Cabinet Conclusions)
CAB 24 (Cabinet Memoranda)
CAB 27 (Cabinet Committees – various)
CAB 29 (Minutes and other documents relating to various international conferences)
CAB 53 (Committee of Imperial Defence: Chiefs of Staff Committee Minutes and Memoranda)
CAB 63 (Papers of Maurice Hankey)

FO 371 (Foreign Office: General Correspondence)
FO 408 (Confidential Print: Germany)
FO 800 series (papers of ministers and officials who served in the inter-war Foreign Office)

PREM (various classes containing material relating to the Prime Minister's Office)
PRO 30/69 (James Ramsay MacDonald Papers)
WO 32 (various War Office files)

Private papers

Arthur Balfour (British Library)
Stanley Baldwin (Cambridge University Library)

First Earl of Birkenhead (British Library: India Office Collections)
Alexander Cadogan (Churchill College Cambridge)
Viscount Cecil of Chelwood (British Library)
Austen Chamberlain (University of Birmingham Library)
Neville Chamberlain (University of Birmingham Library)
Winston Churchill [Chartwell Papers] (Churchill College Cambridge)
Duff Cooper [Norwich Papers] (Churchill College Cambridge)
Marquess of Crewe (Cambridge University Library)
Eyre Crowe (Bodleian Library Oxford)
Philip Cunliffe-Lister [Swinton Papers] (Churchill College Cambridge)
Marquess Curzon of Kedleston (British Library: India Office Collections)
Viscount D'Abernon (British Library)
Seventeenth Earl of Derby (Liverpool Record Office)
Anthony Eden [Avon Papers] (Birmingham University Library)
Maurice Hankey (Churchill College Cambridge)
Viscount Halifax [First Earl of Halifax Papers] (Borthwick Institute York)
Viscount Halifax [Irwin Papers] (British Library: India Office Collections)
Samuel Hoare [Templewood Papers] (Cambridge University Library)
Lord Lloyd (Churchill College Cambridge)
Eric Phipps (Churchill College Cambridge)
Walter Runciman (Newcastle University Library)
John Simon (Bodleian Library Oxford)
William Strang (Churchill College Cambridge)
Robert Vansittart (Churchill College Cambridge)

Published documents

Documents on British Foreign Policy, 1919–1939 (Series 1, 1A, 2, 3)
Parliamentary Debates (House of Commons): 5th Series
Parliamentary Debates (House of Lords)
British Parliamentary Papers (various command papers)

Newspapers and magazines

Daily Express
Daily Herald
Daily Mail
Daily Telegraph
English Review
Morning Post
The Times

Memoirs, diaries and contemporary writings

Amery, L.S., *My Political Life*, 3 vols (London, 1953–55).
Amery, L.S., *The Leo Amery Diaries*, 2 vols, John Barnes and David Nicholson, eds (London, 1980–83).
Asquith, Herbert, *Memoirs and Reflections, 1852–1927* (London, 1928).

Avon, Earl of (Anthony Eden), *The Eden Memoirs: Facing the Dictators* (London, 1962).

Avon, Earl of (Anthony Eden), *Another World, 1897–1917* (London, 1976).

Avon, Earl of (Anthony Eden), *British Foreign Policy Speech to the East and West Fulham Conservative and Unionist Association, May 1935* (London, 1935).

Birkenhead, Lord, *The Speeches of Lord Birkenhead* (London, 1929).

Bruce, H.J., *Silken Dalliance* (London, 1947).

Brockway, A. Fenner, *Inside the Left: Thirty Years of Platform, Press, Prison and Parliament* (London, 1942).

Butler, Lord, *The Art of the Possible: The Memoirs of Lord Butler* (London, 1971).

Cadogan, Alexander, *The Diaries of Sir Alexander Cadogan, OM, 1938–1945*, David Dilks, ed. (London, 1971).

Cato, *Guilty Men* (London, 1940).

Cecil of Chelwood, Viscount, *All the Way* (London, 1949).

Chamberlain, Sir Austen, *Down the Years* (London, 1935).

Chamberlain, Sir Austen, *The League of Nations* (Glasgow, 1926).

Chamberlain, Sir Austen, *The Austen Chamberlain Diary Letters*, Robert Self, ed. (Cambridge, 1995).

Churchill, Winston, *The Second World War*, 4 vols (London, 1955).

Ciano, Count, *Ciano's Diplomatic Papers*, Malcolm Muggeridge, ed. (London, 1948).

Clynes, J.R., *Memoirs*, 2 vols (London, 1937).

Curzon, George Nathaniel, *Persia and the Persian Question* (London, 1892).

D'Abernon, Viscount, *An Ambassador of Peace*, 3 vols (London, 1929–30).

Dalton, Hugh, 'British Foreign Policy, 1929–31', *The Political Quarterly*, 2, 4 (1931), pp. 485–505.

Dalton, Hugh, *Call Back Yesterday* (London, 1953).

Dalton, Hugh, *Political Diary of Hugh Dalton, 1918–40, 1945–60*, Ben Pimlott, ed. (London, 1986).

Davidson, J.C.C., *Memoirs of a Conservative*, Robert Rhodes James, ed. (London, 1969).

Duff Cooper, Alfred, *Old Men Forget: The Autobiography of Duff Cooper* (London, 1953).

Gregory, J.D. *On the Edge of Diplomacy: Rambles and Reflections, 1902–1928* (London, 1928).

Haldane, Richard Burdon, *An Autobiography* (London, 1929).

Halifax, Earl of, *Speeches on Foreign Policy by Lord Halifax*, H.E.E. Craster, ed. (London, 1940).

Halifax, Earl of, *Fulness of Days* (London, 1957).

Hankey, Maurice, *Diplomacy by Conference: Studies in Public Affairs, 1920–1946* (London, 1946).

Hardinge of Penshurst, *Old Diplomacy* (London, 1947).

Harvey, Oliver, *Diplomatic Diaries of Oliver Harvey, 1937–1940* (London, 1970).

Henderson, Arthur, *The League of Nations and Labour* (London, 1918).

Henderson, Arthur, *Labour and Foreign Affairs* (London, 1922).

Henderson, Nevile, *Failure of a Mission: Berlin, 1937–1939* (London, 1940).

Henderson, Nevile, *Water Under the Bridges* (London, 1945).

Hore-Belisha, Leslie, *The Private Papers of Hore-Belisha*, R.J. Minney, ed. (London, 1960).

Ismay, Lord, *The Memoirs of General the Lord Ismay* (London, 1960).

Jones, Thomas, *A Diary with Letters, 1931–1955* (Oxford, 1955).

Jones, Thomas, *Whitehall Diary*, 3 vols (London, 1969–71).

Kennedy, A.L., *The Times and Appeasement: The Journals of A.L. Kennedy, 1932–1939*, Gordon Martel, ed. (Cambridge, 2000).

Kirkpatrick, Ivone, *The Inner Circle: Memoirs of Ivone Kirkpatrick* (London, 1959).

Lindsay, David (Earl of Crawford), *The Crawford Papers*, John Vincent, ed. (Manchester, 1984).

Lloyd George, David, *War Memoirs of David Lloyd George*, 2 vols (London, 1938).

MacDonald, J. Ramsay, *War and the Workers: A Plea for Democratic Control* (London, 1915).

MacDonald, J. Ramsay, *The Foreign Policy of the Labour Party* (London, 1923).

Morel, E.D., *Morocco in Diplomacy* (London, 1912).

Nicolson, Harold, *Diaries and Letters*, 3 vols (London, 1966–68).

Parmoor, Lord, *A Retrospect: Looking Back over a Life of more than Eighty Years* (London, 1936).

Peterson, Maurice, *Both Sides of the Curtain* (London, 1950).

Ponsonby, Arthur, *Parliament and Foreign Policy* (London, 1914).

Purcell, A.A. and Morel, E.D., *The Workers and the Anglo-Russian Treaty* (London, 1924).

Rennel Rodd, Sir James, *Social and Diplomatic Memoirs*, 3 vols (London, 1922–5).

Riddell, Lord, *Lord Riddell's Intimate Diary of the Peace Conference and After, 1918–1923* (London, 1933).

Shinwell, Emanuel, *The Labour Story* (London, 1963).

Simon, Viscount, *Retrospect: the Memoirs of the Rt Hon. Viscount Simon* (London, 1952).

Snowden, Philip, *An Autobiography*, 2 vols (London, 1934).

Stimson, Henry, *The Far Eastern Crisis: Recollections and Observations* (London, 1936).

Steed, Henry Wickham, *Through Thirty Years*, 2 vols (London, 1924).

Strang, Lord, *The Moscow Negotiations*, 1939 (Leeds, 1938).

Strang, Lord, *Home and Abroad* (London, 1956).

Temperley, A.C., *The Whispering Gallery of Europe* (London, 1938).

Templewood, Viscount, *Nine Troubled Years* (London, 1954).

Vansittart, Lord, *The Mist Procession: the Autobiography of Lord Vansittart* (London, 1958).

Webb, Beatrice, *Beatrice Webb's Diaries, 1924–1932*, Margaret Cole, ed. (London, 1956).

Selected secondary sources

Adams, R.J.Q., *British Politics and Foreign Policy in the Age of Appeasement* (Basingstoke, 1993).

Adams, R.J.Q., *Bonar Law* (London, 1999).

Aitken, William Maxwell (Lord Beaverbrook), *The Decline and Fall of Lloyd George, and Great was the Fall Thereof* (London, 1963).

Andrew, Christopher, 'British Intelligence and the Breach with Russia in 1927', *Historical Journal*, 25, 4 (1982), pp. 957–64.

Babij, Orest M., 'The Second Labour Government and Maritime Security', *Diplomacy and Statecraft*, 6, 3 (1995), pp. 645–71.

Baer, George W., *The Coming of the Italian-Ethiopian War* (Cambridge, Mass., 1967).

Baer, George, W., *Test-Case: Italy, Ethiopia and the League of Nations* (Stanford, 1976).

Bagehot, *The English Constitution* (London, 1993).

Beck, Peter, 'Politicians Versus Historians: Lord Avon's "Appeasement Battle" against "Lamentably Appeasement-Minded" Historians', *Twentieth-Century British History*, 9, 3 (1998), pp. 396–419.

Bell, Peter, *Chamberlain, Germany and Japan, 1933–4* (Basingstoke, 1996).

Bendiner, Elmer, *A Time for Angels: the Tragicomic History of the League of Nations* (London, 1975).

Bennett, G.H., *British Foreign Policy during the Curzon Period, 1919–1924* (Basingstoke, 1995).

Bennett, G.H., 'Lloyd George, Curzon and the Control of British Foreign Policy', *Australian Journal of Politics and History*, 45, 4 (1999), pp. 467–82.

Bennett, Gill, 'British Policy in the Far East, 1933–1936: Treasury and Foreign Office', *Modern Asian Studies*, 26, 3 (1992), pp. 545–68.

Bennett, Gill, *A Most Extraordinary and Mysterious Business: the Zinov'ev Letter of 1924* (London, 1999).

Best, Anthony, *Britain, Japan and Pearl Harbour: Avoiding War in East Asia, 1936–1941* (London, 1995).

Bialer, Uwe, *The Shadow of the Bomber* (London, 1980).

Birkenhead, Earl of, *Frederick Edwin, Earl of Birkenhead* (London, 1933).

Birkenhead, Earl of, *Halifax: The Life of Lord Halifax* (London, 1965).

Birn, Donald S., *The League of Nations Union, 1918–1945* (Oxford, 1981).

Boadle, Donald Graeme, 'The Formation of the Foreign Office Economic Relations Section, 1930–1937', *Historical Journal*, 20, 4 (1977), pp. 919–36.

Bond, Brian, *British Military Policy Between the Two World Wars* (Oxford, 1980).

Bourette Knowles, Simon, 'The Global Micawber: Sir Robert Vansittart, the Treasury and the Global Balance of Power, 1933–1935', *Diplomacy and Statecraft*, 6, 1 (1995), pp. 91–121.

Bruegel, Johann Wolfgang, *Czechoslovakia before Munich: The German Minority Problem and British Appeasement Policy* (Cambridge, 1973).

Busch, Briton Cooper, *Hardinge of Penshurst: A Study in the Old Diplomacy* (Hamden, Ct, 1980).

Caputi, Robert J., *Neville Chamberlain and Appeasement* (London, 2000).

Carley, Michael Jabara, 'A Fearful Concatenation of Circumstances: the Anglo-Soviet Rapprochement, 1934–36', *Contemporary European History*, 5, 1 (1996), pp. 29–69.

Carley, Michael Jabara, *1939: The Alliance that Never was and the Coming of World War II* (Chicago, 1999).

Carley, Michael Jabara, 'A Situation of Delicacy and Danger: Anglo-Soviet Relations, August 1939–March 1940', *Contemporary European History*, 8, 2 (1999), pp. 175–208.

Carlton, David, 'Great Britain and the Coolidge Naval Conference of 1927', *Political Science Quarterly*, 83, 4 (1968), pp. 573–98.

Carlton, David, 'Great Britain and the League Crisis of 1926', *Historical Journal*, 11, 2 (1968), pp. 354–64.

Carlton, David, *MacDonald versus Henderson: the Foreign Policy of the Second Labour Government* (London, 1970).

Carlton, David, *Anthony Eden: A Biography* (London, 1981).

Carlton, David, *Churchill and the Soviet Union* (Manchester, 2000).

Cassels, David, 'Repairing the Entente Cordiale and the New Diplomacy', *Historical Journal*, 23, 1 (1980), pp. 133–53.

Catterall, Peter (ed.), *Britain and the Threat to Stability in Europe, 1918–1945* (Leicester, 1993).

Ceadel, Martin, *Pacifism in Britain, 1914–1945: The Defining of a Faith* (Oxford, 1980).

Charmley, John, *Duff Cooper: The Authorised Biography* (London, 1987).

Charmley, John, *Lord Lloyd and the Decline of the British Empire* (London, 1987).

Charmley, John, *Chamberlain and the Lost Peace* (London, 1989).

Chisholm, Anne and Davies, Michael, *Beaverbrook: A Life* (London, 1992).

Churchill, Randolph S., *Lord Derby: King of Lancashire* (London, 1959).

Cline, Catherine Ann, 'E.D. Morel and the Crusade against the Foreign Office', *Journal of Modern History*, 39, 2 (1967), pp. 126–37.

Cockett, Richard, *Twilight of Truth: Chamberlain, Appeasement and the Manipulation of the Press* (London, 1989).

Colvin, Ian, *Vansittart in Office* (London, 1965).

Connell, John, *The Office: A Study of British Foreign Policy and its Makers, 1919–1951* (London, 1958).

Corthorn, Paul, 'The Labour Party and the League of Nations: the Socialist League's Role in the Sanctions Crisis of 1935', *Twentieth-Century History*, 13, 1 (2002), pp. 62–85.

Cosgrave, Patrick, *R.A. Butler: An English Life* (London, 1981).

Cowling, Maurice, *The Impact of Hitler: British Politics and British Policy, 1933–1940* (Cambridge, 1975).

Craig, Gordon A., 'The British Foreign Office from Grey to Austen Chamberlain', in Gordon A. Craig and Felix Gilbert (eds), *The Diplomats, 1919–1939* (Princeton, 1953), pp. 15–48.

Cromwell, Valerie and Steiner, Zara, 'The Foreign Office before 1914: A Study in Resistance', in Gillian Sutherland (ed.), *Studies in the Growth of Nineteenth-Century Government* (London, 1972), pp. 167–94.

Cross, J.A., *Sir Samuel Hoare* (London, 1977).

Crossman, Richard, *The Diaries of a Cabinet Minister*, 3 vols (London, 1975–77).

Crowe, S. Eyre, 'Sir Eyre Crowe and the Locarno Pact', *English Historical Review*, 87, 342 (1972), pp. 49–74.

Crowe, Sibyl and Corp, Edward, *Our Ablest Public Servant: Sir Eyre Crowe GCB, GCMG, KCB, KCMG, 1864–1925* (Braunton, 1993).

Crowson, N.J., 'Conservative Parliamentary Dissent over Foreign Policy during the Premiership of Neville Chamberlain: Myth or Reality?', *Parliamentary History*, 14, 3 (1995), pp. 315–36.

Crowson, N.J., *Facing Fascism: the Conservative Party and the European Dictators, 1935–1940* (London, 1997).

Crozier, Andrew J., *Appeasement and Germany's Last Bid for Colonies* (Basingstoke, 1988).

Davis, Richard, *Anglo-French Relations before the Second World War: Appeasement and Crisis* (Basingstoke, 2001).

Dockrill, Michael, *British Establishment Perceptions of France, 1936–1940* (Basingstoke, 1998).

Dutton, David, *Austen Chamberlain: Gentleman in Politics* (Bolton, 1985).

Dutton, David, *Simon: A Political Biography of Sir John Simon* (London, 1992).

Dutton, David, 'Simon and Eden at the Foreign Office', *Review of International Studies*, 20, 1 (1994), pp. 35–52.

Dutton, David, *Anthony Eden: A Life and Reputation* (London, 1997).

Dutton, David, *Neville Chamberlain* (London, 2001).

Dutton, David, '1932: A Neglected Date in the History of the Liberal Party', *Twentieth-Century History*, 14, 1 (2003), pp. 43–60.

Ferris, John Robert, *The Evolution of British Strategic Policy, 1919–1926* (Basingstoke, 1989).

Fischer, Conan, *The Ruhr Crisis, 1923–1924* (Oxford, 2003).

Fisher, John, 'On the Glacis of India: Lord Curzon and British Foreign Policy in the Caucasus, 1919', *Diplomacy and Statecraft*, 8, 2 (1997), pp. 50–82.

Fisher, John, *Curzon and British Imperialism in the Middle East, 1916–1919* (London, 1998).

Gerth, H.H. and Wright Mills, C., *From Max Weber: Essays in Sociology* (London, 1957).

Gibbs, N.H., *Rearmament Policy* (London, 1976).

Gilbert, Martin, *The Roots of Appeasement* (London, 1966).

Gilbert, Martin, *Winston S. Churchill*, Vols 4–5 and Companion Parts (London, 1975–82).

Gilmour, David, *Curzon* (London, 1994).

Gilmour, David, 'Empire and the East: the Orientalism of Lord Curzon', *Asian Affairs*, 26, 3 (1995), pp. 270–7.

Glenny, M.V., 'The Anglo-Soviet Trade Agreement: March 1921', *Journal of Contemporary History*, 5, 2 (1970), pp. 63–82.

Goldstein, Erik, 'Great Britain and the Greater Greece, 1917–1920', *Historical Journal*, 32, 2 (1989), pp. 339–56.

Goldstein, Erik, 'The Evolution of British Diplomatic Strategy for the Washington Conference', in Erik Goldstein and John Maurer (eds), *The Washington Conference, 1921–22* (London, 1994), pp. 4–34.

Goldstein, Erik, 'The Evolution of British Diplomatic Strategy for the Locarno Pact, 1924–1925', in Michael Dockrill and Brian McKercher (eds), *Diplomacy and World Power* (Cambridge, 1996), pp. 115–35.

Goldstein, Erik, 'Neville Chamberlain, the Official British Mind and the Munich Crisis', *Diplomacy and Statecraft*, 10, 2–3 (1999), pp. 276–92.

Goldstein, Erik, 'The British Official Mind and the Lausanne Conference, 1922–23', *Diplomacy and Statecraft*, 14, 2 (2003), pp. 185–206.

Goodlad, Graham D., 'The Liberal Nationals, 1931–1940: the Problems of a Party in Partnership Government', *Historical Journal*, 38, 1 (1995), pp. 133–43.

Gorodetsky, Gabriel, *The Precarious Truce: Anglo-Soviet Relations, 1924–1927* (Cambridge, 1977).

Grayson, Richard, *Austen Chamberlain and the Commitment to Europe* (London, 1997).

Grayson, Richard, *Liberals, International Relations and Appeasement: The Liberal Party, 1919–1939* (London, 2001).

Grenville, J.A.S., *Lord Salisbury and Foreign Policy at the Close of the Nineteenth Century* (London, 1970).

Hall, Hines H., 'The Foreign Policy-Making Process in Britain, 1934–1935, and the Origins of the Anglo-German Naval Agreement', *Historical Journal*, 19, 2 (1976), pp. 477–99.

Hamilton, Mary Agnes, *Arthur Henderson: A Biography* (London, 1938).

Hanak, H, 'The Union of Democratic Control during the First World War', *Bulletin of the Institute of Historical Research*, 36, 94 (1963), pp. 168–80.

Hardie, Frank, *The Abyssinian Crisis* (London, 1974).

Heller, Richard, 'East Fulham Revisited', *Journal of Contemporary History*, 6, 3 (1971), pp. 172–96.

Herman, John, *The Paris Embassy of Sir Eric Phipps: Anglo-French Relations and the Foreign Office, 1937–1939* (Brighton, 1998).

Hill, Christopher, *Cabinet Decisions on Foreign Policy: The British Experience, October 1938–June 1941* (Cambridge, 1991).

Hinsley, F.H. (ed.), *British Foreign Policy under Sir Edward Grey* (Cambridge, 1977).

The History of the Times, Vol.4, Parts 1–2 (London, 1952).

Howard, Anthony, *RAB: The Life of R.A. Butler* (London, 1987).

Howard, Christopher, 'MacDonald, Henderson and the Outbreak of War, 1914', *Historical Journal*, 20, 4 (1977), pp. 871–91.

Hughes, Michael, *Inside the Enigma: British Officials in Russia, 1900–1939* (London, 1997).

Hughes, Michael, *Diplomacy Before the Russian Revolution: Britain, Russia and the Old Diplomacy, 1894–1917* (London, 2000).

Hughes, Michael, 'The Development of Methodist Pacifism, 1899–1939', *Proceedings of the Wesley Historical Society*, 53, 6 (2002), pp. 203–15.

Hughes, Michael, 'The Foreign Secretary Goes to Court: Sir John Simon and his Critics', *Twentieth-Century British History*, 14, 4 (2003), pp. 339–59.

Hughes, Michael, 'The Peripatetic Career Structure of the British Diplomatic Establishment, 1919–1939', *Diplomacy and Statecraft*, 14, 1 (2003), pp. 29–48.

Jacobson, Jon, *Germany and the West: Locarno Diplomacy, 1925–1929* (Princeton, 1972).

Jennings, W. Ivor, *Cabinet Government* (Cambridge, 1936).

Johnson, Gaynor, 'Curzon, Lloyd George and the Control of British Foreign Policy: A Reassessment', *Diplomacy and Statecraft*, 11, 3 (2000), pp. 49–71.

Johnson, Gaynor, 'Das Kind Revisited: Lord D'Abernon and German Security Policy, 1922–1925', *Contemporary European History*, 9, 2 (2000), pp. 209–24.

Johnson, Gaynor, 'Lord D'Abernon, Austen Chamberlain and the Origins of the Treaty of Locarno', *Electronic Journal of International History*, 2 (2000).

Johnson, Gaynor, *The Berlin Embassy of Lord D'Abernon, 1920–1926* (Basingstoke, 2002).

Jones, Ray, *The Nineteenth-Century Foreign Office: an Administrative History* (London, 1971).

Jones, Raymond A., *The British Diplomatic Service, 1815–1914* (Gerrards Cross, 1983).

Jones, Raymond A., *Arthur Ponsonby: the Politics of Life* (Bromley, 1989).

Kennedy, Gregory C., 'Britain's Policy-Making Elite, the Disarmament Policy, and Public Opinion, 1927–1932', *Albion*, 26, 4 (1994), pp. 623–44.

Kennedy, Paul, *The Realities behind Diplomacy: Background Influences on British External Policy, 1865–1980* (London, 1981).

Kent, Bruce, *The Spoils of War: The Politics, Economics and Diplomacy of Reparations, 1918–1932* (Oxford, 1989).

King, Peter, *The Viceroy's Fall: How Kitchener Destroyed Curzon* (London, 1986).

Kitching, Carolyn J., *Britain and the Problem of International Disarmament, 1919–1934* (London, 1999).

Kitching, Carolyn, J., *Britain and the Geneva Disarmament Conference* (Basingstoke, 2002).

Koss, Stephen, *The Rise and Fall of the Political Press in Britain* (London, 1990).

Lammers, Donald, 'The Second Labour Government and the Restoration of Relations with Soviet Russia', *Bulletin of the Institute of Historical Research*, 37, 95 (1964), pp. 60–72.

Lammers, Donald, 'From Whitehall after Munich: The Foreign Office and the Future Course of British Foreign Policy', *Historical Journal*, 16, 4 (1973), pp. 831–56.

Larner, Christina, 'The Amalgamation of the Diplomatic Service with the Foreign Office', *Journal of Contemporary History*, 7, 1–2 (1974), pp. 107–26.

Lockhart, John Gilbert, *Viscount Halifax* (London, 1935–36), 2 vols.

Louis, William Roger, *British Strategy in the Far East, 1919–1939* (Oxford, 1971).

Lyman, Richard W., *The First Labour Government* (London, 1957).

Mackintosh, John P., *The British Cabinet* (London, 1962).

Magee, Frank, 'Limited Liability? Britain and the Treaty of Locarno', *Twentieth-Century British History*, 6, 1 (1995), pp. 1–22.

Maiolo, J.A., *The Royal Navy and Nazi Germany, 1933–39: A Study in Appeasement and the Origins of the Second World War* (New York, 1998).

Maisel, Ephraim, *The Foreign Office and Foreign Policy, 1919–1926* (Brighton, 1994).

Manne, Robert, 'The Foreign Office and the Failure of Anglo-Soviet Rapprochement', *Journal of Contemporary History*, 16, 4 (1981), pp. 725–55.

Marks, Sally, *The Illusion of Peace: International Relations in Europe, 1918–1933* (London, 1976).

Marks, Sally, 'The Myths of Reparations', *Central European History*, 11, 3 (1978), pp. 231–55.

Marquand, David, *Ramsay MacDonald* (London, 1977).

Maurice, Sir Frederick, *Haldane, 1915–1928: The Life of Viscount Haldane of Cloan* (London, 1937–39).

Mayer, Arno, *Political Origins of the New Diplomacy, 1917–1918* (New Haven, 1959).

MacDonald, Callum A., *The United States, Britain and Appeasement, 1936–1939* (London, 1981).

McKercher, B.J.C., 'Austen Chamberlain's Control of Foreign Policy, 1924–29', *International History Review*, 6, 4 (1984), pp. 570–91.

McKercher, B.J.C., 'A Sane and Sensible Diplomacy: Austen Chamberlain, Japan and the Naval Balance of Power in the Pacific Ocean', *Canadian Journal of History*, 21, 2 (1986), pp. 187–213.

McKercher, B.J.C., 'Belligerent Rights in 1927–1929: Foreign Policy versus Naval Policy in the Second Baldwin Government', *Historical Journal*, 29, 4 (1986), pp. 963–74.

McKercher, B.J.C., 'Of Horns and Teeth: The Preparatory Commission and the World Disarmament Conference, 1926–1934', in McKercher, B.J.C. (ed.), *Arms Limitation and Disarmament: Restraints on War 1899–1939* (Westport, Ct., 1992), pp. 173–202.

McKercher, B.J.C., 'Old Diplomacy and New: The Foreign Office and Foreign Policy, 1919–1939, in Michael Dockrill and Brian Mckercher (eds), *Diplomacy and World Power, 1890–1950* (Cambridge, 1996), pp. 79–114.

McKercher, B.J.C., 'From Disarmament to Rearmament: British Civil–Military

Relations and Policy-Making, 1933–1936', *Defence Studies*, 1, 1 (2001), pp. 21–48.

McKercher, B.J.C., 'Austen Chamberlain and the Continental Balance of Power: Strategy, Stability and the League of Nations, 1924–1929', *Diplomacy and Statecraft*, 14, 2 (2003), pp. 207–36.

McKercher, Brian and Roi, M.L, 'Ideal and Punchbag: Conflicting Views of the Balance of Power and their Influence on Interwar British Foreign Policy', *Diplomacy and Statecraft*, 12, 2 (2001), pp. 47–78.

MacMillan, Margaret, *Peacemakers: the Paris Conference of 1919 and its Attempt to End War* (London, 2001).

Mejcher, H, 'British Middle East Policy, 1917–21: The Inter-Departmental Level', *Journal of Contemporary History*, 8, 4 (1973), pp. 81–101.

Meilinger, Philip S., 'Clipping the Bomber's Wings: the Geneva Disarmament Conference and the Royal Air Force, 1932–34', *War in History*, 6, 3 (1999), pp. 306–30.

Michie, Lindsay W., *Portrait of an Appeaser: Robert Hadow, First Secretary in the British Foreign Office, 1931–1939* (Westport, Ct., 1996).

Middlemas, Keith, *Diplomacy of Illusion: the British Government and Germany, 1937–39* (London, 1972).

Middlemas, Keith, and Barnes, John, *Baldwin: A Biography* (London, 1969).

Mills, William C., 'The Nyon Conference: Neville Chamberlain, Anthony Eden and the Appeasement of Italy in 1937', *International History Review*, 15, 1 (1993), pp. 1–22.

Mills, William C., 'The Chamberlain–Grandi Conversations of July–August 1937 and the Appeasement of Italy', *International History Review*, 19, 3 (1997), pp. 594–619.

Mills, William C., 'Sir Joseph Ball, Adrian Dingli, and Neville Chamberlain's "Secret Channel" to Italy 1937–1940', *International History Review*, 24, 2 (2002), pp. 278–317.

Morgan, K.O., *Consensus and Disunity: the Lloyd George Coalition Government, 1918–1922* (Oxford, 1979).

Morrell, Gordon W., *Britain Confronts the Stalin Revolution: Anglo-Soviet Relations and the Metro-Vickers Crisis* (Waterloo, Ont., 1995).

Morrisey, Charles and Ramsay, M. A., 'Giving a Lead in the Right Direction: Sir Robert Vansittart and the Defence Requirements Sub-Committee', *Diplomacy and Statecraft*, 6, 1 (1995), pp. 39–60.

Naylor, John F., *A Man and an Institution: Sir Maurice Hankey, the Cabinet Secretariat and the Custody of Cabinet Secrecy* (Cambridge, 1984).

Neilson, Keith, 'Pursued by a Bear: British Estimates of Soviet Military Strength and Anglo-Soviet Relations, 1922–1939', *Canadian Journal of History*, 28, 2 (1993), pp. 189–221.

Neilson, Keith, 'The Defence Requirements Committee, British Strategic Foreign Policy, Neville Chamberlain and the Path to Appeasement', *English Historical Review*, 118, 477 (2003), pp. 651–84.

Neville, Peter, 'Nevile Henderson and Basil Newton: Two British Envoys in the Czech Crisis, 1938', *Diplomacy and Statecraft*, 10, 2–3 (1999), pp. 258–75.

Neville, Peter, *Appeasing Hitler: The Diplomacy of Sir Nevile Henderson, 1937–1939* (Basingstoke, 2000).

Neville, Peter, 'Sir Alexander Cadogan and Lord Halifax's "Damascus Road"

Conversion over the Godesberg Terms, 1938', *Diplomacy and Statecraft*, 11, 3 (2000), pp. 81–90.

Neville, Peter, 'Lord Vansittart, Sir Walford Selby, and the Debate about Treasury Interference in the Conduct of British Foreign Policy', *Journal of Contemporary History*, 36, 4 (2001), pp. 623–33.

Newman, Simon, *March 1939. The British Guarantee to Poland: A Study in the Continuity of British Foreign Policy* (Oxford, 1976).

Newton, Scott, *Profits of Peace: The Political Economy of Anglo-German Appeasement* (Oxford, 1996).

Nicolson, Harold, *Curzon: the Last Phase, 1919–1925* (London, 1934).

Noel-Baker, Philip, *The First Disarmament Conference 1932–33, and Why it Failed* (London, 1979).

Northedge, F.S., *The Troubled Giant: Britain among the Great Powers, 1916–1939* (London, 1966).

Northedge, F.S., *The League of Nations: its Life and Times, 1920–1946* (Leicester, 1986).

O'Halpin, Eunan, *Head of the Civil Service: A Study of Sir Warren Fisher* (London, 1989).

Orde, Anne, *Great Britain and International Security, 1920–1926* (London, 1978).

Orde, Anne, *British Policy and Reconstruction after the First World War* (Cambridge, 1990).

O'Riordan, Elspeth Y., *Britain and the Ruhr Crisis* (London, 2001).

Otte, T.G. and Pagedas, Constantine A. (eds), *Personalities, War and Diplomacy* (London, 1997).

Parker, R.A.C., 'Great Britain, France and the Ethiopian Crisis, 1935–1936', *English Historical Review*, 89, 35 (1974), pp. 293–332.

Parker, R.A.C., *Chamberlain and Appeasement: British Policy and the Coming of the Second World War* (Basingstoke, 1993).

Parker, R.A.C., *Churchill and Appeasement* (Basingstoke, 2000).

Peden, George C., *British Rearmament and the Treasury, 1932–1939* (Edinburgh, 1979).

Peden, G.C., 'Sir Warren Fisher and British Rearmament against Germany', *English Historical Review*, 94, 370 (1979), pp. 29–47.

Petrie, Sir Charles, *The Life and Letters of the Right Hon. Sir Austen Chamberlain KC, PC, MP*, 2 vols (London, 1939).

Pugh, Michael, 'Pacifism and British Politics', *Historical Journal*, 23, 3 (1980), pp. 641–56.

Pugh, Michael, 'An International Police Force: Lord Davies and the British Debate in the 1930s', *International Relations*, 9, 4 (1988), pp. 335–51.

Richardson, Dick, *The Evolution of British Disarmament Policy in the 1920s* (London, 1989).

Riddell, Neil, *Labour in Crisis: the Second Labour Government, 1929–1931* (Manchester, 1999).

Rhodes, R.A.W. and Dunleavy, Patrick (eds), *Prime Minister, Cabinet and Core Executive* (Basingstoke, 1995).

Rhodes James, Robert, *Anthony Eden* (London, 1986).

Robb, Janet Henderson, *The Primrose League, 1883–1906* (New York, 1942).

Roberts, Andrew, *The Holy Fox: A Biography of Lord Halifax* (London, 1991).

Robertson, James C., 'The British General Election of 1935', *Journal of Contemporary History*, 9, 1 (1974), pp. 149–64.

Robertson, James C., 'The Hoare–Laval Plan', *Journal of Contemporary History*, 10, 3 (1975), pp. 433–64.

Robbins, Keith, *Appeasement* (Oxford, 1997).

Rock, William R., *British Appeasement in the 1930s* (London, 1977).

Roi, Michael, *Alternative to Appeasement: Sir Robert Vansittart and Alliance Diplomacy, 1934–1937* (Westport, Ct., 1997).

Ronaldshay, Earl of (Dundas), *The Life of Lord Curzon*, 3 vols (London, 1928).

Rose, Inbal, *Conservatism and Foreign Policy during the Lloyd George Coalition, 1918–1922* (London, 1999).

Rose, Norman, *Vansittart: Study of a Diplomat* (London, 1978).

Rose, Norman, *The Cliveden Set: Portrait of an Exclusive Fraternity* (London, 2000).

Roskill, Stephen, *Hankey: Man of Secrets*, 3 vols (London, 1970–74).

Rostow, Nicholas, *Anglo-French Relations*, 1934–36 (London, 1984).

Ruggiero, John, *Neville Chamberlain and British Rearmament* (Westport, Ct., 1999).

Satow, Sir Ernest, *A Guide to Diplomatic Practice* (London, 1917).

Sharp, Alan J., 'The Foreign Office in Eclipse, 1919–1922', *History*, 61, 202 (1976), pp. 198–218.

Sharp, Alan, *The Versailles Settlement: Peacemaking in Paris – 1919* (Basingstoke, 1991).

Sharp, Alan, 'Lord Curzon and British Policy towards the Franco-Belgian Occupation of the Ruhr in 1923', *Diplomacy and Statecraft*, 8, 2 (1997), pp. 82–96.

Sharp, Alan and Stone, Glynn (eds), *Anglo-French Relations in the Twentieth Century: Rivalry and Co-Operation* (London, 2000).

Shay, Robert J., *British Rearmament in the 1930s: Politics and Profits* (Princeton, 1977).

Skidelsky, Robert, *Politicians and the Slump: the Second Labour Government, 1929–1931* (London, 1967).

Smith, Malcolm, *British Air Strategy Between the Wars* (Oxford, 1984).

Stafford, Paul, 'Political Biography and the Art of the Possible: R.A. Butler at the Foreign Office, 1938–1939', *Historical Journal*, 28, 4 (1985), pp. 901–22.

Stambrook, F.G., 'Das Kind: Lord D'Abernon and the Origins of the Locarno Pact', *Central European History*, 1, 3 (1968), pp. 233–63.

Steiner, Zara, 'The Last Years of the Old Foreign Office, 1898–1905', *Historical Journal*, 6, 1 (1963), pp. 59–90.

Steiner, Zara, *The Foreign Office and Foreign Policy, 1898–1914* (Cambridge, 1969).

Steiner, Z.S. and Dockrill, M. L., 'The Foreign Office Reforms, 1919–1921', *Historical Journal* 17, 1 (1974), pp. 131–56.

Steiner, Zara, 'On Writing International History: Chaps, Maps and Much More', *International Affairs*, 73, 3 (1997), pp. 531–46.

Stewart, Graham, *Burying Caesar: Churchill, Chamberlain and the Battle for the Tory Party* (London, 1999).

Strang, Bruce G., 'Two Unequal Tempers: Sir George Ogilvie-Forbes, Sir Nevile Henderson and British Foreign Policy, 1938–1939', *Diplomacy and Statecraft*, 5, 1 (1994), pp. 107–37.

Strang, Bruce G., 'Once More Unto the Breach: Britain's Guarantee to Poland, March 1939', *Journal of Contemporary History*, 31, 4 (1996), pp. 721–52.

Swanick, H.M., *Builders of Peace* (London, 1924).

Tanner, Duncan, 'The Development of British Socialism, 1900–1918', *Parliamentary History*, 16, 1 (1997), pp. 48–66.

Taylor, A.J.P., *The Origins of the Second World War* (London, 1963).

Taylor, A.J.P., *Beaverbrook* (London, 1972).

Theakston, Kevin, 'The Biographical Approach to Public Administration: Potential, Purpose and Problems' in Kevin Theakston (ed.), *Bureaucrats and Leadership* (New York, 1999), pp. 1–16.

Theakston, Kevin (ed.), *British Foreign Secretaries since 1974* (London, 2004).

Thomas, Martin, *Britain, France and Appeasement: Anglo-French Relations in the Popular Front Era* (Oxford, 1996).

Thompson, J.A., 'The Peace Ballot and the Public', *Albion*, 13, 4 (1981), pp. 380–92.

Thompson, John M., *Russia, Bolshevism and the Versailles Peace* (Princeton, 1966).

Thompson, Neville, *The Anti-Appeasers: Conservative Opposition to Appeasement in the 1930s* (Oxford, 1971).

Thorne, Christopher, 'The Shanghai Crisis of 1932: the Bases of British Policy', *American Historical Review*, 75, 6 (1970), pp. 1616–49.

Thorne, Christopher, 'Viscount Cecil, the Government and the Far Eastern Crisis of 1931', *Historical Journal*, 14, 4 (1971), pp. 805–26.

Thorne, Christopher, *The Limits of Foreign Policy: the West, the League and the Far Eastern Crisis of 1931–1933* (London, 1972).

Thorpe, Andrew, 'Arthur Henderson and the British Political Crisis of 1931', *Historical Journal*, 31, 1 (1988), pp. 117–39.

Thorpe, D.R., *The Uncrowned Prime Ministers* (London, 1980).

Thorpe, D.R., *Eden: The Life and Times of Anthony Eden First Earl of Avon, 1897–1977* (London, 2003).

Trommer, Aage, 'MacDonald in Geneva in March 1933', *Scandinavian Journal of History*, 1, 3–4 (1976), pp. 293–312.

Ullman, Richard, *Anglo-Soviet Relations, 1917–1921*, 3 vols (Princeton, 1961–72).

Vysny, Paul, *The Runciman Mission to Czechoslovakia, 1938: Prelude to Munich* (Basingstoke, 2003).

Waterfield, Gordon, *Professional Diplomat: Sir Percy Loraine of Kirkharle, 1880–1961* (London, 1973).

Watt, Donald Cameron, 'Chamberlain's Ambassadors', in Michael Dockrill and Brian McKercher (eds), *Diplomacy and World Power* (Cambridge, 1996), pp. 136–70.

Webb, Sidney, 'The First Labour Government', *Political Quarterly*, 32 (1961), pp. 6–44.

Webster, Andrew, 'The Disenchantment Conference: Frustration and Humour at the World Disarmament Conference, 1932', *Diplomacy and Statecraft*, 11, 3 (2000), pp. 72–80.

White, Stephen, *Britain and the Bolshevik Revolution: A Study in the Politics of Diplomacy, 1920–1924* (London, 1979).

Williams, Andrew, *The Attitude of the Labour Party Towards the USSR, 1924–1934* (Manchester, 1989).

Williamson, Philip, *National Crisis and National Government: British Politics, the Economy and Empire, 1926–1932* (Cambridge, 1992).

Williamson, Philip, *Stanley Baldwin: Conservative Leadership and National Values* (Cambridge, 1999).

Williamson, Philip, 'Christian Conservatives and the Totalitarian Challenge, 1933–1940', *English Historical Review*, 115, 462 (2000), pp. 607–42.

Wilson, Keith M. (ed.), *British Foreign Secretaries and Foreign Policy: from Crimean War to First World War* (London, 1987).

Wilson, K.M., 'A Venture in the "Caverns of Intrigue": the Conspiracy against Lord Curzon and his Foreign Policy, 1922', *Historical Research*, 70, 173 (1997), pp. 312–36.

Winkler, Henry R., 'Arthur Henderson', in Gordon A. Craig and Felix Gilbert (eds), *The Diplomats, 1919–1939* (Princeton, 1953), pp. 311–43.

Wrench, John Evelyn, *Geoffrey Dawson and our Times* (London, 1955).

Wrigley, Chris, *Arthur Henderson* (Cardiff, 1990).

Index

Murray, Gilbert 81, 101
Mussolini, Benito 114, 117, 120, 125, 126, 144, 158

naval disarmament 95, 96
Near East policy 23–4
News Chronicle 101, 136, 186
newspapers *see* press, the
Newton, Basil 167
Nicolson, Harold 17, 65, 169
Noel-Baker, Philip 111
Norman, Montagu 184
Northcliffe, 1st Viscount 31
Northedge, F. S. 164

Observer 101
Oliphant, Sir Lancelot 126, 145, 161
O'Malley, Owen 50
Optional Clause 83, 84, 86–7
Ormsby-Gore, William (later Lord Harlech) 104, 130, 138
Ottawa Conference (1932) 106

Palmerston, 3rd Viscount 1
Paris embassy 18, 19
Paris Peace Conference 4, 13, 81
Parmoor, Lord 42, 45, 49
Passfield, Lord (Sydney Webb) 40, 87
Peace Pledge Union 206
Persia 29–30, 31, 73
Perth, Lord 167
Peterson, Maurice 126, 134
Phipps, Sir Eric 146–7, 167, 180
'Plan Z' 171, 176, 177–8
Poincaré, Raymond 23, 27, 42
Polish guarantee 184–6
Ponsonby, Arthur 39, 41, 45, 49, 50, 197–8
post-First World War years 4–5
power: as a term 6, 193–4
Pratt, Sir John 109
press, the 10, 31–2, 69–70, 74, 75, 88, 101, 107, 205–6
prime ministerial interference ix
Primrose League 33
public opinion: and Austen Chamberlain 69–71; and Curzon 10, 30–4, 205; and Hoare, Samuel 132, 134; impact on foreign policy 10–11, 205–6; war scare (1935) 182
Purcell, A. A. 50–1

Reading, 1st Marquis of 8, 99, 206

rearmament 14, 118, 144, 148, 151, 183, 199
remilitarisation: of the Rhineland 148–9
reparations 4, 14, 27, 29, 45, 53, 91–4, 93–4, 106
Rome–Paris–London axis 120–1
Roosevelt, F. D. 156–7
Roosevelt's initiative 156–7, 160, 163
Ruhr crisis 27, 29, 53
Rumania 186
Rumbold, Horace 85
Runciman, Walter 105
Runciman Mission 176
Russia, Soviet *see* USSR
Russian Trade Agreement 77

Salisbury, 3rd Marquess of 1, 2
Samuel, Herbert 106
Samuelite Liberals 101
sanctions 149
Sargent, Sir Orme 121, 145, 155, 163, 167, 168, 174
Satow, Ernest 193
Scrivener, Patrick 126
sea power 13–14
'secret channel' 154, 157, 158, 164, 202
security 111–15 *see also* collective security
Selby, Walford 83
service department heads 203–4
Shinwell, Emmanuel 41
Simon, Sir John (later 1st Viscount): Anglo-Italian relations 159; appeasement 203; assessment of 121–2; and the Cabinet 104–8; criticism of 100–2; European situation (1934–35) 117–21; expectations of role 193–4; and the Far East crisis 108–11, 115–17; and the Foreign Office 102–4; and the House of Commons 206; Macmillan's opinion of ix; and the media 101, 107, 114; Munich crisis 181; and officials 9; personality 208, 209; political career 101–2; and the press 205; public image 11, 107–8; World Disarmament Conference (1932) 111–15
Sino-Japanese conflict 102
Smith, Sir Frederick *see* Birkenhead, Lord